THE NATURE OF HUMAN CONFLICTS

D1097531

THE NATURE OF
HUMAN CONFLICTS

OR EMOTION, CONFLICT AND WILL

AN OBJECTIVE STUDY OF
DISORGANISATION AND CONTROL
OF HUMAN BEHAVIOUR

BY

A·R·LURIA

PROFESSOR OF PSYCHOLOGY AT THE ACADEMY OF COMMUNISTIC
EDUCATION; RESEARCH ASSOCIATE, STATE INSTITUTE OF
EXPERIMENTAL PSYCHOLOGY, MOSCOW

Translated from the Russian and edited by

W. HORSLEY GANTT

PHIPPS PSYCHIATRIC CLINIC, JOHNS HOPKINS UNIVERSITY; COLLABORATOR
IN PROF. PAVLOV'S LABORATORY, INSTITUTE OF EXPERIMENTAL
MEDICINE, LENINGRAD, 1924-29

With a foreword by ADOLF MEYER
PROFESSOR OF PSYCHIATRY, JOHNS HOPKINS UNIVERSITY

GROVE PRESS, INC.   NEW YORK

TO

H · M · K

FOREWORD

THERE ARE several reasons which make the publication in English of our Moscow colleague especially welcome. In the first place, it represents a mode of approach constituting a characteristic expansion of the Russian school of laboratory work in the clinical field, little known and little cultivated in the English-speaking countries. We are therefore grateful to the author and to the translator and to the publisher for giving us access to a work refreshing on many counts. Professor Luria offers us a true psychobiology and not largely neurologising tautologies, in remarkably close contact with the sense of the work of Lashley and other American workers but definitely occupied with human problems. He shows a much greater applicability of laboratory methods to the human being than is generally expected in our environment, without surrendering to a sidestepping in merely physiologising concepts. Another point that is bound to impress one is the combination of practical interest with a remarkably consistent perspective of methodology in the midst of a phase of cultural and political life which among us is too often used as an excuse for neglect of strictly scientific programmes.

These are a few of the reasons why it is a pleasure to give a word of warm welcome and gratitude and introduction to this account of the unusually ingenious results of factual and methodological contributions that cannot help proving a genuine contribution to psychiatric work and interests apt to be somewhat onesidedly treated in psychiatric practice.

ADOLF MEYER

Baltimore, May, 1932.

vii

TRANSLATOR'S PREFACE

M Y INTEREST in the scientific work being accomplished in Soviet Russia—a nation whose vigour, versatile talents, and potentialities we must not ignore nor minimize—as well as the stimulating record of experiments that Professor Luria gives us here, has led me to undertake the translation of this book. My sojourn of six years in the Union of Soviet Socialistic Republics as the first American following the Revolution to do extended research in the laboratories and medical institutes of the new Russia just emerging from chaos, my intimate and cordial relations there with the scientists and my admiration of their zealous strivings and achievements, together with my natural interest in the problems Luria illuminates, have made the opportunity to cooperate in the presentation of another scientific book from Russia too great a temptation to let pass.

Now, out of the USSR where the dogma of Marxian materialism all but reigns supreme, comes this record of experimental work from one who likes to style himself a "Marxian materialist-psychologist" telling us among other interesting things that we can control our behaviour and showing us how; whether this is in effect freedom of the will each reader may decide according to his own philosophical predilections. The author suggests many new theories, and whether we agree with them all or not, the record of experiments upon which these hypotheses concerning human nature are everywhere based must command our serious attention. And we can but welcome this attack upon the many questions of our psychical existence (for "mankind will possess incalculable advantages and extraordinary control over

human behaviour when the scientific investigator will be able
to subject his fellow men to the same external analysis as he
employs for any natural object"[1]) if we have a real interest
in psychobiology or the science of the total higher nervous reactions (and their contributing factors) of the organism; for we
are gradually coming to the view expressed by a philosopher-
scientist-psychiatrist that "all human functioning must be
brought within the scope of natural science"(Adolf Meyer).

I have made a close translation of the actual experimental
work, without alterations or omissions. Owing to the large size
of the book, however, the discussions I have sometimes con-
densed; Chapter XI and particularly Chapter XII I have ab-
stracted quite freely without adhering to the style of the author.
In the association tests the words given are translations of the
Russian except where otherwise indicated. In cases in which
there seemed to be a phonetic relation between the word-stimulus
and the word-reaction I have translated the Russian word too,
but not unless such a relation was evident. Figures 85, 111, and
130 were lost and they and their references in the text have
been omitted. All the kymographic records have been traced
under my supervision, as the originals could not be photographed.

With deep appreciation I acknowledge the valuable aid ren-
dered me in this translation by the following: Dr. Roger Brown
Loucks for a careful reading of the manuscript, and for
suggestions regarding some of the psychological terms; Miss
Ruth M. Muellerschoen for re-drawing most of the charts, and
also, together with Mrs. Helen Luber Soffer, Mrs. Frank Gosnell
and Miss Frances Hall for technical aid with the manuscript.
Especial credit is due Mr. Saxe Commins for his participation
in the editorial work, and altogether the publishers have spared
no pains nor consideration to present the book in a manner
befitting its scientific merit.

W . H O R S L E Y   G A N T T

---

[1] Pavlov's *Lectures on Conditioned Reflexes,* p. 95, Liveright Publishers,
New York.

T HE RESEARCHES described here are the results of the experimental psychological investigations carried on at the State Institute of Experimental Psychology, Moscow, during the period of 1923-1930. The chief problems of the author were an objective and materialistic description of the mechanisms lying at the basis of the disorganisation of human behaviour and an experimental approach to the laws of its regulation. The first of these tasks forced the author to investigate the whole series of phenomena in which the disorganisation of human behaviour was clearly expressed: the problem of the diffuse, acute affect, of trauma and neurosis. An analysis of these states and the description of the symptoms characterising acute affect, as well as its traces, are given in the first part of the book.

The study of affects and neuroses and their psychophysiological mechanisms suggested to the experimenter that it was not profitable to seek for the causes of the affective processes in the peripheral apparatus, but that the affective disorganisation of behaviour was connected primarily with central changes—with the disturbances of human activity, and hence with profound changes in all the systems of psychological function, the correlations of which are fundamentally modified during the state of affect. To accomplish this it was necessary to create artificially affects and models of experimental neuroses which made possible an analysis of the laws lying at the basis of the disintegration of behaviour. The experiments with artificial conflicts, outlined in the second part of the book, constitute an approach to the psychophysiological structure and dynamics of affect.

Notwithstanding the fact that the material of this book is

treated psychophysiologically, the author remains withal a psychologist. This is shown in the principles laid down at the beginning of the work and in the closing chapters. The author starts from the fundamental idea which he has sought to express elsewhere—that the complex forms of organisation and disorganisation of human behaviour can in nowise be explained as a simple play of neurophysiological processes, that no phenomena of elementary neurodynamics can elucidate those configurations of integrated behaviour specific for the human as a social subject. It is more probable that elementary neurodynamics, as observed in the human, is comprehensible only by an analysis of those higher forms of organised behaviour connected with the culturally created psychological functions, as for example, the involved behaviour of work, speech, and complex indirect operations. The inclusion of neurodynamics in the system of such higher psychological functions brings about a specificity of its organisation.

The desire to study the development of these higher forms of the regulators of human behaviour led at first to genetic experiments whose purpose was to investigate the regulation of behaviour in early childhood, and to experiments dealing with pathological material in which models of these regulations were created in an experimental situation; thus we were able to study the mechanism of the control of behaviour. Part III is devoted to this subject.

In this latter series of experiments the author attempts to define his universal psychological point of view. Whilst dealing with the experimentally manifested psychophysiological mechanisms of affects, complexes, and conflicts, he does not become a psychoanalyst; nor a behaviourist in objectively analysing the psychophysiological structure of the disintegration and integration of the psychical apparatus; and least of all does he attempt to deduce the laws of higher activity from simple neurodynamical processes.

The author does not believe that the problems of the most complicated forms of human behaviour can be solved by the laws of the dynamics of tendency nor by the analysis of the conditioned reflex connections playing a rôle in the nervous system; the solution of this problem will be attained only by a careful description of the specific systems of behaviour produced in the process of the social historical development, which are distinguished by the peculiarities of the human, and without which the organisation of the higher neurodynamics remains incomprehensible.

The author desires to thank the publishers for their interest in producing a book requiring so much labour. He feels especially flattered that such an authoritative scientist as Doctor Gantt should take upon himself the difficult and onerous task of translating these investigations; without his participation it would have been well-nigh impossible to acquaint the American readers with these experiments. Furthermore, the author gratefully acknowledges the help of Prof. H. M. Kallen and Prof. Langfeld who have been instrumental in bringing this book before the American psychologists.

A. R. LURIA

TABLE OF CONTENTS

*

PART TWO

PSYCHOPHYSIOLOGY
OF THE CONFLICTING PROCESSES

✳

PART THREE

THE GENESIS OF THE REACTIVE PROCESSES AND THE PSYCHOPHYSIOLOGY OF THE CONTROL OF BEHAVIOUR

THE NATURE OF HUMAN CONFLICTS

CHAPTER I

THE PROBLEMS OF DISORGANISATION
OF BEHAVIOUR

---

1. THE PROBLEMS OF
DISORGANISATION OF BEHAVIOUR

WE are concerned here with the investigation of the disorganisation of human behaviour, with the mechanism of its falling and rising. Certainly we are not the first on this path; therefore, the necessity to define its methodological position and to indicate how our concepts diverge from those of former dissertations.

Our work should begin with the establishing of our fundamental approach to human behaviour, the terminology and inherent principles.

Correct and worth-while work in this epoch of the growth of science is possible only when terms and concepts strictly correspond with that which we wish to express. The labours of many authors known to us are unsuccessful because new thoughts have been concealed in old and inadequate expressions; primitive concepts are not suitable for the development of knowledge. In numerous other researches with which we are acquainted, the new terms employed do not convey new ideas but are cluttered with old truths not requiring a departure from the concepts inherent in the former terms.

Words express definite conceptions, and the successful author first chooses carefully thought-out words in order that carefully thought-out methodological conceptions will constitute the basis of his investigation.

We should begin our work with a consideration of the conception of organisation and the outline of these principal ideas which we include under this term. The twentieth century has brought a remarkable change in the style and content of scientific thought, an enormous progress in manufacturing technique on the one hand, and, on the other, of scientific thought. Many authors hope that the complicated forms of human activity will be easily explained from an analogy to machines and that the time is near when the most vital processes will be conceived as the mechanism of a machine remarkably more complicated than a machine made by the human hand but run along the same general principles. It would be an interesting work to follow the complete history of the twentieth-century natural science of analogy, built by the investigators, a history of those models which are accepted as a basis for the construction of ideas concerning forms and mechanisms of human vital activity. This history should reveal many naïve sources of human thought, and certainly there is not a more attractive territory than the history of naïve philosophy. This tendency to introduce naïve concepts, to explain the nervous system on the basis of analogies with artificial things is more common in the study of behaviour than anywhere else.

The idea of the nervous system as a most complicated system, of a series of separate apparatuses, acting, thanks to very delicate and changeable connections, in a manner comparable to the telephone system, was considered the basic theory of nervous activity almost from the very first. But in the second half of the nineteenth century it appeared that we had already reached the limit of understanding the secret of this complicated machine. I remember the antiquated formula upon which was based the history of diseases in the psychiatric institutes of that time. On the principal sheet was drawn a colored chart of the brain. An investigating physician had to register thereon with great exactness those affections which "lie at the basis of the disease."

The model of the telephone station, a brilliant criticism of which has been recently given by K. S. Lashley,[1] has been continually introduced in neurological conceptions, even up to the present time. Together with this there were a series of conceptions always introduced when the fundamental laws of human behaviour were mentioned.

On this basis, concealed almost in every structure of psychoneurology were the conceptions having to do with the structure of the psychical apparatus, considering them as a series of separate and self-sufficient mechanisms arranged by the help

[1] K. S. Lashley: *Basic Neural Mechanisms in Behaviour*, Psychological Review, 1930.

of the connecting excitations and inhibitions in a definite relation with one another.

In effect, if the whole nervous apparatus consisted of separate neurons, and the brain were nothing more than a centralisation of them and their conduits by which they are connected, then all the laws of behaviour must be inevitably evidenced in those laws which already hold for the individual neurons. The whole of behaviour might be understood merely as a preservation of equilibrium between the separate apparatuses of the nervous system; its pathology as a destruction of this equilibrium.

Here we immediately come into a circle of the basic conceptions which are used in almost all contemporary psychoneurology, and which unavoidably ensue from the analogy upon which it was constructed.

The elementary processes of excitation and inhibition are the basic ones which are found in every nerve cell; they are carried throughout the whole organism, and the most eminent objective school of psychoneurology attempts to explain every process of behaviour in the terms of excitation and inhibition. At any given moment certain cells of the nervous system are in a state of excitation, others in a state of inertness, and yet others in a phase of inhibition. The normal behaviour of the human is consequently examined as a preservation of a certain equilibrium between the inhibitory and excitatory processes.

In pathological cases this equilibrium is disturbed first of all; and the behaviour deviating from the normal is the activity which is primarily characterised by the predominance of the inhibition and excitations.[1]

In all these cases the processes of excitation and inhibition are generally the same elementary processes which occur in the isolated nerve preparation, and the inhibitory or excitatory activity of the systems is governed not by specific laws having to do with the structure of the whole organism, but by the law of the above elementary physiological processes.

But can we express all the forms of organisation or disorganisation of human behaviour in terms of elementary inhibition and excitation? Does this conception explain adequately those phenomena, the analysis of which is treated by psychoneurology?

Researches in human behaviour, both normal and pathological, lead us to doubt the adequacy of these fundamental conceptions. The facts which we observed convincingly show that behaviour

[1] See I. P. Pavlov: *Lectures on Conditioned Reflexes*, International Publishers, New York.

cannot be explained as an equilibrium of the separate systems, that the concept of elementary inhibition and excitation (not being included in the highest and specific whole) are completely inadequate, and that the disease of any of the mechanisms does not by any means always call out the same affect, and often causes general changes, comprehensible only from a most complicated functional reciprocity of the internal behaviour.

We shall purposely take an example of an organic illness in which the disease of a special system might lead us to believe that there would result only a partial and organic disturbance in the activity of the organism. A very simple example is that of aphasia, in which there is a disturbance of the complicated function of speech and symbolic activity. Let us examine the behaviour here. The thing that strikes us most forcibly is marked confusion. Experimentally the aphasiac cannot elaborate fairly simple acts nor complete an elementary chain of actions; a complicated situation causes confusion; a more difficult problem, complete disorganisation of the behaviour.

Can we understand this case as only a failure of a separate system, or can it be expressed in terms of inhibition and excitation? It is with the greatest difficulty that we state the facts before us in such elementary terms, because of not having included them in a more complex whole, nor having preceded our construction with the analysis of that complicated structure of reciprocal relations into which these functions enter.

An attempt to express this state as a complicated mosaic of inhibition and excitation does not by any means satisfy us. Undoubtedly both the forces of neuro-dynamics—excitation and inhibition—are included in our phenomena; but it would be a naïve representation to presuppose that they are created from those elementary processes which are easily observed in the nerve preparations. Inhibition and excitation are included here in a higher complex whole, and may be understood only on this basis. Entering into the whole, they inevitably acquire a new qualitative significance, inhibiting as well as organising the rôle of speech. Can this be only according to the terms and basic elements of identity with those primitive functions which are known to the physiologists?

The characteristic mechanisms of complicated human behaviour can be understood only on a basis of adequate conceptions. But these conceptions should first take into account the whole organisation of behaviour: its structure and dynamics.

The structure of the organism presupposes not an accidental

mosaic, but a complex organisation of separate systems. This organisation is expressed paramountly in a functional correlation of these systems, in that they do not combine one with the other in an accidental way, but they unite as very definite parts into an integrated functional structure.

The basic features of this total structural organisation of behaviour is a functional inequality of the different systems entering into it; certain systems appear as governing and regulating, others as subordinate, executing one or another function. It is clear that the significance of these in the system of organisation is not always the same, and the whole activity of the organism can be understood only as a dynamic system, a conditioned activity of its component parts. It is difficult to describe this system in terms of inhibition and excitation; it is considerably more adequate to consider here the conception of organisation and disorganisation, regulating the destruction of the system of behaviour. In these we see a far greater possibility of understanding the dynamics of behaviour than if we approach the subject from those mechanical conceptions which we have described above.

The behaviour of the aphasic would be more comprehensible to us if we attempted to depict him in the terms of organisation and disorganisation. We will then proceed on the basis of those concepts only. The destruction and organisation would thus be completely comprehensible to us. The cortex and especially its highest parts have for a long time been described as having a regulating function; this function was discussed in a series of special investigations (we still have our own opinion here) on speech and symbolic activity. By this fact, speech and the higher psychological processes were separated from a series of other processes playing a special, regulating and leading rôle in behaviour. It is comprehensible that an injury to these should call out not a partial destruction of definite processes, but the destruction of the whole system of behaviour which is shown to be incapable of functioning with a destroyed executive regulating system. The confusion which we observed in the behaviour of the aphasiac, the uncertainty of all his activity, the disorganisation of his behaviour, which has been so brilliantly described by Head,[1] is comprehensible if we direct our attention to the neuropsychiatric apparatus as a system of separate partial apparatuses capable of being inhibited or stimulated. We shall proceed from this conception of organisation of behaviour con-

[1] Henry Head, *Aphasia*, Vols. 1 and 2, London, 1928.

nected with an apportioning of the executive regulating systems.

The mechanisms of inhibition and excitation serve us admirably to understand the processes of regulation and destruction, but they participate as a part of the mechanisms in the general purpose, and will be best understood only in the light of the complicated dynamic relation of the separate systems of the organism.

Organisation and disorganisation of human behaviour, conditions, laws and forms appear thus as the most important problems of psychobiology [1] and these which have concerned us for a number of years refer precisely to this chapter of the science of personality.

We have pointed out the chief principles lying at the basis of our researches; but we will now describe some of the concrete steps taken in the realisation of these principles.

The conception of "organisation" is to a certain degree opposed to a mechanical conception of the organism as an equilibrium of its component parts, in that it is adequate for an analysis of some of the more complicated processes of human behaviour. Nevertheless, it will remain a barren explanation as long as we do not give to it a more sharply defined specific content.

The conception of structure and organisation does actually make up most of the new psychoneurology, and based on these concepts are the latest ideas expressed by Köhler, Koffka, Wertheimer, K. Goldstein, Lashley, Child and others.

We must clearly define a number of ideas which arose during the early part of our work.

The conception of organisation and destruction still does not disclose those mechanisms which lie at their base, and the most varied dynamic relations may be concealed behind these terms. The history of scientific thought shows that two methodologies of false construction may be easily associated with the principle of organisation. The first of these is included in its universality. Having accepted it as a basis, we, too, easily see in it a certain general law, which appears equally in mechanics, in physics, and in neuropsychiatry and social life; and many authors have proceeded along the path of the universality of this principle. The logical consequence of this procedure is the wish to carry the complicated forms of organisation of behaviour into general laws which have already been observed in physics.

---

[1] We use this term psychobiology (instead of the more vague and general ones—psychoneurology, etc.) as applied by Adolf Meyer to indicate the organismal personality with all of its functions.—*Translator.*

Many psychoneurologists, having proved that approximately analogous laws govern the complicated forms of behaviour as they do tension in the physical world, cannot find in this wealth of relation any specific function not found elsewhere outside of human behaviour and without which it remains inaccessible for study. In particular, the extension of the principle of organisation into the domain of a general law inevitably leads us to ignore and misunderstand the details of human neurodynamics and the highest and specific forms of behaviour always remain beyond the field of vision of the mechanists. The opposite danger is represented by those who connect the principles of organisation with a vital structure.

Is it necessary to say that precisely these structures, counting the higher forms of organisation as the products of some special forces, exclude every possibility for a scientific investigation of the mechanism of this organisation and replace analysis with the postulation of some new existence, obscure and not adaptable to analysis? It should not confuse us that the best minds [1] often made a mistake precisely here, and that, abandoning the principle of integral activity of the organism, they proceeded to the recognition of a new and specific force bringing about this integration. The mistake does not arise here from a false principle; but it points only to a defect of methodology.

We begin with the view that in the organisation of behaviour there are some general laws operative, dependent upon the inclusion of some special vital forces. The organisation of adult human behaviour is the product of a fairly complicated and long development. The forms of organisation of behaviour in the first stages of this development are certainly something else than those forms of organisation which differentiate more complex behaviour, and we can the sooner say this development proceeds along the path of dominating the primitive laws, rather than along the path of simple repetitions of them in their new stages.

The problem of human behaviour proves, as we think, to be the problem of development, and only on this path can we attain to an understanding of the mechanism lying at the basis of the activity of the human personality.

The material in this book (which is discussed in detail in Part Three) makes us think that the genesis of organised human behaviour is through the development and inclusion of all the new regulating systems, which overcome the primitive forms of

[1] See Monakow and Mourgue: *Introduction biologique à l'étude de neurologie et de la psycho-pathologie*, 1928.

behaviour and transfer them to that which is a new and a more systematised organisation.

There is every reason to suppose that the primitive forms of organisation of behaviour, characterised by the sub-cortical type of activity, are completely transformed into the processes of the highest development, and the question of age ceases to play the leading rôle in general behaviour. This replacement of one type of behaviour with another is connected with the development of newly regulated systems, coming into conflict with the primitive sub-cortical activity and overcoming it, creating all the new forms of organisation.

These new forms of organisation are not at all organised—as many authors think—by the development of inhibition and the restraining influence of the cortex on sub-cortical activity. The development of neurodynamics from early childhood to an adult age results in a gradual overcoming of a primitive diffusion in the activity of the nervous system and the elaboration of the new functionally organised forms of behaviour. In this process, the higher cortical mechanism does much more than play a simple negative rôle; it is owing precisely to this participation in behaviour that there are included those regulating systems, which transfer the organisation of behaviour to the higher and higher stages and create new forms heretofore not existing.

The development of the child results not only in the inhibition of the primitive forms of activity of the nervous system; it proceeds along the path of the general development of regulation which begins with the primitive aspects of instinctive capabilities, and, with the help of the development of the higher psychological mechanisms, it approaches the most complicated forms of control of its behaviour. The inclusion of these activities in the behaviour of the child began with the complicated organic mechanism and then with the higher cultural systems conditioning new forms of organisation. This conception completely loses any universal character it may have for us, and at the same time it is by no means necessary to include here any conception of vital forces. In a completely concrete analysis of the organisation of behaviour, we think of it as a function of definite regulating systems, unequal at the various stages of the development of behaviour, and fully accessible through scientific analysis.

If in the examination of the principles lying at the basis of organised behaviour, we began with the idea of development and structural scheme of behaviour, different at the various stages of development, then we should carry with us the same idea when we pass over to an investigation of the disorganisation of human behaviour.

One feature is shown by a characteristic found in nearly all our works dealing with an investigation of the peculiarity of disorganised human behaviour. Although many authors studying human behaviour (normal) always attempted to understand its general structure, they failed to do this when they passed over to the investigation of such processes as affect, conflict, and neurosis. To investigate in this territory the existing structures, to find lawfulness in chaos, of course, seemed far more complicated and sometimes more or less senseless; and confirming "that affect is a disease of the mind," the majority of authors decided not to examine it as a form of behaviour obeying its own particular law, and were satisfied with a simple description of the various pathological states.

When science attained the possibility of studying objectively psychological phenomena, a new phase was reached, but in the main there was no improvement. Such authors decided that to speak of disorganisation of behaviour as a psychological subject was fairly difficult, and that when the person "loses his equilibrium" the behaviour falls under the influence of certain physiological processes, losing its specific psychologically organised character. The same affect, or neurosis, and this was still more marked with psychoses, began to be considered as physiological or pathological phenomena; and in its study they considered sufficient a description of the several physiological symptoms characterising it. The James-Lange theory of emotion was the theoretical justification of such a capitulation of psychological investigation and the transfer of the whole domain of affect to pure physiology.

It is thus perfectly clear, that, proceeding along this path, science naturally rejected the theory of disorganisation of behaviour, which for many years was substituted by a physiological symptom complex of disorganisation. Neither Wundt nor those who followed him avoided this difficulty, and the present investigator, attempting to work in this field, finds that he is building on air, or, in any case, on very uncertain ground.

The difficulty of this symptomatological point of view concerning affect and disorganisation of behaviour was overcome by the physiologists themselves. Cannon's researches proved that the separate physiological symptoms do not by any means completely describe affect, and for a satisfactory explanation we must consider the whole function of the organism. In the actual exposition of the problem, Cannon [1] showed convincingly that the affect itself can be understood only as a function of the animal's behaviour, and that its structure cannot be completely investigated in those structural relations which characterised the behaviour of the animal in a concrete situation and which evoke in the cortex, and through it in the sub-cortical apparatus, a very definite configuration of excitation.

From a different angle this problem was approached by another great physiologist—Pavlov.[2] His brilliant experiments showed clearly that affect is not a completely specific state with constant characteristics and definite symptoms. The affect itself can be understood only with the total behaviour of the animal, and it is a product of this activity, the result of a definite disturbance in the behaviour. Pavlov obtained very definite affective "breaks," an acute disorganisation of behaviour, each time that the conditioned reflexes collided, when the animal was unable to react to two mutually exclusive tendencies, or was incapable of adequately responding to any imperative problem.

In both of these cases—in the investigations of Cannon and Pavlov—they directed more attention to the affect than to the disorganisation of the behaviour, and abandoning the description of the separate symptoms, they considered with all seriousness the question of its causation, mechanism, and dynamics.

If the affect stands in dependence upon the general activity of the organism, and is manifested when something happens to this activity, then it is perfectly clear that in its study we must use other methods and conceptions than those which were ascribed to it in the descriptions of the various physiological symptoms. At the same time, there was introduced a new necessity, a psychical concept. The investigator began from an entirely new point of view to be interested in the question of the relation of affect to the general activity and its structure, to verbal behaviour, to general forms of regulation of human activity; he began to approach the structure of its different types, its influence upon the social activity of the human. These problems, which were without meaning or non-existent in the physiological examination of affect, took the first place in its examination by the psychologists.[3]

---

[1] W. B. Cannon: *The James-Lange Theory of Emotions,* American Journal of Psychology, Dec. 1927.
[2] I. P. Pavlov, *Lectures on Conditioned Reflexes,* International Publishers, N. Y., 1929.
    In using the term "psychological," we do not by any means consider a subjective study of affect obligatory. We simply want to say that the problem

Many psychologists [1] have attempted, so it seems to us, to introduce affect into the system of active human behaviour; but in the study of affect as a part of the system of pure psychology John Dewey (1) was perhaps the first to show the close connection between emotion and human activity, advancing the hypothesis that emotion appears when human activity is obstructed. Watson (2), Kantor (3), Marston (4), Mac-Curdy (5), came to the same conclusions from their investigations, showing that emotional behaviour actually depends upon how freely the tension which is produced in the nervous apparatus as a result of one or another condition is discharged. Finally, K. Lewin (6), attempted to show, in a series of carefully executed experiments, a more sharply marked relation between the processes of tension, discharge, and affection.

For the psychologist studying affect, a fairly stable theoretical basis is thus laid down, and we now see that in this question several general points of view are admitted, and the concrete investigation begins.

If the affect actually is determined by activity, then, on the basis of the concrete investigations, we should expect that precisely this is to be a fundamental supposition in the experimental study of affect, and that the investigation of disorganisation of behaviour proceeds exactly along the path of the study of affect as a form of human activity. But to our regret we have not yet been able to confirm this. The psychological experiment turns out to be a conservative psychological theory, and the scores of psychological laboratories continue to concern themselves with a description of the individual characteristics of the affective symptoms—of respiration, heart beat, mimicry, psychogalvanic phenomena—completely forgetting to study the function of those separate moments in the general dynamics of behaviour, and to connect this study with the participation of those systems which in the organisation of behaviour and in its disorganisation undoubtedly play the decisive rôle. In order to do this, we study the symptoms, mechanism, dynamics of affect, as one of the

of affect is introduced in the method of studying personality and its active behaviour.

[1] 1. J. Dewey: *The Theory of Emotion*, Psychological Review, 1, 1894; 2, 1895.

2. J. B. Watson: *Psychology from the Standpoint of a Behaviorist*, 1919, New York.

3. J. R. Kantor: *Principles of Psychology*, 1924-1926. *The Psychology of Feeling and Affective Reactions*, American Journal of Psychology, 1923. *An Attempt towards a Naturalistic Description of Emotion*, Psychological Review, 1921.

4. W. M. Marston: *Emotions of Normal People*, 1928.

5. J. T. MacCurdy: *Psychology of Emotions*, 1925.

6. K. Lewin: *Wille, Vorsatz und Bedürfniss*, 1925. *Die Entwichlung der modernen Willenspsychologie und Psychotherapie*, 1929.

existing forms of disorganisation of human behaviour. We try especially to think of the conditions of the origin of this disorganisation, of those systems which play decisive rôles, and to apply to physiological processes the methodology of psychology, not for a minute forgetting that we are studying the structure and function of human behaviour.

2. THE PATH OF INVESTIGATION

THE work on our problem proves that in order to study in as detailed a way as possible the mechanism of disorganisation of human behaviour and to establish certain laws, we should first take into consideration the fact that the disturbance of behaviour during the affective processes or in neuroses is not always the same, but that its destruction may be of several different types and that it follows its own special laws. The disorganization of behaviour must also have its own structure, and we should investigate it first as we do the structure of the organic psychological processes. This problem is far from being a simple one, and it is necessary to define those paths which lead us to its successful solution.

But first we should challenge the attempts of the subjective study of the problem before us. Empirical psychology, trying to divine the details of the affective processes through penetrative introspection, gave us an excellent description of the emotional states, but was completely powerless to create any kind of stable basis for the mechanics of affect, and even less for a dynamic explanation of these emotions. The barrenness of the idealistic psychology indicated, more than anywhere else in its study of emotion and affect and in the detailed descriptions of the various "mental phenomena," that there had been no further progress in the advance of our realistic knowledge concerning the mechanisms of human behaviour.

It is clear that the failure of the pure subjective analysis cannot force the psychologist along the path of the study of "simultaneous affect" of the bodily phenomena to investigate the structure and dynamics of affective processes. That step which Wundt formally took to direct attention to affective psychological-physiology was a great stride forward in the history of psychological science; however, many decades after the first physiological method of study of affect, it was apparent from the trials of Wundt that there were many methodological errors, and that the application of his method, although an enormous revolutionary impetus, could not really elucidate the matter.

Turning to the physiological paths of investigation of emotion, Wundt in reality could not abandon his phenomenal apparatus, and he approached it with those methodological principles which guided him in all of his psychological investigations.

The basic methodological position of the majority of the psychologists of that time consisted in the recognition of the fact that the psychologist must first of all describe that which he observed and must analyse it subjectively. On the other hand, in the decomposition of the observed phenomenon into its elementary components, many psychologists, as well as the natural scientists of that epoch, considered this their chief problem.

This descriptive mosaical stage proved ruinous for psychology, delaying its development for several decades. The ordinary work of the psychologist consisted in enumeration of the separate phenomena accompanying one or another psychological process, leading to a certain generalised theoretical situation, at best only to an explanation of the described phenomena. The problem of the structure of the whole process usually was relegated to an empirical description of the separate phenomena and symptoms, and the theory of explanation in nearly all the works of the psychologist-empiricist was fatally separated from the observed facts by an abyss.

In the investigation of the affective processes this method demanded much attention and led to an establishment of that view of the affective processes which lay at the basis of Wundt's psychological method of the study of emotion. This point of view might be expressed paradoxically: affect is not an act of behaviour but is a reaction to a series of psychological symptoms. This reached its paramount theory in the peripheral theory of emotion.

Observing the emotional processes, investigators saw that they depended upon many parallel phenomena: acceleration or slowing of association, change in respiration, frequency of pulse, and distention of blood vessels. Attempting to explain the physiological origin of affect, the positively minded authors usually directed their attention to those phenomena whose interrelations they understood very poorly but which seemed to them to be the source of the affective states. This assertion stood for a time as the basis of the peripheral theory of emotion, and affect began to be described "as the union of certain motor innervations in the vegetative symptoms."

The peripheral symptoms of emotion were first investigated a long time ago; but their study had led to no definite results. In spite of a multitude of attempts to discover in the separate psychological symptoms an adequate reflection of the affective process, all these trials to establish a unified and clear-cut picture of the psychological emotional state, producing exact changes in the breathing, pulse, and vaso-dilators were unsuccessful. One and the same affect in the hands of different authors gave far from the same symptoms accompanying varying and frequently completely different combinations of physiological changes. Wundt's attempts, and also those of many other authors, to defend the position of the exceedingly complicated theory of emotion, did not make the physiological symptoms a more stable basis for the study of affect, and the recent publications of the detailed experimental data [1] at best give us the right to say that affect is connected with a certain disorganisation of the ordinary course of the vegetative normal processes.

The more serious defects of all those attempts to study the affective processes by describing the individual physiological symptoms prove, however, the complete impossibility of comparing these symptoms with the details of human behaviour and the futility of drawing any definite conclusions about the structure of the psychological processes. But do the established physiological symptoms give us the possibility to say anything about the degree of activity or passivity of the process under consideration, about whether there is at its basis some conflict or experience resulting from an external trauma; is there here any vacillation of the subject, or is the process characterised by a continued uniform disorganisation?

These questions cannot find in the physiological symptoms any kind of answer, because the processes lie in an entirely different plane from that of our problems. We inquired into the structure of behaviour and attempted to find an answer in the analysis of the individual physiological changes of behaviour, which it was possible to understand, however, only from the general structure of the whole process.

Precisely this last assertion changes our relation to the accompanying physiological symptoms. Considering then their secondary affects, arising as a result of the general change in behaviour, we consider them upon the structure of this behaviour and we certainly are not astonished that, in the change of this structure, the reciprocal relations of the different vegetative

[1] Löwenstein: *Experimentelle Hysterielehre,* Bonn, 1923.

symptoms are completely altered. On the contrary, all attempts to study the structure of the affective disorganisation of behaviour without considering the alteration in the behaviour itself appears to us wide of the mark. The bad beginning cannot, in any case, lead to successful results; for the basic factor producing these secondary symptoms, having different significance in the varying structure of behaviour, is senseless and already destined to fail.

It is thus natural that all our attention, which was earlier given to the different physiological symptoms, should be transferred to the investigation of the alterations in the structure of behaviour during affect; from an observation of the peripheral symptoms, we turn to the study of the structure of the central processes, and it is here that we expect to find the key to a possibly complete understanding of the whole disorganisation of behaviour.

In thus shifting our attention to the central processes, we are in step with the leading physiologists. The researches of Cannon [1] are of extraordinary interest; he showed experimentally that the complete excision of the viscera did not result in a decrease of emotion, and that the animal after the operation gave evidence of all the signs of affective behaviour, in spite of the fact that the visceral components were completely absent. These experiments confirm that the physiological changes usually considered as the basis for the affective processes, in reality, are only secondary and accompanying processes, the diminution of which does not remove the affect. For the James-Lange theory, as well as for the ordinary physiological method, attempting the study of the effect of behaviour on the basis of unified secondary symptoms, these experiments are fatal, and scientific thought is proceeding along another path in the study of affective experiences and affective behaviour.

The investigation starting from the active processes of behaviour is, as we think, more adequate for the study of affect and affective disorganisation. Only in the alterations of the active forms of human activity can we hope to find a suitable reflection of that structure of the affective processes in which we are interested. Many motives forced us along this path.

On the one hand, there are a series of causal dynamic considerations. We begin with the hypothesis that the affective disorganisation of behaviour is connected intimately with the Fate of the active processes. The affect appears when something happens with the organised phenomena of activity; therefore, it should be reasonable to hope to obtain a more adequate structure of the affective process by the investigation of the fate of the active functions connected with this process.

[1] W. B. Cannon and others: *Some Aspects of the Physiology of Animals Surviving Complete Exclusion of the Sympathetic Nervous System*, American Journal of Physiology, 1929.

The second consideration follows immediately after the first: only a system of active behaviour—speech or motor—appears capable of manifesting an actual structure, changing under the influence of the affective behaviour. All the interesting events for us, which cannot be expressed by the physiological symptoms, are fully obtained in the structure of the active "spontaneous" acts.

We may at a glance trace here the variation and conflict of the experimental, active or passive, character of its reaction, the disturbance of the process and its control. The complicated character of the behaviour, directed to a known external activity, allows us with great exactitude to estimate not only the general character of the disturbance, but indeed to ascertain in which system of activity, in which of its phases, "beginning, or concluding motor," arose those changes calling out the characteristic disorganisation of behaviour. We turn here, consequently, in a new direction in the investigation of the affective processes, replacing the study of the symptoms by the investigation of the structure, switching from the path of physiology to that of psychology.

Taking upon ourselves the problem of the study of the structure and dynamics of the processes of the disorganisation of human behaviour, we should stand firmly upon the ground of the psychological experimenters; we should on the one hand, produce the central process of the disorganisation of behaviour; on the other hand, we should try to reflect this process in some system accessible and suitable for examination. The motor function is such a systematic, objectively reflected structure of the neuro-dynamic processes concealed from immediate examination. And there lies before us the use of the motor function as a system of reflected structure of hidden psychological processes. Thus we proceed along the path which we call the combined motor method.

The motor functions of the human being serve as the subject of study of the great majority of authors. These fall into two general groups: in one group, as, for example, Hamburger, Foerster, Magnus, Kleist, Gurevitch, movement is the subject of the entire investigation. The problem which these authors face consists in studying the development of movement, coordination, and motor formulæ, and their destruction in certain diseases of the nervous system. They investigate the motor function physiologically as one of the component parts of the vital activity of the organism, frequently concealing symptoms indicative of the very serious disturbance of the nervous system.

The other group of investigators proceed in a different manner. The motor activity of the human being offers them not the goal but only a means of studying the complicated psychological-physiological processes. They are interested in the structure of movement *per se*, but only as a reflection of certain changes concealed from immediate observation. Therefore, not all of the details of the motor activity, but only those which are directly connected with the psychological changes are of interest to the investigators of this group (Sommer, Löwenstein, Isserlin, Kraepelin, Lehrman, Kornilov). To this group belong those investigators who have tried to find a reflection of the complicated psychological processes in certain partial motor functions, as, for example, in handwriting.

The first group of authors are distinguished for their detailed neurological analysis of the motor functions; whereas the second group, for whom the motor activity is only a door to the recognition of those processes which are of interest, consider this analysis of the motor indicators of much less importance, and indeed some of the investigators possess only a slight technical ability. However, this has not disturbed the essential principles of their work, because, in this case, not the structure of movement itself but only a reflection in it, of the complicated psychological processes, is for them the chief subject of research. The transfer of the main topic of discussion to the reflection of the hidden psychological processes at once makes the investigation more complicated. The problem arises to differentiate the motor changes which are the products of the psychological influence from those resulting from the organic peculiarities of its activity—the problem appears here with all its preciseness, and can be decided only by a very careful, detailed, and comparative analysis.

In this classification our work as a whole is more closely allied with the second group of investigators. We are only very slightly interested in the motor activities of the subject *per se;* with the constitutional typical analysis of the differences of movement, flow of speech, coordination, intensity, and speed of movement—these do not interest us insofar as they are not connected with the structure of the psychological processes. In our investigation we should constantly meet with the study of the motor activities; but these will serve us only as a path to the concealed psychological processes, only the systemic reflection of their structures. Therefore, our studies are not typological but are functional.

The chief problem of this investigation is to explain the laws of the disorganisation of human behaviour, the conditions under which they arise, and the way in which they are overcome. Therefore, we should study the structure of the disappearance and origin of this behaviour in those reactions entering into its real composition.

We rejected the view that in order to study the reflection of the disorganisation of behaviour it was necessary to investigate the changes of the vegetative activity. We will not follow along the same path as the physiologists of the nervous system, and we shall not incorporate into the bases of our method the investigation of how the reflexes change under the influence of a general disturbance of the structure of behaviour. The investigation of the reflex activity is hardly more suitable in itself as an index of the structure of the changing human behaviour than is the isolated study of the vegetative system. The reflex movement, composing perhaps the genetic basis of behaviour, enters into the composition of active behaviour only as a separate category, defined by the most complicated circumstances and mechanisms of personality, and losing its form in the active behaviour. To investigate the reflection of the structural changes in behaviour in the elementary reflexes would be to carry the investigation along under great disadvantage, forcing the complicated processes to be revealed inadequately by an elementary and slightly changing phenomena; therefore, it is entirely unsuited for a complete description of function.

Studying the objective forms of reflection of the complicated central changes, we do not intend to explain this complicated structure of disorganisation of human behaviour in elementary units. This would be contradictory to our fundamental methodology. In our opinion, the adequate can be expressed successfully only in the adequate, and the structure of the disturbed behaviour can be revealed only in those fractions of behaviour accessible for study: this should include in its composition all the basic mechanisms, the basic instances which enter into the whole behaviour.

We have become convinced of the necessity of accepting as a basis for our method of study, the spontaneous movements, having included them in a known experimental system, in an attempt to investigate the characteristic changes of the disorganisation of behaviour. Certainly, the affect causes great fluctuations in the motor activity; if the affect is not accidentally related to the section of the human behaviour we are studying, if we consider the given disorganisation of behaviour to consist in the particularities of the systems of behaviour under investigation, then the disturbance will be involuntarily and definitely expressed in the sections of activity which we will record. We shall study the involuntary destruction of the voluntary movements; we consider this a more adequate path to a better understanding of the disorganisation of behaviour.

One objection which can be raised to our desire to accept the study of the voluntary movements as a basis will be that involuntary fluctuations occur. In order that our problem will be successful, it is necessary that it should be actually possible to divide these involuntary changes from the voluntary. In a word, it is essential that the voluntary be stable. But many psychophysiologists seriously doubt that the voluntary movements satisfy this requisite. Even its name indicates a certain volition, a certain instability; hence the impression that we are building our investigation on sand and that the voluntary movements we obtain fluctuate each time, and that we cannot estimate accurately these variations underlying the affective changes.

Voluntary movements are not less regular nor less stable than the reflexes, and to a certain degree even more so than the mechanical movements which are always taken as a model of stability and exactitude. It is true, however, that in one respect there is a real difference between the mechanical movement and organic movement, particularly voluntary movements. While mechanical movements, arising under the same conditions, always have the same form, the organic movements undoubtedly are characterised by a great plasticity—under the same conditions they may not be of identical form in the separate details, but they remain, however, absolutely identical in their general scheme, in their fundamental "motor formula."

The presence of such a movement-formula is the recognised characteristic for all voluntary movements, and the variations of this usual motor scheme are no more voluntary than the change of form in any mechanical movement. If, in the scheme of movements, any change occurs, we may rightly look for certain organic or functional situations which may have altered the scheme; therefore, precisely this analysis of voluntary movement can prove to be the path to a sufficiently exact diagnosis of the concealed destruction of the nervous apparatus and the fluctuations of those conditions under which the nervous apparatus performs its duties.

A voluntary movement within its own scheme reveals a far greater stability than we might suppose, and from this point of view it is no less advantageous, fundamentally, for the study of the concomitant disorganisation of the behaviour than an involuntary movement, and any doubt as to its stability can be dissipated in the first analysis of the material.

In Figure 1 we see a cyclographic record of three motor strokes taken on one and the same photographic plate.

We have taken purposely an example of a fairly complicated voluntary movement, in which we might expect the maximal variation and instability of form; this illustration shows us, however, that there is no essential variation: three complex voluntary movements are identical in the scheme, within its limits, and they so resemble one another that we are often unable in the same record to differentiate them. These slight digressions which we find between the trajectories of these three movements do not lead to any confusion, because they do not represent a situation of the scheme but only an inconsiderable variation in its performance, by no means changing the fundamental "movement-formula."

If this is the state of affairs with a comparatively complicated movement, then with similar movements it is much more evident, and many inherited reactions (let us say the movement of the toes) during one and the same trial usually reveals such stability that even a detailed analysis proves that its basic form is preserved. An examination of the claim that the voluntary movements are unstable proves that this statement does not correspond to the facts, and we have sufficient grounds to accept voluntary movements as a basis for our study.

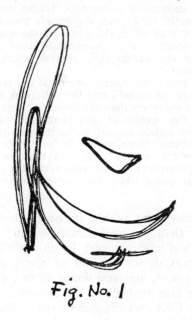

Fig. No. 1

CYCLOGRAM OF THREE MOTOR STROKES

We have shown above that if we desire to trace the structure of the internal changes which are inaccessible to direct observations, we can follow their reflection in the voluntary motor functions, and that the existing conditions enabling us to investigate the central process wherein arises that disorganisation of interest to us, should not be unsuitable for the reflection of the motor processes. We must find such a system of activity which will include in its parts and central process the affective disorganisation concerned, and the motor process which should be capable of reflecting the central activity and its fate, not as something foreign but as a special phase, included in the whole structure. Only under these conditions of the participation of the central changes and motor-reflected processes in one general structure can we hope to represent adequately in our study all the phenomena arising in the concealed concatenation of changes.

We find such a possibility in the principle of the active union of the central and motor activity. Certainly if we combine in one functional system two activities—the central and the motor—we can record that every central change is necessarily reflected primarily in that motor system, which is formed into a united whole, and only secondarily evokes certain changes in the physiological system to which it spreads. Such a division of the united dynamic structure, including in itself the central part concealed from direct study and the motor functions capable of being objectively registered, is the basic combination of the motor method by the help of which we have acquired the essential material dealt with in this volume.[1]

We can very easily create a model of such a united system of activity in which the character and fate of a certain concealed function can be reflected in the structure accessible for a direct experimental analysis of the objective process. In order to do this, it is sufficient to confront the subject with the following simple problem: The subject must reply to a word given him by the first thought which enters his mind, linguistically, pressing at the same time the finger of the right hand on the receiver of an apparatus lying in front of him. Here we stimulate in our subject two systems of activity which are connected with each other so closely that they are set in motion by two simultaneously occurring activities of one and the same process. Actually, the proposal to answer a given word by any other word excites in our subject a certain central process of a very complicated order, and close to the speech system. Analysing it psychologically, we can in some cases see its associative process; in others its primitive fate; in still others, its reintegration with the origin of the whole image of the details contained in the word, or the production of some other details entering together with what is represented in the word-stimulus into one and the same formation.

We are not here concerned with the phenomenal existence of this process; and our attention is directed chiefly to the fact

[1] A special article describes the details of this method: *The Union of the Motor Method and the Investigation of the Affective Reaction,* State Institute of Experimental Psychology, Moscow, 1928; *Die Methode der Abbildenden Motorik und ihre Anwendung an die Affektpsychologie,* Psychol-Forschung, Band 12, 1929.

that we are able to evoke a definite, very complicated neuro-dynamic process, concealed from immediate observation and, after a certain period, leading to the speech response. This neuro-dynamic process can be now entirely organic and regular, now it may meet in its path a certain obstacle with which it collides, and the result is a certain disorganisation. It is obvious that the neurodynamic process, lying at the base of the habitual associative answer, is actually different from the characteristic of the intel-lectual process, vacillating with and obstructed by the affective tone or by passing through different variations to the specific reactions. In all these cases, the structure of the neurodynamic processes will be, of course, very different, and to the direct and objective analysis it appears inaccessible. Our problem consists in trying, experimentally, to carry the destruction to this struc-ture, and by means of this application to lay emphasis on the analysis.

The union of the motor reaction with the speech response serves precisely this purpose. By connecting the language response to the motor reaction of the hand, we create, so to speak, a system which is capable of reflecting objectively the whole dynamic character for the central neurodynamic process of the attention. By uniting the word response and motor reaction into a single process we have a method by which we can estimate the actual changes in this obscure process as necessarily reflected in a clearly defined process, and we see that the differences in the neurodynamic structure of the central process are reflected in the evident differences of structure in the motor curve. Pre-cisely this union of both functions into a single active system leads us to believe that every sharp fluctuation and every tendency to a speech response, and, even more so, every marked affective disorganised character of the central process does not remain without influence on the structure of the compounded motor reaction; and analysing it, we have at hand a very objec-tive means for drawing conclusions concerning the structure of the internal neurodynamic process.

We employed the combined motor method in our experiment, some of the details of which we shall describe.

The subject is seated in a comfortable armchair in front of a table, holding in his hand a special device. The right hand lies on the table so that the finger tips can be used to compress the pneumatic bulb; the left hand during the experiment holds also an analogous apparatus. This is shown in Figure 2.

In our routine experiment there is given a word-stimulus, to which the subject must answer by another word, and simultaneously he presses

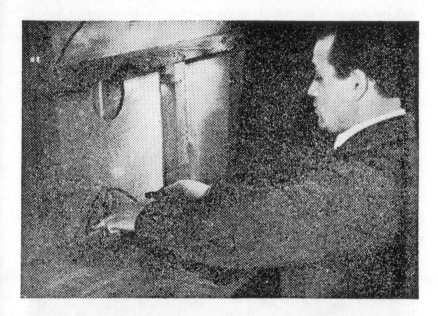

FIG. NO. 2

SUBJECT DURING EXPERIMENTATION

FIG. NO. 3

with the fingers of the right hand the pneumatic bulb, connected with a recording drum, while the left hand remains passive, holding the weight without producing any movement. The moment of stimulation is registered by closing an electrical key by the experimenter, and the instant of the response, by means of a sensitive membrane (Shirsky's system) which is operated by the subject's voice.

Figure 3 shows the metal capsule especially constructed over the pneumatic bulb. The finger of the right hand is pressed simultaneously with the speech response. Every slightest tremor of the hand is registered. Each pressure of the finger corresponds to the ascent of the curve on the drum, and a decrease in pressure [1] to the descent of the curve.

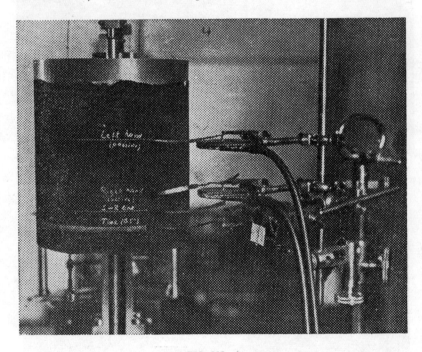

FIG. NO. 4

SPECIMEN OF RECORD

As was mentioned above, the (active) hand rests on the bulb, the left (passive) remains on the weight. The latter is thus held, in order to make its position less stable; hence it can be used as a sensitive indicator, as we shall see, the neurodynamic excitation by a general overflow of tremor. This is registered on the drum at the same time as the pressure of the right hand.... In the usual experiment, the kymograph ordinarily turns with a speed of one centimeter per second.

[1] The pressure of the finger on the pneumatic appliance and its record will be hereinafter referred to simply as *pressure.—Translator.*

We obtained, in this way, a record simultaneously of three very important lines as shown in Figure 5.

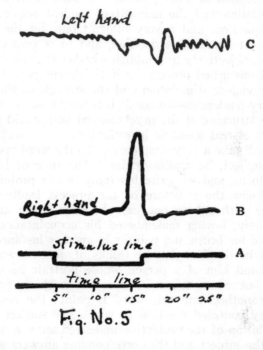

A = the line of speech reaction, the time being in fifths of a second.

B = the curve of the active right hand which in most experiments is smooth in the latent period, giving a regular rise associated with the speech reaction.

C = the curve of the passive left hand fluctuating with the tremor.

Besides these three curves, representing the intellectual process, and the active and passive motor response, there is sometimes added a fourth curve to record the respiration and pulse, as the part of the cycle of symptoms which arises from the vegetative system. In this manner we are able to see the reciprocal evidences of the entire system, the changes in which enable us to investigate the structure induced by our neurodynamic disturbance.

The application of our method can be best shown by an example—that of the "enigmatical latent period." The structure of the latent period of any complex reaction actually represents an enigma for the majority of psychologists, for it seems that in this study there are no other paths besides the subjective, and that the establishment of the objective neurodynamic structure of this time interval, when the reaction has not been expressed, is a hopeless problem.

The question of what process is hidden between the moment of stimulation and the moment of evident response remains a crucial question, and a very difficult one, for the psychologist. To refuse to make this decision, and to recognise that we are powerless objectively to establish whether the reaction is a result of the undisturbed process, or if the latent period is connected with the violent stimulation and the struggle of the several contradictory tendencies—to admit this would mean giving up hope that the structure of the psychological acts would sometimes be a subject of real scientific investigation.

We shall take a very simple case. To the word "portrait" given to our subject, he replies "paint." The time of his reaction is known to us, and we write his reply in our protocol. However, do we know the structure of the process leading him to the reaction? Although in one case he may arrive at this answer immediately, having remembered his acquaintanceship with an artist and his brush and paints; in another instance, the answer may not be the first that he thinks of, for the word "portrait" may remind him of a person whose portrait he might like to possess but whose name he does not wish to pronounce. He chooses another, and this word is paint; the result is only a secondary confused reaction to which our subject arrived after the inhibition of the protective undesired answer. The introspection of the subject and the corresponding answers sometimes can call out such a structure of the associative reactions; in other cases when the inhibition of the first reaction suggests an affective character, and is connected with some unpleasantness, compromising his impressibility (such a case is for us most interesting) we do not have any basis to hope for frankness in our subject, and the structure of the latent period is concealed from us. In the event we have before us a criminal not admitting his crime, or an hysteric concealing his affective complexes, this door is closed even more tightly in front of us, and the hope to investigate the structure of the latent period by a subjective analysis vanishes completely.

Even with a full and "honest" statement of the subject, we cannot consider the situation altogether favourable. If we can here recognise the content of the repressed word and the motives behind the repression, then the neurodynamic structure of this process does not stand out any clearer for us. Is the process connected with a certain neurodynamic excitation, or does it represent here only a general tendency to the expression of some complicated or repressed impulse—all these questions are inaccessible to a subjective analysis, and the most detailed answer does not facilitate the task of the experimenter here.

We do not obtain much of value in this instance from the introduction of such simultaneous symptoms as respiration, pulse, plethismogram, psychogalvanic reflex. In the most favourable situation these indicators reveal only some details of the general affective tone, but the structure of the process here remains obscure.[1] Did the repression of the first word which came into the mind of the subject have a place here, or was it simply the affective tension? This cannot be reflected, simply because the structure of the action of behaviour cannot be recorded in physiological symptoms having no control over such a structure.

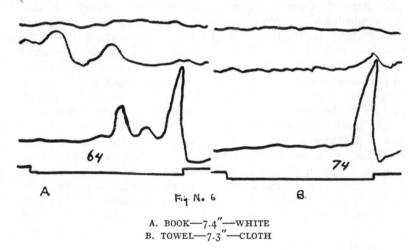

Fiq. N. 6

A. BOOK—7.4″—WHITE
B. TOWEL—7.3″—CLOTH

For the objective expression of such a structure of the associative process we connect it with the voluntary motor activity, which should completely reflect its neurodynamics; and we have this possibility in our combined methods. Figure 6 gives us an example of how this structure of the latent period can be reflected in the combined motor process.

We give here two reactions from one of our subjects: M., who, two days preceding the experiment, murdered his fiancée, and

[1] L. Binswanger, *Über das Verhalten des psychogalvanischen Phönomens beim Associationsexperiment*, Diagnostic Associationstudien, C. Jung, II, 1910. O. Löwenstein, *Die experimentelle Hysterielehre*, 1923. W. W. Smith, *The Measurement of Emotions*, 1923.

came to our laboratory after his arrest. The position of the murderer was known to us: the fiancée resisted strongly and wounded M's hand. In order to stop the flow of blood M. had to take the kitchen towel, tear off a piece and wrap it around his hand, and with this convincing evidence he was caught. We confronted our subject by two word-stimuli, one of which, "book" was indifferent to him, and the other "towel," was connected with an important moment of the event. The two reactions are almost equal in time, and both are normal in the character of the responses: book—7.4"—white, and towel—7.3"—cloth.

The external signs do not give us any reason to speak of the structures of these reactions; but we have every right to believe that the structures should be different, and that the response to the latter stimulus was not the first which occurred to the subject. The characer of the combined motor reaction convinces us that the supposition is correct; while in the first reaction the latent period shows no upheaval; in the second we unmask the motor reaction, which is not completed, is inhibited, but is sufficiently clearly expressed, and the structure of the motor response points to two clashes of the reactive process, from which only one, the latter, was expressed in the speech response, the first being inhibited in the speech but revealed only in the motor reaction.

The mechanics of this process is clear enough. The combined motor pressure is connected not only with the explicit word response, but in the tendency to the speech answer, and the reaction occurring in the mind is shown in the motor tension of the first compression of the bulb, before the word was spoken, and before it was inhibited. The tense motor reaction clearly shows us not only the peculiarities of the neurodynamic latent period, but it gives us data concerning the structure of the process concealed from view.

We can easily be convinced that we have before us an adequate reflection in the motor structure of the neurodynamic process, and that the "motor attempt to the reaction" is, in effect, the correlation of the concealed and unexpressed speech symbol.

We may compare the facts we have obtained in the combined motor method with those of the subjective response, and such a comparison shows that the correspondence of structures is here evident. Figure 7 gives us a section of the graphic protocol illustrating this.

The word "work" is the word stimulus. "Work" is presented to one of our subjects, and the result is: work—5."—well, day. The answer shows in its structure this reaction:

"At once there began within me the word 'day,' but it seemed that it had no connection with what you said to me. Therefore, I began to inhibit it, but, then nevertheless, I decided to say it."

The structure of the combined motor curve reflects very clearly the character of the observed introspective process. After one second following the giving of the stimulus, we disturbed the light motor pressure, also the inhibitory pressure, and then in the second trial, and even in the third the appearance of the pressure is shown with the newly responding reaction of the subject. The expression of the active curve is clearly defined if we compare it with the character of the passive curve of the left hand; these curves reveal that which is unexpressed, and which, of course, does not manifest any signs of the structure of the process before us.

We have a complete confirmation that the motor function is actually reflected here in the structure of the unexpressed newly associated process, when in the experimental conditions we artificially create such a structure, and after this we express it in the motor function.

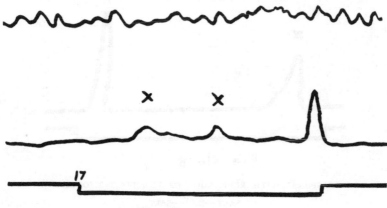

Fig. No. 7

ATTEMPT TO REACTION

We suggest to the subject, while in the hypnotic state, that with the presentation of the definite word-stimulus, he think of some indecent word, and if the hypnosis is sufficiently deep, our suggestion will undoubtedly have effect. The subject actually thinks of some indecent word but his education and training will not allow him to utter it; he represses it and speaks another word, one which serves in the given case as a substitute and which is more suitable for utterance. Thus we artificially arrive at the structure of the reaction, and we shall see that the combined motor method is able to express this structure objectively.

Figure 8 shows such an example. To the subject *Nor* in the hypnotic state it was suggested that after the word "salt" he should think of some indecent association. In the experiment we obtained some exceedingly characteristic data following the series of perfectly normal responses. This reaction is obtained after the word "salt" (salt—17"—salt; salt—6.6" "valley." "I myself do not know why.") The subject's answer showed that the first word he thought of "was not fit to utter," he inhibited it and said the first word he thought of afterwards. The combined motor curve is a sufficiently accurate reflection of the structure; 8/10 seconds after the presentation of the stimulus we saw a marked motor impulse quickly becoming inhibited, and only 6 seconds after there follows the final reaction, corresponding to the frank speech response.

Here the combined motor curve is capable of showing not only the symptoms of the known changes in the process, but reflects fairly adequately its structure.

In the cases which we have examined, the combined motor method is a satisfactory reflection of the inhibited and the unexpressed parts of the associative process, and we may confidently expect that in expressing the structure of the organised process, it is also capable of revealing the disorganisation of this structure.

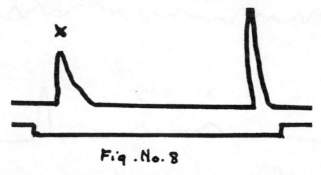

Fig. No. 8

RESPONSE WITH REPRESSION OF THE FIRST THOUGHT

SALT—6.6″—SALT

In the experiments with association we frequently meet with cases in which the excitatory process begins to have a markedly affective character, losing its organisation and passing over into a definitely disorganised, chaotic state. We meet with a similar situation when our stimulus collides with some affective focus, stimulating and actuating affective traces. In these cases the presented word-stimulus does not evoke the organic intellectual process, but it gives to both a typical confusion, which is evident to observation as a certain affective excitation, inhibiting the associative process and expressing itself in various vegetative symptoms. Is this destruction of the process reflected in the combined active curve? We may not answer this question categorically. If the affective process consists at basis in the delay of the adequate answer and in the disorganisation of the activity, then precisely in the active motor curve directly connected with the central associative process we may primarily expect a change of the reflected structure. We are limited here to only one example, because all our investigations are concerned with the study of the structure of the disorganised behaviour, and of the functions which we have destroyed.

The subject "St," with whom we chose to demonstrate how our method disorganised the affect reaction, is accused of the murder of the woman found on the front steps of a certain house, strangled with a strap. We give him a number of language stimuli, and among these the word "train" [Russian = *poyezd*]. The subject understands this word as "belt" [Russian = *poyus*] and gives the reaction, "strap."

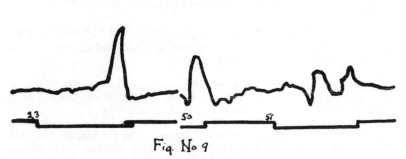

Fig. No 9

COMPLEX REACTION OF "ST"

23. TRAIN—3.2″—STRAP   50. WATER—1.0″—LAKE
51. STRAP—4.0″—WELL, FUR COAT

Figure 9 is a graphic representation of this reaction. The registration of the speech answer showed only a slight delay in comparison with the normal reaction, and this led to the supposition that there was a connection with the situation of the crime. The combined motor method very clearly reveals the neurodynamic declination characteristic of the given process. Soon after the presentation of the stimulus there begins in the active motor curve a typical tremor showing that for this latent period there is a central excitation, and that precisely the presence of this reaction differentiates it from the others. We do another experiment giving to the subject, after an interval, the word "strap." He answers to it by a very delayed reaction: strap—4.0″—well, fur coat.

Looking at the combined motor curve we are convinced that it is completey disrupted, and that for this reaction there is substituted an extreme neurodynamic excitation, completely disorganising the whole process.

On inspection the curve of the combined motor method shows us an equivalent neurodynamic excitation, concealed behind each given reaction, and enables us to evaluate immediately the degree of its affect.

The examples which we have given here show that the combined motor curves can reflect not only the neurodynamic destruction, combined with the associative process, but indeed their structural peculiarities. This latter possibility, of course, does not involve any expressive physiological system, and only the active motor method, combined with the central process in a unified functioning system, is capable of expressing the structure of the neurodynamic process ordinarily hidden from direct observation.

We can very easily prove this by comparing the results with those obtained in the passive motor method reflecting the destruction of the neurodynamic process.

To perform such control experiments means the repetition of the large number of those carried out by R. Sommer, which have been more recently perfected technically by O. Löwenstein. The analysis of these authors' data shows that the affective disorganisation of behaviour can be reflected in the passive motor processes of the human, but that its reflection can in nowise reveal here the real structure itself of the changing central processes; on the other hand, that it is unstable and indefinite. Registering the passive fluctuating curve of the four extremities, of the head, and the added curve of respiration and pulse, we cannot, properly speaking, confidently tell precisely where the disorganisation of the behaviour is reflected; if in one experiment it conditions a marked fluctuation of the curve of the right hand, and in the other experiment we may expect an appearance of these destructions in the tremor of the feet, or the movements of the head, etc.

Every evoked affective destruction in one of the expressive systems creates a corresponding discharge of excitation. Therefore, its reflection in one of the systems exposes the reflection in other systems; to predict with a lesser or greater degree of accuracy precisely where our destruction appears is next to impossible, and the work of Löwenstein proves this without doubt.

We have had many occasions to observe the fact that the excitatory reinforcement of innervation of the legs, by affect, gave all the symptoms which we would expect from the records of the arms. This led the authors to register the maximal number of expressive systems, increasing the number of chances that the reflection of the affect will be registered in one of these systems.

In the method we have evolved, we have chosen another way. This allows us to dispense with the parallel registration of a large number of systems. In joining the active motor curve with the central processes, we obtain a united system of activity, and have every reason to believe that in this active motor system there is reflected the changes occurring in the central processes. The presence of two, or a maximum of three, registered systems (actively combined hand, passive hand, and one of the vegetative systems) is in this case sufficient to obtain a complete representation of the structure of the processes under consideration.

What we have said brings us to the conclusion that, refusing the principle of the active combination of the motor reaction with the central processes, we surrender substantial ground in the study of the objective systems of the processes of disorganisation of behaviour, and to a great extent we pass over to the influence of accident, which can, thanks to some change in excitation which we fail to measure, at any moment alter our passive system so that it becomes an entirely inexpressive system.

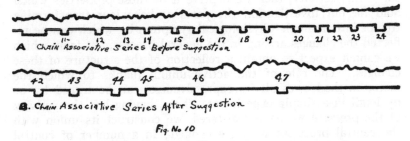

A Chain Associative Series Before Suggestion

B. Chain Associative Series After Suggestion

Fig. No 10

REFLECTION OF AFFECT IN THE TREMOR OF THE HAND

A = CHAIN ASSOCIATION BEFORE SUGGESTION
B = CHAIN ASSOCIATION AFTER SUGGESTION

In Figure 10 we see an example of how an attempt to trace the reflection of extreme affective processes in the general tremor often does not lead to results corresponding with the speech reaction, after this has already given the stimulus for the pressure by the hand; the intensity of this pressure is shown here unconnected with the intensity to the speech reaction, and there were such fluctuations in the methods that the motor curve ceased to be an adequate reflection of the central processes.

To the subject "Z" in a hypnotic state a very disagreeable experience was suggested. Before and after the suggestion we have two chains of the associated series: the first flowed very smoothly and without appreciable obstacles, whilst the second was connected with the suggested unpleasantness, and was, therefore, strongly affective. The contents of both of the chains, as well as the length of interval between the separate words and the control experiments conducted by our usual method, convincingly proved that the second series differs significantly from the first precisely in its exclusive affectiveness. If this affect, however, is expressed in our usual combined motor method by the marked disorganisation of the active curve, then in the application of the passive method—the curve is incomparably less expressive, the registration of the tremor of the passive movement of the hand and the inhibition has lost chiefly its ability to reflect the structure of the adequate process.

Figure 10 shows that if the general character of our data in this case changes, then neither its structure nor the clear-cut accompanying destruction with the separate critical reaction makes it possible to describe accurately the location and character of the affective process.　If we subtract from the motor curve this activity, then we deprive it of those properties which hold for our investigation the parts of behaviour transforming tremor into a simple physiological symptom by which can be reflected the changes arising in the general process, but from which we cannot expect to obtain a reflection of the structure of these changes.　The rôle of the active union, thanks to which the motor method owes all its expressiveness, can be traced by us in detail in a simple experiment, where, having left the activity of the pressure we have registered, we construct its union with the central processes we have evoked; in a number of control experiments, designed especially for this purpose, we told the subject to answer, as ordinarily, with the first word he thought of, not, however, combining his answer with the pressure of his hand, but compressing only after the answer had been given.

In this case we do not evoke any discoordination of movement and of speech response; by displacing the movement we destroyed that unified motor structure which was produced by the combined language and motor reaction. The physiological character of the process was changed. The subject, having reacted already after this, gave himself a stimulus by the compression of the hand, the intensity to this compression is here not connected with the intensity of the language reaction. Such a slight alteration in the method was sufficient to cause the motor curve to fail in an adequate reflection of the central process.

We give as an example of such a variation of the method, Figure 11, showing two reactions in the same subject. Both of these reactions, according to all the data, are in the highest degree effective; this is proven by the extreme inhibition and the absence in the first cases of the response and many

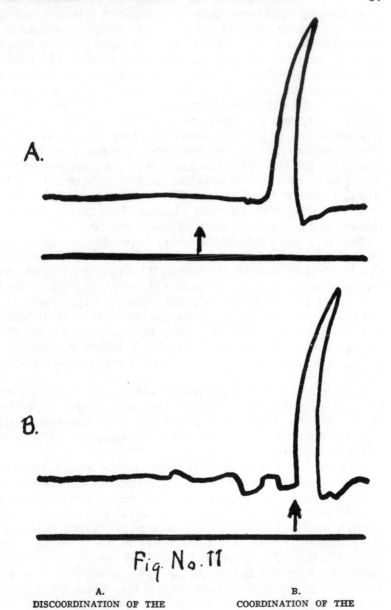

Fig. No. 11

A.
DISCOORDINATION OF THE
PRESSURE

B.
COORDINATION OF THE
PRESSURE

A. TIMID—14.4″—(SIGH) "I WON'T SAY ANYTHING."
B. WAIT—5.8″—MEETING

accompanying symptoms. Only one condition was different in these two experiments; in the first case we gave this subject instruction on the delay of the motor response; in the second instance, we proceeded as in our customary manner. The results were widely divergent. A great delay in one of the associated processes in the first case is not accompanied by any motor symptoms; the right gave during the course of the whole latent period a very smooth, dead, inexpressive curve, and its active pressure is clearly separate from the whole process seen here. The second case presents entirely other symptoms, bearing witness to the fact that the motor action is here a process of limited connection, with a central associated activity reflecting its inadequacy; precisely, therefore, the affective character of this reaction is reflected with sufficient clearness here in the observed changes of the motor function of the latent period.

Only an active combination makes it possible to express the internal process inaccessible to direct observation, in the completely adequate external symptoms. With this active union, we create, so to speak, a unified acting structure, into which enter the obscure as well as the externally expressed symptoms. The changes of one side of the structure are inevitably reflected from the changes of the other side, and with this we are able to study the inadequate character of the highest psychological processes, where the direct observation of these processes is unattainable for us.[1]

The application of our method, combining the associated experiment with the motor reaction, has still another important characteristic: reflecting the affective process into completely objective symptoms, it at the same time makes possible a more suitable comprehension of affect.

After the experiments of C. G. Jung and the psychoanalytical method we consider it useless to try artificially to evoke affect in the subject by irritation of his fecal masses or by discharge over the ear; each of the subjects had had in his past experience shown a wealth of affective traces such as to obtain a significant affect sufficient to call out these traces in life, to bring them into realisation. The associated experience serves this purpose admirably. It would be utterly fallacious to suppose that the associative processes obey those rational laws which are enumerated in ratiocinative logic. The greatest authors in the history

---

[1] We will not give here the different details and the possibilities of the method. They will be found in our work: *Die Methode der Abildungen Motorik,* Psycholog. Forschung, Bd. 12, 1929.

of psychological thought always come to the conclusion that the current affective associative processes are conditioned by the living experience of personality and that the deciding rôle in it can be played by those affective traces which, in view of the "affective complexes" were separate in the personality and often condition its apperception as well as its active associative functions.

The word-stimulus which we represent has many chances of falling in the territory of such affective traces, and calling out in life a marked affective reaction. In such cases, when we take a number of subjects in a marked affective state or people whose affective complexes are already activated, such as students before an examination, criminals immediately after arrest, or neurotics and emotionally labile persons, the chances of producing affective reactions by means of word-stimuli are greatly increased, and a carefully chosen inventory of stimuli will almost unfailingly provoke in the subjects a clearly defined affective process. Having produced the affective association, we necessarily stimulate some disorganisation of behaviour which is evident to observation for a certain length of time. This "model affect" spreads not only to the system of activity connected with the associative process, but manifests all the signs of the affective disorganisation of behaviour. The appearance of the affective stream is accompanied by a destruction of the course of the higher speech process; it creates a certain conflict, goes over then to the motor functions, and can, under given circumstances involve even the autonomic system. In a word, we have a model affect very suitable for investigation, and including the most important symptoms of the affective disintegration.

With these possibilities we may now venture to begin our work. With the help of the associative experiment, we are able to evoke a known affective state, and by means of the combined motor method we will analyse its structure. We begin with an analysis of the ordinary affective processes, and we shall attempt to choose those which lead to a clearly defined disorganisation of human behaviour. When we pass over more fully to the investigation of the processes of disorganisation, we create artificial obstacles and conflicts in speech, and again we attempt to trace their reflection in the combined motor method. Finally, not abandoning our methodological ground, we essay to study the genesis of these processes of disintegration, and to elucidate those examples by means of which the human surmounts this destruction, systematically taking possession of his own behaviour.

PART ONE
PSYCHOPHYSIOLOGY OF THE
AFFECTIVE PROCESSES

CHAPTER II

THE INVESTIGATION OF MASS AFFECT

1. THE PROBLEM OF
NEURODYNAMIC INVESTIGATION OF AFFECT

THREE fundamental problems arise before psychologists who study the disorganisation of human behaviour during affect: the study of symptomatology, the mechanics and the dynamics of affect.

Symptomatologically, the questions of affect have been further investigated than others connected with the problems of affective disorganisation. However, it is impossible to say that we know enough about the symptoms of the destruction of human behaviour to group them in a clearly definite picture. A majority of the symptoms described in the psychological literature give only partial and incomplete material to the theory of the disorganisation of behaviour. Describing the symptoms of the affective state, the authors almost never deviated from a single representation of affect as a system of disorganisation of active human behaviour. Therefore, the symptoms enumerated by psychophysiologists and psychologists differ considerably. The problem of functional reciprocity of these symptoms, the separate symptoms of the affective state, playing the leading rôle, remained altogether insufficiently studied, and only a further investigation will enable us to decide this problem.

In a given investigation, we attempt to proceed precisely along this path. Having taken as a basis the active behaviour of the subject, we set ourselves the problem to describe not all the symptoms with his affective behaviour, but only those which allow us to establish in what way the affect is reflected in the disorganisation of active behaviour. Our work was thus much more limited than a general investigation of the whole symptomatological affect.

From such a point of view, attacking the problem of the disorganisation of behaviour, we met at once two extreme aspects of affect, whose governing laws it is necessary to describe. We saw that the affective destruction of the disorganisation of behaviour by no means represents a short chaotic record of a brief period of behaviour in a structural state. We are in a position to describe the structure of the affect and show that it varies widely in different instances.

While in some cases we come upon a distinct diffuse affective state, where all of the behaviour is for a time disorganised, in others there stands out before us a conspicuous contour of the concentrated affect, which appeared only surrounding definite stimuli and extended only to several reactive systems manifesting a very definite structure, whose forms and interrelations we are able to study. These interrelations and the laws governing them bring us to the conclusion that, properly speaking, a structural state does not exist, and that even the affective chaos, produced in the behaviour by certain difficulties and affective conditions, is not an accidental destruction, but always manifests lawfulness. To study these interrelations and their laws is not easy, because every concentrated affect inevitably tends to pass into a diffused state of disorganisation, and because the great complexity and the emancipation from the higher regulating mechanism which appears during the state of affect makes the laws governing these phenomena very confusing. Before the investigator, however, describing the destruction of behaviour during affect remains the problem of how to approach it, how to get at the deformations; in other words, to describe those structures of the laws governing the apparent chaos.

This brings us to the second question—the study of the mechanics of the affective states. Although the symptomatology of affect has been described to a certain extent there is much less material concerning the relations of the mechanics of the affective destruction of the behaviour. Besides, a few physiological researches (preeminently those of I. P. Pavlov and W. B. Cannon), there are practically no others discovering in the disorganisation of behaviour any constant laws, formulating the processes of affective destruction into fundamental rules. The matter becomes still more involved when we begin to speak of definite physiological laws as well as rules relating to this activity which is disorganised during the affective disturbance. Here authors usually prefer to end their investigations, pointing out that under the influence of the affect the behaviour is disorganised, the separate systems form the general regulators and the diffuse excitation suppresses the normal vital activity of the organism. To gainsay this is impossible, and likewise one cannot state that it is the concluding stage of the investigation. On he contrary in that chaos of behaviour which arises during the acute affect we can sooner see a problem which becomes the starting point for the investigation, behind which we must necessarily seek for the laws manifested in this disorganisation. At the basis of the affective disturbance of behaviour, is there some alteration in the adequate mobilisation of the excitation, or does the affect change the very structure of the reactive process? If the affective state is connected with the abolition of the normal standards of movement, then what forces lie at the basis of this fact? Does the affective disturbance influence only the active system, or, under certain circumstances, is it connected to other spheres, extending into the passive motor and vegetative systems? All these questions are essential, not only in the symptomatological description but also in the psychophysiological investigation which should attempt to establish definite laws lying at the basis of the affective disorganisation of human behaviour.

Obviously these laws can be established only in conjunction with the study of the conditions producing the affect and the circumstances governing its organisation. The mechanics of the affect is comprehensible only in the light of the dynamics of the affective state. The interrelations of the separate symptoms observed by us, the character of the affective disturbances and their extension into various regions of activity are far from being equal, whether we study the affective disturbance directly under the conditions producing the trauma, or turn our attention to the investigation of the difficult situation which is brought about and becomes dominant. The relations of the personality to the production of the affective situation can modify the whole mechanics of the affective disturbance, and in the investigation of the affects besides this relation of the personality, there may be obtained the false impression that the laws of the mechanics of the affective state do not have any existence. Here, as in many psychological investigations, we come face to face with the fact that the course of the processes becomes comprehensible only when we take into account the leading rôle played by the higher forms of behaviour and the more complex psychological systems. Extended by the study of the dynamics of affect, its genesis and destiny, its dependence upon the general setting of the personality, and upon the ability of the personality to overcome the affective disorganisation, our investigation proceeds from the limits of the neurodynamical analysis and becomes, in its broader significance, truly psychophysiological.

All these problems should be studied by us in actual experimental material, which is suitable for analysis and which is capable of showing an affective disorganisation in its acute forms. The material afforded by the mass affect of scholastic examinations, criminals, and artificially produced affects will be first considered in our analysis.

2. AFFECT OF EXAMINATION: SITUATION AND MATERIAL

FIRST we shall take up the analysis of behaviour connected with a fairly acute traumatic situation—the situation of the student examination.

For our experiments with the examinations we use a very simple characteristic: on the one hand, there is the situation which is produced by the somewhat intensive affective phenomena. Everyone who recalls the state of the average student facing an important examination will remember that his behaviour is far from normal, and that an intense affect usually governs all of his activity; on the other hand we undoubtedly have a case of mass affect connected with a very definite situation. This is certainly an advantage for the experimenter: the structure of the affect, which we have already spoken of, can be observed in a large number of subjects simultaneously. As equal stimuli are present in all of the cases, we may be assured that the same factor is operating in the production of the affective results.

Such a procedure brings before the experimenter numerous possibilities. Comparing the reaction of many subjects in one and the same affective situation, the experiment can be conducted with a statistical accuracy which is very difficult to attain in separate experiments with affect.

The situation of the examination has another distinct advantage: it allows the experimenter to discover in the mass of the material the dynamics of affective states. Our experiment can be arranged in situations differing in the degree of their traumatic action; the investigator can study students before very difficult, average, and comparatively easy examinations; doing the experiment at varying times from the examination, studying its *"Fern-* and *Nahe-Wirkung,"* he can trace the extension of qualitative changes in the structure of the affective processes; finally he has an opportunity to investigate the student before as well as after the examination, and to explain the specific course of the affective process in relation to the degree of the affective trauma and affective tension.

The number of experiments and the uniformity of the situation make it possible for the psychologist to study the question of the mechanics and dynamics of affect, not only in general but from the standpoint of typology. If the traumatic situation of the examination acts on the subjects unequally, if the personalities controlling the neurotic labileness of the nervous system are separated very distinctly, then the psychologist has an opportunity to expand his investigation into many typological problems.

Three chief problems standing out in bold relief before the psychologist can be formulated as the problems of the mechanics, the dynamics, and the typology of the mass affect:

What symptoms characterise the behaviour of subjects experiencing similar mass affect? In the disorganisation of which basic mechanism is it expressed? What dynamics are present, and how do they depend upon the main traumatic situation? And, finally, how are the typological peculiarities of the neurodynamics in this traumatic situation disclosed?

An experimental answer to these questions will be attempted in the ensuing pages.[1]

A. EXPERIMENTS WITH THE SITUATION OF "PURGATION"

1. MATERIAL AND EXPERIMENTS

THE experiments which we shall now take up lead us at once to the situation of more acute affect.

These experiments were made in 1924, and are of exceptional interest for the psychologist studying the affect of the situation connected with "cleansing" or "purgation" in the higher schools.

The overcrowding of the higher schools and universities, which, during the revolution, were open to everyone, regardless of their preparation,

---

[1] We know of only a very few works dealing with the experimental psychology of the examination. One of the earliest of these is: T. G. Schnitzler, *Experimentelle Beitrage zur Tathesandsdiagnostik,* Zeitschr. f. angew. Psychol. Bd. 2, S. 51-91. The author uses material before the examination and before operations. Two of our papers (in conjunction with L. P. Leontiev) concerning material of the examination are: *Investigations of the Objective Symptoms of Affective Reactions,* Problems of Contemporary Psychology, 1926; and *Examination and Psyche,* Moscow, 1929. The material of these furnishes the basis of the present chapter.

the lack of equipment in the laboratories, the want of control of the academic progress of the students on the one hand, and on the other hand, the social class standing of the students (often the presence of persons not active in the revolution and even inimical to it)—all this explains the general scrutiny of the student bodies during the Spring of 1924, the so-called *chistka* ("cleansing"). Every student had to appear before a special commission. This commission went into his academic record, his social-political inclinations, collected information on his past and academic activity, and then made its decision. In the case of an unfavourable judgment, the student was expelled from the university, and thus all of his work and future plans came to naught. If he passed the censorship of the commission he continued his academic course.

Naturally this situation far exceeded in its traumatic character the usual school examination; we thus had very specific conditions for the investigation of an acute mass affect.

Thirty students were examined in the series, nineteen women and eleven men. In contra-distinction to other authors (Schnitzler) who investigated subjects half a day before the examination, we took students directly from the line awaiting examination, so that some of them were examined only a few minutes after our experiment.

From among these, eleven were experimented on twice: the first time we experimented upon them immediately before going into the examination, the second time immediately following the examination. Thus we were able to evaluate the result of the trauma which standing before the commission represented for them. The fact that the outcome of the "cleansing" was unknown to the student beforehand gave us a possibility of performing our experiment under comparatively pure conditions, excluding the influence of the fortunate or unfortunate result, and tracing the pure (relatively, of course) process of testing the student *per se.*

In this series of experiments, as well as in all the others described in this book, we applied the method of associated motor reactions, giving the subject a speech stimulus, and recording the speech responses connected with simultaneous motor pressures. In each of the subjects, reactions were taken to thirty word-stimuli. The experiments were performed after a short preliminary training, sufficient for the understanding of the instructions and for the establishment of the corresponding coordinations. After the test the experiment was repeated.

The comparative study of the speech reactions (their latent period, the character of the responses) and their reflection in the corresponding motor system (the intensity and form of the motor curves, their variability and coordination) made it possible to evaluate the general character of the dynamics of the affective process.

2. THE SYMPTOMS OF THE DIFFUSE AFFECT

THE general behaviour of our subjects demands our attention and gives evidence that most of them are in a state of intense excitation. Fidgeting in the chair, and many agitated movements characteristic of a general excitability, marked excitability of attention, sometimes compensatory loud laughing—all of this creates a typical picture.

Here is a section of a typical protocol:

Subject No. 26. Very excited, talking loudly, fidgeting in his chair, striking his hand on the table, continuously conversing in spite of being asked to keep quiet; scolding. He responds to the stimulus in fluctuating tones, sometimes in an ordinary voice and again very boisterously. Further investigations reveal a marked variability in the strength of the motor pressures; sometimes he strikes the dynamoscope. Toward the end of the experiment he says he cannot continue the experiment as he must wait his turn in the line. The experiment stopped here.

The general excitability and the marked instability of behaviour is clearly evident in this subject; these features are typical of the behaviour of all our subjects, and are reflected in the graphic protocols. The diffuse affective state is shown in the motor reactions of the subject; it makes his reactions unstable, deprives him of the possibility to coordinate the movements, and brings out neurodynamic symptoms characteristic of affect.

We shall give a comparative example of the characteristic experimental conditions of behaviour in three subjects—young people of nearly the same age and development. The first of these was a control who was ignorant of the "cleansing" as well as of the purposes of the experiment; the other two were students tested immediately preceding their appearance before the commission.

Figure 12 contains the graphic protocols of these experiments.

The above reactions show that our control subject is very calm. Several fundamental symptoms characterise his behaviour under the conditions of our experiment; all of these can be seen in the protocol. They are:

1. The speech reactions of the subject are rapid and stable. The average speed of the speech answers equals 1.4″, and the variation of this in the separate cases is very small. In the graph we see how short are the intervals between reactions, showing how little energy the subject expends in responding to the given word-stimulus. An analysis of the speech responses shows that the stability in the associative activity is not attained at the expense of the quality of the speech reactions (for example, a change to a stereotyped answer, etc.), but that a relatively complex psychical activity can flow in distinct and stable forms.[1]

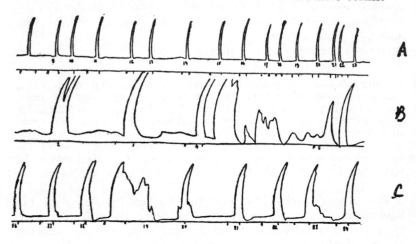

Fig. No. 12

ACCOMPANYING MOTOR REACTIONS IN STUDENTS DURING "CLEANSINGS"
A. NORMAL SUBJECT   B. AND C. STUDENTS

2. The motor reactions of the subject have a regular and standard form, and show a more or less equal intensity of pressures. The variability of the forms here is entirely lacking, and the fluctuation of intensity is insignificant, one pressure differing from the other by not more than 1-2 mm.

3. The behaviour is characterised by a complete coordination of the separate systems. The movements of the hand occur

[1] In a special work dealing with the genesis of speech reactions in the child (*Speech and Intellect in the Development of the Child*, Moscow, 1928) we showed that such an organised and stable character of the reactions (a normally adequate associative process and a normal stability of the reactive period) is shown in the history of the development and is generally established at twelve to fourteen years of age.

simultaneously with the speech reactions. The space between them is not occupied by one of the accompanying reactions or by impulsive reactions of the hand not dependent upon the speech process, and the whole neurodynamical apparatus works with a maximal coordination.

We may summarise these three features of the normal adult's behaviour as follows: here there is a very exact organisation, a regulation of the behaviour, which is the property of the normal work of the developed neuropsychical apparatus, and which is fully established at this stage of activity by the time adolescence is reached.[1]

One may say that the whole behaviour of the subject is characterised here by a preliminary elaboration of that associative and motor formula which, further, is stably and automatically present in all of the reactions.

Precisely these properties of the regulation of the neurodynamical process are destroyed in the state of acute diffused affect. Curves 2 and 3 show this in the above figure. We have here analogous reactions of the subjects during the excitation of the acute affect present immediately before the session with the commission. The features are entirely different from those just described.

1. The speech reactions to the word stimuli occur much more slowly, although the subjects are in no sense inferior intellectually to the control. Not infrequently we meet cases here where the subject cannot respond to the first word coming into his mind in less than 5.7″ or even 10″. The average reactive time of our subjects is 2.29″, while normally this time does not exceed 1.5-1.7″ (Jung), attaining this speed already in children 14-15 years old (Luria).

This fact indicates the serious changes which the affect causes in the course of the higher psychological processes; the figures show that the acute affect, as a rule, inhibits the intricate associative process, obstructing it and bringing about that state of the person long since past, a state which is characterised by a serious obstruction of the associative reaction.[2] The affect provokes a functional lowering of the associative possibilities.

This fact, that the affect ruptures the organised course of the associative processes, is shown in the greatly increased vari-

[1] In subsequent chapters we show that this regulation of the higher processes is genetically a fairly late development, and comes about as the result of the overcoming of the primary diffusion of behaviour. See Part Three.

[2] A. R. Luria, *Speech and Intellect in the Development of the Child*, Moscow, 1928.

ability of the speech reactions. The time expended on the speech
responses fluctuates, and together with the quickly flowing associations we usually meet very slow ones, and in the state of
affect we say that those elaborated earlier formulæ of the associative reactions, which characterise the behaviour of the normal
adult, are lost.

We applied in these investigations a very simple means of calculating
the variability. Taking into consideration the fact that deviation is a
result of the inhibition of the individual responses, we express the variability in the difference between the median and the average of the
arithmetical sums of the reactive time, considering that the whole of
the instability of the series is shown in the size of this difference. If in
the normal case this difference comes to zero, then in our experiments it
can be expressed by an average figure of 0.30" (17% of the basic size)
but this represents a very considerable instability of the series.

The subject in the state of acute affect not only inhibited his
associative reactions, but as a rule he was not able to produce
these reactions with any degree of stability (even though delayed). The failure of coordination in the human experiencing
the affect begins with a falling out of the higher regulations,
and, as we shall soon see, disturbs the coordination connected
with the motor sphere.

The destruction of the organisation of the associative processes
under the influence of the affect appears in the character of the
speech responses.

We have in the cultured adult, as a rule, during quiet periods,
almost a hundred per cent of adequate associations; the primitive forms of the associative reactions (the extra signalising
response to the direct stimulus, the stereotyped repetition of
one and the same answer, the reaction of senseless words) are
met with only on rare occasions.

The facts of our material give other evidence. Only 81.7%
of all the responses were complete, 10.8% were of a primitive
nature and 5.3% showed prominent symptoms of speech excitability and speech discoordination.

These data give an active picture for the examinations. In
our material we met cases where the associative processes did
not influence the affect and where all the disturbances could be
attributed to the somewhat delayed and unequal reactive times;
the subject responded by adequate associations but the process
itself of the associative response produced in him considerable
tension; this process, usually automatic and easy, became deautomatised under the influence of the affect, and this was

expressed in the character of the delayed reactive period of the deautomatised process and the increase in its variability. Here we meet for the first time with one of the chief laws characteristic of the mechanics of the affective process. The affective state causes a great disturbance in the associative process which is only dispelled by a number of secondary forces; the associative process in the affective state is entirely another psychological structure than that which is seen in the associations of ordinary subjects. In these cases when for some reason such a secondary elaboration of the associative processes fails, it is plain why the subject should give a perverted series of the associative reactions, entirely disorganised in character. We begin to see a chain of senseless extra-signalising responses; every accidental stimulus—the portfolio on the table, the eyeglasses of the experimenter, picture drawn on the wall—all these began to activate the subject, taking him away from the experiment, and producing "accidental responses." We obtain an associative series ordinarily foreign to the cultured adult and usually seen only in the earlier stages of development or, in peculiar forms, in definite neurotic states.

The extra-signalising and senseless reactions, the auditory and stereotyped responses indicate that the acute affect destroys the normal associative activity, throwing the subject back on the primitive psychological structures. These we shall take up below.

2. The unusually acute changes evoke the affective process plainly in the motor coordinations of the subject. In Figure 12 (curves 2 and 3) the motor disturbances clearly indicate that the reactive process of the subject in the state of diffused affect takes on entirely other forms; he is not able to produce those distinct and strictly coördinated movements which characterise the reactions of the normal, composed person, the motor-formula is quickly lost and the reaction acquires an organised, automatic quality. Looking more carefully at the curves given, we are able to see that in the affect there were contending several fundamental mechanisms proper to the reaction of the normal person. These disturbances of the motor system are not exceptional, individual cases; our statistics show that before the "cleansing" 26.9% of all the reactions were disturbed in form, having lost the appearance of the regular coordinated pressure; in many of the subjects the movements showed a sharp tremor between the separate reactions; in several there was a complete loss of coordination in the movements of the hand with the speech reactions, and the motor pressure occurred much earlier than

the speech. Figure 13 contains a part of the protocol of the experiment on such a subject.

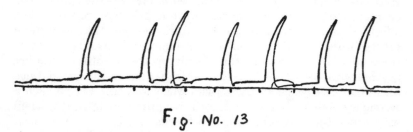

$$F_{ig.} \ No. \ 13$$

DISCOORDINATION OF THE MOTOR REACTIONS IN AFFECT

A detailed analysis of the material indicates that the existing mechanism here consists in this: the impulses connected with the excitation break down the ordinary regularity of the movements, proceed without obstruction to the motor area, destroy the coördination, and give to the movements their impulsive, excitatory character.

The detailed analysis of these mechanisms will be given below; they bring us to the establishment of the chief movements in the mechanism of affect. Now, with the aid of two concrete examples, we shall attempt to approach closer to this mechanics of affect.

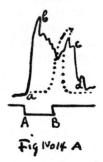

Fig No14 A

As a typical example of the first, we give the reaction in Figure 14A; the scheme is typical and allows us to see more clearly the properties of the mechanisms manifested here. At the point A we give the subject the word-stimulus "wall," and at Point B we have the response, "stone." We might expect that the motor reaction would be coördinated with this response and that it would proceed along the path corresponding to our points in the scheme. But the record indicates otherwise. Instead of after the definite, latent period, in the course of which the motor impulses were inhibited, giving an organised motor pressure coordinated with the speech response, the subject gives an entirely different picture: the motor system is separated in it from the speech reaction; the motor impulse (a-b) comes only after the presented stimulus and is completely uninhibited in the active part of the motor pressure; the inhibition is produced by the absence of the simultaneous speech response; it now begins later, in the passive part of the curve, and is manifested in the slowly appearing tremor (b-c); the organised shortening of the active pressure (c-d) we see considerably later in the point B of the speech reaction.

This example first brings before us a law of affective behaviour, which we shall encounter many times later on. That disorganisation and discoordination of behaviour present in every case of acute affect, consists in this, that in the affective state the motor setting has a tendency to be directly realised, the excitation does not meet with any delay, with any inhibition, and immediately proceeds to its terminus. That which is injured here is the restraining system, the barrier which inhibits the direct appearance of the motor act, causing its coordination with other active systems. The regulating, inhibiting impulses here are delayed, and come into action only after the appearance of the active movement, in its passive portion ("c" at the beginning of the passive part of the curve). The whole curve is deciphered as the result of the disturbed and delayed regulating inhibition, taking place on the basis of the sharply increased impulsiveness.

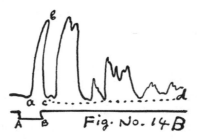

Fig. No. 14 B

The second example is taken from the above figure; it makes possible the addition of a second law to the first one, developing our viewpoint of the mechanics of the affective processes. For analysis we take a similar reaction, No. 4 in curve No. 2. To the subject experiencing the acute affect, there is given the word-stimulus "unfortunate," to which he answers "student"—clearly a connection with the chief affect of the reaction. The motor reaction (a-b-c) is connected with this response (see Figure 14 B), and it flows as a normal and regular pressure. However, there is an actual change following it: instead of the expected even line following the free interval as it occurs in normal subjects, the subject gives several discoordinated sharp pressures, not connected with the speech responses and occupying all of the free interval. It becomes clear to us that the period following the reaction is characterised by a strong affective excitation, that the excitation was not entirely absent in the normally occurring reaction, that the reaction provoked a considerable process, having disturbed all of the ensuing behaviour and spread into the following discoordinated activity. It is evident that under certain circumstances the stimulus present in the affective state produces larger quantities of excitation than it does in the normal; this excitation apparently is not brought about only by the stimulus; the stimulus seems to play the rôle of a catalyst of a considerable amount of excitation present in the subject. On the other hand the reaction itself to the given stimulus is insufficient to remove the excitation, the reaction cannot overcome those masses of excitation which were called out by it. As a result we have that definite picture appearing in the figure: the excitation not connected with impaired restraints in the affect comes out in several unorganised and spontaneous motor impulses.

Such a picture is not exceptional.

3. CONCENTRATED AFFECTIVE FOCI

THE example which we have just given suggests to us the question: In the person experiencing affect, does the stimulus always activate considerable masses of excitation which he cannot control, or does this occur in special instances?

The experiment answers this question for us very definitely; as a rule we have similar cases only when the stimulus is not indifferent for the subject, when it falls on that complex setting which constitutes the chief focus of the given affect. We return to the example just cited. The stimulus which was presented to our subject was the word "unfortunate"; the principal affective focus of the subject was connected with the situation of the awaited trial. It is naturally the word "unfortunate" which was assimilated in the content of this complex, and the answer "student" given by the subject confirms this. Such a situation explains the results in the experiment with affects. Evidently the stimulus presented activated the excitation which was connected in our subject with the traumatic situation. The experiment shows us that the given mechanism is largely a result of the activated affective complex rather than a process characterising an acute affect.

The results of this series confirm our position. We presented to our subject very dissimilar word-stimuli. Some of these were neutral in their relation to the traumatic situation (indicated by i), others directly stimulated the system of these affective traces (k), the third appeared doubtful, sometimes stimulating the affective traces in the case of the corresponding setting (c).

A list of our word-stimuli follows:

1. day (i)	11. cleansing (k)	21. pillow (i)
2. dress (i)	12. gun (i)	22. court (i)
3. sleep (i)	13. constitution (c)	23. roll call (k)
4. unfortunate (c)	14. to cut (i)	24. already (c)
5. occurrence (c)	15. commission (k)	25. to fear (c)
6. pen (i)	16. pipe (i)	26. brush (k)
7. student (c)	17. broom (c)	27. gold (i)
8. examination (k)	18. to surrender (k)	28. tomorrow (i)
9. book (c)	19. wall (i)	29. to hurry (i)
10. end (k)	20. lame (k)	30. to remain (c)

Thus eight words of the list were critical (k), nine were doubtful (c), and thirteen indifferent (i). The stimuli (end, cleansing, commission, roll call), relate directly to the situation—the academic examinations; *brush* was included in the critical group owing to its connection with *cleansing, to clean; lame* was connected with one of the most strict members of the examining commission; *to surrender* was connected with one of the most traumatic moments of the situation, the giving up of the students' documents. The stimuli relating to the doubtful group included words which under certain circumstances might be associated in thought with the given complex.

The stimuli arranged on such a principle allow us to investigate the state of affect in our subjects, the specific reactions directly connected with the traumatic situation of the stimuli on the basis of the reactions to the neutral indifferent stimuli. The data show that the reactions to such critical stimuli are differentiated on the basis of those disturbances characterising the behaviour of subjects during our experiment. It was sufficient to present a stimulus taken from the traumatic situation to produce a rupture of the affect which disturbed the intellect and disorganised the motor activity of the subject.

The simple statistical facts show that the reaction to these critical stimuli are different from those to the neutral ones. Table 1 gives the figures relating to reactive periods in the cases of the associations to the different groups of word-stimuli.

TABLE I

Character of stimuli	M	Am	Am—M
indifferent	1.69″	1.95″	0.26″
critical	2.19″	2.44″	0.25″
doubtful	1.88″	2.20″	0.32″
post-critical	1.73″	2.18″	0.35″

M = median; Am = Average

The average reactive time depends upon the character of the stimulus. These figures show that the average time required for the response in the case of the critical stimuli is 30% more than the time in the case of the indifferent stimuli. There is considerable delay in the reaction to the doubtful stimuli. The reactions connected with the traumatic situation are distinguished by a distinct increase of their periods, notwithstanding the fact that qualitatively the associative reaction is almost the same in both cases, and even in the answers to the doubtful and critical stimuli it is somewhat lower.

The statistics give, in the case of the neutral stimuli, 85.9% of the complete associative reaction, while in the critical stimuli this is lowered to 78.3%, and in the doubtful even to 76.1%.

Our subject, to whom we present the word connected with the critical situation, is not able to respond to it with the speed usual for him, and adequate responses require a much longer time.

In Table 2 we have a statistical summary showing the average speed of the reactions to the different word-stimuli. It is easily seen that the answers to the neutral stimuli occur quickly, while those to the stimuli connected with the traumatic situation are maximally delayed.

Such a picture of the disturbed behaviour, in the case of the reactions directly connected with the affective complexes, were studied in relation to the symptoms of the motor disorganisation. Table 3 shows that quantitatively the motor disturbances in these cases are greater than in the others; such a marked destruction of the motor reactions occurs here two and a half times more frequently than in the responses to the indifferent stimuli.

The following conclusion may be drawn from this material: the presentation of stimuli directly connected with the traumatic

TABLE 2

Средняя скорость реакций

на отдельные раздражители (медианы)

[по всем исследованиям кроме группы „B"]

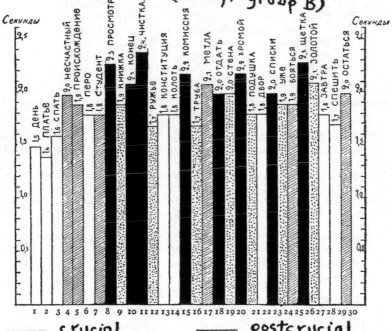

(THE NUMERALS UNDER THE COLUMNS REFER TO THE WORDS
GIVEN IN THE LIST 1-30 PRECEDING TABLE I)

situation to the subject during the state of affect usually produces an obstruction of the associative processes and a marked
disturbance of the motor reactions. These properties of the disturbed behaviour in the case of the critical reactions are not by

any means accidental; an analysis shows that these reactions cause a wave of disturbances lasting some time after the critical reactions. In Table 3 we see that following it, the post-critical reactions (they are themselves indifferent) have a considerably delayed period and are characterised by an increased number of sharply disturbed reactions. An analysis of the concrete cases indicates that the critical stimuli produce a marked obstruction of the associative processes and condition a specific structure of the reactions.

TABLE 3

Character of Stimuli	Normal reaction	Intensely disturbed reactions	Slightly disturbed reactions
indifferent	86.9%	9.8%	3.3%
critical	70.9%	23.3%	5.8%
doubtful	80.4%	15.2%	4.4%
post-critical	79.0%	15.1%	5.9%

The number of motor disturbances are dependent upon the character of the stimuli.

The associative process is broken under the influence of the affective stimulus; our data make it possible to point out the types of action of such a stimulus on the associative process.

1. The more acute influence of the affective stimulus is expressed in the complete failure of the reactions in that affective "desert" whose presence has been shown in the works of M. Wertheimer. Here are examples of such reactions:

Subject 27
      examination—3.5"—absence of response
      cleansing   —4.0"—I can not answer that
Subject 33
      student   —3.0"—I do not know
      examination—2.6"—I do not know
      commission —2.4"—I do not know
      broom   —2.2"—I do not know
Subject 17
      commission—5.2"—absolutely nothing

2. A characteristic feature is the failure to hear the critical stimulus. This symptom is never met with in the case of the indifferent stimuli:

      Subject 3   commission—3.0"—I did not hear
      Subject 14   end   —4.0"—I did not hear
      Subject 18   book   —6.0"—the devil take it, I didn't hear it.

3. A large number of speech responses to the critical stimuli are of an externally disturbed nature; this symptom, pointed out by C. G. Jung, is connected with that conflict which is excited by the affective stimulus,

destroying the associative process and weakening those regulators of behaviour, about which we have spoken above. Examples of such reactions follow:

Subject 9
    brush—4.6″—t ... yellow
Subject 14
    cleansing—1.6″—pro ... *proshla* (it is finished)
Subject 15
    cleansing—8.4″—cleansing ... what shall I say? A good method

4. Finally in the last group there are cases of internally disturbed reactions in which the disturbance is connected not with the motor functions of speech but with the associative process itself. The extrasignalising, senseless and particularly the stereotyped reactions make up the forms here. Examples:

Subject 6
    unfortunate—1.0″—house
    student   —1.4″—house
    cleansing   —2.2″—house, etc.

We shall concern ourselves with a special analysis of similar disturbances again later on; in the analysis of the facts obtained in criminals, subjects under hypnosis, and in neurotics we shall meet with similar examples. Now we should like to emphasise the fundamental fact that the affective situation does not simply influence qualitatively the intellectual processes but actually changes the whole reactive structure.

4. THE DYNAMICS OF THE AFFECTIVE PROCESSES

WE shall discuss here all the investigated symptoms and the dynamics of the affect. That setting which we have investigated twice in our subjects, directly before and immediately after the traumatic situation, gives us some experimental material on the dynamics of the affective process. How does the behaviour of the subject change after passing through the affective situation? The figures obtained indicate very clearly that already the tension of the affective situation (passing before the examining commission without being informed of the outcome) is sufficient to decrease markedly the affective symptoms. The associative reactions, after the passage through the traumatic situation, occur much more quickly (an average of 1.75″ instead of 1.95″ obtained in this group in the first experiment); the acute motor disturbances are also much less in the repeated experiment—14.4% instead of the earlier 20.6%.

We are led to believe that the passing through the traumatic situation is connected with a diminution of the affect, that the affective influence of the situation is more connected with the situation of expecting the trauma than with the trauma itself, and that the latter leads to some sort of solution of the tension. *Entspannung* is the term applied to this phenomenon by the Berlin school of psychologists.

The control experiment shows that the decrease of the affective symptoms is explained by the fact that in the interval between the two experiments the subject went through the situation of cleansing and the psychological picture of his behaviour was different in a special series. In order to find out the influence of the simple repetition of the stimuli we tried two successive experiments. In both cases there was almost no change. The average reactive time of the first experiment was 2.29″, and of the second, 2.27″. The control entirely excluded any influence of simple repetition. It is positive that the above given diminution of the affective symptoms is connected not with the repetition of the experiment but with the change in the psychological conditions.

The fundamental affective complex under the tension of the traumatic situation appears in the very special mechanism of the affective dynamics. The principal changes produced consist in this: the affective focus loses its exceptional affective significance, and the changes take on a diffused form, equally extending to all the reactions of the subject. Tables 4 and 5 illustrate this.

TABLE 4

Character of the stimulus	Reaction time before "cleansing"	Reaction time after "cleansing"	Difference
indifferent	1.58″	1.62″	+0.04
critical	2.01″	1.86″	—0.15
doubtful	1.60″	1.55″	—0.05
post-critical	1.84″	1.65″	—0.19

Reactive time before and after the traumatic situation.

TABLE 5

Character of the stimulus	Before "cleansing"	After "cleansing"	Difference
indifferent	14.3%	11.1%	— 3.2%
critical	30.4%	19.6%	—10.8%
doubtful	23.4%	14.3%	— 7.1%
post-critical	18.4%	14.3%	— 4.1%

Quantity of acute motor disturbances before and after traumatic situation.

Both these tables showing the dynamics of the two important symptoms of the affective disturbance give similar results. In both cases the repeated experiment after the "cleansing" show a marked decrease of symptoms in the cases of the critical and post-critical reactions. In the second experiment they take place more quickly and with fewer motor disturbances. This process is noticeable only in the indicated group of reactions; the re-actions not connected with the main affective complex give in the repeated experiment a picture almost unchanging in com-parison to the first experiment; the tension of the affective situa-tion produces a disturbance of the chief affective complex, not causing any actual change of reactions in the neutral stimuli.

The affective complex in the diffused affective state represents here different degrees of inertia; the connections of the traumatic situation put the affect under tension, but there remains some general, diffused disturbance of behaviour.

B. EXPERIMENTS WITH THE SITUATION OF THE SCHOOL EXAMINATION

1. MATERIAL AND EXPERIMENTS

THE second series of experiments, performed in the Autumn of 1927, made use of analogous situations. We chose the problem of the ordinary school examination through which every student of the university must pass.

We had a greater wealth of material here than in our first series. We used 109 subjects, 51 men and 58 women, varying from 18 to 35 years of age. As in the first group of experiments, the subjects were tested twice, once just before the examination and then immediately afterwards, before the results were known to the student. Most of the students were taking mathematics and physics, although some were from the department of social sciences. Certainly the affective situation here was much less severe than in the previous series, but, as will be seen below, there were definite signs of affect present even here.

The subject was given 30 word-stimuli, 6 of which related to the situation of the examination, the other 24 being indifferent:

1. field	11. *examination*	21. *passed*
2. wall	12. boot	22. roll (bread)
3. winter	13. house	23. air
4. wanted	14. *formula*	24. school
5. time	15. glass	25. *commission*
6. pen	16. fire	26. wood
7. book	18. bird	27. butter
8. spoon	17. watch	28. *acceptance*
9. flowers	19. *physics*	29. smoke
10. water	20. courtyard	30. bell

(In the instances where the subject was from the department of social sciences, Numbers 14 and 19 were substituted by words from those subjects.)

These experiments were completed by testing the blood, for catalytic activity, of the students during the state of diffuse affect.[1]

2. NEURODYNAMICAL SYMPTOMS OF DIFFUSE AND CONCENTRATED AFFECT

THE results of the investigation with the students taking examinations gave similar pictures to those seen in the first series. Therefore, we shall discuss in detail only the data which are specific for this group.

The situation of the examination was much less traumatic than that of the "cleansing"; nevertheless, the psychological structure of both was analogous. This may be seen from the following table:

TABLE 6

Reactive Time	First experiment	Repeated experiment	Difference
Average figure: M	1.8″	1.6″	—0.2″
	2.2″	1.8″	—0.4″
Indifferent stimulus (M)	1.7″	1.5″	—0.2″
Critical stimulus (M)	2.2″	1.8″	—0.4″
Post-critical (M)	1.9″	1.6″	—0.3″
Average Variation			
Average figure: M	0.9″	0.6″	0.3″
Average figure: Am	—	—	—
Indifferent stimulus	0.7″	0.6″	—0.1″
Critical "	1.6″	1.0″	—0.6″
Post-critical "	0.8″	0.7″	—0.1″

Period of the speech reactions in the experiments with the situation of the examination.

In table 6 we see the facts relating to the velocity of the speech reactions in our experiments. The average reactive time, expressed in $Am = 2.2″$, is markedly inhibited in comparison with the usual reactive time in the normal subjects; we see here a considerable inhibition in the speech reactions, even up to 8-9-9, 5 seconds, which almost never happens in the normal.

A great disturbance of the accompanying motor reactions corresponds to the marked delay of the associative process; the movements indicate that these delays are not connected with the simple lowering of the energetic tones of behaviour, as occurs,

[1] Luria, et al: *Examination and Psychical Reactions*, Moscow, 1930.

for example, in fatigue or in drowsiness, but they are the result of a diffuse excitation, breaking the normal associative process.

TABLE 7

	Intense motor disturbance			Whole motor disturbance		
	Before examination	After examination	Difference	Before exam.	After exam.	Difference
Average	70.7%	3.8%	− 6.9%	22.7%	13.2%	− 9.5%
Indifferent stimulus	5.3%	3.8%	− 1.5%	13.3%	9.9%	− 3.4%
Critical stimulus	19.0%	7.3%	−11.7%	30.8%	16.3%	−14.5%
Post-critical	6.5%	2.1%	− 4.4%	15.8%	8.1%	− 7.7%

Disturbed motor reaction in the experiment with the situation of the examination

Table 7 shows that 22% of all the motor reactions of the subject in the pre-examined state show the signs of the motor disturbances and that 10.7% of these signs are markedly disturbed.

Both of these figures almost exactly coincide with the results obtained from those students who had to go before the "cleansing" commission. A detailed analysis convinces us that the inability to find the adequate association quickly, as well as the accompanying motor disturbance, is a result of that specific affective state present in the student awaiting examination. This and the other series of symptoms are particularly evident in the reactions connected with the situation of the examination, and such stimuli as, "examination," "accept," "commission," "to judge," etc., exhibit a sharp increase in the reactive periods (2.2″ instead of 1.7″ of the indifferent stimuli). A considerable variation in the speed of the reactions (mV = 1.6″ instead of the normal 0.7″) and the distinct concentration of the motor disturbance connected with the speech reactions (19.0% of the intense motor disturbances instead of the 5.3%).

Two tables are given illustrating this. Table 8 shows the average reactive time to the separate word-stimuli presented to the subject; Table 9 indicates the quantity of motor disturbances corresponding to each given case. Hence the following fact can be established: all the stimuli relating to the situation of the examination show a sharp increase of the corresponding symptoms, and we are able to choose from among the number of all the stimuli those connected with the affective situation, being guided only by the objective data.

It is evident that the situation connected with the examination

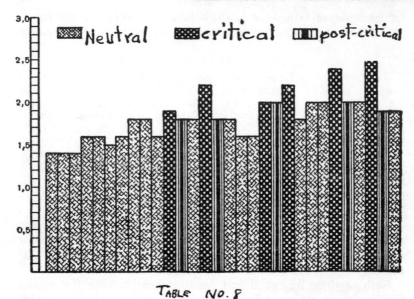

TABLE NO. 8

AVERAGE SPEED OF REACTIONS TO WORD-STIMULI

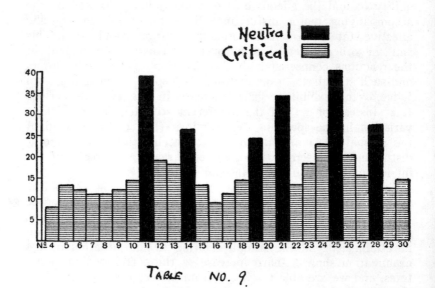

TABLE NO. 9.

MOTOR DISTURBANCES IN REACTIONS TO WORD-STIMULI
(ORDINATE = NUMBER OF DISTURBED REACTIONS; ABSCISSA = WORD-
STIMULUS NUMBER)

creates a special affective complex but this complex is characterised by a group of symptoms entirely suitable for objective study.

A thorough analysis permits us to point out that for this situation those mechanisms are characteristic which we have established in the first series. As we have already stated, the delayed reaction in critical cases in no wise can be related to any form

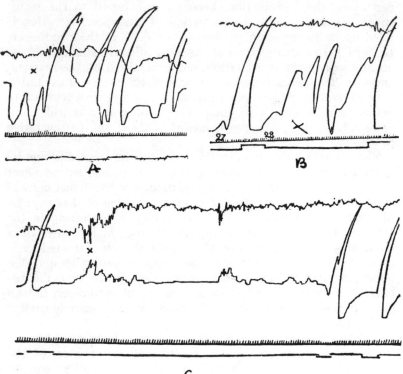

A   B

C

Fig. No. 15

MOTOR REACTIONS IN AFFECT (STUDENT BEFORE EXAMINATION)

of hypotonus; the facts prove that there is present here, more likely, the reverse process: the delayed reaction is accompanied always by intense motor excitation, and this again indicates that behind these retardations there occur profound changes in structure in the reactive processes themselves.

In Figure 15 we have an example of several reactions to the word-stimuli "accept" and "commission." It is clear that according to structure the reactions differ sharply from the normal, co-ordinated movement. In response to the stimulus connected with the traumatic situation our subject is not able to carry out a very simple organised movement; the regulating motor impulses strive to free the movements from their inhibitors, and they become chaotic-excitatory. In our cases the stimulus often produces the direct motor impulse, i.e., the excitation, immediately destroying the coordination, becomes transferred to the motor sphere; and the whole latent period of the speech reaction is filled up by independent pressures (curve A) or their rudiments (curve C). In another group of cases the affective stimulus causes an intense process of excitation, not neutralised by the reaction, and after the speech response we see a distinct trace of excitation appearing in the whole cycle of spontaneous pressures (curve B); before us is again a panorama of that phenomenon which undoubtedly is the psychophysiological basis of the perseverative processes.

The affect of the examination consists in, according to its psychophysiological mechanisms, exactly the same as the affect observed in the above series: the destruction of the higher cortical regulations, and the weakening or even breaking of that regulating restraint which underlies every excitation occurring in the nervous system of the adult. First, the higher regulating mechanisms suffer from the affect, and the unobstructed excitation begins to flow into the motor sphere, distorting and disorganising the behaviour. Recent analyses prove that the behaviour in the state of affect causes the organism to revert to long past, primitive stages of development of the neurodynamical mechanism.

In the state of affect the person is not able to complete organised systematic actions; he is deprived, as it were, of the possibility of carrying out a chain of facts with identical, equally spaced links; he cannot perform five equal movements, give five speech responses with uniform speed. As an intricate machine, the regulating part of which is disjointed, turns out imperfect products, deviating from the standard by various defects, so the person in a state of diffuse affect loses the ability to give several regular, organised reactions.

In Figure 16 we give the velocity of the speech reactions in a normal, control subject (curve A) compared with an analogous curve of a student before examination (curve B). That which we see here shows how far the disturbance of the regulating systems caused by the affect has proceeded; the majority of

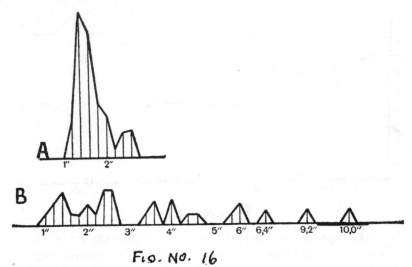

Fig. No. 16

CURVE OF DISTRIBUTION OF THE REACTIVE TIME

A = CONTROL SUBJECT   B = SUBJECT BEFORE EXAMINATION

the reactions in a normal subject is inclined to a definite medium type; the reactions of the affective person are very unstable in associative activity and he is not able to elaborate any stable, standard reactions; the disturbance of the regulative functions is evident here: the organism in the state of affect ceases to turn out a standard product.

Two other curves taken also from the normal and affective subject are given in Figure 17. They show the intensity with which the separate motor reactions occur. An analogous picture is seen here: the separate motor pressures in the normal subject (curve A); the subject in a state of affect preceding examination is not able to perform a cycle of movements with equal intensity, and the curve (B) acquires a broken irregular character.

All these phenomena are much decreased after the affective trauma is removed, and a student after examination usually gives considerably accelerated speech reactions, a decrease of their variability, and a smaller number of motor disturbances (see Tables 6 and 7). There is no doubt that this diminution of the symptoms of the disturbed equilibrium is the result of the removal of the affective situation of the examination. Especially evident are our figures showing that first, after the examination, the reactions to the critical stimuli are changed; precisely in these cases occurs

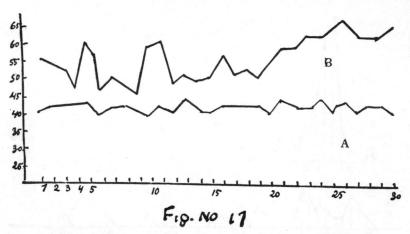

Fig. No 17

DISTRIBUTION OF INTENSITY OF ACCOMPANYING REACTIONS

A = CONTROL SUBJECT   B = STUDENT BEFORE EXAMINATION

the noticeable reestablishment of the normal type of the reactive processes. The whole process of such reestablishment we may consider with assurance an occurrence due to the removal of the affective focus. All the facts convince us that the entire structure of the psychophysiological processes are markedly altered after the affective focus has disappeared, and if we compare the curves in Figure 18, we see how in one and the same subject the character of the neurodynamic processes takes on entirely new forms compared with those existing in the preexamination state.

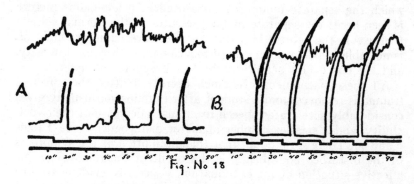

Fig. No 18

A = REACTION OF SUBJECT C BEFORE EXAMINATION
B = REACTION OF SUBJECT C AFTER EXAMINATION

3. TYPOLOGICAL DATA

THE mass character of the data obtained makes it possible to analyse typologically the reactions of the personality in the traumatic situation.

Our material clearly shows that the various subjects during the experiment do not conduct themselves at all similarly; while the behaviour of some of them is characterised by a very intense excitability, others remain rather calm and do not express an acute disturbance of coordination nor those marked affective symptoms which are so evident in the first group.

In Figure 19 we submit two sections of the graphic protocols:

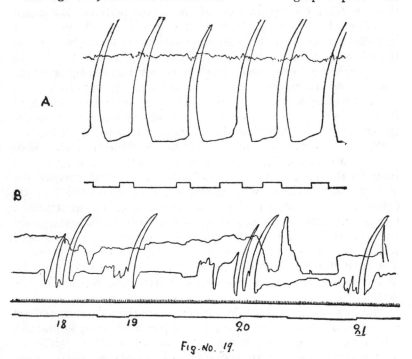

Fig. No. 19.

A = ACCOMPANYING MOTOR REACTIONS OF A STABLE SUBJECT
B = ACCOMPANYING MOTOR REACTIONS OF A LABILE SUBJECT

the first of these is a characteristic experiment with the subject belonging to the *reactive-stable* group; the second is characteristic for a group which we conditionally term the *reactive-labile*. These are both taken from experiments done directly on students waiting in line for the examination. The cardinal difference of the structure of behaviour in the two cases is evident from a glance at the curves; the reactive process of the first subject is characterised by his complete coordination and the relative regularity of his work; we do not see here sharp fluctuations in the time of the speech responses; the accompanying motor pressures are accurate during the speech responses, and regular in their successive forms; all the behaviour is characterised by an obvious regulating process, the preliminary and impulsive reactions being absent. An entirely different picture is seen in the behaviour of the second subject; his general conduct reflects this disorganisation; the stimuli produce rather marked and unequal delays of the speech reactions, and at the same time an acute discoordination of the motor activity. We again encounter those phenomena mentioned previously. Almost every stimulus provokes in this subject a direct motor impulse, often following immediately after the given stimulus and long before the speech reactions; frequently it is not limited by a single impulse and the subject gives numerous separate impulsive pressures. Again we are led to believe that every excitation beginning in the subject at once passes over without any obstruction to the motor sphere, conditioning the unorganised motor activity.

We come to this fact: in different subjects the traumatic situation acts dissimilarly. In some it does not produce an actual basis for the reactive process, specific for each complex reaction—with a characteristic preliminary delay of excitation and its consequent organised transfer to the motor area, i.e., the structure remains unchanged; in others the affect disturbs fundamentally the normal structure of the reactive processes, destroying that which we conditionally designate as the "functional barrier." The excitation becomes diffuse, directly extending over into the motor region, causing an unorganised impulsive rupture of the activity.

The two examples given do not constitute the only cases: about 30% of our subjects (30 cases) give a picture of intense reactive lability; on the other hand, 25% showed reactive stability—an unvarying relation to the traumatic influence. There arises the question: with what facts are the characteristics of these two groups connected?

The first supposition is that some of our subjects fear the examination, while the others, feeling secure and well prepared, conduct themselves with *sang-froid* before the ordeal. Special control experiments, however, indicate that the symptoms obtained in both cases are almost identical in the well-prepared as well as in the incompetent students; the degree of fitness apparently does not play a rôle here. It is a fact that some students manifest acute affective reactions before the examination, and others are calm, but the cause of this remains an open question.

A more detailed study of the personality of students belonging to these groups throws some light on the situation. What are the characteristics of those students found in the experiments to be reactively labile? The following table gives us some hints concerning the answer to our problem:

REACTIVE LABILE		REACTIVE STABLE	
Subject—Character of motor reaction	Symptoms	Subject—Character of motor reactions	Symptoms
1. impulsive	fatigue, anemia	1. normal	exhaustion
2. "	anemia, affective instability	2. "	normal
3. motor disturbance	increased knee jerks, fatigue	3. "	"
4. hysterical	hyperthyroidism	4. "	increased reflexes
5. "	fatigue	5. "	normal
6. tremor	?	6. "	"
7. separate motor disturbances	neurasthenia	7. "	affective reactions
8. "	neurasthenia after commission	8. "	normal
9. impulsive	constitutional neuropath	9. "	"
10. deformed reactions	neurasthenia	10. "	normal
11. unstable	neuropathic depression, affective excitability	11. tremor in intervals	"
12. *irradiated* excitation	normal slight tremor of hands	12. normal	"
13. hysterical	normal neurasthenia after examination	13. "	"
14. labile motor reactions	anemia	14. "	"
15. hysteria	fatigue irritability	15. "	anemia
16. hysteria	hysteria	16. normal	normal
17. hysteria	?	17. normal	normal
18. labile	?	18. "	"

REACTIVE LABILE		REACTIVE STABLE	
Subject—Character of motor reaction	Symptoms	Subject—Character of motor reactions	Symptoms
19. labile	normal	19. normal	fatigue, anemia
20. labile	"	20. "	normal
21. Irradiated disturbance of the motor reaction	arteriosclerosis	21. "	"
22. inhibition of reactions	?	22. "	neurasthenia after
23. hysteria	normal	23. "	normal
24. irradiated	vitium cordis	24. "	normal
25. concentrated disturbances	anemia, tremor of fingers		
26.	hysteria		
27. concentrated disturbances	"		
28. "	fatigue, headache increased reflexes		
29. pathological movements	"		
30. irradiated excitation	nervous, palpitation, excitability		
31. labile motor reactions	fatigue, headache		

Here we see the facts which suggest several differences of the reactive processes of the subject. It seems that the characteristic defect of the structure of the reactive processes observed are met with in people having a functionally damaged nervous system; exhaustion and anemia, increased reflexes—these are the processes which are generally operative in trauma of the organised behaviour; the facts are especially conspicuous if we collect them into a table (Table 10).

We see that the results characterising the reactive labileness of our subjects in the face of a traumatic situation is connected with the neuropathic status; only 13% of those of the reactive labile group are normal, according to the first medical investigation conducted; and conversely, only 16% of those reactively stable subjects show neuropathic results in the medical examination. The degree and character of the reactions of the personality to the affective situation are primarily connected with the neuropathic status, with that fatigue or weakness of the nervous system seen in many of our mental workers. Obviously these neuropathic defects create the conditions which deprive the human of the ability to resist the traumatic situation and lead to inadequately intense reactions to that situation.

TABLE 10

Psychobiological characteristics	Reactively labile	Reactively stable
Normal, healthy	13%	64%
With neuropathic symptoms (psychasthenia, hysteria, etc.)	61%	16%
With somatic defects	13%	20%
Undiagnosed	13%	0

Analysis shows that two main features appear here: first the unconditioned sensibility of the nervous system, and, second, special defects in the cortical regulators of excitation, in consequence of which every arising excitation manifests the tendency to pass immediately to the motor sphere.

We shall see how these two factors are characteristic of the psychophysiology of the functional neurosis, and it is not surprising that they are especially conspicuous in the traumatic situation of the subjects whose ordinary behaviour manifests neuropathic traits.

Here we witness the confluence of affect and neurosis. The affective situation provokes a reaction similar in structure to that of the neurosis; it creates, as it were, a temporary actual neurosis, which is most distinct in those subjects already having a neuropathic disposition.

The experimental investigation of the reactions of subjects to a traumatic situation is indeed the path to the diagnosis of their neuropathic constitution. There have been many instances where the subjects of our experiments, giving a picture of reactive labileness have, after 6 or 7 months of strenuous living, become ill with neurasthenia, showing that our research may serve as an early diagnosis to neuropathic disease.

Nevertheless, we meet with hundreds of cases in which the defects show only some slight functional weakness of the nervous system; and we cannot be led to consider them as neuropaths. Under ordinary circumstances their behaviour hardly deviates from the normal. However, we can with assurance expect that the very first experience with a vital difficulty will produce an upset and perhaps an actual neurosis. For the diagnostics of such a neurotic disposition we have a definite method—this is the method of putting the subject in some temporary situation giving rise to an analogous difficulty, and investigating the influence on the deformation of the reactive processes. The disturbance and the production of primitive, diffuse forms of excitation will definitely indicate the typological features characteristic of the personality.[1]

[1] This will be discussed in detail in Part Two of this volume.

CHAPTER III

THE INVESTIGATION OF AFFECT IN CRIMINALS

1. PROBLEMS AND MATERIAL

TWO CONSIDERATIONS incline the psychologist studying the mechanism of affect to the investigation of criminals. The first of these has to do with the strength of the affective traumata and the experiences which we are able to observe in criminals.

Psychologists occupying themselves with the affective life of the human have always attempted to study the actual affect which severely disorganises the whole activity of the organism. In these attempts psychologists hastened to use various artifices, wasting much ingenuity in trying to produce a marked affective reaction—by shooting a revolver close to the ear of the subject, or showing pictures supposed "to remind him of something very disagreeable," or giving quinine, or demonstrating fecal masses, etc.[1] In all these cases the psychologists seeking to produce a stable acute affect most often were unsuccessful; the state obtained was not sufficiently stable or well enough expressed; or it was too artificial and shallow, not penetrating to any depth of the personality. This state was usually an emotional reaction to a partial situation, and one that never revealed the affect peculiar to the personality.

The study of criminals and its inter-relations has many advantages. If we are lucky enough to obtain for experimental investigation a person who has just committed a serious crime, for example, a murder, and who was arrested after this crime, we are able to see very intense affective behaviour. Ordinarily the affect is obtained here from two sources: one, the affective experi-

---

[1] Numerous such methods are described in: D. Brunswick, *The Effect of Emotional Stimuli on the Gastro-Intestinal Tone*, Journal of Comparative Psychology, 1924, Nos. 1 and 3.

ence, which still exists, connected with the crime itself; this happens especially when the subject has committed the crime spontaneously, without previously forming a systematic plan, as occurs most often with murderers; they therefore have a very strong affective disturbance. The more serious and the more unusual the crime, i.e., the sharper the conflict with the common social setting, the more intense will be this *primary affect* of the criminal. From this there usually proceeds a secondary affect. In the given case it is associated not so much with the crime itself as with the situation of the arrest, and with the expected possible punishment. The very deprivation of freedom evokes, as we can well understand, affective reactions: the awaiting of the sentence, generally associated with the feeling of no escape and indefiniteness, produces this secondary affect; and it is natural that this affect is stronger than the mere seriousness of the crime. In cases of murder and very important crimes in which the criminal may expect execution, this secondary affect attains its maximum.

We can understand how suggestions (and it is not uncommon to meet cases in which the subject shows only the secondary affect, without the primary) concerning the arrest, the accusations, suspicions, etc., relating to the crime furnish us with precisely such a structure of the process.

As a rule, in all of these cases we meet with an affective behaviour of exceptional strength depending upon the seriousness of the crime, the labileness of the nervous system, and how soon we observe the culprit after the crime. It is obvious that the psychologists investigating the affective mechanics cannot easily overlook such material. The investigation of affect in criminals is an exceedingly interesting problem.

Along with this there arises before the psychologist another problem which is specific to the given material. If, during the investigation of the affect arising in the situation of the examination, we were primarily interested in the symptoms of the diffused affective states, then in the study of the behaviour of criminals the first problem is the establishment of the affective traces connected with the crime.

Can the psychologist studying the affective traces in the criminal objectively establish his participation in the crime?

The investigation of the influence of the scholastic examination on the psychobiological reactions of students proved to us that the definite trauma causes not only a general affective reaction of the subject, but a series of concentrated affective traces connected with this trauma. Studying the behaviour of such a subject we obtain a series of completely objective symptoms, showing us which group of trials are connected with the affective experiences. This makes possible the establishment, with some degree of certainty, of the diagnosis of the trauma in the student, founded exclusively on the facts obtained by objective investigation.

Is such a diagnosis possible when in the psyche of the subject there remain traces of the committed crime? This question is of great interest to the psychologist. It is obvious that every criminal after some known offence does not experience a "general affect"; his affective experiences are concentrated around very definite associations with the crime-complexes. And if the psychologist is in a position experimentally to establish the value of such an affective trace which is present in the criminal but not in others (even in those suspected of the crime), then the problem of the study of the affective traces of the crime ceases to be a purely academic one and takes on a new meaning.

It is not of so much interest for us to show that the employment of the acute affect concentrated on the definite traces represents a great convenience for the investigator as it is for us to be able to study this affect in the different stages of the given psychological drama (the arrest, accusation, sentence, pardon), for this affords us a special means of studying the affective dynamics.

We have produced exceptional conditions for the study of the above-mentioned questions. Thanks to the organisation of a special laboratory in Moscow (The "Procurator") it was possible for us to carry out our experiments very successfully.

In contradiction to many other people occupied with the psychological testing of criminals (Jung, Wertheimer, Ritterhaus, Löeffler, Heilbronner, Ph. Stein, O. Löwenstein and others), we were in a position to perform our experiments on subjects who had been arrested a few hours or days before, instead of those criminals who had been already liberated. When the conditions of the experiment required it, we obtained criminals before they were questioned and before they were told of the cause of their arrest. In special experiments we could trace the influence of the examination and of the sentence, repeating our experiments after the trial in the same way that they had been done before. Finally, we succeeded in performing a number of experiments on arrested people who were not guilty, but were by mistake suspected in one or another crime.

During five years of investigation we collected material relating to about fifty subjects, the majority of whom were murderers or suspected of murder. In special investigations directed to the affect and complexes of the criminals we will discuss in detail the analysis of all our material. Here we must of necessity limit our discourse to a few special, illustrative, and typical cases.

2. ACTUAL AFFECT IN CRIMINALS

WE shall first take up the symptoms of the actual diffuse affect which we observed in our subjects. With confidence we can say that never, during all of our work on human affect and conflicts, have we seen people experiencing so sharp an affect, with so much disorganisation of behaviour. No kind of laboratory experiments can create such an acute and prolonged affect as that which we often observed in people a day or more after the crime and only several hours following the arrest.

It would be possible to fill pages with a description of how our subjects conducted themselves, with what specific characteristics the behaviour of normal people differed from that of a murderer. For years during our investigation we saw subjects in whom traumatic experiences of the day evoked an affective stupor, and who came to us in a stuporous state; we saw persons whose behaviour was characterised by a general tension, in whom there had been no premeditation of a murder; there were those in whom every movement showed excitation, and there were others, externally calm, reacting toward the crime as to a completed irrevocable event, and awaiting their punishment. Finally, and this occurred most frequently, there came to us people traumatised by their arrest, who expressed astonishment and positively denied all participation in the crime, and then, appearing in our laboratory some days later, after confession of guilt in the murder, evidenced depression connected with the expected punishment.

Let us return, however, to our chief problems. We shall limit our description to only the psychophysiology of those states. By what is the psychophysiological picture of the experienced affect characterised in the criminals? What mechanisms guide the behaviour in such a situation?

We did all the experiments in our ordinary laboratory setting, presenting to each subject a series of word-stimuli and registering the accompanying associations and movements. We were less interested in the changes in the series of organic symptoms accompanying the affective state in the subject (vegetative changes, variations in breathing, pulse rate, etc.); we were more concerned with the question of what characterised the behaviour of the subject when he was in a state of acute affect. The comparative material permitted us to draw several conclusions concerning the specific mechanisms of the subject's behaviour while he was in the state of acute affect. We shall discuss a few of the fundamental mechanisms.

(a) *Difficulty of Establishing Organised Forms of Behaviour*

We have already noted that in the state of acute affect it is difficult and often impossible to elaborate any kind of regular and stable forms of behaviour. The organism appears to be incapable of establishing any standard behaviour, any stable system of coordination, any constant reactive formula. The actions seen in the state of acute affect are characterised by their own accidental nature and lack of organisation, giving the impression that the organism is not able to establish the above stable automatisms, but it seems impelled to adapt itself to every stimulus presented. As a result we observed an unstable system of reactions, practically useless for the elaborations of stable reactive standards. This rule is primarily seen in the language reactions of our subject, while the normal subject responds to the stimuli with remarkable stability, easily forming his own standard of speed in the language answers, but the criminals whom we have studied are completely unable to do this; the establishment at a definite average of speed completely fails to appear here, the process is in the highest degree deprived of its automatisms, and the subject reacts with astonishing variable speeds.

In Figure 20, we find the curves of the reactive periods in eight of the criminals examined by this method.

All these eight cases were murderers, who came under our investigation two or three days after committing the murder, immediately after their arrest. During the examinations all of them were in a state of maximal affect. The curve of distribution which we give shows no kind of regularity, and there are usually not even the peaks generally obtained in the standard reactions. Such a phenomenon is entirely lacking in our subjects; the affect excludes the formation of those "reaction patterns" which are so quickly formed in our normal cases.

The fact that our subjects do not give stable reactions during the time of the tests is not explained by want of intelligence, or the unusual conditions of the experiments; those subjects of the same intelligence become quiet after the first two or three reactions, and they elaborate their characteristic standard of speed and preserve it during the whole time of the experiment. In

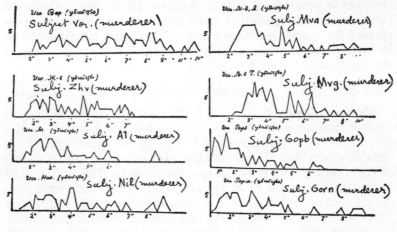

Fig. No. 20

Figure 21, we give two examples: two control subjects, of the
same social position and development as our criminals, under-
going the experiment for the first time but having no knowledge
of the crime and not knowing why they were investigated, remained calm, giving perfectly regular curves of distribution of
the reactive time with sharply defined peaks.

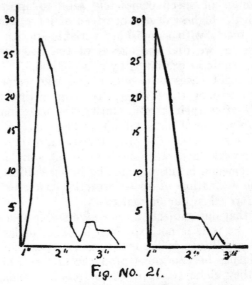

Fig. No. 21.

CONTROL SUBJECTS

It is obvious that the affect destroys one of the fundamental functions of behaviour: the function of the establishment of organised forms, the elaboration of which has in American psychological literature received the name of "reaction patterns" (we refer to them as "reactive formulæ"). This function of elaboration of standard forms we may consider established for language reaction by the tenth or twelfth year. The affect causes chaotic forms in the subject, characteristic of the linguistic reaction of a child seven or eight years old. In Figure 22, we have analogous curves of distribution of speed of the linguistic reaction in three children; the first of whom is eight years old (with some mental retardation), the second, fifteen years old and the third a normal child of twelve years and eight months.[1]

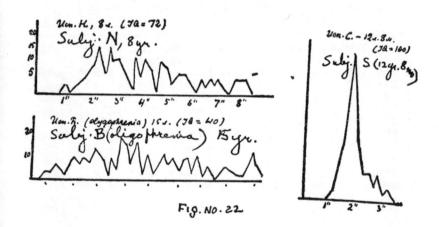

Fig. No. 22.

The curves show that, in the child twelve and one half years old, the standard setting of the language reactions at a definite speed is already established, and the behaviour at this stage of activity is completely organised; this organisation is not present in the eight-year-old mentally retarded child, and the process shows a complete deterioration in the idiot, who was unable to form standard reactive formulæ in these complicated functions.

Only in the youngest child and in the idiot do we see that disintegration in the coordination of the language reactions which we observe in criminals, although here we do not have a simple return to the previous stage, but at the same time, while the

[1] These curves are taken from the author's book, *Speech and Intellect of the Developing Child*, Moscow, 1928.

children have not yet reached complex organised forms of reactivity, the affect experienced by the criminal is devoid of these organised forms. Below we shall again see that this external picture of destruction has in the two cases a very different basis, and that the destruction in the elaboration to the standard forms of reactivity in the criminal leads to the action of those affective traces which in him are unusually real; however, the psychophysiological law here is unassailable: there is a sharply expressed inability to establish stable reactive formulæ, and the passing over into chaotic and accidental reactions.

TABLE II

Subject	Crime	Reaction time	Variation (absolute)	Per Cent	Subject	Crime	Reaction time	Variation (absolute)	Variation (in %)
1 Vorn.	Murder	5.9″	2.9″	48%	17 Shik.	Suspected of Murder	1.6″	0.4″	25%
2 Mva.	"	2.0″	0.4″	20%	18 Filat.	"	3.2″	1.0″	30%
3 Bva.	"	2.2″	0.4″	18%	19 Skorob.	"	2.2″	0.8″	35%
4 Sm.	"	2.5″	0.4″	16%	20 Mosg.	"	5.6″	3.8″	68%
5 Step.	"	2.2″	1.0″	45%	21 Ivan.	"	1.9″	0.4″	21%
6 Zhv.	"	4.0″	1.4″	35%	22 Bib.	"	2.6″	1.2″	46%
7 Mva.	"	4.2″	1.0″	24%	23 Zogr.	"	3.0″	1.4″	46%
8 Mbg.	"	4.0″	1.2″	30%	24 Kram.	"	1.8″	0.6″	33%
9 Agaf.	"	4.0″	0.8″	20%	25 Vora.	"	2.3″	0.5″	22%
10 How.	"	3.2″	1.4″	43%	26 Vas.	"	1.4″	0.4″	28%
11 Gorb.	"	2.0″	1.2″	60%	27 Bel.	"	2.4″	1.0″	42%
12 Fil.	"	3.0″	1.2″	40%					
13 Drob.	"	1.6″	1.4″	25%	Average		2.9″	1.1″	34%
14 Agap.	"	3.2″	1.8″	56%					
15 Nigam.	"	4.0″	2.2″	55%					
16 Dborn.	"	2.4″	1.2″	50%					

Speed and stability of the language reaction in 27 criminals—murderers and those suspected of murder.

In Table 11 we give the figures which are characteristic here. We have chosen twenty-seven criminals; sixteen of these were murderers, eleven were suspected of murder; all of these came to us immediately after their arrest.

We submit the average time of the language reactions and the average variation in each of these; the first shows a marked retardation (in several as much as four to six seconds); the picture of No. 2 is especially characteristic. If the variability of the normal adult subject reaches not more than 0.2″ to 0.4″, or 20%

to 25% of its average speed,[1] then here we not infrequently meet with a variability of $1''$-$1.8''$, $2.0''$ and the deviation is often as much as 40% or 60% of the average time, practically twice as much as the normal.

We intentionally give here not only the group of murderers but also those suspected in the murders; they both give practically the same result, and, as we shall see further on, it is necessary to search for the specific differences between them in other indicators.

The impossibility or, at least, the difficulty of establishing in the affect a stable reactive formula finds its cause deep in the nature of the process. The facts which we established concerning language reactions apply also to the motor reactions, accompanying the speech.

We usually obtained in our normal subjects stable accompanying reactions very easily; even after two or three trials, the pressure of the hand became connected with the language reaction in a stable manner, and later on it became automatic. We did not, as a rule meet, in our normal subjects, cases who forgot to press the bulb. The curves of the pressure correspond to each language reaction and give an equal or nearly similar series of almost equivalent pressures, certainly not varying in their form and very slightly varying in their intensity.

We see an entirely different picture in people experiencing an acute diffused affect. The accompanying motor reaction is here very unstable; the subject often "forgets" to make the connection between the language response and the motor pressure, and this forgetting enters into the system, and is shown by the difficulty of obtaining stable automatic motor reactions in such a state. On the other hand when the subject gives the motor reaction, he is not able to elaborate any definite standard reactive formula, and the pressures are unequal, showing the different degrees of underlying excitation.

In Figure 23 we call particular attention to the series of ordinates characterising the intensity of two different motor reactions in two of our subjects. The first of these demands special attention. We see instability of the accompanying motor reactions; now they are present, now absent. At first, until the 30th reaction, we have a series of decreasing motor pressures. Ordinarily the usual series of pressures preserves its strength for some twenty-

---

[1] For an index of the variability we take the coefficient ZW_0—ZW, i.e., the upper quartile. This is conditioned by the fact that the usual sharp decline occurs in our material only on the side of the inhibition, i.e., increased reactive time.

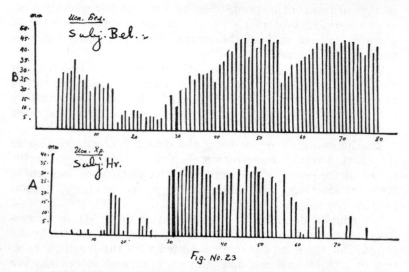

Fig. No. 23

INTENSITY OF ACCOMPANYING REACTIONS DURING AFFECT

five reactions, and then the reactions begin anew to become irregular, in places falling out altogether. The whole series proves that even such a simple act as the movement of the hand, which is associated with the speech response, cannot be firmly elaborated in this subject; his behaviour during the experiment convincingly shows that at the basis of this lies the acute disturbed affect. The subject "Hram" was suspected of a very serious crime, and though she did not know anything about what she was suspected of, she was severely traumatised by the sudden arrest in a small town in the provinces and her unexpected removal to Moscow. During the time of the experiment she cried, and was very confused and agitated. In Figure 24 we give a sample from the continuous protocol obtained during the experiment with this subject; it shows variations of the reactions.

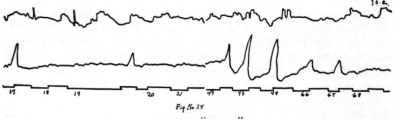

Fig No. 24

SUBJECT "HRAM"
THE ACCOMPANYING MOTOR CHANGES DURING A DESTRUCTIVE AFFECT

In some cases the associated motor pressures are regular (Reaction 17); in others (Reactions 18, 19, 21), they are very much decreased; in still others (Reaction 19) the motor pressures are delayed. We do not have a general picture here, and the last protocol with acute excitatory pressures shows us that in this subject we cannot establish any typical model reactions; sometimes the pressure is not as much as 3 mm., other times it reaches 40 mm., at times it is lacking altogether. In the last cases we actually have a complete failing of the motor component of the reaction, and the curve concealed by a constant tremor shows that here even the attempts to accompany the speech by the motor pressures have disappeared. The neurodynamic picture lying at the basis of the reaction is astonishingly unorganised; the disturbed excitation leads to a marked energetic destruction in some cases, and in others to a complete failure of the motor innervation.

The affect gives a picture of complete destruction in the regulation of the disturbed excitation; the activity begins to be separated entirely by other factors than those observed in the normal person.

BUT HERE THE RESULTS DEPEND UPON VOLUNTARY COOPERATION OF S ... HE MUST ATTEND TO THE TASK

We append here three parts from one and the same protocol, in the same subject, and we obtain three completely different pictures, as if there were three different people reacting. The intensity of the pressure, the form of the coordination, the violence of the disturbance show here complete differences and varied instabilities.

(b) *The Instability of the Dynamics of the Excitation in the Reactive Series*

We immediately come to the second factor characterising the behaviour of the affectively excited subject. Whilst in the normal subject, the energy of the different reactions revealed considerable stability in the course of the whole reactive series, in the affective subject it often varies. We chose cases where the motor reactions in the experiment had a tendency to become extinguished toward the end, and the subject began to make a weak slow pressure. In our protocols we have the reverse of this case—when having begun with comparatively weak motor reactions the subject passes during the time of the experiment into an increasing excitation, and this dynamics of excitation is shown in an acute change of the motor curves. Tracing the dynamics of the motor reaction we obtain a graphic picture of the dynamics of the excitation during the given period of time.

Let us return to the reactive series b, illustrated in Figure 23. Before us we have the subject "Bel" accused in the same murder in which he was suspected.... Before the beginning of the experiment "Bel" conducted himself calmly, but during the time of the experiment he became excited; this is reflected in the dynamics of his motor reactions, and although in the beginning of the series his usual reactions reached 15-25 mm., gradually the intensity of the pressure became 45-50 mm., increasing the intensity of the reactive disturbances.

As in the first case, the subject was unable to maintain a more or less equilibrated standard in the expenditure of energy; this lack of equilibrium, however, is not so much a result of an incapacity to form a fairly stable organised set of reactions as much as an expression of the definite dynamics of excitation in the course of the experiment. The affect is characterised here by the impossibility to establish definite standards in the expenditure of energy, and involving in activity constantly more and more of its mass. The behaviour is characterised by the mobilisation of the activity, extending far beyond the limits of the ascertained norms of the first reaction.

Such instability of an expenditure of energy, the comparatively uneven profile of the experiment, the unequal limits of the energies of the different portions of the experiments is revealed in almost every part of the protocol; and the variability of the motor pressures, a summary of which is given in Table 12, often attains to 35-50% of the basic average intensity for that subject, but in special cases reaches even beyond their limits.

The energetic inequalities in the different parts of the behaviour is a very characteristic symptom for the affective state.

The figures given in the table are by no means uniform, but they show only that the simple statistical analysis here is not always sufficient. Two factors have an unequal influence on the data obtained: first, our subjects are far from being in the same affective states; the extreme cases are represented by Nos. 1, 23, 24, 25, 27, and these give a uniformly maximal variation in the reactive disturbances. Secondly, a bare analysis of the intensities of the motor pressures is not of great advantage because a considerable number of the motor reactions, and at almost the same height, show a sharp disturbance in their form. Therefore a simple mensuration of the intensities of the pressures according to their heights is futile; behind the external form very interesting figures may be concealed, and it is on this account often an unsuccessful process.

TABLE 12

No.	Subject	Crime	MV M.	MV Abs.	in %	No.	Subject	Crime	MV M.	MV Abs.	in %
1	Vorn	Murder	?	?	?	15	Dorn.	Murder	28	9	32%
2	Mva.	"	Extreme	pressures		16	Shish.	Suspected	36	8	22%
3	Bva.	"	22	F	32%			of Murder			
4	Sm.	"	37	6	19%	17	Fil.	"	45	5	11%
5	Step.	"?	?	6	30%	18	Skorob.	"	42	11	26%
6	Zhv.	"		8	27%	19	Mosg.	"	58	8	13%
7	Mvg.	"	22	9	40%	20	Ivan.	"	20	24	120%
8	Mva.	"	28	6	21%	21	Bib.	"	28	9	32%
9	Agaf.	"	83	16	19%	22	Zagr.	"	35	4	11%
10	Gorn.	"	106	10	95%	23	Hram.	"	11	8	73%
11	Gorb.	"	23	F	30%	24	Vora.	"	25	24	98%
12	Filat.	"	25	6	24%	25	Vas.	"	?	?	?
13	Drob.	"	43	13	30%	26	Bel.	"	47	8	17%
14	Agap.	"	36	17	39%	27		"	30	23	77%
							Average		—	—	35%

Intensity of the motor reactions and their variability.
M = median; MV abs. = variation absolute;
MV % = median variation in per cent.

(c) *The Diffuse Excitatory Character of the Reactive Processes*

If we wish to indicate the specific peculiarity of the excitation characteristic of the disturbed affect shown by our subjects, then we should have to repeat emphatically that which we said in the analysis of the cases of mass affect. The chaotic behaviour of our subjects is characterised by the same impulsive excitation, the identical discoordinated reactions, the same actuality of the large mass excitation given by the reactions of the subjects who were not in a state of neutrality.

We had best submit one of our observed examples of sharply disturbed affect.

Subject Vorn, fifty years old, a baker who was accused of the murder of his wife with whom he had lived recently in a state of divorce. The murder occurred in a half-lit corridor of the apartment. The neighbour of the wife of Vorn heard her cries from the corridor, "Vasily (name of her husband) has killed me." Responding to the cries, she found the wife in a pool of blood, and carried her into the next room where she died before the arrival of the doctors. The autopsy revealed stab wounds from a knife in the region of the abdomen.

Vorn was arrested the same day in his own apartment. He was accused of the murder, but he denied it, claiming that someone killed her in order to obtain the use of her things. Two days after the murder Vorn was passed on to us for investigation.

The behaviour of the subject during the experiment was marked by acute excitation: wiping his forehead, fidgeting about in the chair, and in the intervals between stimuli, he smacked his lips and muttered something to himself; from time to time, there was a quick movement of the feet, and the speech responses were now very deep, almost whispers, now in a high-pitched tone of voice.

The features which are common for all the behaviour are: the tendency of the immediate excitatory reactions to every stimulus, and diffuse excitation in the motor system during the intervals when there is no stimulation. The whole series of word-stimuli are responded to by answers containing many words, and it shows marked disturbances in form as follows:

13. to cut—8.6″ to cut—no—to cut bread—what
20. coat—2.2″—well, coat, black—
27. paper—2.4″—paper—written—read—clean.
39. iron—16.0″—iron—iron—iron—well iron goes in the car.
48. sister—11.0″—sister—well sister—well, what of it?

The organised associated activity of the subject is sharply disturbed, often the stimulus does not evoke immediately a definite word-reaction; the latent period, however, is filled with the speech excitation, the subject repeats many times the given stimulus aloud, seeking to find the proper answer. In all the instances the word given by the subject is not the prepared product of the answer thought of during the latent period; the reactive process is diffuse, it is not distributed over the phase of internal preparation and subsequent realisation of the answer, the excitation directly extends to the speech area, and a series of unorganised speech impulses is clearly shown in the changing structure of the reactive process.

An especially marked category of such a form of excitation appears every time the subject makes a connection between the stimulus given him and the situation of the crime. This happens, however, at almost every step in the experiment:

13. to cut—6.5″—to cut ... well ... to cut bread ...
14. window—8.0″—(confused, muttering to himself).
15. wife—16.0″—this you have asked in vain, what you ask is to no purpose, we have not cut anyone, nor thought about it. ...

16. neighbour—8.2″—well, neighbour, well, Ivan, Sergei....

24. blow—10.4″—why a blow ... you can strike a blow on the table.

25. belly—7.8″—well, my belly aches today....

26. corridor—30.0″—well, this you ask in vain, dear Sir, we were not there in the corridor....

79. fear—13.8″—fear—well, what of it—well, here in this room where there is more fear than—but why?

80. grieve—6.8″—one can grieve for his relatives and others, my daughter grieves that my wife has been cut up. It is a pity.

An acute excitation, with confusion, whose contents arise in traumatic situations is seen very clearly in the associated processes here without requiring further explanation.

The affective process, however, may have other results than simply the excitation referred to above. In many cases the answer becomes echolalic, or perhaps there is no speech response at all; the subject does not form any association to the word given him, and instead we get a long period of silence:

23. hand—9.4″—well, hand—

24. blow—4.8″—well, what ... well ... blow

25. belly—3.4″—well, belly, what?

26. corridor—4.4″—corridor ... well ... corridor ...

43. wound—39.0″—well, wound ...

50. jealousy—33.0″—(coughs, clears throat, no answer) ...

88. to love—31.0″ (refuses to answer)

89. to change—11.0″—to change nobody ...

90. confection [1]—26.0″—(refuses).

91. to walk—17.5″—(moves his lips, sighs, but the reaction is absent).

Many serious considerations lead us to believe that these cases of silence and echolalia do not differ in principle from those responses accompanied by an acute excitation of the speech area; we are inclined to put both of these into one group. Evidently the examples of excitation are only partial stages in which the impaired excitation destroys every associative process. The general behaviour, the fragmentary symptoms of the speech excitation, and finally the structure of the accompanying motor reaction confirms us in this belief.

In Figure 25 we submit a part of the graphic protocol of this subject in order to show how deeply the functional disorder of the neurodynamic processes extended. We have purposely chosen the reaction of the repeated experiment (after a hundred previous reactions in the subject). We cannot say anything, however, of

[1] In the room of the murderer there were found 5 lbs. of confectionery which were probably bought by V. to persuade his wife to live with him again.

the establishment of the coordination of the movements here; the latent periods are filled with marked tremors signalising the extreme excitation correlated in the central process, the signs of the motor excitation usually begin with the trace of the given stimulus and occupy the whole latent period; the excitation which has just begun dominates the innervation and manifests a tendency to spread over all the free intervals (see the characteristic series after reaction No. 7); the general excitation produces tonic and rigid pressures (note slow beginning in reaction No. 8); the active pressures often are not coordinated with the speech responses. In a word, we observe neurodynamic chaos which does not, at first sight, manifest any lawful regularity.

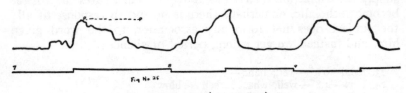

Fig No. 25

SUBJECT V. (MURDERER)

7. LAMP—4.6"—WITH A LAMPSHADE.
8. OATS—4.5"—WELL, ASHES IN A SACK
9. KIND—5.7"—A KIND HUSBAND, A KIND PERSON

A closer examination, however, shows that this chaos is wholly a result of the definite neurodynamic changes observed in the affect and related to certain fundamental forms. Here we shall discuss only those of their characteristics illustrating the curves taken from the protocols of our various subjects.

1. Each central obstacle produces disturbance of the motor excitation, often prolonged until after the speech reaction.

2. The given stimulus frequently causes a direct motor impulse, not connected with the speech function, acting as a catalyser of that motor excitation whose setting is characteristic of the behaviour of the subject.

3. The speech reaction given to the subject, connected by a command with a single short motor pressure calls out a series of motor impulses not altogether contained in the speech response and appearing in a succession of diffused motor pressures.

4. Every foreign impulse (endogenous excitations—thoughts entering the mind or external stimuli: noises, etc.) produces a direct transference of energy to the motor area and becomes manifest as a number of spontaneous motor disturbances.

All these laws may be summarised in a principle which we have stated above: the disappearance of the reactive structure under the influence of the affect, the exclusion of the higher regulating functions and the transformation of the excitation into a process of diffused character. This occurs markedly every time

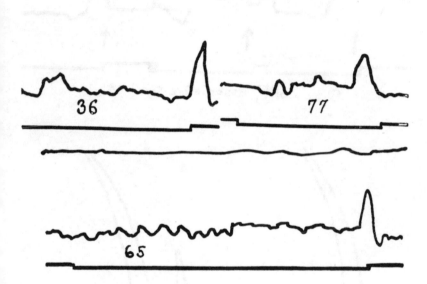

Fig. No. 26.

SUBJECT "ST." (MURDERER)

36. MARIA—5.0"—BUT I HAVE ALREADY SAID I DO NOT KNOW, WELL, PAPER.
77. DEEP—5.0"—DEEPLY
65. CHANGE—8.2"—CHANGE..

the stimuli bring back to the subject the situation of his arrest.

We shall give only some of the curves illustrating these laws.

In Figure 26, we have some typical reactions of one of our subjects: "St." arrested for rape and murder. In this case the normal pressures are confused with sharply uncoordinated motor impulses, in which every obstacle in the speech reaction evokes

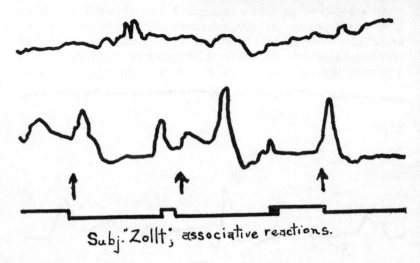

Subj. "Zollt"; associative reactions.

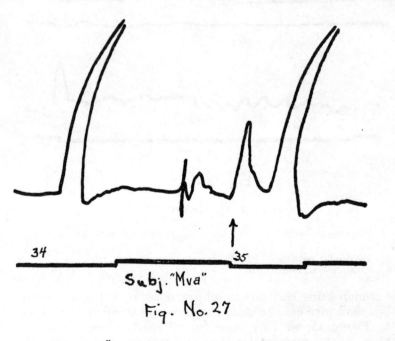

34

35

Subj. "Mva"

Fig. No. 27

34. FAITH—2.4"—LAVATORY
35. POND—2.6"—TO RINSE

many impulsive pressures, going over into an acute, diffused tremor. This tremor usually terminates in a successful response (see reaction No. 65), and fills up the whole latent period with an obstructed reaction, appearing as the motor correlate of the destruction. There has hardly been a single one of our subjects in whom we have not seen, in greater or lesser degree, this phenomenon.

In Figure 27 we give examples of two subjects in whom there is an individual catalytic action of the speech stimulus.

The stimulus we give calls out, as a rule, a direct motor reaction. It catalyses, so to speak, the excitation existing in a concealed form, at once connecting it with the motor apparatus. This group of examples is characteristic of that motor setting established to a direct impulsive muscular reaction, which we encounter in greater or less degree in every subject during the state of affect. It is evidence of the weakness of the "functional barrier," of that difficulty to control excitation, to partition it from the motor area, which is characteristic of a functional neurosis as well as of the actual affect.

Finally, Figure 28 gives two typical cases where the excitation beginning in the latent period is not connected with the reaction being tested, but is prolonged into several successive spontaneous impulses. In these two instances we first come into contact with the mechanism of perseveration, which will occupy our attention later on.

All of this explains the mechanics of those cases (the examples of which are given in the curves of Figure 27) characterised by the sudden and incomprehensible appearances of the spontaneous impulses occurring during the intervals free from stimuli.

All the examples prove that in the state of affect the reactive process acquires a diffused character, but that the behaviour is characterised by a constant and direct transference of each excitatory process to the motor area.

After this it becomes clear to us why, in such a state as we have in criminals only a few days separated from the crime and from the arrest by only several hours, the motor reaction should produce so large a number of disturbances never met with in normal subjects.

In Table 13, we have a group of murderers and those suspected of murder who were the objects of our research. The figures reveal that the number of disturbances accompanying the motor feaures vary widely, but only in three or four of our cases are they lower than ten per cent; as a rule our subjects give from twenty to thirty per cent of such disturbances, and frequently this figure is considerably higher.

It is characteristic in these cases that the secondary affect is built up on the primary affect of the crime, but there is another group in which the affect is connected only with the arrest, and sometimes with the suspicion; in both of these groups, as far as the relations of the accompanying motor system are concerned, there is no remarkable difference; the irradiated disturbances of the motor reactions occur in nearly equal degree here as well as there.

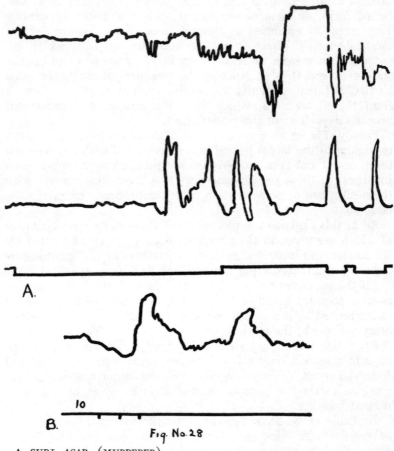

Fig. No. 28

A. SUBJ. AGAP. (MURDERER)
    TO THROW AWAY—22.0″—WHAT TO THROW AWAY...A FLOWER
B. SUBJ. FIL. (MURDERER)
    10. FISH—2.8″—MEAT

TABLE 13

No.	Subject	Crime	Motor disturbance	No.	Subject	Crime	Motor disturbance
1	Vorn.	Murder	100%	15	Nigam.	Murder	14%
2	Mva.	"	26%	16	Dvorn.	"	?
3	Bva.	"	21%	17	Shish.	Suspected of	5.5%
4	Sm.	"	45%			murder	
5	St.	"	44%	18	Fil.	"	8.5%
6	Zhv.	"	10%	19	Skor.	"	0
7	Mva.	"	27%	20	Mozg.	"	16%
8	Mvg.	"	60%	21	Ivan.	"	17%
9	Agaf.	"	?	22	Bib.	"	44%
10	Gorn.	"	22%	23	Zagr.	"	76%
11	Gorb.	"	11%	24	Hram.	"	56%
12	Fil.	"	100%	25	Vora.	"	100%
13	Drob.	"	?	26	Vas.	"	4%
14	Agap.	"	20%	27	Bel.	"	20%

Even where there is a considerable variation in the quality and quantity of the motor disturbances it depends mostly upon those individual and typological differences which we shall further on [1] have an opportunity to see in more detail.

3. THE DIAGNOSTICS OF THE AFFECTIVE TRACES IN CRIMINALS

THE problem of the actual diffused affect in the criminal is interesting but still not specific for this material. The special question here is that of the possibility of discovering the experimentally psychological path of the affective traces of the crime, and in such a way to establish the diagnosis of the participation in the crime.

If, in the experimental seance, there is actually an objective and scientific means of establishing traces of the person's past and especially concerning his affect and traumata, then it is perfectly natural that for psychology there is opened up an enormous territory, very interesting both theoretically and practically.

The question of the experimental diagnostics of participation is certainly not a new one, and its history is exceedingly interesting. Even a quarter of a century ago the problem of the experimental psychological determination of participation in crime was discussed by the well-known criminologist H. Gross, and many investigators worked on it, constantly applying the methods of the associative experiment. Jung, Wertheimer, Heilbronner, Löffler, Rittehaus, Stein, A. Gross, and others attempted to use the method of the experimental diagnostics of participation. Freud

[1] See Chapters III, B, 3, and also Chapters VIII and IX.

and Stern have occupied themselves with this question; Münsterberg and other criminologists have studied the problem hopefully, and in 1910-11 there was not a more fashionable topic in psychology than the artificial manifestation of traces of the affective past. The subject was then dropped for about a decade after the appearance in 1911 of Lipmann's monograph. . . .

There were two reasons for the disappointment connected with these researches: the majority of the investigators did not use actual criminals, and the psychologists created artificial situations which they intended to be similar to the crimes, but which were, of course, deprived of the affect connected with the actual crime. The criminals who did come into the hands of the investigators were usually accidental or they were ruined for this purpose by cross-questioning, trials, or conviction and consequent psychical disease. . . . Also there were some disappointments arising from the method itself; the associative experiment produced traces of definite affective complexes, and, therefore, it was not suitable to record objectively the phenomena. The elaborated method of analysis of the associative reactions and the appearance of the symptom complexes was insufficient; the accessory difficulties might produce symptoms similar to the affective, but fairly complicated complexes might be reflected in other systems than that of the associative system. In the attempt to estimate the accompanying affective traces of the symptoms it became necessary to employ auxiliary methods not purely objective.

Now there appeared a new cycle of investigations, attempting to employ the objective registration of psychophysiological processes, and often more modest questions. . . . Beginning with Tarchanov, Veraguth, Binswanger and other authors, they tried to apply to the diagnostics of the affective traces a method of the physiological reflexes. Others—Benussi, W. Smith, and Larson—used the respiration, the pulse, and the destruction of certain internal structures of equilibrium as an objective establishment of concealment and lying. Finally there was a third group from among the old investigators, like R. Sommer, who attempted to trace the reflection of the affective traces in the involuntary movements (Löwenstein, M. Seelig).

Our researches are more closely allied to the last group, exhibiting however some radical changes in the establishment of the questions. In contrast to the former experimenters, we were able to use as material actual criminals taken usually before investigations and cross-questioning. Thus we were sure that we obtained material characterised by a continuous and strong affect; and, in contradistinction to the latter investigators, we made use of the reflection of the affective traces not in the passive system but in the active behaviour measured by our new method.

Both of these factors enable us to place the question of the experimental diagnostics of participation on a more objective basis.

The behaviour of our subjects during the time of the experiments showed that not only is the simple diffused affect (about which we have spoken above) characteristic, but there is manifest a sharply marked area of affective disturbance. This focus appears each time that the word-stimulus touches the situation of the crime and causes marked changes in the graphic record as they are objective symptoms connected with the criminal complex.

We arranged all of our experiments in such a way that the undifferentiated word-stimuli were of equal value for the subject, and such as were connected with the situation of the crime entered into the structure of the criminal act. We estimate that every such word, by virtue of its entrance into the general affective complex, calls out in the psyche of the subject all this complex, with its entire affective tone,[1] and we are able in the person who has participated in the crime to witness the manifestation of symptoms characterising the disturbed affective focus.

Here we unavoidably come to an explanation of the difficulty: the subject is in such a position that he most of all desires to avoid compromising himself, and he applies all of his strength in order to conceal and inhibit what is going on in his mind. The symptom is not only seen in the subject, but simultaneously in the tendency to inhibit the disturbance.

Two questions arise:

1. Can we objectively establish the symptoms appearing in the response to the critical stimuli, so that we can differentiate the participating criminal from an innocent person?

2. Can we objectively establish them under the conditions of that resistance by the subject who is trying to conceal the appearance of the compromising affective traces?

We can best answer these queries by submitting the material from three typical cases. The first of these is one of murder where confession was obtained before our experiment; the second case was one in which the subject denied his participation in the murder, but proof of his guilt was forthcoming later; and finally the third represented one of a less serious nature—pilfering—but all the conditions remained as formerly.

CASE NO. I

Eighteenth of January, 1925, Mva., 28 years old, came to the porter of the house in which she lived and reported that she had found her husband (Mv.) in the bed, murdered, with a crushed skull and a cut throat. An investigation was quickly made and it was revealed that the murder was committed by Bv. living in that apartment, at the request of the wife (Mva.) of the murdered man—for this she promised him 18 rubles

[1] At present it is immaterial to us whether we speak of the conditionally evoked reaction, as Pavlov does, or of the law of redintegration, according to Hollingsworth. For us it is essential that the stimulus be able to call out in the given case the whole complex related to that situation from which it is taken.

(ten dollars) and the overcoat and cap of her husband—and that Mva. herself, as well as the wife (Bva. 32 years old) of the murderer, took part in the killing.

The course of events was as follows: It was arranged that Bv. kill Mv. after a drinking party which was to take place in the apartment of Mv. and his wife. After the carousal, Mva. left the house, thinking that when she returned her husband would have been killed. However, when she came back she found nothing had happened, and she went to Bv. who said that he had not yet been able to get an axe, and he asked her to return again in a half an hour, promising that her husband (Mv.) would be dead after that time. When Mva. returned, Bv., remaining in the apartment with his wife (Bva.) and with Mv., had killed him with a blow of the axe, put him in the bed and covered him with a blanket, after which he began to break into the cupboard, thinking that he would find valuables there. Entering about this time, Mva. assured herself that her husband was dead, put on the samovar, took a basin and washed the bloody spot from the floor. It was previously decided that the body should be thrown into a neighbouring pool but this was not done, and it remained in the bed.

Both of the women, Mva. and Bva., were arrested. They did not deny that the murder was committed by Bv., and the only doubt was in the degree of their active participation. Bva. said that the murder was done at the request of the wife of the murdered man, but Mva. reported that it was on the initiative of Bv. and his wife, Bva.

As a control, a woman on the same intellectual level of those arrested, 32 years old, was taken.

The experiment was carried out the 22nd of December, 1925, four days after the crime. The subject was given 75 word-stimuli, which were then repeated: 12 of these were directly connected with the situation of the crime, several were chosen so that in a certain setting they could be connected with this situation.

We submit the list in full:

1 house	20 paper	39 to allow	58 oven
2 forest	21 *overcoat* (k)	40 overshoes	59 foot
3 hours	22 train	41 amber	60 hut
4 eyes	23 *cap* (k)	42 horse	61 bed
5 glass	24 flowers	43 *Jacob* (k)	62 snow
6 bread	25 money	44 letter	63 *basin* (k)
7 lamp	26 white	45 blanket	64 floor
8 oats	27 weather	46 polka	65 knock (c)
9 spectacles	28 candle	47 tobacco	66 *blow* (k)
10 kind	29 *sin* (k)	48 *husband*	67 water
11 rock	30 glue	49 table	68 *axe* (k)
12 to go	31 quarrel	50 red	69 gums
13 bucket	32 rye	51 dress	70 trough
14 window	33 Peter	52 pipe	71 love
15 neighbour	34 cotton	53 wine	72 change
16 pie	35 pond	54 *cupboard* (k)	73 head
17 lake	36 iron	55 vestibule	74 god
18 carriage	37 advice	56 to promenade	75 salt
19 tea	38 Maria	57 *to .crush*	

The facts we obtained manifested the acute symptoms of affect, remarkably concentrated about those cases in which the stimuli presented to the subject are connected with the situation of the crime. Table 14 gives a statistical review of these facts.

TABLE 14

Subject	Reactive time				Motor disturbances			
	Index stimulus	Critical stimulus	Post-critical stimulus	Coefficient of critical inhibition	Index stimulus	Critical stimulus	Post-critical stimulus	Coefficient of critical disturbances
Mva.	1.75″	2.9″	2.1″	+64%	6%	83%	100%	+77%
Bva.	1.75″	3.4″	2.2″	+94%	3%	73%	82%	+70%
Control	2.2 ″	2.0″	2.0″	—10%	36%	25%	18%	—11%

Notwithstanding the fact that the critical stimuli we have chosen are not always accepted by the patient as such, and, on the contrary, other stimuli which we estimate to be indifferent, often are taken by the subject as connected with the situation of the crime—notwithstanding this, the reactions to the group of critical stimuli are characterised by a sharp increase of inhibition and by a marked rise in the number of disturbed accompanying motor reactions.

Practically all these cases of acute inhibition of the speech reactions and almost all the instances of the motor disturbances coincide with the stimuli connected with the situation of the crime.

Although the first reactions in both of these cases have a normal course,

Subject, Mva.	Subject, Bva.
5 glass—1.6″—frame	5 glass—1.2″—mouth (perseveration)
6 bread—1.9″—knife	6 bread—1.3″—salt
7 lamp—1.6″—fire	7 lamp—0.8″—tea (perseveration)
8 oats—1.6″—land	8 oats—2.0″—wheat
9 spectacles—1.6″—glass, etc.	9 spectacles—1.6″—(perseveration) etc.,

the words connected with the situation of the crime produced inhibition in both cases:

Subject, Mva.   Subject, Bva.

43 Jacob—4.0"—calling Jacob   13 bucket—3.8"—what shall I an-
44 vestibule—6.0"—vestibule to   swer you—ladle
     paint   21 overcoat—3.4"—the coat
57 to crush—13.0"—to crush, Oi!   25 money—3.4"—paper
     I do not consider it neces-   29 sin—4.8"—what shall I say
     sary to do this,   now, I don't know—hours
68 axe—4.0"—to cut wood with   31 quarrel—4.0"—peace

As can be seen from the above summary, these inhibitions are not accidental; it is characteristic that all the post-critical reactions are in a certain degree inhibitory; the experiment when repeated shows inhibition in the same groups of stimuli.

The affective character of all the delayed reactions appear in bold relief when we pass over to the analysis of the accompanying motor reactions. In Figure 29 we see records of the experimental graphs from both subjects; we compare here the average motor reactions to the indifferent stimulus with the motor reactions of those cases in which the given stimulus was connected with the situation of the crime.

We see that even if the external course of the associative reaction appears calm, in reality there is concealed behind it an acute neurodynamic change; the excitation in all these cases shows the connection of the given stimuli with the affect, and we are able to reestablish in the recorded reactions the separate components of the affective situation of the crime.

CASE 2

On the 15th of January, 1926, a body of an unknown man was found in a pile of snow, in a courtyard of a house. The body was lying on its back, in underclothes, with the *valenka* (Russian felt boots) beside it. The head had been split by a heavy instrument, on the body were stab wounds, and the whole body was dirty with coal dust. Tracks in the snow led to a blacksmith shop, and there the instrument of the murder was found—a sledge-hammer bespattered with blood, and the remains of a charred, bloody shirt.

The owner of the blacksmith shop, Sm., 30 years old, was suspected. The murdered man was the porter from a neighbouring house, and he and Sm. often drank together. It was found that the day before the murder they were seen together, drinking in a saloon. The preliminary investigation showed that on the morning of the 15th of January, Sm. went to his blacksmith shop by an unusual way which led through the court where the body lay, but by a roundabout path. After arriving there, he then went to church, which was not his custom, and remained some time. It was also brought out that during the night of the 15th of January he was at home and did not sleep, but smoked a great deal.

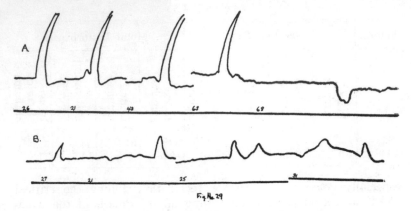

Fig. No. 29

A. SUBJECT MVA. (PARTICIPANT IN MURDER)

26. NORMAL REACTION; 21. OVERCOAT—2.8″—TO HAND IT UP; 43. JACOB—4.0″—CALLING JACOB; 63. BASIN—2.8″—TO WASH IT; 68. AXE—4.0″—TO CUT WOOD WITH.

B. SUBJECT BVA. (ACCOMPLICE IN MURDER)

27. NORMAL REACTION; 21. COAT—3.4″—THIS—JACKET; 25. MONEY—3.4″—PAPER; 31. QUARREL—4.0″—PEACE

On being arrested, he denied any participation in the murder. Our experiment was done the 16th of January, 1925, i.e., one day after the crime. Among 70 word stimuli (the general list remained without change) there were fourteen which had a direct relation to the situation of the crime:

15. porter	30. hammer	46. body	61. tracks
16. quarrel	36. blow	51. knife	70. blood
27. money	44. spot	59. to cut	
29. boots	45. shirt	60. to drag	

As in the previous case, during the experiment stimuli were introduced which could, under the given conditions, be associated with the situation of the crime.

The results we obtained were closely analogous to those of the former experiment. Table 15 gives a list of the critical stimuli showing a marked concentration of all the affective symptoms. The control subject in this case, as well as in the previous one, does not give any symptoms relating precisely to these complexes. Thus in the criminal the reactions to the stimuli connected with the crime show considerable inhibition and an increased number of disturbed motor reactions, notwithstanding the fact that the subject denied his participation in the crime. These facts are

TABLE 15

Subject	Reactive Time				Motor Disturbances			
	Index stimulus	Critical stimulus	Post-critical stimulus	Index of critical inhibition	Index stimulus	Critical stimulus	Post-critical stimulus	Index of critical inhibition
Sm.	2.0″	3.1″	2.5″	+30%	32%	62%	54%	+30%
Control	1.6″	1.6″	1.6″	0	16%	8%	12%	− 8%

especially convincing when we recall that among the critical words we introduced stimuli calling up the details of the situation of the crime, which otherwise are entirely indifferent.

Just as in the case before this, the first stimuli give a quick and adequate reaction:

    5. pie—1.6″—sugar
    6. hay—1.8″—wood
    7. horse—2.4″—wolf
    8. matches—2.0″—iron
    9. butter—1.9″—kerosene

The delayed reactions coincide either with the critical stimuli or with those directly following them, and this comes out as a clear picture of the details connected with the affective complexes:

    15. porter—3.6″—hut
    21. money—4.6″—love
    29. boots—3.1″—wood
    30. jacket—4.4″—*boots* (*perseveration*)
    36. blow—4.1″—to talk
    49. body—4.0″—wood
    56. snow—3.5″—water
    61. tracks—3.6″—wood
    70. blood—3.8″—death

    18. quarrel—2.0″—to scold
    19. falsely—*4.3″*—is

    61. tears—3.6″—wood
    62. lamp—*4.0″*—to light

Besides these cases we have not met with a single instance in our experiment of a definite inhibitory reaction, and the connection of the delay with the affective complex is obvious. The fixed motor disturbances convince us again that behind these delays lie the conflicting excitatory processes.

Figure 30 illustrates the disturbances in our subject. When we recall that these disturbances are strictly concentrated, arising from entirely normal motor reactions, we are able to understand how the symptoms that we obtain furnish us with objective evidences of a series of traces which are connected in our subject with his crime, in spite of all the energy he applies in order to conceal the fact of his participation.

We have had an opportunity to investigate repeatedly and in detail this subject and the reactions which occurred in him and

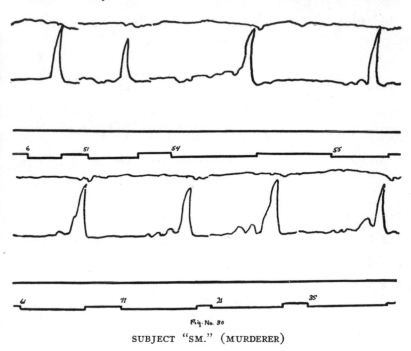

Fig. No. 30

SUBJECT "SM." (MURDERER)

6. NORMAL REACTION; 51. KNIFE—2.8″—TO CUT BREAD; 54. DRUNK—5.6″
—FOOL; 55. TO CRAWL—3.2″—TO SLEEP; 61. TRACKS—3.5″—WOOD; 71.
BLOOD—3.8″—DEATH; 21/N. MONEY—3.4″—TO LIVE; 35/N. HAMMER—
3.8″—TO CARRY

their symptoms, comprehensible only after the investigation had established the whole situation of the crime, and Sm., having denied his participation, had confessed it.

Here is the picture of this crime: on the 14th of January Sm. and his friend, the janitor, were in the saloon, and upon leaving they started to the blacksmith shop, intending to empty another bottle there. When they had arrived Sm. asked his friend when he was going to pay him the two-ruble debt which he owed. When this was answered in the negative, Sm.

grabbed the hammer and struck him on the head. The wounded man fell and began to groan and crawl on the floor. Sm. became very frightened, and, according to his story, he grew sorry for the struggling man and finished killing him with a knife; after this he removed the outside clothing which was spattered with blood, burned it and buried the body in the courtyard, where it remained.

After giving this history of the crime, the disturbances coinciding with such stimuli as money, blow, knife, hammer, drunk, to crawl, tracks, quarrel, etc., are easily understood.

CASE 3

On the 13th of May 1926, in one of the Moscow factories, a window had been broken and a ventilator stolen. The janitor, Uv., 28 years old, was suspected. He was arrested and accused of the theft, but denied it.

The experiment was done on the 15th of May 1926, two days after the crime. As a control we used a man 28 years old, similar in development to Uv. but ignorant of the purpose of the experiment.

Along with the fifty word-stimuli were seven relating to the situation of the crime:

19. money	28. window	39. glass	44. instrument
26. ventilator	33. to break	40. to shatter	

This case is characterised by two distinguishing signs: the subject would not admit his guilt, and the crime was very slight in comparison to those we have described; this is shown by the diminished acuteness of the accompanying affect.

However, here the group of stimuli connected with the situation of the crime produced a marked concentration of all the symptoms (see Table 16), and practically only the critical reactions in our subject are characterised by signs of disruption. As in the

TABLE 16

Subject	Reactive Time				Motor Disturbances			
	Index	Critical stimulus	Post-critical	Index of critical inhibitions	Index	Critical stimulus	Post-critical	Index of critical inhibitions
Uv.	2.4″	4.2″	3.4″	+33%	15%	86%	40%	+71%
Control	1.8″	1.8″	1.6″	0	12%	16%	0	+ 4%

cases cited above the graphic charts show quiet, regular movements, separate foci of reactions having a delayed speech response and considerable motor excitation. These reactions are so strongly connected by their content with the situation of the crime that the separate details stand out before the investigator very boldly.

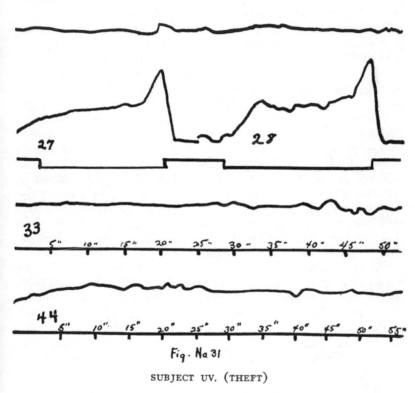

Fig. No 31

SUBJECT UV. (THEFT)

27. NORMAL REACTION; 28. WINDOW—4.2″—BIG; 33. TO SHATTER—25.0″—TO SHATTER . . . WHY TO SHATTER? 44. INSTRUMENT—20.0″—INSTRUMENT. . . . I DO NOT KNOW. . . . WHY? ALREADY I SAID I DO NOT KNOW . . . INSTRUMENT . . .

Figure 31 gives us several reactions typical of Uv. We purposely employ at first reactions almost similar and not showing any special disturbances; the simple associative experiment is not suitable to bring out this difference. The neurodynamical processes lying behind the external reactions are very different, and the fact that the accompanying motor curve is in one instance regular, and in the other is distinguished by characteristic impulses and acute tremors, indicates what a considerable amount of excitation is concealed behind this externally calm picture.

The accompanying motor reactions make possible here the establishment of objective symptoms which with the definite group of answers in the subject are connective affective traces, but these affective traces lead us directly to the establishment of the factors associated with the situation of the crime.

We have chosen three characteristic cases. In a separate report we have analysed them in detail, but here we are concerned with the fact that in almost all of these instances the affective traces of the crime are manifested in our experiment by a group of objective symptoms usually relating to the inhibitions of the corresponding speech reactions, and by the characteristic signs of excitation reflected in the motor area. We are now convinced that by a purely experimental method the psychologist is able to answer positively the question of the possibility of an objective diagnosis of criminal participation.

There can naturally be raised an objection to the method of our experimentation: even in those cases when the suspect denied his participation in the crime, he was accused, and this obviously produced in him an affective reaction. Is it not true that we are investigating this reaction of accusation, thinking that we have before us the affective traces of the crime?

We have two answers to this very just complaint. First, we hardly ever give to the subject stimuli directly connected with the charges. Usually, and in other experiments this is especially clear, the entire list of critical stimuli is confined to the details of the situation of the crime, and these are unfamiliar to nonparticipants and those who may be arrested by mistake. The presence of the symptoms connected with these details are evident signs of participation.

On the other hand we give the actual facts, challenging and abrogating this objection. We succeeded in making a series of experiments before any conversation with the people arrested, before they were accused of anything, and these experiments gave us affective symptoms by no means weaker than those which might be introduced; and, on the other hand, we had an opportunity to perform experiments on persons arrested by mistake and who did not participate in the crime, and such experiments indicated without doubt the complete absence of symptoms connected with the crime in those who were not guilty. We shall discuss one of these cases in detail.

4. NEGATIVE EXPERIMENTS

ONE of these cases is of especial interest on account of the unusual material, as well as the definite results, which it brings to us.

CASE 4

In February, 1927, in one of the Moscow railroad stations, there was found a sort of basket addressed to the city of Bryansk. The basket appeared suspicious, was opened, and in it was the body of a woman clothed in a tunic. She had been killed with a sharp instrument; the corpse was tied about with ropes and wrapped in pieces of paper and squeezed into the basket.

The paper which was around the body indicated the place where the murder had been committed; on it was written the name of the restaurant "The Bear." This paper was apparently taken from one of the tables.

Simultaneously with the finding of the corpse, Citizen Sh. of Kiev received a letter containing a baggage check. The letter advised him that he might obtain his wife in Bryansk and it was signed "Unknown." The writer of this letter apologised that he could not send the body to Kiev, as he did not have enough money. Citizen Sh. was summoned to Moscow and there he recognised in the basket the body of his wife.

Subsequent investigation established the fact that the basket was transferred by a drayman, given him as freight. The baggage receipt was signed, evidently by a fictitious name, Kartusov.

The suspicion in this murder fell upon several people, and after a few days the following seven were arrested:

1. Iva, 26 years old, the proprietress of the apartment in which Citizen Sh. of Kiev usually lived.

2-4. Bva., 33 years, Zagr., 24 years, Hran, 30 years, friends of the murdered woman living in Kiev.

5-6. Vor., 45 years, Vas., 46 years, the first being a pensioned invalid, the second an unemployed person; both of these lived in Moscow, and, according to information obtained, met with Citizeness Sh. in the last days of her life.

7. Vel., formerly a hair-dresser having known the murdered woman in Kiev and then having met her in Moscow.

All of these subjects were brought to the laboratory immediately after their arrest, and none of them was questioned before experimentation. Bva., Zagr., and Hran. were taken in Kiev and immediately brought to Moscow, where they were met at the train and at once transferred to the laboratory. Thus we had at our disposal exceedingly pure material; none of them had any knowledge of why they were arrested.

The subjects were given a series of 80 word-stimuli among which were the following fifteen critical words:

21. basket	36. baggage	52. Kartusov	63. check
24. train	38. station	54. dray	(receipt)
25. "The Bear"	43. freight	56. woman	70. Bryansk
30. letter	49. cashier	58. load	

76. Marusya (name of the murdered woman)

It is comprehensible that the first thing that we meet in this material is the marked affect shown by the subjects, especially the women arrested in another city and brought to Moscow without telling them the exact motive of the arrest. There was present, of course, an especially acute affect; they sobbed and cried during the experiment and were entirely incapable of concentrating on the long list of words and became quickly fatigued—the picture of acute affect. We call attention to the fact that the above-given characteristics of diffuse affect were obtained primarily on the basis of the experiments done on these subjects. There was a comparatively long reactive time and great variability, extreme disturbance of the character of the motor curves, showing the presence of an intense excitatory process.

However, in all of these experiments we did not find any traces of affects regularly concentrated about the critical group of words. The affect showed a diffuse character and the reactive symptoms of the disturbances were met with in the neutral as well as in the critical stimuli.

Table 17 gives a statistical summary of the results.

TABLE 17

Subject	Reactive Time				Motor Disturbances			
	Index stimulus	Critical stimulus	Post-critical stimulus	Index of critical inhibition	Index stimulus	Critical stimulus	Post-critical stimulus	Index of critical inhibition
1. Iva.	1.8″	1.9″	1.9″	+ 5%	15%	7%	21%	− 8%
2. Bva.	2.8″	2.8″	2.0″	0	48%	64%	50%	+16%
3. Zagr.	2.8″	3.6″	3.6″	+29%	88%	78%	50%	−10%
4. Hran	1.8″	2.0″	1.8″	+10%	55%	36%	44%	−19%
5. Vor.	2.2″	2.4″	2.3″	+ 9%	—	—	—	
6. Vas.	1.4″	1.6″	1.2″	+14%	5%	0	0	− 5%
7. Vel.	2.4″	3.2″	2.6″	+33%	15%	28%	21%	+13%

The figures describe a picture differing widely from that which we have just seen in our other three cases.

We are often confronted with the situation in which the figures obtained are not convincing, and we become irritated when the figures do not correspond to the results which we should like to see. Our subject, however, is complicated, and the living, human personality is not always adequately expressed in simple figures; in such cases a concrete analysis aids in bringing to light the obscurities.

Figures, nevertheless, give us a fairly definite picture. In the majority of our subjects the reaction to the critical stimuli is not more inhibited than the reaction to the indifferent stimuli; in all subjects, even those seeming to have some inhibition in the critical reactions, it was not much more than the probable error (exceedingly large in the diffuse and unstable series) and in no measure can it be taken as authenticated.[1] In our experiments the fact that the critical stimuli do not represent a specific affective group of reactions is clearly evident from the accompanying motor curves whose average appearances do not differ from that of the general disturbances.

Here we submit parts of our protocol, which prove that our critical stimuli do not differ essentially from the others:

Subject Iva.	Subject Bva.	Subject Hram.
19. wall—1.2"—walls	19. wall—2.2"—floor	19. wall—2.2"—rock
20. spectacles—2.0"—eyes	20. spectacles—1.8"—eyes	20. spectacles—6.4"—What shall I say, eyes
21. *basket*—1.4"—wolf	21. *basket*—2.0"—to sell	21. *basket*—2.2"—fish
22. clock—2.4"—chair	22. clock—1.8"—watch chain	22. watch—1.8"—case
33. brush—3.4"—shoes	29. Rostov—2.6"—Don	33. brush—2.2"—stick
34. wheel—2.2"—horse	70. ring—2.4"—finger	34. ring—1.2"—cart
35. *baggage*—2.8"—dress	71. to paint—3.2"—to smear	35. *baggage*—1.8"—bag
36. hare—2.2"—cat	72. *Bryansk*—2.0"—station	36. hare—2.4"—forest
37. station—3.4"—buffet	73. chemise—2.0"—to sew	37. *station*—2.4"—cars
38. pie—2.6"—curds	74. overcoat—1.6"—to put on	38. pie—1.8"—flour
39. grass—1.8"—plow		39. grass—4.4"—well, earth

[1] Thus in the subject Zagr., we have an increased reactive time during the critical stimuli equal to 29%, while as an average variability the whole series has a value of 42%; thus, more than 20 reactions have a reactive time greater than 3.4" and the index of the reactive time in the critical stimuli can, of course, not be accurately estimated.

We cannot give here the reactions to all the critical stimuli in our subjects; but in another place we shall take up this in its detailed analysis.[1] One thing is clear: notwithstanding the different cases of the observed inhibition coinciding with the critical stimuli, we do not meet here with the picture of a definite group of reactions which we can call "critical"; the experimenter becomes impressed with the fact that the subjects in this group lack those affective traces which we had formerly seen.

The character of the separate reactions to the critical stimuli are well illustrated by two portions of our graphic protocols shown in Figure 32. The subjects here described belong to two different reactive types: the motor system of one is relatively stable, and during the experiment he is quiet except for a tremor of the left hand (the subject was an alcoholic). The second, judging by the symptoms, belongs to the reactive labile type; he is not able to coordinate accurately his movements with the given speech reactions, the disturbance is irradiated over the motor system (the experiment was complicated somewhat, owing to the fact that the right hand was paralysed and the left hand had to be used instead); in the given subject the general affective tone is coloured by his confusion and by his not understanding why he was arrested and brought to experimentation. The general tone of the reactive processes in both cases is different; but in both we have a common factor; the reactions to the "critical" stimuli are just the same as to the others, and the neurodynamic character of the process concealed from us does not differ from that in the other reactions of the subject.

In connection with this, Figure 27 A is of especial interest; the complete disorganisation of the reactive process is evidence of a very marked diffusion of the affect in subject Zagr. From this, however, we can not find the disturbances which would allow us to point out in our patient very active affective traces; on the contrary, all the results can be attributed to the diffused reaction caused by the traumatic situation of the arrest.

We shall use one of the cases from this series in our analysis. The following is evident: in a number of our subjects we obtain a picture of diffused affect without concentration of the affective symptoms connected with the situation of the crime. In these instances we can speak of the differential diagnosis of participation in crime and the separation of the guilty from those who have been by mistake arrested innocently; or expressed in the

[1] *The Affects and Complexes of Criminals,* Chapter VII.

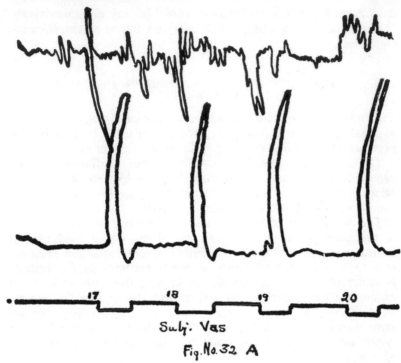

Subj. Vas

Fig. No. 32 A

17. SPECTACLES—1.4″—EYES; 18. BASKET—1.8″—EGGS; 19. WATCH—1.4″
—O'CLOCK; 20. FREIGHT—1.4″—BETEL

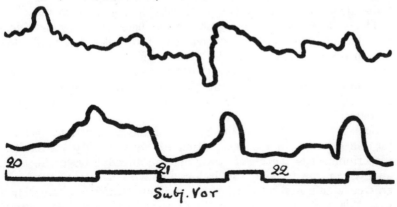

Subj. Vor

Fig. No. 32 B

20. PEN—3.6″—TO WRITE; 21. GOOD—2.6″—AT THE BAZAAR IS A POND;
22. WATCH—3.8″—TO KNOW THE TIME

language of psychology, between those having a diffused state of the actual affect and the concentrated traces of the affective complexes.

5. THE DYNAMICS OF THE AFFECTIVE PROCESSES IN CRIMINALS

THE affect of the criminal which we are studying is an affect of vital significance. Therefore, we may expect to find here a peculiar and definite manifestation of its dynamics.

The criminal is certainly far from being indifferent to his experiences; but, on the contrary, he puts himself in an active relation to this experience; its trauma, urging him into activity, conditions the dynamics of his behaviour.

The acute state of the trauma, complicated by the necessity of concealing it, bound in by the fear of expressing itself, creates in the criminal a state of exceedingly acute affective tension; this tension is very probably exaggerated because the subject is under the fear of disclosing his crime; the more serious the crime, the more marked the affect, and the greater the danger of disclosing it, the more this complex is suppressed, and we have already seen what a remarkable destruction of the most important neurodynamical functions characterises the behaviour of the criminal.

That the state of the criminal in whom the tension cannot find exit anywhere may become actually insufferable is beautifully illustrated in the pages of great literary productions.

The suppression of the complexes is here truly insufferable, and the subject experiencing them is certainly not in a condition to remain passive during the course of this affect; he must orient himself in such a way that he discharge the tension and save himself from an external play of excitation, which upsets all of his behaviour and keeps him incessantly under the fear of detection.

Such a tension is undoubtedly one of the most serious factors for the criminal in the recognition of his guilt. By confession the criminal has the means to avoid the affective traces, to find an exit for the tension, to discharge that affective tonus which created within him an unbearable conflict. Confession can eliminate this conflict and restore the personality in a certain degree to a normal state, and this is its psychophysiological significance.

The psychophysiological rôle of confession has been evaluated for a long time; the ancient teaching concerning catharsis considered confession in offences an expiation; Christianity in its use of confession always employed this psychological principle of alleviation, and brought about avoidance of the affective traces by having the subject relate the sins troubling him to an official of the church; finally, all psychotherapy, and especially every therapeutic system of psychoanalysis proceeds from this principle, which is connected with the transfer of the complexes and a relief of the tension in the consciousness. This principle, so well established in the various therapeutic processes, is directly connected with the powerful process of elimination of the affective complexes; and precisely this is the specific value of the therapeutic effect of psychoanalysis.

In the situation of crime, we may expect the influence of such avoidance in especially marked forms. Admission of guilt removes from the criminal those restraints which controlled each of his steps and every one of his thoughts and created an exceedingly acute conflict of very marked tension; thus confession is a path to the relief of affect and to the reestablishment of a more normal functional life.

From the psychophysiological investigation of crime and confession, we may expect, consequently, extreme changes in the behaviour compared to what it was before confession, the removal of acute symptoms of affective traces connected with the crime, and, finally, the removal of the suppressed complex striving to express itself in some activity, the control of which is weakened. On the contrary, the confession should give us a psychophysiological picture of discharge, ventilation, and, connected with this, a certain calmness of the behaviour. The experiments on the psychophysiology of confession arouse in us, then, a deep theoretical interest.

We shall now discuss a case which well illustrates the psychophysiological picture of the processes we have described.

CASE 5

On the 28th of January 1927, in a garbage can in the courtyard of one of the Moscow houses was found a body of a half-dressed woman, whose head was crushed by some kind of heavy instrument. Investigation traced her back to a dwelling occupied by seasonal workers, where there was living at that time only one person, a house painter, Fil., 47 years old. In the room were found traces of blood, and in the stove an unusual bulk of ashes and the charred remains of a woman's dress. It seemed that the body was carried from the room in the garbage can between 5 and 7 o'clock on the morning of that day. The rigidity of the body, however, made us think that the murder was done at least a day before.

The painter, Fil., was arrested immediately without warning and brought to the laboratory. After the experiment he was cross-questioned but he did not admit participation in the killing. During the next two weeks he was put in prison, and twice questioned; on one of these occasions he related the following story:

On the evening of the twenty-sixth of January, he met a strange woman on the street to whom he proposed that she spend the night with him, and to this she agreed. Fil. escorted her to his house, they drank a bottle of vodka together and then they lay down to sleep. During the night he awoke, feeling that the woman was searching his pockets. He began to curse her and hit her on the head, first with his fists, and then with a stick of wood; the woman fell down, and he, being drunk and confused, went to sleep again. In the morning he saw that the woman was dead. He searched her to find the money that she had stolen from him, removed her coat, and took it to the market and sold it "in order to recover from his spree." Returning home he burned the clothes which were stained with blood, and put the body under the bed, where it remained all night long. Having decided to hide the body in the garbage can, in the morning he took it down, placed it there and covered it up. About the crime itself, according to him, he did not remember much, because he was extremely intoxicated.

We did three experiments on him: one immediately after his arrest (two days since the murder), and before the questioning, on the same day after the questioning but before he had acknowledged his guilt, and finally two weeks later, immediately after his confession. This permitted us to follow step by step the whole dynamics of his affective processes.

In the first and second experiments he was given thirty-five word-stimuli, among which the critical were: *hammer* (afterwards it was shown that this had no relation to the crime), *stove*, *garbage*, *dress*. Here we obtained two series of valuable associations.

In the last experiment there were eighty critical word-stimuli, and these were in addition to those given below: 41. *overcoat*, 44. *woman*, 48. *stick* (of wood), 49. *head*, 53. *body*, 56. *blood*, 64. *to trickle*, 65. *sign*, 70. *trial*, 74. *cross-questioning*.

The first thing that we noticed characterising the behaviour of the subject in our first meeting with him was, as we might expect, an intensely diffuse affect, disturbing all of his actions and making all of his psychological operations unstable.

Table 18 shows that his reactive time as well as the character of the accompanying motor acts are distinguished by instability. The average reactive time of his speech reactions was fairly slow and extremely unstable, the curve of its distribution very

TABLE 18

Experiment	Reactive Time		Motor Reaction		
	Median	MV.	Intensity	Normal	Disturbance
Before questioning	3.0″	40%	25mm 24%	45%	55%
After the first questioning	3.2″	22%	15mm 80%	0	100%
After confession	2.0″	30%	47mm 8.5%	86%	14%

diffuse; the accompanying motor pressures were extremely unstable in their intensities, and a large per cent of them were greatly distorted in form. Such were the characteristics of the psychophysiological state of the subject immediately after arrest, before he was accused.

The first cross-questioning was accompanied by his accusation, but it did not lead to his confession. With what psychophysiological changes was this accompanied? The results can be seen in Table 18: they are characterised by a sharp exacerbation of the affect. The speech reactions begin to occur more slowly, the motor reactions finally become uncontrollable, and we observe the characteristics of the diffuse affective process, which we have noted above: the established stable standard reactive forms are destroyed; the subject is not able to make two movements similar in their intensities and forms; the motor excitation acquires an acute, irradiated character, and the number of motor disturbances is increased to one hundred per cent. It is obvious that the accusation produces an acute precipitation of the affect.

In Figure 33 cuttings from our graphic protocols illustrate this. True, the neurodynamics of the first experiment show the signs of an acute impulsiveness; the possibility of the elaboration of definite standard forms of reactions (reaction patterns) are absent, and the subject is very unstable, giving movements varying in intensity; but only in the second experiment, after the accusation, did this process of disorganisation take on its actual acute character. The general diffused excitation produces here a marked irradiated tremor, the functional delay of the excitation is finally destroyed, and each impulse directly extends into the motor area, markedly disturbing the coordination, and we have before us a characteristic picture of the diffused reactive process, disturbed by the acute affect. It is evident that the representation of the accusation revived the acute affective traces, transforming the affect into an actual state, and there being no path of exit to his affect, there resulted a sharp state of conflict.

This acute state of the affective tension is certainly connected with the manifestation of special traces of affective groups associated with the crime; the reactions having a direct connection with the situation of the crime are characterised by symptoms of an especially marked inhibition and disturbance; after the cross-questioning these disturbances in the critical cases became more acute, and we are impressed by the marked actualisation of the concrete affective traces, under the influence of the questioning; although in the first cases we encountered most often the mechanism of the consequential, perseverative disturbances; in the second experiment, the whole series of disturbances have a sharply expressed actual character:

First Experiment	*Second Experiment*
74. garbage—4.2″—earth	24. garbage—5.6″—no, earth
25. nail—5.2″—iron	25. nail—5.8″—wood
27. clothing—2.4″—cold	27. clothing—7.8″—well, boots, I do not know what to say.
28. butter—0.2″—butter	28. butter—9.2″—milk

The acute dispersed excitation, entering into the behaviour of the subject, is characterised by a factor which we think is very important; it explains much in the mechanism of the affective dynamics and elements of confession. We call this mechanism the *suppressed complex;* it consists in this: the affective traces, not having been eliminated, have a tendency to express themselves, notwithstanding the strong resistance of the subject, and actually they do manifest themselves in those cases where the control of the behaviour is diminished and the behaviour follows the course of the lower automatisms.

After the first questioning, when Fil. denied his guilt, we gave him an opportunity to associate freely, telling him to say any words that came into his mind. The series that we obtained as usual consisted, in a fairly superficial chain of associations, of frequent repetitions of the stimuli given him in the experiment; in this series, however, the tendency to reproduce confusedly the series of words was well marked, and the jumble of reproduced words appeared to be exactly those words which were directly connected with the situation of the crime. Here are the words:

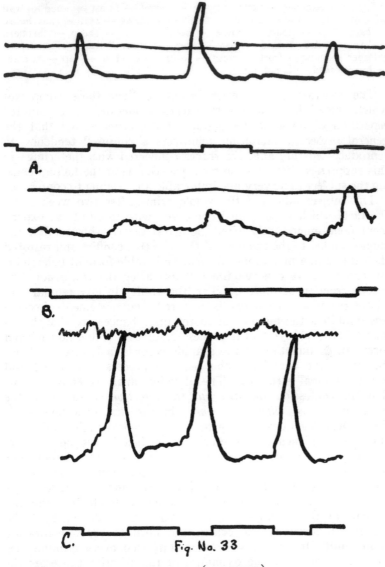

Fig. No. 33

SUBJECT FIL. (MURDERER)

A. REACTION BEFORE QUESTIONING
B. REACTION IMMEDIATELY AFTER QUESTIONING AND CONFESSION
C. REACTION ONE WEEK AFTER ADMISSION OF GUILT

Scythe — hammer — axe — scythe — shovel — forest — wood — wall
window — electrical — ceiling — boots — *clothing* — *shed* — warehouse
— bath house — court — house — horse — cow — sheep — shepherd
— hay — water — sand — clay — earth — *dung* — *garbage* — *dirt* —
galoshes — snow — frost — grass — forest — *clothing* — cap — sweater
— hut — *shed* — bread, etc.

The free associative series brings to light those complexes
which should have been very carefully guarded. The jumbled
repetition of some of the details of the crime shows that the
general dispersed excitation manifests a confused tendency to
reproduce separate affective traces connected with the crime; in
this suppressed affective complex, we see one of the factors causing the subject to be very uncomfortable and leading to confession.

The subject admitted the whole crime after two weeks, and
the facts which we obtained compared with those of the experiment done immediately after the arrest clearly showed that the
confession led to the removal of the affective conflict and restored
the subject to a much more normal and stable form of behaviour.
In Table 18, we can see these facts: after the confession, the
speech reaction becomes quicker, the ability to give regular and
stable reactive movements is restored, the movements become
less inhibited, the number of motor disturbances are sharply reduced, the neurodynamical process assumes a stable and normal
form. An examination of the graphic records in Figure 33 shows
that after the confession the reactive process is restored and
has its normal structure. The detailed analysis convinces us
that the confession *smooths out the affective character of the
traces connected with the crime;* in the first experiments all
the critical reactions were attended by considerable inhibition,
but this phenomenon was much diminished in the last séance.

The process of confession of a crime is of great importance
psychophysiologically. The annihilated conflicting character of
the process, leading to the removal of the affective traces, does
away with the affective tension which characterises the behaviour of the criminal for some time from the date of the
trauma produced by the crime, and until the open confession
of his guilt. Of course, we cannot state that every criminal has
equal reactions; for the dynamics of the affective processes the
chief interest lies in which of them are actually connected with
the crime; the delay of confession produces a much more intense conflict; precisely in these cases is the influence of the
removal most marked

We still have a certain doubt which has not disappeared

even after the above discussion. Can the given results lead to an actual confession; or can it be that the time elapsed after the crime weakens the excitation arising from the arrest?

Certainly the time influences the dynamics of affect and so does removal; however, the material which we bring forth indicates that one factor of the removal was sufficient to alter sharply the picture of the reactive processes.

We shall cite only one very typical case: the subject Gorn, who committed the murder, was arrested and carried through the experiment, and then cross-questioned, and immediately afterwards he confessed; then he was again experimented on. The setting and the whole procedure (the arrest, both experiments and cross-questioning) were done in the course of several hours, and this allowed us to eliminate the factor of time, and to show that the confession actually changed the character of the psychophysiological processes. Table 19 summarises the results. We see that the confession produced an immediate fall of the reactive time and a diminution of all the symptoms connected with the affective traces of the crime. Obviously there remained considerable excitation (30% of disturbed reactions in the repeated experiment), but this can be attributed to the fact that in both cases the affective state did not have time to recover. The remaining changes, however, are sufficiently sharply expressed in the experiment to show the results of confession. In spite of this, that here we have a subject who is not trying to conceal and deny his guilt, the confession after the cross-questioning is most brilliantly reflected in the affective dynamics.

TABLE 19

	Reactive Time				Motor Disturbances				
Experiment	Index	Critical	Post-critical	Index of critical inhibition	Total	Index	Critical-	Post-critical	Index of critical inhibition
Before confession	5.2″	2.8″	4.3″	2.6″—54%	22%	14%	44%	31%	+ 30%
After confession	2.6″	2.8″	2.6″	2.2″— 9%	30%	18%	28%	38%	— 16%

Subj. Gorn: The Dynamics of the Symptoms in Relation to the Confession.

Confession in crime has its own serious psychophysiological correlate; the confession, itself, appears in many results of the peculiar affective factors, of the definite dynamics of affect, whose removal it produces. In the light of psychophysiological analysis its mechanism becomes clearer to us, and, at the same time, we are able to understand the psychophysiological basis of such phenomena as the Christian Confession or catharsis of the ancients. It is perfectly obvious that precisely these mechanisms are operative in the therapeutic action of psychoanalysis, the neurodynamic analysis of which must represent one of the most interesting pages in the program of the further psychophysiological experimentation.

6. THE AFFECTIVE COMPLEX AND THE STRATEGY OF THE PERSONALITY .

WE should be greatly mistaken if we thought that our subject remains completely indifferent during our experiment and passively awaits the expression of the affective traces in his definite external symptoms.

In our situation the matter is really just the reverse: the subject is always highly interested in order that he shall not demonstrate or disclose his affective traces; threatening him in case of discovery of the crime is the fear of punishment which always keeps him on guard, and if he is not forced into confession, then this fear conditions a certain strategy of the subject, designed to conceal the traces of his participation.

It is difficult to state how much of this strategy is conscious. Often the measures employed by the criminal to conceal his guilt are skillfully devised; frequently they are naïve and perceptible even to the inexperienced. The psychology of criminal strategy is exceedingly interesting, constituting an enormous problem, proceeding directly from our investigations. One problem, however, directly connected with our experiments, we cannot pass over in silence.

A peculiar strategy is already manifested by the subjects in our experiment, and we are often witnesses of the process of the accouchement of the strategical measures in an entirely new setting for our subject. We should like here to dwell on only one of these measures, met with, however, very often.

Jung [1] has already brought out the fact that associations connected with the affective complexes have a tendency to assume primitive forms. The response through extrasignalising, senseless or perseverative, or phonetic reactions, Jung considers one of the most pathognomonic signs of the affective complex. Our

[1] *Diagnostische Associationstudien*, 1910.

material wholly confirms this position, and the reason that we do not emphasize it more in this work is only because this feature of the affective symptoms has already been most thoroughly studied.

The fact that we should like to bring out here consists in this: the simple associative reaction, formerly connected to the symptom of the affective complex, *is often converted in our subjects into a measure which they use as an aid in trying to avoid the manifestation of the affective symptoms.*

In effect, the simple extrasignalising or phonetic reaction relieves the subject of that difficulty in which the critical stimulus connected with the situation of the crime puts him, and this reaction allows him to give a neutral answer, having avoided the compromising one. Precisely such a character of the primitive reactions causes the criminal to make a connection with the primitive, simple type of reaction, to elaborate a stereotyped, extrasignalising or echolalic reaction every time that the stimulus presented to him steps on dangerous ground, as far as the manifestation of the complex is concerned.

In all of our material we have hardly met with a single case which did not have the signs of the lower forms of associative reactions; in the beginning it was manifested as a symptom of the confusion created by the affective complex; however, the symptom of the affect quickly passes over into a means of its repression, and we begin to see with remarkable regularity a linking up with the primitive type of reaction every time that the stimulus touches a part of the affective situation.

In the more acute cases of dispersed affect we have a manifestation of echolalia during every acute affective stimulus, as for example:

Subject Vn. (accused of the murder of his wife; she was killed in the corridor by a knife stab in the abdomen).

23. hand—9.4″—hand
24. stab—4.8″—stab
25. abdomen—3.4″—abdomen, what of it
26. corridor—4.4″—corridor, well . . .
43. wound—39.0″—wound
44. knife—5.9″—knife

Here we see that *echolalia* is again an evident symptom of the affective process; the dispersed inhibition shows that it cannot yet be used in the speech reaction as a means of suppressing the affect.

However, in the further experimentation when the dispersed

affect was less acute, and the subject was quieter we already find the signs of a more ordinary reaction as a means of the subject avoiding the affective response. The quick and confident manner of making the reaction and the manifestation of stereotypy or echolalia each time during the presentation of the critical stimulus may serve as a true sign of the fact that the reaction has already become here a factor in the behaviour.

We shall give several examples from our protocols:

Subject Sm., a blacksmith, who killed the janitor of a neighbouring house (see above Case 2), and at the beginning of the experiment, showed an acute disturbance to the critical stimuli, as for example:

> janitor—3.6″—hut (with motor disturbances)
> body—4.0″—wood, etc.

In the further experimentation, stereotyped responses appeared whenever a critical word was presented. As a result of such a linking up we obtained:

> 36. blow—4.1″—to speak
> 39. business—2.6″—to speak
> 48. neighbour—1.8″—to converse
> 59. to cut—1.6″—to speak
> 68. to die—2.8″—to converse
> 15. but janitor—2.3″—to speak
> 36. blow—1.4″—to converse.
> 39. but business—2.2″—to converse.
> 48. but neighbour—1.6″—to speak
> 59. to cut—2.0″—to speak
> 60. but to drag—8.0″—to speak
> 61. but tears—1.8″—to speak
> 68. but to die—3.2″—to speak

The assuredness of the responses and the reactive times show us that the stereotyped answer permits of the suppression of the affective course of the reaction.

Subject Gor. after a quarrel, killed his neighbour with an axe, and gave such a picture, following several considerably disturbed reactions, for example:

> 27. to cut—12.2″—I can't think of anything ... finger
> 96. quarrel—3.6″—scold,

he gives a stereotyped character of reaction with almost every critical stimulus,

> 36. quarrel—2.4″—person
> 50. to fight—2.2″—person
> 55. mouth—1.6″—person
> 57. blood—4.2″—person, etc.

Subject Mv. (murderer of sister-in-law) having given adequate associations, after presentation of words having to do with the murder, gives a stereotyped reaction. This can be considered partly as an inhibition after the affective shock, partly as a linking up with a primitive type of reaction:

71. *valley*—14.5″—old woman
72. mushrooms—10.2″—well, birch mushroom
73. teeth—3.2″—*white*
74. book—4.2″—*white*
75. fish—4.0″—*white*
77. thread—3.0″—*white*

A similar fact we see in subject Drob. (murderer of his fiancée), after presentation of words referring to the killing he shows echolalia:

55. Nousha—2.0″—Nousha
56. to hide—1.6″—to hide
57. head—1.2″—head
58. rape—2.6″—rape
59. night—1.6″—night
60. meeting—1.6″—meeting

All the above cases show, that by means of linking up with the primitive reactions, principally that of *stereotypy*, the subject is able to avoid the compromising reactions, and often also the manifestation of affective symptoms. We submit a section from the graphic protocol showing the stereotyped reactions of subject Sm. which we have described above.

36. BLOW—4.1″—TO SPEAK
37. BUSINESS—2.6″—TO SPEAK
59. TO CUT—1.6″—TO SPEAK
68. TO DIE—2.8″—TO SPEAK
36. BLOW—1.4″—TO SPEAK
61. TEARS—1.8″—TO SPEAK

If we compare Figure 34 with those critical disturbances typical for this subject, which he gives in those cases where he does not employ the linking up with the stereotyped reaction (see Figure 30), we will be able to understand the rôle played by the strategy made use of in the domination of the affective reaction and in the suppression of the affective symptoms.

If we recall the large number of similar linkings which we have met with in our experiments it will be clear to us why it is necessary for us to make a correction, and after this the symptoms characterising the participation in the crime stand out in bolder relief.

We may obtain perfect analogies of the strategy of the subject in comparatively pure form in experiments with artificially produced repressions. We read a story to the subject, asking him to conceal everything that he had heard; then we performed an experimnet with him analogous to that which we had done with the criminals.

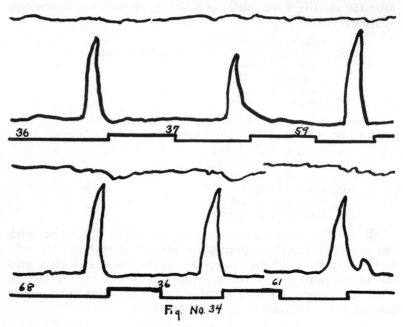

Fig. No. 34

SUBJECT SM. (MURDERER)

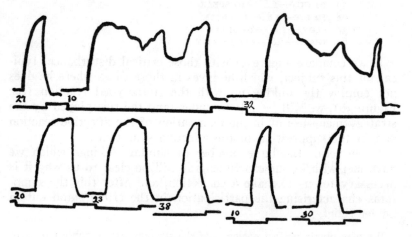

Fig. No. 35

27. NORMAL REACTION; 10. ALTAR—6.4″—HOUSE; 32. CANDLE-HOLDER—
6.6″—BUSY; 20. CROSS—2.8″—FAITH; 23. CHURCH—2.4″—FAITH; 38.
IKON—2.2″—FAITH

This material is not recorded here; but it showed us that the problem of concealment is far from easy, and that the method we successfully applied called out critical symptoms in connection with the attempt to hide the traces of the tale known to the subject.

Here we applied the method which we have used above. The appearance of the stereotyped responses was most often the means employed by the subject in avoiding the repressed traces.

In Figure 35 is given the graphic protocol from one of such experiments. To the subject it was proposed to conceal a tale read to him about a church robbery. In the beginning of the control experiment he gave several reactions which were exceedingly compromising for him; after this by giving stereotyped answers he avoided the compromising symptoms. The gradual domination of the stereotyped answers, as a means of adaptation, are clearly seen here, thanks to the accompanying motor curves.

CHAPTER IV

THE INVESTIGATION OF COMPLEXES PRODUCED DURING HYPNOSIS BY SUGGESTION

1. PROBLEMS AND MATERIAL

W E HAVE discussed in detail the problem of symptomatology of the affective processes and the problems of their dynamics. From the material available we have shown that the affective foci can play an important rôle in human behaviour and that their course, which disrupts the normal activity, itself is subject to some constant laws. We have analysed the mechanisms of affective disorganisation, using as an actual affect the expectation of a traumatic situation, as well as those affective traces left in the psyche of the person after previous trauma.

In both cases, we have come to the necessity of establishing accurately all the symptoms shown by the affect; the mechanics of its disrupting rôle, and the dynamics of its development. For these purposes the material we used was indispensable; but still it appeared to be far from sufficient for the full analysis of the process.

The psychologist, as compared with the physicist and the chemist, finds himself in a very unfavourable position; even with the best possible experimentation he usually has to admit regretfully that a great many of the facts he analyses are beyond his control, not capable of being recorded, and that he does not hold in his hands nearly all the ends of the process under his research. The psychologist envies the chemist, who can easily and completely reconstruct the processes which he analyses, artificially decomposing and uniting substances, synthesising the object of his research and following up the lawfulness of the structure he has obtained artificially. From envy comes desire, and difficulties evoke energy to combat them; this is why the experimental psychologist with extraordinary perseverance has again and again returned to the task, being entirely in possession of material and coming as close as possible to that freedom felt by the physicist; the chemist and partly the biologist, in their respective fields.

The ideal for the psychological experimenter has become the possibility to reconstruct artificially the phenomenon under examination, because only this enables one to keep it entirely under control. The psychologist's ideal became a method by which it would be possible to produce in a laboratory a model of the phenomenon analysed, by which he could bring into the psyche a new ingredient and could follow up the changes provoked in it by these artificially created factors.

That desire of the psychologist to possess knowledge of the process, by artificially creating it, appears especially justified in the study of the mechanics of affect. In fact, when we analyse the elaborated affective reactions we can never be quite sure that the process under our research is known to us in sufficient detail; we have purposely taken those affective situations which follow the cycle of the affective complexes rather closely; we have attentively studied the mass situation of examination or the individual situation of crime; but we could not at all be sure that the affective traces, considered by us as central, in reality did not conceal behind them many situations unknown to us and very much more traumatic to the subject than those evident.

We tried to rely on the objective analysis of the changes, which are brought into the neurodynamics of the subject analysed by the traumatic situation; however, we still worked largely in the dark, because the objective situation of the trauma naturally never quite corresponds to its reflection in the psyche of the personality, and that psyche, which is defined by the very complicated past experience, was entirely omitted from our record.

It is quite comprehensible, therefore, that only an artificial insertion of an affective complex into the psyche of the subject, which complex is known in all details, can create for the psychologist a situation where it would be easier for him to record all the factors forming the affective reaction. The course of our experiments has shown us that way.

The work on the artificial creation of affective feelings is not easy; it is especially difficult if the psychologist wants to obtain, not a simple affective reaction to some disagreeable irritation, but a more or less genuine affective feeling somewhat acute and stable, and one which could only artificially be inserted into the

psyche of the person under test during the experiment. Here
are discarded automatically the methods commonly used in the
psychology of affects. The method of shocks and the varieties
of the "method of impression" by Wundt usually create very
superficial affective reactions, and do not leave in the psyche,
deep affective traces.

We decided to follow the course of artificially creating some
affective complexes or rather their short-term models, feelings
which provoke a natural emotional reaction of the person under
test, and leave conspicuous traces for a certain period of time.
We had to create feelings of important intensiveness and stability,
and for that end we used hypnotism.

We suggested to the person under test, while in a sufficiently
deep hypnotic state, a certain situation, more often a disagreeable one, in which he was playing a rôle irreconcilable with his
habits and contrary to his usual behaviour. We made those suggestions imperatively, and forced the person under hypnotism to
feel the situation suggested with sufficient painfulness; we thus
obtained an actual and rather sharply expressed acute affect.
After awakening the person under test and following the awakening by amnesia (a suggested one or a natural one), we had a
subject who was "loaded" with certain definite affective complexes, which mostly remained unknown to himself, but which
were recorded by us in almost all important details.

We inserted into the psyche of the person under test definite
affective contents, and were thus able to see how those contents
were met by the personality of our subject under test, how they
became obscured by certain details and were liable to certain
changes, how they became affective traces, and how they continued to act on the behaviour of the person deprived of the
knowledge of them, and, as if becoming models of unconscious
complexes, showed a number of extremely interesting symptoms,
which were much more comprehensible to us than to the person
under test. Having created the artificially affective traces, we
were able to verify their symptomatology in pure form and their
appearance in the state of sleep and in the state of awakening;
discontinuing at our will the suggestion or making it deeper,
we were in a position to follow up the special dynamics of the
affective traces; and when we evoked analogies of the natural
affective states formerly recorded by us, we could better understand the data, of which we were previously only passive ob-
servers.

We have a good number of tests, the majority of which were made by us in 1924-1925. They all were subjected to the following standard operation: the person under test was put to sleep, and a traumatic situation previously prepared was suggested to him. After the suggestion was made, an amnesia was suggested to the person (in control cases the amnesia was not suggested and we observed a natural post-hypnotic amnesia) and he was awakened. Before the hypnosis, we used a number of word-stimuli—a part of them having a direct bearing on the complex which later was suggested to him; and we obtained the usual series of associated answers with connected motor reactions. Simultaneously we recorded a free number of chain associations, which were connected with the respective motor pressures. That operation was repeated a second time after the suggestion was made to the person in his post-hypnotic state; after this the subject was again put to sleep and the suggestion made was countermanded. After his second awakening, he was tested again in the same way. The whole experiment, therefore, proceeded thus: Test No. 1, hypnotic suggestion, Test No. 2, countermanding the hypnotic suggestion, Test No. 3 (see above).

The first test gave a general background to the psyche of the person in a state practically normal for him; the second test was a critical examination of the changes which were found in the psyche after the insertion of an artificial affective complex; the third test was to give material which would be characteristic of the reestablishment of a certain status after the time that the affective complex was "drawn away" out of his psyche. The whole series [1] was to make it possible to follow up in detail the complete dynamics of the affective processes.

2. SYMPTOMATOLOGY OF THE SUGGESTED COMPLEX

THE suggestions that were given by us in a hypnotic state were usually received with active objections, and we clearly saw that we were inflicting a certain temporary psychological trauma in the person under test, inciting in him a very sharp affective state.

---

[1] We wish to remember here with gratitude the names of the friends who helped us in those very difficult tests—Dr. G. Z. Iolles, Paris, and Dr. R. V. Valenitch, Moscow, and V. I. Zabrejnev, Leningrad, who were my patient collaborators during two years, and I owe to their fine and able technique the results obtained. One of my nearest collaborators, Mr. B. E. Varshav, did not live to see the end of my work, and to his memory and his faithfulness to science and to his deep interest in the problems of the human being must be dedicated many pages of this book.

The affectiveness of the reaction to the suggestion made was evident from the simple observation of how the personality met the affective situation suggested to him: restless defensive movements, trembling during sleep and unwillingness to take at once the suggestion, the acute conflict which follows and great sensitiveness to the situation which was inserted into his psyche, and, finally, often tears. This is the picture of that psychological operation which certainly every psychologist has observed, when using hypnotism as a method of research.[1]

Here is a typical example from the statement of such a suggestion:

The person under test, K., a student of obstetrics, 23 years old, is in a fairly deep hypnotic sleep, and it is suggested to her that a woman comes to see her with the request to produce in her an abortion, which K. has no right to do. The suggestion meets in her an obstacle. The doctor: "You are sitting at home and there is a woman who comes to see you and is imploring you to perform an abortion on her and that nobody should know that. She offers you 7 *tchervontsi* ($35.00). You hesitate because this is prohibited, but later you agree." The person under test (interrupting): "I will not do it." The doctor: "But I suggest to you that you should agree." K.: "I tell you I will not." The doctor: "The woman is imploring. She has no other way out and you are agreeing." K.: "No." The doctor: "You have agreed and the woman has gone away."

The person under test easily feels the suggestion; her face changes, she trembles, makes restless movements on the couch and she is ready to cry.

Further, the situation of the operation is suggested to the person under test. She feels it very painfully.

After the suggestion of the affective situation, the subject is awakened; to the question of how she feels she answers that she feels very bad, that something very disagreeable has happened, but she does not know what.

When asked to remember the cause of her disagreeable feeling she answers that she cannot remember anything, but a heavy sensation remains. From the past test, she only remembers that the doctor counted to six (the beginning of the hypnosis) and held up his fingers (which actually occurred in the first phase of her sleep); the rest is entirely beyond her consciousness.

---

[1] The acute character of the test required certain precautions. We excluded beforehand all hysterical persons. The test was prepared by a series of sittings. At every séance there were present three persons, and a physician followed the course of the experiment.

Two points are here of unquestionable interest. First—a very marked submission to the suggestion. Second—the entire elimination from the consciousness of what occurred. In fact, the suggestion is taken here not at all as something alien and not concerning the personality or being outside of it. The personality reacts very sharply to the suggestion given; it comes into an active conflict with the situation suggested, and that conflict creates a sharp and acute affective reaction. It is by the nature of this reaction and the participation in it of the entire personality that the situation thus obtained is entirely different from the commonly known experiments with "evoked emotions" by giving agreeable and disagreeable stimuli, which were used in the school of Wundt. The emotion actually begins where the action or the active appearance of the personality tested starts. Suggesting a conflict connected with some *action*, we obtained an affective reaction. This is one of the fundamental ideas of this book, and we will deal with it later in special experiments.

The situation suggested by us becomes distinctly affective. Therefore, it is even more interesting that the person under test entirely forgets the suggestion after awakening, and that only a few signs, like a heavy feeling, a general anxiousness, etc., remain as symptoms of the fact that in the subject's past there is concealed some severe trauma.

We have before us an entirely new structure of the affective process, compared to those previously analysed. A strong emotion is hidden here in the past and is concealed not only from the experimenter, but also from the personality itself; it is removed from consciousness, though apparently it is still active. It is quite natural that in this connection we should expect symptoms entirely different from those which we observed in cases of the marked and evident emotions.

We took three "samples" which were characteristic for the state of the person under test in his normal post-hypnotic condition, and finally after the suggested trauma was countermanded. We performed upon him an associative experiment, recording the motor reactions which followed, and as well a part of his free behaviour during a certain period of time by asking him to say everything that came into his head, and we also recorded the neurodynamic correlations of that process. All this gives us good reason to believe that we find in our records a sufficiently clear cycle of symptoms to reflect the general state of the personality.

Our material gives us quite extraordinary data, markedly differing from what we have observed before. In Table 20, we give a short summary of the figures superficially characteristic of our material. That summary gives us but little possibility to talk about the changes which were evoked during the course of the organised processes within our subject by the suggestion inserted into his psyche. We note here a certain retarding of the associative processes, and an increase of the variations of the reaction time after the suggestion was made. This is not a direct influence of the hypnotic sleep, because in the third test—after the second hypnotic sleep—the associative processes follow faster and with more stability than in the beginning.[1] It is quite obvious that the changes that have occurred in the subject during his first hypnosis showed certain difficulties in his associative activity, due to its disorganisation and to the fact that the reactions lost their stability. However, this data cannot be considered sufficiently clear and equal in all cases. In five cases out of ten, in which the figures were summarised, they do not give any distinct deviations, and from the first appearance the activity of the subject tested may appear as not having been subject to any marked changes.

The accompanying motor reactions show considerably more alarming signals. While usually a number of motor disturbances in the normal associative series amount to zero, which explains the quiet and sufficiently organised behaviour of the subject under test, we observe that after the affective complex has been introduced into the psyche, the reactions became considerably less quiet, from 30 to 40% of them, in several cases, being followed by conspicuous motor disturbances. However, this also appears to be not equally constant with all persons under test, and a number of our hypnotists have produced sufficiently organised reactions also after the affective complex was introduced into the psyche.

We obtain a picture, which at first is not sufficiently clear, although it shows certain consequences of the subject's first hypnotic séance. Apparently the summary statistical survey does not seem to be sufficient here, and the process cannot be expressed in terms of general and scattered changes, which were so clearly observed in subjects passing through the phases of acute affect.

---

[1] The latter is due to some excitation, which naturally appears after the series were repeated three times and which definitely prevails over the inhibitory process still remaining after the hypnotic sleep.

TABLE 20

Subject	Situation	Reaction Time			Average Variations			Motor Traumata			Remarks
		Tests			Tests			Tests			
		1st	2d	3d	1st	2d	3d	1st	2d	3d	
1 Kar.	Sit. B.	1.6"	1.8"	1.7"	0.4"	0.6"	0.2"	6%	27%	12%	
2 Kar.	Sit. C.	2.0"	1.8"	1.4"	0.6"	0.6"	0.4"	0	40%	0	
3 Kar.	Sit. D.	2.0"	2.0"	1.6"	0.2"	0.4"	0.3"	20%	30%	6%	
4 Che.	Sit. C.	1.4"	2.1"	1.2"	0.2"	1.5"	0.1"	0	28%	3%	40% of motor reactions oc-
5 Zub.	Sit. C.	1.0"	1.6"	1.2"	0.3"	0.2"	0.3"	0	x	0 x	cur without coordination
6 Zub.	Sit. B.	1.6"	1.8"	1.8"	0.2"	0.2"	0.2"	3%	3%ox	6%	
7 Vyg.	Sit. C.	1.6"	2.1"	—	0.6"	1.2"	—	—	—	—	Suggestion is not accepted
8 Shv.	Sit. A.	1.4"	2.0"	1.0"	0.4"	1.0"	0.2"	—	—	—	Suggestion unsuccessful
9 Shv.	Sit. B.	1.5"	3.2"	1.8"	0.5"	0.8"	0.4"	—	—	—	
10 Shv.	Sit. C.	1.6"	1.8"	—	0.2"	0.4"	—	—	—	—	
Average		1.57"	2.02"	1.46"	0.33"	0.69"	0.26"				

However, our impression sharply changes when we try to replace our summarised description by a differential analysis; if we consider what characterises the subject's reactions to the stimuli differing as to their contents, we observe that the second post-hypnotic experiment is distinctly different from the first one, and that with the help of our method *we succeed in producing models of complexes,* which *almost entirely reconstruct all the symptoms characteristic for the natural affective traces in the personality.* What is the more interesting is the amazing lawfulness which we observe in the appearance of these traces, the subject's complete unawareness of them, and the astonishment which he shows when meeting unexpected symptoms of difficulties and disturbances in cases "critical" for him.

We prepared a list of word-stimuli which we showed to our subjects under test, that list was made up so that, along with words indifferent to him, we inserted word-stimuli which were immediately connected with the traumatic situation suggested to him. The unequal character of the reactions to those stimuli constituted the symptoms which differentiated the first from the following. In the first test, all stimuli appeared to be more or less neutral for the experimental subject; in the second, there was a distinct difference. Part of them remained entirely neutral, another part connected with the suggested complex invariably began to show considerable symptoms of destruction. This happened constantly, and even crude statistical data showed definitely a concentrated group of severe reactions. In Table 21 we have a summary of the data characteristic of the average reaction time during the answers to the word-stimuli connected with the suggested trauma, as well as to the neutral ones.

Table 22 gives a summary of the motor symptoms in the same cases.[1]

An examination of these tables proves that we have before us artificially obtained symptoms entirely similar to those which we observed in cases of natural affective traces. The difference lies only in this: three varying situations, which are usually observed in different subjects, are here shown in three tests with the same subject. The first test deals with a man who is in a state of emotional balance, whose behaviour is entirely organised; the second, a personality with a marked apparent central affect (similar to the one we have observed with criminals or with hysterical

[1] Table 22 gives only six cases out of ten. In four cases certain errors in the apparatus prevented a statistical survey of the symptoms.

TABLE 21

Subject	Situation	First Test Excitation	First Test Inhibition	Second Test Excitation	Second Test Inhibition	Third Test Excitation	Third Test Inhibition
1 Kar.	Sit. B	1.6" 1.95" 2.0"	+21%	1.7" 2.5" 1.6"	+46%	1.4" 2.1" 1.6"	+50%
2 Kar.	Sit. C	2.0" 2.5" 1.7"	+25%	1.7" 2.5" 1.8"	+46%	1.2" 1.6" 1.4"	+30%
3 Kar.	Sit. D	1.9" 2.1" 1.9"	+11%	1.7" 2.4" 1.8"	+41%	1.4" 1.6" 1.6"	+14%
4 Che.	Sit. C	1.4" 1.6" 1.8"	+14%	1.8" 3.4" 2.2"	+88%	1.2" 1.2" 1.2"	0
5 Zub.	Sit. C	1.0" 1.3" 1.7"	+30%	1.7" 2.0" 1.6"	+18%	1.3" 1.3" 1.2"	0
6 Zub.	Sit. B	1.4" 1.4" 1.6"	0	1.8" 1.8" 1.9"	0	1.6" 1.8" 1.8"	+12%
7 Vyg.	Sit. C	1.6" 1.4" .9"	−14%	1.8" 3.3" —	+83%	— — —	—
8 Shv.	Sit. A	1.4" 1.2" 1.8"	−14%	2.0" 3.0" 2.2"	+50%	2.0" 1.9" 1.8"	−10%
9 Shv.	Sit. B	1.3" 1.6" 1.4"	+23%	2.2" 3.2" 2.5"	+46%	2.0" 2.0" 1.8"	0
10 Shv.	Sit. C	1.4" 1.8" —	+28%	1.8" 2.0" —	+12%	— — —	—

TABLE 22

Subject	Situation	First Test			Second Test			Third Test			Remarks
1 Kar.	Sit. B	4%	0	0	8%	50%	17%	0	20%	0	
2 Kar.	Sit. C	0	0	0	18%	83%	20%	0	0	0	5. Disturbance expressed in discoordination.
3 Kar.	Sit. D	15%	37%	0	20%	50%	20%	5%	25%	0	6. The complex is evident here.
4 Che.	Sit. C	0	0	0	0	15%	0	6%	0	0	
5 Zub.	Sit. C	0	0	0	0	15%	0	6%	0	0	
6 Zub.	Sit. B	0	0	0	0	10%	0	0	0	0	

people); the third one shows again a picture of a more or less quiet state with but few traces of the past experiences or of the reactive (sometimes completely eliminated) affect.

In fact, the first test shows that there is no conspicuous difference in the different groups of reactions, and the relations which are characteristic for one of the groups do not exceed the limit of the average probable error. The motor area is fairly stable in all cases, and the reaction time is rather uniform. The second test verifying the psyche of the experimental subject, after the hypnotic complex has been inserted into it, produces an entirely different picture; the general background of the reaction remains somewhat quiet, but it brings out a distinctly serious complex. As distinguished from the cases which we showed above the complex of disturbances remains a strictly concentrated focus, and does not create any acute, frank affect; the reactions to the indifferent stimuli remain unchanged. (They occur just as rapidly and without any marked increase of motor disturbances.) On the other hand, the reactions of the stimuli connected with the situation produced by suggestion are given with distinct retardation and with equally distinct motor disturbances. We obtained here artificially constructed complexes of considerable stability and concentration. All these facts disappear again in the third test, when, by a second hypnotic sleep and countermanding the suggestion, we bring about an artificial elimination of the complex introduced into the psyche. The control experiments convinced us that the symptoms obtained are actual products of the suggestion and that we have created, in fact, under laboratory conditions a certain model of experimental complex with removed or partly removed trauma and conflicts. We have a number of tests where the associative experiment was brought in after the hypnotic sleep, which was not followed by a traumatic suggestion. We also have many tests where our suggestion was not accepted by the subject under test. In all those cases, the control test shows that the personality of the subject is not actually influenced by any important traumata, and the associative experiment does not give us any characteristic symptoms of the concealed affect.

Obviously the hypnotic suggestion can provoke an artificially created affective complex, but for this we must have definite conditions.

We shall first describe the peculiarities of such an artificially constructed complex, and then by means of a comparative analysis try to ascertain the conditions which must be present during its elaboration. The hypnotic method, allowing us to vary the conditions of provoking such traces, is especially adapted to our purpose here.

We shall select, therefore, two tests, typical for cases in which the suggested affective situation was accepted by the person under test, and in which we succeeded in obtaining an actual model of the artificial complex. We choose these two cases because they allow us to point out distinctly two directions in which the symptoms of affective traces are elaborated.

TEST NO. 1: SUBJECT UNDER TEST, CHES. 23 YEARS OLD

The following situation is suggested. (Index situation C.) "You are in great need of money. You go to a friend in order to borrow from him; he is not at home. You decide to wait in his room and suddenly notice on his bureau a fat wallet with money. You open it and find many five ruble notes. You make a decision; you quickly take the wallet and conceal it on your person. You cautiously go outside and look around to see if you are detected. You have stolen money and now you are afraid that there will be a search in your home and that they will discover you."

In this case, we have reconstructed through hypnosis a situation similar to those, traces of which we have often observed in our tests with criminals. The suggestion was accepted by our subject fairly well, and after it was it was possible to study the affective complex artificially inserted into our subject in whom it remained unconscious.

We performed three tests with the subject before the suggestion, after it, and when the suggestion had been countermanded. In all the cases, twenty-eight word-stimuli were presented, of which eleven were connected with the situation of the suggested complex.

Quite naturally in the test all stimuli were at first equally indifferent, and evoked equally rapid reactions. The basic condition may be characterised by an entirely normal reactive background, by equal and adequate associative answers and by the absence of any motor disturbances. (See Figure 36A.)

A. EXPERIMENT BEFORE THE SUGGESTED COMPLEX

6. MONEY—1.2″—GOLD
8. PAPER—1.6″—MONEY
7. SNOW—1.8″—RAIN
9. CHIFFONIER—1.6″—LINEN

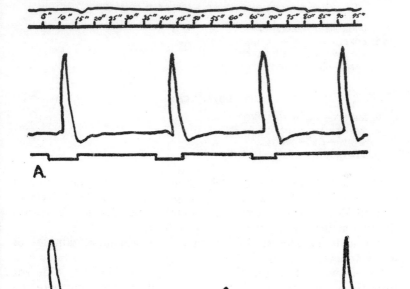

A.

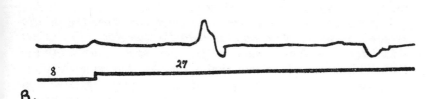

B.

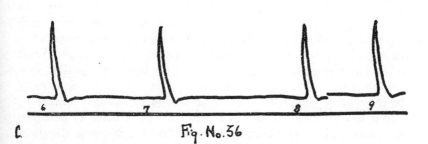

C.

Fig. No. 36

B. EXPERIMENT AFTER SUGGESTED COMPLEX

5. BOOK—1.6″—EDITION
26. CORRIDOR—1.8″—TO GO
6. MONEY—4.0″—TO CARRY
8. PAPER—3.6″—PORTFOLIO

C. SUBJECT CHES.

6. MONEY—1.4″—TO COUNT
8. PAPER—1.2″—TO TAKE
7. SNOW—1.2″—RAIN
9. CHIFFONIER—1.2″—LINEN

The picture, however, entirely changes after the suggestion is given. The subject wakes up from his hypnotic sleep and declares that he does not feel very well, but he does not at all realize the reason for the change of his condition.

We again experiment with him and obtain data, samples of which follow:

It goes without saying that these data are distinctly different from those we received in our first test. Both there and here the subject is not conscious of any definite affective complex. His association in the second test follows just as quietly and normally in the beginning as in the first test, until the first critical stimulus, which immediately shows a distinct retardation, and a reaction, markedly changed and slowed down.

It is the same in all the other cases, *and every time the subject responds to the words connected with the complex with distinct retardation and shows a curve of pressure reaching almost to the limit.* (Figure 36.) It is remarkable that the subject gives these symptoms without any suspicion of the complex suggested and only by the end of the experiment begins vaguely to remember the "dream" suggested to him. (Figure 36.) Such unconsciousness of the affective traces is what produces the specific nature of the symptoms under observation. As distinguished from what we have seen in cases of an acute active affect, the affective traces have here a marked concentrated character and are given only in response to the critical stimuli presented to the subject. When removed from consciousness, the affect begins to be considerably cut off from the motor area, and shows up only when some corresponding stimulus is powerful enough to make it active.

We always obtained such a concentrated character of affective symptoms, when we succeeded in introducing hypnotically into

Stimulus	First Test Reaction Time Seconds	First Test Reaction Word	First Test Motor Disturbance	Second Test Reaction Time Seconds	Second Test Reaction Word	Second Test Motor Disturbance	Third Test Reaction Time Seconds	Third Test Reaction Word	Third Test Motor Disturbance
1 thunder	1″	lightning	None	1.2″			1.0″	lightning	None
2 chair	1.4″	board		1.4″	sit down		1.2″	table	
3 hand	1.2″	leg		1.6″	walk away	+	1.0″	leg	
4 smoke	1.2″	fire		1.2″	flame		1.2″	fire	
5 book	1.4″	note book		1.6″	read		1.0″	write	
6 *money*	1.2″	gold		4.0″	carry		1.4″	count	
7 snow	1.8″	rain		2.1″	pour		1.2″	rain	
8 *wallet*	1.6″	money		3.6″	pocketbook	++	1.2″	take	
9 *bureau*	1.6″	laundry		3.4″	napkin		1.2″	laundry	
10 darkness	1.4″	light		1.2″			1.2″	light	
11 candle	1.4″	lamp		2.0″	burn		1.2″	burns	
12 need	1.2″	walk		2.0″	intrude		2.6″	request	
13 *fat*	2.0″	spoke		3.4″	thin		1.6″	thin	
14 *theft*	1.1″	theft		3.4″	gun	?	1.0″	theft	
15 warehouse	1.2″	merchandise		2.4″	things		1.2″	merchandise	
16 blue	1.5″	white		1.8″			1.0″		
17 together	1.4″	apart		3.8″	friendly	?	1.2″	apart	
18 *search*	1.6″	play		4.2″	hide		1.8″	trying to find	
19 open	1.8″	lock		2.2″	lock		1.2″		
20 carpet	1.6″	table		1.8″	floor		1.2″	floor	

the subject certain affective traces. Sometimes these traces come out more distinctly, and instead of obtaining a general retardation, we obtained centers of strong excitement, in cases when the presented stimulus made the suggested affective trace active. However, the concentrated nature of the affective symptoms remained also here unchanged.

We will now quote the second case, which duplicates that picture with some variations:

TEST NO. 2: SUBJECT UNDER TEST, KAV., 20 YEARS OLD

The following situation is suggested (Situation B): "You are sitting in your room and are studying. A child of your neighbour's, a boy of about six, comes into your room. He shouts and disturbs your studies. You ask him to stop; he does not listen to you.... You get angry, and forgetting yourself, take a stick and beat the boy, first on his back and then on his head. There are some wounds on his head and he cries. You feel very much ashamed and you do not understand how such a thing could have happened to you, how you could beat up a child, and you try to forget it."

As distinguished from the first suggestion quoted above, this one is of an acute conflicting nature. We suggested the situation with a definite purpose; it is entirely unacceptable for the moral standing of the personality, we make it still more complicated by suggesting repentance, the desire to forget and remove the occurrence. The protocols show that the suggestion was actually taken with sufficient intensity. Following is a part of the protocol of the first hypnotic trance of the subject.

The situation is suggested to the subject. She reacts very vividly to the suggestion, shown by her facial expression. The suggestion is followed by these questions:

Experimenter:—Why did you beat him?
Subject:—He was bothering me.
Experimenter:—Is it right to beat a child?
Subject:—But if he annoys me.

At once it is seen that we succeeded in suggesting to the subject a certain situation. However, that situation did not appear to be conflicting. The detailed question which followed later during the second hypnotic sleep shows the whole picture, and makes it evident that the suggestion was accepted in a sufficient affective situation. Here is that question:
Experimenter:—What did you see in your dream? Something disagreeable?
Subject:—Me...no.

Experimenter:—Try to remember what you saw.

Subject:—I was sitting . . . at the table, was working on psychology . . .

Experimenter:—What happened afterwards? You will remember that it will not provoke in you any disagreeable feelings.

Subject:—To our neighbours' came Marussa with her child. When they went to sleep he made some noise and was crying.

Experimenter:—And then what?

Subject:—I was sitting . . . I cannot possibly study when there is noise . . . I went to him and asked him not to make any noise . . . then I pulled his ears. First he laughed, then he cried . . . my conscience began to torture me.

Experimenter:—But you did not beat him?

Subject:—No, I never beat children.

Experimenter:—And you did not beat him with a stick?

Subject:—Yes, I beat him, but not with a stick, and then my conscience tortured me.

The protocols give a convincing picture that our suggestion created in the subject a considerable conflict. The very difficulty with which the given suggestion is reconstructed, even in the second sleep, shows that it was connected with some shifting of considerable force. The refusal to remember that she has beaten the child and the gradually concealing reminiscence, first that she has "pulled his ears," then that she has "beaten him but not with a stick"; all this shows how much the situation suggested was unacceptable to the personality. The statement repeated twice, that "my conscience has tortured me," shows its considerable affectiveness. We have evidence that we introduced into the psyche of the subject a situation which provoked in her an acute affective state. That state, however, appears to be separated from the consciousness of the subject, and after the awakening we obtained the answers to what happened during the hypnotic sleep:—"It seems to me that during my sleep, I went to the next room, but what for, I do not know." "Did you dream of something?" Answer: "Nothing."

The subject has, as usual, after the sleep a slightly heavy feeling, but does not remember any disagreeable happenings.

The same way as in the test shown above, the reactions of the subject after the hypnotic sleep are in the beginning undisturbed, almost as usual.

There are hardly any symptoms differentiating the three tests, which were taken in three entirely different psychological situations. There is an abrupt change, however, when the first stimulus is introduced, which is connected with the affective situation suggested:

	First Test		Second Test		Third Test	
Stimulus	Reaction Time in Seconds	Reaction Word	Reaction Time in Seconds	Reaction Word	Reaction Time in Seconds	Reaction Word
1 Work	1.6″	Good	1.8″	Interesting	1.2″	Heavy
2 Curtain	1.8″	White	1.8″	+	1.0″	+
3 Balcony	1.7″	Light	1.6″	Large	1.2″	Light
4 Forest	1.4″	Dark	1.9″	+	———	
5 Couch	1.2″	Soft	1.2″	+	1.4″	+
6 Sail	1.7″	White	1.4″	+	1.8″	+
7 Foot	1.2″	Small	1.2″		1.2″	+

The stimuli connected with the situation suggested in the first test usually show a normal picture (with the exception of two or three cases where we apparently met with natural complexes). On the other hand, in the second test, all the critical stimuli

	First Test		Second Test		Third Test	
Stimulus	Reaction Time in Seconds	Reaction Word	Reaction Time in Seconds	Reaction Word	Reaction Time in Seconds	Reaction Word
8 *Boy*	1.9″	Mischievous	2.2″		1.4″	
9 *Back*	1.2″	Clean	2.4″	Bends	1.9″	Bent
10 Night	1.6″	Dark	1.2″		1.4″	
11 Leaves	1.4″	Yellow	1.8″		1.2″	
12 Dress	1.8″	Red	1.9″		1.2″	
13 *Angry*	4.0″	I do not know what for	6.5″	At a dog	6.0″	At a dog
14 Rose	2.0″	White	1.2″		1.2″	
15 Window	1.4″	Large	2.0″	Light	1.8″	Large
16 *To beat*	2.0″	A girl	2.0″	A dog	3.4″	A dog
17 Book	2.0″	Interesting	1.8″		1.8″	
18 *Stick*	1.4″	Black	2.6″		2.2″	
19 *Hair*	1.6″	Brown	2.6″		2.4″	
20 *Hit*	2.4″	A dog	9.6″	A cat	2.2″	A cat
21 Freedom	2.4″	I don't know	2.1″	Equality	1.8″	Equality
22 Repair	1.8″	Of a building	1.4″		1.4″	Building
23 *Wound*	1.4″	Of the face	2.6″		1.8″	
24 *Tears*	2.0″	Bitter	1.6″	Boisterous	1.6″	
25 Laugh	1.4″	Merry	3.2″		2.0″	Gay

showed distinct retarding of the answer and equally distinct motor disturbances. *The subject tested shows symptoms of a complex about which she herself cannot say anything, but which are well known to us.*

18. STICK—1.4″—BLACK
19. HAIR—1.6″—
20. TO HIT—2.4″—DOG

3. BALCONY—1.6″—BIG
7. FOOT—1.2″—SMALL

13. TO BECOME ANGRY—6.5″—AT A DOG

20. TO HIT—9.6″—CAT

These symptoms follow with great regularity and form typical disturbances for the affect. In Figure 37 we show examples of the graphs which characterise accurately the neurodynamics of our subject. In the first, as well as in the second test, the general background of the reactive processes remains stable. On that background are distinctly shown the different reactions connected with the suggested situation. In the same figure are curves describing the neurodynamics of these reactions. It can be clearly seen that the stimulus provokes a noticeable excitement, expressed in reaction No. 20 in a peculiar motor storm, filling the whole latent period and becoming manifest in the tremor of the left hand.

Of considerable interest is the nature of the breathing in these cases: The critical stimulus when presented provokes here a noticeable retardation of the expiration, showing a change in the ratio of inspiratory to expiratory duration, the symptomatology of which, for some emotional situations, was described in detail by Benussi and by a number of other authors.

The examples cited above show a picture of symptoms so marked that if even the contents of the affect are unknown we could successfully point out the elements of the affective situation, basing our conclusion on the objective analysis of the symptoms. In the experiment we are again convinced that we have artificially reconstructed the structure of those psychological processes which usually can be observed in people passing through an acute traumatic situation, in hysterical people, and finally in normal subjects whose affective traces we have analysed.[1]

---

[1] This book does not include the special work dealing with the objective study of neurodynamics of normal and pathological complexes.

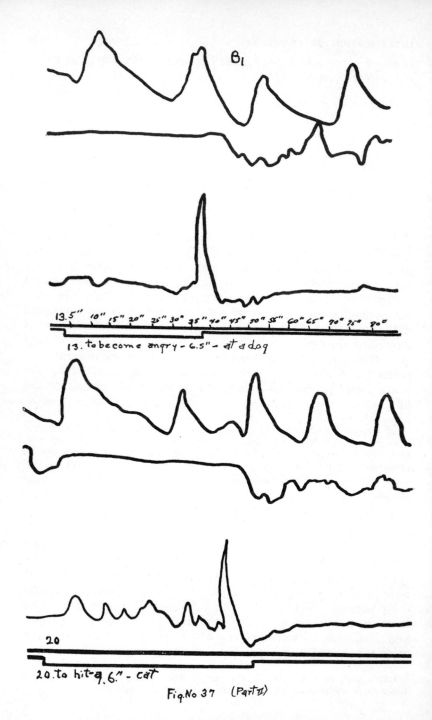

β_1

13.5″ 10″ 15″ 20″ 25″ 30″ 35″ 40″ 45″ 50″ 55″ 60″ 65″ 70″ 75″ 80″

13. to become angry – 6.5″ – at a dog

20

20. to hit – g. 6.″ – cat

Fig. No 37   (Part II)

The suggested complex appears to be stable to the extent that its symptoms remain even in the third test in spite of the fact that the suggestion was countermanded. Some of the reactions quoted above show this. (See reactions Nos. 13, 16, 18, and 19), and we may confidently state that the process started by us appears to be much deeper than a short suggestion, and that we have before us a natural reaction of the personality, and one which has cut rather deeply into that personality.

3. NEURODYNAMICS OF A SHIFTED AND CONSCIOUS AFFECT

THE two cases quoted above have one important characteristic: the affective symptoms have here a distinctly localised character. They appear only when the corresponding stimulus provokes them, leaving the general background of the reaction almost entirely unchanged.

We obtain a picture very different from the one of a scattered affect, and similar to what we have observed in cases when time, smoothing out the acuteness of the affect, had transformed its scattered character into concentrated traces, which only showed in single critical instances. (See Chapter III.)

However, in our case we have an entirely different structure of the process. The lack of the scattered disturbances is due here to quite other factors. We believe that the concentrated nature of the traces, not passing into the irradiated disturbance of the behaviour, is a result in this instance of the disconnection of the affective complex from consciousness, which we frequently noted before. The disruption from the consciousness is connected here with separation from the motor area, and this is actually, in our opinion, the important neurodynamic mechanism of shifting.

We encountered an affect every time when some beginning activity was retarded and the potentially powerful activity of the organism was inhibited. This we have pointed out in the preceding pages. The affect begins when something happens to the human activity. There are two ways of checking it—either by giving an outlet to the tension which accumulated as a result of the retardation, or by removing it from the motor area. We have seen how the first way appears in the act of admission. We must be ready to meet the second one in the post-hypnotic act of forgetting the complex.

We come here to a question which is of vast importance in psychology, as well as in the pathology of psychological situations. The amnesia which we artificially created in our case, insulating the traumatic picture from consciousness, actually provokes a process quite similar to the process of shifting. The authors who described the latter (beginning with Freud) have often pointed out that the active side of the insulation from the consciousness must be viewed as insulation from the motor area. That insulation must mean, that after having lost its immediate connection with the motor area, the traumatic and conflicting group of affective traces ceases to have the possibility of influencing the behaviour in a definite way. The connection of the consciousness with the motor area is itself one of the most interesting problems of psychology. A number of American authors (M. F. Washburn and others) have given it their serious attention. In future tests, the relation will be clearly shown: Removal from the consciousness—insulation from the motor area, consciousness—spread into the motor area.

If the mechanism of the post-hypnotic "removal" of the affect is nothing but its separation from the motor area, it is quite clear that, being insulated from it, that affect does not influence it in any noticeable way. On the contrary, every time it appears in consciousness, noticeable disturbances of activity and a distinct affective tone ensue.

Our tests make it possible to observe what neurodynamic factors are being evoked by the consciousness of the suggested affect. For this, the associative experiments, used here, seem specially well adapted. Each stimulus connected with the situation suggested provokes distinct disturbances in the reactive process. With this, however, each such stimulus is another step toward the breaking up of the barrier which separates the affect, already introduced into the psyche, from the consciousness.

By means of hypnotic suggestion, we have constructed a model of an affective complex, disconnected from the motor area and from consciousness. By using a prolonged associative experiment we may also build a model of the very process of its becoming conscious. That process is the more important to us, as it then makes it possible to trace the neurodynamic mechanisms connected with that consciousness.

In the cases quoted above, we already have some elements of such consciousness of the situation suggested, under the influence of the "critical" word-stimuli. We may, however, construct a much fuller picture of such "experimental psychoanalysis," if we adopt prolonged and more adequate observations.

The process of the shifted complex becoming conscious during the experiment is so interesting that we shall dwell on it in more detail.

We take here the test to which we have briefly referred:

Test No. 3: Subject Kar., 20 years old, student of obstetrics. The following situation is suggested: (Situation D). "You have been graduated in obstetrics and started to work in a maternity hospital. You are at home and a woman comes to see you and asks you to produce in her an abortion so that nobody should know it. She offers you money for this. You hesitate, because this is against the law. The woman implores you with tears in her eyes. You feel sorry for her and you agree. You take your instruments, put them in a suitcase, and proceed to the sick bed. You ascend a narrow staircase, ring a bell, and an old woman opens the door. You are very excited and start the operation. But immediately a hemorrhage begins and you cannot stop it. You see a pool of blood on the floor. The sick woman is very weak, you have made an error in your operation and you fear for her life...."

The situation, suggested by us, is accepted by the subject very actively, and it undoubtedly creates an acute affective reaction. This is already shown in the extract from the statement which we quoted in the beginning of this chapter. However, in spite of the affective nature of the situation suggested, it appears to be entirely disconnected from consciousness, and after awakening, our subject refuses to remember anything of what happened to her during the hypnotic sleep. We might say that we have constructed here an "experimental unconsciousness," and further tests convince us that this unconscious affective complex remains very active and becomes an actual and entirely conscious affect, after certain means are employed. The object of our test is to trace the *neurodynamic correlations of that gradual consciousness,* and in this way clear up the problem of the psychophysiology of the conscious and inhibited affect.

We shall use here a method, which should help us to evoke the affective traces introduced by us into the psyche and simultaneously to record the whole dynamics of their gradual realisation. After having constructed an "experimental unconsciousness," we would naturally employ, as a method, "experimental psychoanalysis." The free chain associations were the best means for our purpose. Being determined not only by the logical, but also by the affective data of the personality, they showed beyond doubt the inhibited affective complexes. The acute character of the suggested affective complex, assured us that even a small number of free associations would bring it out. Finally, the fact that the procedure was followed by a recording of the whole system of expressive symptoms made it possible not to deviate here from our method of psychophysiology.

In one important respect the method of our chain associations was distinctly different from the method of psychoanalytical research. It was entirely included within the limits of psychophysiological experiment, and herein lie its strong and weak points. The complex, the appearance of which we have studied, was known to us beforehand, and this is what made it possible for us to avoid complicated methods and interpretations. We had no ground to believe that our suggestion would be subject to some specially deep symbolic modification, and we expected that it would directly appear already in the first or in the second associative series. Noting all associations that "freely came to the mind," the intervals between them and their connected symptoms, we were able to obtain accurately fixed associative series,[1] and to study in detail their dynamics.

It is quite natural that the experimental, or we would rather say "model," character of our tests limited our possibilities, and entirely excluded extensive research on the problems of the unconscious and of its dynamics. This was not, however, the object of our psychophysiological work.

The free associative series were recorded from our subject under test before the suggestion, as well as after it. As it is possible to compare the symptoms we obtained during our tests of single speech reactions, with photographic snapshots of one section of the psyche, analogously tests with chain associations can be best compared with cinematography. We see before us a number of associations, which, more or less, characterise the state of the psyche within a given period of time, and which afford us a possibility of observing the gradual appearance of the affective complex.

Figure 38 shows sample graphs from our protocols, characterising the state of the neurodynamic processes of the subject under test before the suggestion. The calm motor activity and the equal intervals clearly show the organised character of the subject's behaviour. The summary of reactions given in a chain series brings out the same thing.

1 night	2 door	3 quarrel	4 room
5 wall	6 picture	7	8
9 grass	10 river	11 forest	12 mountain
13 balcony	14 garden	15 flowers	16 lilacs
17 rose	18 nightingale	19 road	20 ?
21 pool	22 night	23 stars	24 couch
25 courses	26 automobile	27 table	28 books
29 notebook	30 pen	31 piano	32 notes
33 stove	34 bed	35 knife	36 fork
37 napkin	38 cow	39 horse	40 cat
41 lamp	42 shade	43 cupboard	

All these data give the usual picture of how the normal associative process occurs, with equally spaced appearance in the

[1] The problem of the structure of the chain series was specially developed by our collaborator, A. N. Leontiev. See his article, *The Structural Analysis of Chain Associative Series*, Russo-German Medical Journal, 1927.

series (4-6, 9-23, 27-37). The study of the intervals between the single reactions has shown here a well organised motor area which reflected a picture of normal neurodynamics.

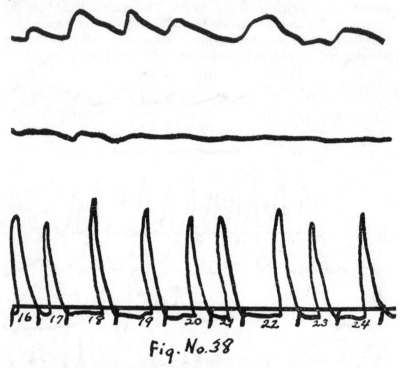

Fig. No. 38

We put the subject into a hypnotic sleep, and introduce into her psyche the affective complex mentioned above. After awakening we again record a similar series of chain associations. We obtained an associative series which are summarised in the following statement:

1 day	2 hammer	3 tapping	4 reflects
5 muscle	6 nose	7 glasses	8 hair
9 eyes	10 hands	11 ring	12 lamp
13 see	14 day	15 shores	16 wave
17 boat	18 river	19 song	20 flowers
21 bridge	22 train	23 road	24 forest
25 village	26 row	27 mud	28 moon
29 month	30 to tap	31 knee	32 shoe
33 flowers	34 daisies	35 automobile	36 book
37 revolver	38 table	39 shelf	40 box
41 suitcase	42 platform	43 depot	44 armchair
45 rocking chair	46 couch	47 floor	

Up to now the series quoted above are in no way conspicuous; the contents and the character of the intervals do not make it in any way different from the series we recorded in the subject's normal state, which were just shown. The graphic records of the accompanying motor reactions which are depicted in Figure 39-A reveals also here a rather normal picture not similar to the one showing the neurodynamics destroyed by an affect.

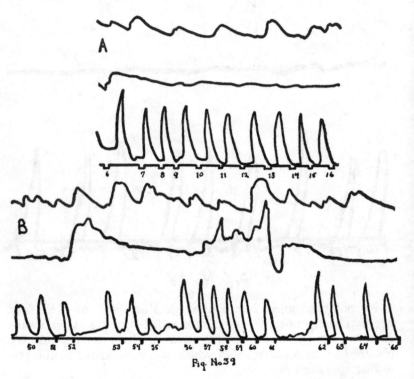

Fiq. No.39

SUBJECT KAR. CHAIN ASSOCIATIVE SERIES AFTER SUGGESTION

A. BEGINNING SERIES
B. CENTRAL SERIES (ORIGINATING COMPLEXES)

All this forces us into the following preliminary conclusions, which, after our observations, seem unquestionable: *The insulation of affective traces from the consciousness simultaneously produces the insulation from the motor area, transforming the active affect into one which is concealed or potential.*

The part of the test shown above does not reveal any symptoms of a concealed affect. However, the appearance of irregular intervals at the end of the chain series, and the presence of some single marked inhibitions is of special interest to us and makes us suppose that some destructive factor has intervened. The protocols disclosed to us this factor: at the end of the associative series there begins to appear persistently the affective complex inserted into the psyche. It provokes a number of associations, which are not yet understood by the subject himself, but which are entirely comprehensible to us who know the contents of the suggestion.

49 cushion	50 to bathe	51 somersault	52 to fight
53 wall	54 picture	55 bath	56 sick woman
57 doctor	58 nurse	59 medicine	60 ether
61 *wound*	62 bandage	63 *forceps*	64 *scalpel*
65 inkstand	66 inkstand	67 pharmacy	68 body
69 clinic	70 road	71 street	72 automobile
73 board	74 pool	75 day	

The subject reconstructs quite unintentionally the situation of the operation, in the chain series, not knowing why that situation has come to her mind, and not being able to explain its contents. However, that not quite conscious reconstruction of a section of the affective situation is followed by a noticeable disturbance of the neurodynamics. Figure 39B is a graph from the record, showing a picture of the connected motor reactions during the appearance of the part which reconstructed the suggested affective situation. That extract convincingly shows *that important symptoms of neurodynamic changes are connected with reconstruction of parts of the complexes in speech series.* Even a few reactions before the situation appears in the associations the motor control of the right hand shows noticeable symptoms of disorganisation, which gradually increase. About the middle of the given group ("the sick woman, the doctor, nurse, medicine") the excitement is switched over to the left hand showing sharp and disorderly movements. Finally, when the central element of the complex situation openly appears (wound, bandage), a distinct tremor of the right hand is evident which shows considerable disturbance in the neurodynamic mechanism. To all this is added a noticeable variation in the breathing (it becomes irregular, sometimes greatly retarded). All these symptoms point to a considerable disturbance of the psychophysiological processes, accompanying the first appearance of the affect in speech.

The later symptoms are more intense; *there is an evident appearance of the affective situation in the consciousness of the subject followed by an acute motor storm, which for a time breaks up any normal reactive process.*

We are able to follow up that entire process in the next associative series, which we record immediately after the subject has completed the above-mentioned series of reactions. It continues for five minutes and includes about ninety reactions; it ends with a total reconstruction of the complex suggested.

After the first appearance of the suggested complex described above, we could certainly expect, that in the following series the complex would appear even more distinctly. After a recess of three minutes we again begin an associative series:

1 night	2 staircase	3 table	4 book
5 day	6 rain	7 icicle	8 pool
9 month	10 building	11 garden	12 river
13 lake	14 boat	15 stars	16 sky
17 board	18 platform	19 lecture	20 glass

Now the structure of the chain series, which is characterised by its intervals is already not the same; it is inserted with con-

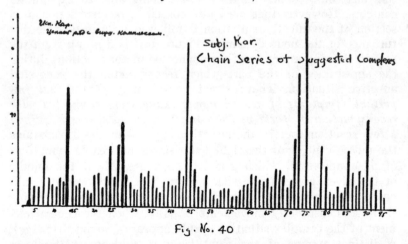

Fig. No. 40

siderable retardations and is exceptionally unstable and disorganised. Figure 40 illustrates this. The structure appears to be quite different if compared with that of the intervals observed on the same subject before the suggestion (and which is shown on Curve 36).

It is quite obvious that the affect has crept into those series more prominently. The following shows the whole picture and makes quite clear the structure of the series shown in the graph; to every section of acute retardation there is a corresponding evident appearance in the series of the elements of the suggested affective situation. The following is the further development of the series:

20 glass	21 ?	22 *operation*	23 *instruments*
24 *woman*	25 street	26 lamp	27 curtain
28 room	29 cupboard	30 carpet	31 picture
32 chrysan-themum	33 piano	34 singing	35 song
36 girl friend	37 *father*	38 *old woman*	39 *mother*
40 *sick woman*	41 *nurse*	42 *don't know*	43 forest
44 river	45 bridge	46 road	47 dress
48 depot	49 wife	50 ?	51 inkstand
52 table	53 revolution	54 book	55 *staircase*
56 blood	57 warm	58 many	59 month
60 gray	61 grass	62 lawn	63 appletree [1]
64 mushroom	65 couch	66 radio	67 chest [1]
68 *wallet* [1]	69 *yellow*	70 *woman*	

71 *I remembered what I dreamt* (the experimenter has told me to do something; go on further, say what comes to your mind).

72 quickly	73 leg	74 hand	75 nose
76 face	77 cheek	78 eyes	79 hair
80 spectacles	81 hammer	82 reflects	83 muscles
84 to swear	85 to fight	86 to laugh	87 to play
88 to joke	89 chair	90 air	91 see
92 sky	93 stars (5)		

The dynamics of the suggested complex become sufficiently clear to us; being disconnected with the conscious area, that complex, nevertheless, shows an insistent tendency to creep into the speech series; being removed every time, it shows, however, a considerable persistence, and after a certain period of time again flows into the free associative series. *The affective complex constructed by us, though not yet being conscious, creates an affective state and determines the flow of the free associative series.* Its appearance is followed every time by a considerable retardation.

Figure 41 shows that the appearance of the traces of the complex in the speech area is invariably followed by an acute motor disorganisation. In section A that disorganisation is a natural

[1] These reactions are connected with situation C, which was suggested to the subject about a week before that test.

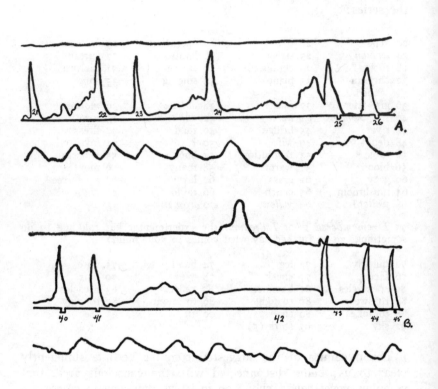

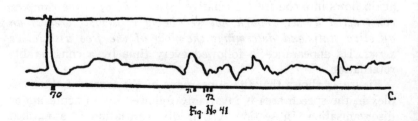

Fig. No 41

reflection of the conflict, which is connected with the appearance in the associative series of the complex links (operation, instrument, woman). Section B demonstrates the neurodynamic equivalent of the removal of the affective part (sick nurse) and conclusively shows that the refusal to prolong the associations ("I do not know what to say") conceals a considerable neurodynamic conflict. After all this, it becomes quite clear that the subject finally arrives at a moment, when the barrier, which separated the affective complex from the consciousness, breaks down, after which the affect appears in an acute and overt form.

The removal of the insulation of the affect from the consciousness and its overt appearance is followed by an acute motor storm, by a model of an affective fit, which breaks down the normal course of the reactive process.

Many things become clear to us after that moment, the graphic course of which is shown on Curve C of Figure 41. What we see here is at the same time a model of an affective fit, and the reactive process of the affective complex. Both these processes are psychologically extremely close to each other, and essentially show the same structure. The reaction is always connected with the breaking of the barrier which separates the affect from the motor area, and with the corresponding switching over of the innervation to the motor area. It seems that these factors enter into the mechanism of the consciousness of the retarded affective complex; the connection between the process of becoming conscious and the reaction of the complexes removed, which is the basis of psychoanalytical therapy, becomes much clearer. In fact, the end of the series quoted above shows with sufficient clearness that after the basic complex has become conscious, the subject is able to pass into a considerably more stable chain of neutral reactions than he had before. A further investigation of the psyche of the subject would show that at the base of the affect we obtain a process very similar to confession, the psychological result of which we have observed before.[1]

On the other hand, the neurodynamic explosion, which appears after the affective complex has become conscious, gives a new aspect to the mechanical structure of the shifting. The insulation from the consciousness and the simultaneous insulation from the motor area seems to be the mechanism which *saves the personality from the over-excitement and from the disorganisation connected with an open appearance of the conflict.* In that respect the con-

[1] Chapter IV, paragraph 5.

struction of a certain functional barrier between the affective centre and the motor area is of decisive importance for the conservation in the personality of the possibility to act normally, without disorganising its behaviour by the affective traces, existing in its past in considerable numbers.

As yet we know but little about the mechanisms which bring about this process. Some physiological analogies allow us to suppose that at the basis of that process lies the "inhibition because of over-excitement," which was described under the name of "parabiosis" in the Russian physiological school.[1] Other suppositions make us think that at the basis of the conflict of the affect may also lie other purely psychological laws, which are connected with the use of some organised and cultural means, acting with the help of speech and a system of intermediate mechanisms. We will study this in the last part of our work, now leaving unanswered this very interesting psychological question.

So much detail in the analysis of one case we have given only on the basis of the clinical method of expression. It seemed to us that the importance of the question deserved its detailed analysis, and that not a statistical summary, but a qualitative examination, should be the most adequate way to this. We could have given other of our experiments. In every one of them we recorded the corresponding series of free chain associations. In every one we obtained data reflecting the same structure of the psychological processes.

In all the cases we examined, we could convincingly describe the *conflicting character* of the process, which appeared in the chain associative series. On the one hand, we invariably observed that peculiar persistency, that "pressure of the complex," which we noted above; on the other hand, we invariably saw attempts to retard the appearance of the complex, to remove it. Finally, the affective complex, not being conscious to the subject, creates a picture of a certain persisting feeling, and we have cases when one and the same group of reactions obstinately repeats itself, five or six times during a five-minute associative series.

Especially interesting are the mechanics of removal of the developing complex, the tendency to go away from it, and to retard its appearance. The conflicting character of that process is evident already from the fact that the passing to a new chain of associations is always followed with considerable inhibition,[2] whereas its structure shows a characteristic, primitive, connecting link. Usually, the replacing series begins either by repeating some past link or by alliteration.

Here is an example, with subject Zub., to which the situation C was suggested (stealing of money):

The first series shows clearly a complex. The subject does not realize it and relates almost the whole situation.

[1] See A. Ouchtomsky and others, *The Theory of Parabiosis*, Moscow, 1927.
[2] See Leontiev, quoted above.

1 window	2 evening	3 solitude	4 snow
5 carpet	6 waiting	7 *money*	8 *need*
9 *fear*	10 white	11 picture	12 *go away*
13 take	14 *open*	15 *approach*	16 window
17 *bureau*	18 chair	19 *yellow*	20 cornice
21 porch	22 secret	23 inevitable	24 *fear*
25 *money*	26 *theft*	30 robins	31 *bureau*
33 couch	34 *approach*	35 *dress*	36 *conceal*, etc.

The persisting character of that series is beyond any doubt. Interesting are the mechanisms, which are used by the subject to remove the persisting associations. This is well demonstrated in the following series:

1 wall	2 stain	3 laces	4 dress
5 meanness	6 evening	11 napkin	12 coast
13 birds	14 bureau	15 fireplace	20 to **fear**
21 *money*			

22 laces (departure to previous link repeating of link No. 3)

24 write	25 *theft*	26 doll (alliteration)	
31 eyes	32 *brown*	33 *to fear*	34 *fear*
35 to be glad	36 *evidence*	37 street (allitera-	44 fireplace
		tion)	
45 *wallet*	46 *money*	47 porch	

48 laugh (departure to the previous links) 21, 42, etc.

These examples hardly leave any doubt that the passing from the persisting, complex section of the chain to the neutral and replacing one is not a simple and quiet process but an acute conflicting act, which is reflected in the structure of the chain links.

4. THE REACTION OF THE PERSONALITY: THE COMPLEX AND THE TRAUMA

THE cases shown above demonstrate that a suggestion of an inacceptable affective situation provoked a rather deep reaction of the whole personality. This is evident from a number of facts, first of all from the active resistance, which our suggestion encountered, from the acuteness with which our suggestion was felt, and finally from the difficulty of removing our suggestion later.

The different reactions of the personality to the suggestion inserted into its psyche enable us to raise the *question about the conditions in which an affective complex* may appear, as well as of its separation from the related, but psychologically entirely different, idea of *trauma*.

Our observations make it possible for us *to state that an affective complex may be created only in the case when the given suggestion (or the given excitement) was accepted by the subject, and, as such, came into a certain conflict with the usual features of the personality.* An opposite case is when the suggestion, though severely traumatic, was not accepted, and it produces an entirely different picture of a *trauma* in its structure. The latter is distinctly different from the affective complex, in that the suggestion made remains alien to the personality, that it does not provoke in it any activity, nor, therefore, any specific conflict. It acts only as an external trauma, provoking quite different neurodynamic symptoms.

All cases which we have studied at present were of the character of artificial complexes, just because of the activeness of the conflict which was evoked in the personality by the suggestion. As a result of this, we also obtained retardation of the critical answers, the motor disturbances, etc., the symptoms of which were described above. The impression was created that the personality valued the suggestion made as its own deed, and felt it as such, sincerely passing through the conflict connected with it.

However, there are often cases distinctly different from these as to their psychological structure; often we do not obtain such a reaction of the personality to the suggestion made. The suggestion is not accepted by the subject, who feels its contents as an external trauma, and does not bring it into the system of *his own* behaviour, and does not react to it with a conflict, which is born *inside* of that behaviour. The psychological picture, which is obtained in these cases, is of considerable interest for the differentiation of the complex from the trauma.

We shall discuss again a case where our test brought about only an external trauma because the suggestion was not accepted and the complex did not appear.

Test No. 4: The subject, SHV, 20 years old. It is suggested that she has stolen money from her friend. (Situation C, text above.)

The vital difference of this test from the others which we investigated is that the subject refused to accept the suggestion. In spite of the sufficiently deep hypnotic sleep, she declared that she did not want to take the money; that if she needed any money she would ask for a loan. The subject felt only an *attempt to suggest to her this situation,* and did not take it as an actual occurrence in which she participated.

The entire course of the test enabled us to evaluate that case as an unsuccessful and unaccepted suggestion which produced a trauma but did not create an affective complex.

The data we obtained during the experiment convinced us that we have before us an entirely different psychological structure, not similar to the one which we observed before. The reactions

Stimuli	First Test	Second Test	Stimuli	First Test	Second Test
1 thunder	1.0" loud	— thunders	16 Blue	1.4" red	2.2" stacking
2 chair	1.2" stands	1.6" sit down	17 together	2" together	1.8" do
3 hand	1.6" lies	1.8" to write	18 *search*	2.2" conceal	3.2" —
4 smoke	— goes	— disappear	19 to open	— to close	1.2" *to find*
5 book	1.6" give	2.0" read	20 carpet	1.6" lies	2.2" to spread
6 *money*	1.6" receive	1.8" *take*	21 *dress*	1.6" hangs	1.4" put on
7 snow	1.6" falls	2.0" winter	22 *lay down*	2.4" conceal	1.6" *take*
8 *wallet*	1.8" money	1.6" *lays*	23 grey	1.8" read	1.8" fog
9 *bureau*	1.4" stands	1.8" *wallet*	24 *notice*	1.8" see	2.0" *not noticed*
10 darkness	1.4" night	1.8" night	25 *friend*	1.8" recognise	2.4" *not see*
11 candle	1.4" goes out	2.0" church	26 hall	1.2" dark	1.6" rooms
12 need	1.4" poverty	1.6" money	27 *look back*	1.4" not looking back	2.2" *not to look back*
13 fat	1.6" thin	2.6" —	28 conscience	1.4" torture	2.6" —
14 *theft*	1.6" to steal	1.6" *to make*	29 paper	1.6" to find	1.6" to lay around
15 warehouse	1.8" to put together	2.2" wanted	30 loan	2.4" pay	1.3" pay

of the subject show a completely frank expression of the inflicted trauma, without any traces of an active conflict.

Above are the records of the associative answers obtained from the subject before and after the suggestion.

These series of answers are distinctly different from those which we observed in the cases quoted above. Here are entirely absent the acute inhibitions which we usually saw in other cases; the associative series follows after the suggestion just as quietly and correctly as before the suggestion. On the other hand, the contents of the associative answers appear to be particularly symptomatic; the subject does not retard the answers connected with the situation suggestion, as happened in the other cases we observed, but quite openly reconstructs the elements of the situation suggested (6. money—take, 8. wallet—lie, 9. bureau—wallet, etc.). He does not show any tendency to conceal them, or to replace them by other neutral reactions.

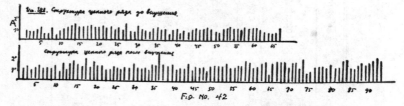

Fig. No. 42

A. STRUCTURE OF CHAIN SERIES BEFORE SUGGESTION (SUBJ. SHV.)
B. STRUCTURE OF CHAIN SERIES AFTER SUGGESTION (SUBJ. SHV.)

An equally correct and quiet character is obtained in a chain associative series which does not differ from the one we recorded before the suggestion, in either its contents or the structure of the intervals.

Figure 42 gives the structure of the intervals of both recorded series, and we clearly see that in spite of any differences in principle, the traces of disorganisation and retardation in the second series are here entirely absent. We purposely prolonged the series recorded after the suggestion up to eight minutes, and have, nevertheless, not obtained any signs of a disturbance, which we expected.

We were ready to abandon our data and admit that our experiment was unsuccessful, had our attention not been drawn to a fact appearing in the important mechanics of that case. The externally equal associative series produced in certain points quite peculiar neurodynamic symptoms, which as a rule were not encountered in other cases. *With the motor area remaining entirely normal we observed noticeable disturbances in the breathing, every time that the association reconstructed an element of the trauma.*

This appeared so constantly that at the end of the analysis we thought that it entirely excluded any possibility of chance. Every time when an element appeared connected with the traumatic situation the breathing was first retarded, and then came a sharp impulsive sigh, from two to two-and-one-half times deeper than the usual respiration of the subject.

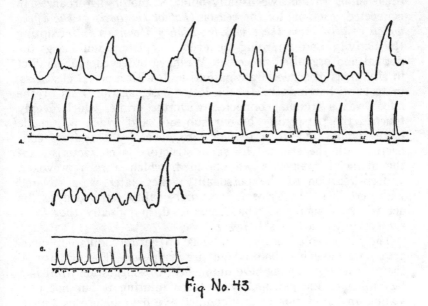

Fig. No. 43

A

ASSOCIATIVE REACTIONS AFTER SUGGESTION

4. SMOKE—?
5. BOOK—2.0″—TO COUNT
6. MONEY—1.8″—TO TAKE
7. SNOW—2.0″—WINTER
8. PAPER—1.6″—
9. CHIFFONIER—?—PAPER

21. DRESS—1.4″—TO PUT ON
22. TO PUT—1.6″—TO TAKE
23. GREY—1.8″—CLOUD
24. TO CHANGE—2.0″—NOT TO CHANGE
26. CORRIDOR—1.6″—CHIFFONIER

B

CHAIN ASSOCIATIONS AFTER SUGGESTION

75. MONTH. 76. TO THINK. 77. BREAD. 78. DOG. 79. RADIO. 80. PHARMACIST. 81. TO ARRIVE,... 99. TO SEEK. 100. DRESS. 101. I DO NOT KNOW. 103. TO BECOME ANGRY.

In Figure 43, we show sections from our graphs. We regret
that we cannot present here the whole record in which the points
we mentioned show up as sharp centres on the background of a
quiet and regular breathing. One thing is at any rate beyond
doubt: the appearance of the sections connected with the trauma
is followed not by the reactions of the hands, which remain
entirely quiet during the whole experiment, but by *vegetative
symptoms.*

The symptoms which we observed in that case are quite comprehensible. In fact, we usually obtained motor disturbances in
connected reactions for the reason *that at the basis of the affect
which created them there was invariably a conflict,* interrupting
the activity and retarding or even completely inhibiting the
normal and organised processes. We have observed that conflict
in situations of school examinations and, with especial clearness,
in tests with criminals. In the latter case, at the basis of the
affect was a trauma connected with the crime, which deeply
touched the personality of our subjects, and which was made
more complicated by a tendency to conceal the feelings connected with the crime. The same structure is characteristic of
the artificial complexes we obtained, which always provoked
a deep reaction of the personality; they later were covered
with certain strata by which the personality responded to the
act which it supposedly has committed, and finally they were
subject to a marked shifting.

The "unaccepted suggestion" has an entirely different character; we have just pointed out its symptoms. The activity of
the personality remains here untouched, the suggestion itself is a
fact alien to the personality, perhaps injuring it but not provoking any hesitation or any conflict. We have before us simply
a case of external violence to the psyche, which may have caused
a trauma, but did not provoke any deep conflict or disturbance.

The symptoms we obtained are a psychophysiological correlation of such a structure of the process, and give us fresh possibilities for its neurodynamic analysis. We may suppose that
if the disturbances in the behaviour, which are connected with
the active affect and affective complex, find their place within
the *system of the active behaviour,* directly connected with the
motor field; that then the feeling of the trauma has an entirely
different psychophysiological structure; the reaction of the human
system to it is featured by a greater participation of the vegetative system which is more distant from the psychological
activity of the personality.

It is quite clear that this statement needs more careful study and cannot be made otherwise than as a hypothetical assertion. However, a number of experimental data, which we shall study later, as well as many psychological and also clinical facts convince us of the correctness of our statement concerning the neurodynamic differences between the complex and the trauma, and concerning their relative influence on the animal and vegetative systems.

Substantial confirmation of the differences between the psychophysiological structures of the complex and the trauma are found in the different pictures of hysteria and traumatic neuroses.

At the basis of one of these diseases usually lies the mechanics of a conflict, of some definite structures, an attraction to one another or towards actual possibility; at the basis of the other lies a traumatic situation. The very symptomatology of both shows that the disturbances which are observed in both cases occur in two entirely different systems. We shall not quote here from the discussion which a few years ago had shown quite different viewpoints on that subject, and which never was clearly or finally decided. We are inclined to believe that only an experimental study of the mechanics which lay at the basis of both neuroses, will make it possible to settle that problem and to outline distinctly the limits between the two cases. Our studies have shown that acute disturbances in the motor area are characteristic of the neurodynamics of hysterical patients; they appear every time when in the reaction of the subject there is reconstructed some part of the affective complex. These disturbances are of distinctly conflicting character, similar to the type of the inhibiting impulses which we have studied above. Such motor disturbances are never observed with traumatic subjects. As a rule, the motor area appears to be very stable there. The stimuli connected with some affective situation do not produce any noticeable motor disturbances, though they may provoke some vegetable symptoms. We had an opportunity to observe a number of traumatic subjects who have committed serious crimes and we have recorded their behaviour in experimental surroundings. We invariably observed with them a picture of acute reactions connected with the situation of the crime, their motor area at the same time remaining quite stable; we were able to reconstruct that picture in our tests with "unaccepted suggestions."

We have dwelt here in some detail on two questions we believe important for the understanding of the affective mechanics.

Their study, with the help of constructing artificial complexes, has shown that the affective processes occur neurodynamically quite near to the motor area, that their insulation from the consciousness is at the same time connected with the insulation from the motor area, and with the passing of the affect into a latent state, from which state it can be evoked with the help of stimuli reconstructing the affective situation. We have observed that the barrier insulating the affective complexes is broken when the complex becomes active; the motor storm which we have observed brings us back the picture of a diffused excitement, which we had occasion to see during the most acute affects.

Finally, we have come to the conclusion that the most important phenomenon in the affective process is connected with the mechanics of the conflict, by which the affective experiences of the personality differ markedly from the action of the simple external traumata.

We could show this only by reconstructing, within an experiment, the situations in which we were interested. It is quite obvious that we should follow that course in order to obtain further data on the mechanics of disorganisation and on the organisation of human behaviour.

CHAPTER V

SOME GENERAL FEATURES AND MECHANICS OF THE AFFECTIVE PROCESSES

E VERY investigation proceeds in cycles, and the attempt to complete one cycle is at the same time an attempt to begin planning the problems of subsequent researches. This is the reason why we have the right to put this chapter about the general mechanics of the affective processes in the middle of the book; it begins the analytical parts of the investigation and also completes the synthetic parts. On the other hand, precisely this leads us to omit the usual long generalising portions of the investigations and to concentrate our attention only on the special details necessary for the continuation of the work in hand.

This we shall proceed to do, with the understanding that our rough generalisations are made with the purpose of defining the problems more exactly.

1. THE PROBLEM OF THE AFFECTIVE SYMPTOMS

WHEN we began analysing the neurodynamical basis of the affective processes by our application of the motor method we had many doubts in regard to the psychological facts. It appeared to us, "if the subject is really in a state of affect his hand trembles." Does this evident fact reveal material for investigation?

We believe that this can be answered in the affirmative, and we decided that the establishment of the principle lying at the basis of this fact defends our position. In the subject in the state of affect the hand trembles—this much is obvious. But in order to establish laws for some of the psychophysiological phenomena of the affective processes from this fact required not one but many years of investigation.

The generalisation proceeding from the results we obtained may be justifiably commenced with some critical work, which indicates that the matter is by no means as simple as one might like it to be. The hands of the subject experiencing the affect do not always tremble, and in order to bring out this fact it is necessary to have very specific conditions. This was taken as our starting point, and we attempted to discover the laws which are manifested in the motor destruction of the neurodynamics of the affective processes. Experiments showed us that the motor disturbance does not always appear in the subject experiencing the affect, and that to include in parenthesis *all the movements* observed during the affect is unconditionally incorrect.

The affective process itself is by no means equally related to all the stages of human activity, but it is connected with special functional zones and it itself requires analysis.

Psychophysiologists studying affect were nearly always very much inclined to localise the affective processes in a special neurological system. Some suppose that the affect has its existence in the sympathetic nerve chains and that it can be detected in the symptoms connected with the activity of this system. Hence the continued and complete attention which the psychologists gave to the study of the symptoms of respiration, pulse, psychogalvanic reaction, distention of the blood vessels, etc. Other authors tended to the view that in order to see the existing mechanism of the affect in the disturbance of the cortical processes it was well to devote more consideration to the phenomena of consciousness, the flow of association, etc.

We have already mentioned that there are two contradictory schools of psychology, one of which inclined to the central origin of emotion and the other to the peripheral. In spite of this, the history of psychology until now has given us investigations dealing only with the objective study of affect through the study of the peripheral symptoms, and following this method have been even those psychologists who did not accept the view that affect is a state in which the normal course of our concepts is disturbed (Wundt). The researches of the Wundt and Lehmann's school took as a basis of such symptoms the fluctuations in the respiration and pulse. Many authors, as for example, Landis, attempted to investigate affect by a study of the phenomena of mimicry; another group took up the psychogalvanic changes. In all these investigations, upon which an enormous amount of labour has been spent, we have to admit that the results are not uniform, and the symptoms of the affective states and their structure are very differently described by different authors. Probably the widest divergence is seen in the attempts to evaluate affect by the change in the respiratory and cardio-vascular symptoms. Even recent views, as for example O. Löwenstein's, devote much attention to the divergencies in the evaluation of the physiological symptoms of such states as negative emotion (*Unlust*). Authors disagree markedly in the evaluations of the symptoms of the various emotional states, and the recent works dealing with the classical views frequently reject the facts that were previously considered to be indisputable.[1]

We have before us a series of contradictions, confirming our view that in the face of undisputed facts obtained by various investigators we should seek for the error in the general methodologies by the use of which these facts are collected and thought out. We believe that the chief error consists in this, that the majority of the authors were inclined to see always in the affective processes a functional connection with a special stable system (often even morphologically strictly defined). Precisely therefore the authors expected to see the affect always expressed by definite symptoms, and obtaining facts which were varied and contradictory they fell into confusion, often ending with the belief that in the chaos of disorganisation it was not worth while to look for any constant relations and laws.

We take just the opposite position. In the revealed unstable affective symptoms we see a result of this, that the *affect is each time a function of a dissimilar structure,* that the symptoms of destruction we study are parts of dissimilar units, and that we should seek for the neurodynamical laws of affect on the basis of the conception, which discounts these dynamic peculiarities.

In the neurodynamical analysis of complexes and traumata we have already shown that the symptomatic affect depends upon the integrated setting of the personality, upon that structure in which is included the reaction to the affective stimulus which we present. Later we shall try to show that the analogy to a static machine must give way to other dynamic conceptions, within which the affective processes are revealed as perfectly law obeying.

The detailed analysis of the affective processes should not proceed from the mechanism of the affect and a morphological system; rather it must be based upon a detailed analysis of the dynamics. Having obtained marked affective symptoms at certain dynamic levels, we must not be surprised if we should observe a subdued picture with completely different affective components in others; we should likewise be prepared to see the affective state

[1] See the work of Kaelas concerning the Wundt school, *The Question of the Nature and Expressions of Emotion,* Psychological Review, I, 3-4, 1918.

in certain settings of the personality have its expression in the
vegetative symptoms; in others, in the cortical. All this does
not speak for the absence of law in the given processes, but for
the varieties of their dynamic structure. The psychologists concerned with the mechanisms related to personality must see their
real problem precisely in the study of these labile structures.

The matter, however, is a little more complicated than we have
just indicated. It would be well to limit the assertion, that in
different cases the affect is expressed now in the vegetative
symptoms, now in the connections of the cortical activity of the
motor symptoms. The "voluntary" motor system does not reveal
the same affective symptoms in the same way in all situations,
and we can state that only under strictly definite conditions have
we the right to expect an appearance of the motor symptoms
of affect.

We shall briefly attempt here to explain all of the material
which we have already given in part.

2. THE CONDITIONS OF MANIFESTATION OF THE AFFECTIVE SYMPTOMS AND THE PROBLEM OF THE SYSTEMS OF EXPRESSION

EVEN when a person is in a more or less acute affective state,
the different motor systems reveal the affect in unequal degrees.

One may think, however, that morphological conditions—the
connection of different motor systems with dissimilar parts of
the nerve apparatus—do not play a decided rôle here. During the
affect, as a matter of fact, the gait may be changed as well as
the movement of the hands in lighting a cigarette, and it can
be shown that only the great differentiation of the motor systems of the hand or of the face is the cause of their unusual
expressiveness.

We take a different point of view; we believe that the degree
of expressiveness of that or another system *depends not so much
on its anatomical position as upon its inclusion in one or another
complicated psychological structure.* Therefore one and the same
motor system can be either expressive or unexpressive, depending
upon what function it is fulfilling at the given moment and to
what psychological structure it belongs. If, for example, the foot
system is ordinarily the least expressive, then this is because it
is ordinarily the least connected with the higher cortical processes
and the least included in those psychological structures which

have the property of maximal labileness and are of maximally conflicting character.

We may at once state that the expressiveness of the motor system is greater, the more it is included in a conflicting system, and on the other hand, it becomes less, with the diminution of its functional connection with the conflict in the personality at the given moment. The expressiveness of the system is conditioned, consequently, not by its morphological but by its *functional* situation. Many very simple experiments compel us to draw this conclusion; they show that in dependence upon different psychological inclusions, one and the same motor system may express the affect in varying degrees. In order to assure oneself of this, it is only necessary to register in one and the same subject, who is in a state of fairly acute affect, a series of hand movements some of which are included in a complicated and conflicting system of psychological operations, some others of which remain isolated. The experiment shows us at once in what degree the expressiveness of one or another system depends upon the functional factors which we have mentioned. We shall bring forth a considerable body of material bearing witness to the correctness of our point of view: in even the most acute cases of disturbed affect the simple movements of the hand, not connected with any complex psychological problems, usually proceed without marked symptoms of destruction, while at the same time the movements included in the complicated psychological structure show a sharply distorted affect.

In a large group of cases we tested out this view, which now seems to us indisputably correct: even the most marked affective states cannot be expressed in motor processes which do not require a preliminary restraint of excitation and *permit a direct manifestation of motor discharge*. This principle can be seen very clearly and investigated in the most primitive movements of an impulsive and direct nature; it is precisely these which remain the least involved in the state of affect, and on the contrary the maximal destruction usually falls on the details of the given motor system in those cases, when it appears, included in the complicated structure requiring preliminary inhibition of the direct impulses and of an already complicated organised response. The comparatively regular character of the primitive motor reaction in the state of affect parallel with the destruction of the complex motor function can be explained precisely by the restoration of the diffused character of the excitation and the destruction of the "functional barrier" isolating the excitation from the direct motor series, as we have mentioned before.

We shall give only one example, which, however, shows very clearly how unequally the affective processes are manifested at the various functional levels. We purposely cite the most marked case of the acutely disturbed affect which we have observed. In Figure 44 we give two series of reactions of the subject Fil., tested by us on the second day after he had committed murder and upon his entering into an acute affective state;[1] we have already observed in this case a continuous and striking disorganisation. From this fact we cannot draw a conclusion; the affect destroys every movement of the hand. It is sufficient for us to record those movements, but in a simpler functional stratum, removing them from the system of accompanying associations—before us there appears an entirely different picture: the same movements which were formerly included in the complicated intellectual structure gave a picture of complete disorganisation. This is registered at a lower level in an isolated form (independent rhythmical pressures). They give us nearly normal additional signs of the disturbed excitation and disorganisation of the neurodynamics. In Figure 44 we record the comparative facts which we have taken as an example of association, undifferentiated by the affective character.

This example shows only that the simple action carried over into the more complicated stages connected with its inclusion in the structure requiring an intellectual process, and the regulated motor impulses lead during the affective state to a complete disorganisation of the activity, and the destruction of those movements whose fulfilment at a lower functional level should certainly be possible.

The fact which we have formulated leads directly to the position we have defined before: the affective *disorganisation* of behaviour begins where the problem of cortical control by the direct diffusion of excitation arises (motor impulsiveness); it disappears where the action permits the direct motor discharge of impulses; the *affect* arises in the place where the conflict begins to be connected with activity.

We have accepted as proven the supposition that the simple rhythmical activity, uninhibited and direct, can occur without marked disturbance, even in the most severe affective states. We must, however, point out the limitations: this is true only when our basic conditions are maintained; the free rhythmical activity can appear without disruption only

[1] The details of this case are given in Chapter IV.

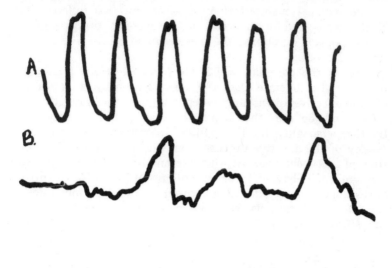

Fig. No. 44

SUBJECT "FIL." (MURDERER)

A. SIMPLE, RHYTHMICAL PRESSURE
B. SIMULTANEOUS PRESSURE OF THE ASSOCIATED REACTION

if it is deprived of its conflicting character, if the mobilised masses of excitation become converted without obstructions and are converted directly into rhythmical motor acts.

But just this situation is not always seen during the state of affect. One of the fundamental laws of affect is that every stimulus mobilises enormous masses of excitation, and that these masses quickly cease to be inadequate to those possibilities of discharge (their realisation)... the consequences of this usually appear as a series of symptoms, which allow us to see the traces of affect in the spontaneous rhythmical acts. The ordinary arhythmia of the spontaneous rhythmical movements arising in the state of affect gradually takes on a character of irregularity. This is an argument for the mobilisation here of an excessively large mass of excitation. The appearance of the most delicate symptoms, frequently the conversion of rhythmical movements into tetanoid forms, and the marked disruption of the usual form of the curves, proves that even on such a primitive level of activity the motor system frequently is not in a state to dominate the affect by the mobilised energies. In such a state our fundamental conditions disappear and even the primitive activity begins to be associated with that conflict causing its organisation.

The unequal manifestation of affect on two different functional levels and in different motor systems brings before us two important questions: the measurement of the affect and the affective types.

Already the material, which we have described above, gives us the right to state that the unequally marked appearances of the affective disturbances depend upon the strength of the affect, and, on the other hand, the degree of resistance offered by the personality to the conflict. In reality, precisely the intensity of the affective process itself and the degree of stabilisation of the behaviour of the personality determine in which stratum (of behaviour) the symptoms of the affective disturbances appear. A general examination of the symptomatology of the affect furnishes us with the material and its mechanisms; the stratified analysis of the motor disturbances gives us the basis of its *functional typology*.

The stratified analysis of behaviour becomes of particular interest in the study of the structure of neuroses. The single flash of the affect passes over into a constant labileness of the nervous system, a constant preparedness for the affective reaction, to the fundamental form of the disrupted behaviour. The affect passes over into a neurosis, and its psychophysiological investigation may open the path to an understanding of its structure. We have collected considerable material in the analysis of affects and complexes in the normal subject as well as in the psychiatric patient, chiefly cases of hysteria, which have not entered into our investigations. But it is this which convinces us of the correctness of the principle of the stratified analysis of affect. If in the normal, according to the constitutional labileness of the subject, the marked disturbance of the motor system appears, as a rule, every time we experience any affective complex, then in the hysterical patient the affective labileness of the neurodynamics is much deeper, and the diffusion characteristic of the affective state already reaches into a primitive stratum of activity, destroying those actions which occur perfectly normally in the person manifesting a more stable neurodynamics.

We have seen neurotics who psychophysiologically differed in the fact that the affective destruction appeared at different levels of behaviour; in some of them even the most primitive actions were destroyed; in others, the affect was reflected in the most complex acts associated with the deep conflict.

Such a stratified analysis of the behaviour of the person or neurotic in an affective state makes it possible for us to approach more closely to the structure of the disorganisation of the human behaviour and to the neurodynamics of the structure of neuroses.

There is no doubt that the neurotic whose behaviour is already disorganised on the lowest, most primitive levels of activity, and the neurotic whose behaviour shows the signs of disturbance only in the intellectual conflicts and affective traces—that these two cases have entirely different neurodynamical structures of their personalities.

The stratified analysis of the affect brings us to the problem of the disorganisation of behaviour, to the problem of the stable and of the easily disorganised personalities. We began with a description of the symptoms of affect, we discussed its mechanism, and we should conclude with the problem of typology and pathology of the behaviour of the personality. We shall also give more of this material in Chapter IX.

3. PSYCHOPHYSIOLOGY OF THE AFFECTIVE SYMPTOMS

WE have shown that the marked disturbances in the motor system occur every time that the movements studied by us fall directly into the sphere of affect; we have come to the supposition that these disruptions arise precisely because the cortical apparatus is not in a condition to dominate the masses of excitation in the affect, and the movement unavoidably takes on an excitatory and destructive character.

The affective processes break up, disorganise the regular neurodynamics of the activity, creating, in the accompanying motor curves which we have been studying, the characteristic motor chaos. The observer can justly raise the doubt: Is this chaos capable of being studied?

We shall try to show that behind this motor chaos lie certain definite laws, and that these laws are a property of the neurodynamics of every affective process. The finding of the laws existing in the disorder, the principle behind the chaos confronting us, is a most difficult and a most unfavourable scientific problem; but is not precisely this a quality of every scientific investigation?

We have taken a subject of our own study of affect, this process of chaotic excitation *par excellence;* we shall try, however, to establish several laws, admitting beforehand our humble pretensions.

The observations on the neurodynamics of the affective states always lead us preeminently to the fact of the *destruction of the higher automatisms*. Then, what was perfectly accessible and simple to attain in the normal state proved difficult and wellnigh impossible to establish in the state of affect. American

authors are inclined in such cases to say that the organism has
lost the ability to produce the standard forms of reaction (reaction patterns); we speak of the destruction of all the regulating
forms of behaviour.

The facts with which we are concerned show this very clearly.
A person who when calm very readily gave stable associated
reactions, standard for that time, during the affect completely
lost this ability and began to react with great irregularity and
with sharp fluctuations in the reactive times. The curves of distribution of speed of the associative reactions, the regularities
in the normal and the chaos in the disturbances of the affect
show how deeply characteristic of the affect are these processes
of disorganisation. The analysis of the accompanying motor reactions, which we have described in the preceding pages, actually
brings us to the same conclusion: instead of regularities in the
organised reaction there arise in the affective state movements
which have lost their regularity and standard character: the
motor reactions do not fit one with the other, lose their similarities, the higher automatic process becomes changed into separate, disrupted, partial movements. The organism ceases to
produce movements agreeing with formerly elaborated "reactive
standards." The destruction of the higher automatisms is a characteristic symptom of affect.

If such a destruction of the higher automatisms is really characteristic of the affective state, then what are the factors behind
these phenomena?

There are two possibilities: either the destruction of the higher
automatisms depends upon the weakening of those very complicated, supporting and regulating psychological functions, or the
character which is subject to the regulating processes actually
changes and becomes much more difficult to regulate.

We have the facts which show that both of these processes
participate here; we are at a loss to say which of these is the
primary one. Further investigation indicates that they are both
causative factors in all probability. For the present we shall
analyse them according to their relation to the psychophysiological problem in hand.

The structure of the affective reaction always demands attention by virtue of its excitability; the first makes an impression
by virtue of that disorganisation which characterises the affective behaviour, and this we can see in each of the adduced
examples. The excitability of the affective behaviour will be
used as our starting point in the analysis.

To what neurodynamical facts can this affective excitation be related? There are at least two groups here, and we shall describe them in detail.

We have good reason for thinking that the affect prepares all the excitation to proceed directly to its motor affect, immediately to call out the motor symptoms. This tendency is reinforced by the fact that precisely in the affect the regulating systems usually manifest some weakness and cease to inhibit special "accidents" not corresponding to the given setting of the impulse.

If we compare the behaviour of a person who is quietly concentrated on his work with the behaviour of another during an affective experience, the specific structure of the affective behaviour will be obvious.

The quietly working process is characterised by an organised preparedness of the "reactive formulæ," the organised choice of movements; and the superfluous and unnecessary movements drop out; the foreign excitation usually does not evoke any motor impulses whatever; the complicated problems which do not operate with ready responses generally evoke a protective inhibition, going on into confusion of thoughts, and during this time all movements are inhibited, and afterwards the excitation is connected with the motor system.

The affect usually gives a picture which is the exact reverse of this: the higher automatisms, so stable in the setting of quiet work, disappear because the person is not in a condition to inhibit any one of his movements; each impulse leads directly to the series of motor symptoms, and continuously fills in completely all the intervals previously occupied by the organised activity. If we say that the affective person cannot be calm, this means, firstly, that he is not in the state to inhibit the beginning excitation, that his reactive processes are of a diffused character, and the barrier separating excitation from its direct transformation into movement is particularly weakened.

Those impulses which are usually manifested in external movements only after their preliminary elaboration and choice, diffuse in the affective subject into the direct motor system, and it is perfectly obvious that such a structure of the reactive process does not create any chaos in its behaviour.

The diffuseness of the reactive process in the affective state leads to a whole series of specific mechanisms, and it is expressed in several laws characteristic for affective behaviour. These have already been given in detail, and we shall now dwell only on some of them.

1. The law of the catalytic action of the stimulus especially characterises that preparedness of the excitation for a direct motor disturbance which we consider typical of affect. This means that in the acute affective state, when the language stimulus is given to the subject, that, instead of evoking a complicated associated process with which the motor reactions have been connected already, there is a catalytic action, causing a direct motor destruction not connected with the associated activity and clearly an expression of the symptoms of the excitation characteristic of the neurodynamic subject.

We have such a peculiar *Kurzschluss* in all cases of affect. This we have already described in the situations of people taking school examinations and in criminals. We were able to observe this phenomenon also in the normal subject during an acute affect. The participation of the maximal excitation, as a rule, affords us the best example of the manifestation of catalytic action of the stimuli. This is shown especially clearly in the examination of neurotic subjects whose affective setting takes on a permanent character.

In Figure 45, we submit two curves taken from our protocols and representing the motor reactions accompanied by the associated responses. The curves come from our experiments dealing with extremely excitable hystero-neurasthenics; the chief curves obtained previously (see Figure 27) contain analogies from other cases. All these curves are strictly typical; they are all constructed according to the same form. In every case the stimulus given to the subject causes a direct motor discharge, entirely spontaneous and isolated from the associated structure. In the first case, the impulsive pressure is immediately inhibited and the final motor reaction is given during the associative response; in the second, the direct impulse appears with the same sharpness; but its inhibition spreads to its passive portion and the whole latent period becomes filled with tonic pressures. The catalytic character of the action of the stimulus is in both cases fairly clear. The last example taken from the experiment with the criminal, and shown in Figure 27, manifests the same mechanism of this process; we see that the free intervals between the reactions are characterised here by spontaneous impulses, which is evidence of the general latent excitation. These symptoms are especially definite in the zones where the excitation leaves its affective traces (such a zone as this is seen after reaction No. 34). The stimulus following the spontaneous impulses acts in a markedly catalytic way, conditioning the direct motor disruptions; the neurodynamic connection between this disruption and the disturbed excitation is likely any minute to be itself destroyed upon the slightest stimulus which may appear.

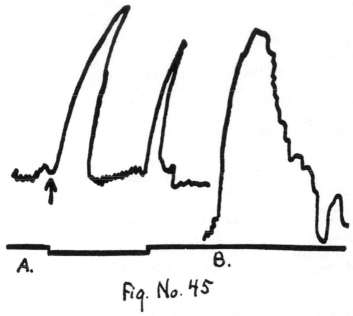

Fig. No. 45

A. SUBJECT GIST. (NEURASTHENIA)   B. SUBJECT ROZ. (NEURASTHENIA)

A series of experiments shows that in the state of affect every stimulus can have a catalytic action; this is especially marked in the stimuli which call out a direct disruption, according to the contents of the affective character. Here the stimulus presented produces a marked irregularity of the excitation and an especially intensive motor discharge. The examples given above in the majority of cases belong to this category; and on this principle are constructed the motor complex reactions.

The catalytic action of the stimuli is not, as a rule, limited to the motor system, but spreads into the speech reactions. Those cases of impulsive responses with subsequent speech excitation, which we often obtain in the affective state, usually owe their origin to this fact. Here the stimulus produces a tendency in the subject to a direct motor excitation and speech discharge which is given even before the subject is in a state capable of forming associations; the consequent signs of the language conflict become quite comprehensible.

We think that this impulsiveness and diffusion of excitation explain many things about the character of thinking during affect. Those *Kurzschlüsse* which are so typical of affective thinking have precisely this neurodynamical base: the constant preparedness to reactions, the inability to inhibit the process in the preliminary stage, not allowing its manifesta-

THOUGHT IN
AFFECTIVE
STATE

tion, and finally the impulsive judgment made suddenly and under the influence of external stimuli—these are the fundamental signs characterising the thinking of the person during the state of affect and the partial thinking of the hysteric. Although we shall not consider in detail the specific peculiarities of the higher psychological mechanisms undoubtedly playing a rôle here, in the psychophysiological analysis we are inclined to connect the indicated peculiarities creating the primitive nature of the thinking in these cases, precisely to the diffuse structure of the reactive processes.

2. The law of the decreased action of the functional barrier relates to the same group of principles; it appears especially well marked in the characteristics of the neurodynamics of the latent period of every complex reaction. At the same time as in the normal state, each reaction precedes some inhibition of all the impulses, and finally their appearance is connected only with the last response—the structure of the affective reaction is somewhat different. The preliminary impulses, as a rule, not only are not inhibited here until the final preparation of the reaction, but they often fill up the whole latent period, extending into the disrupted excitation. The structure of the reaction is transformed from a quiet one into an excitatory disorganisation; from a differentiated reaction into a diffused one.

In every reaction we can see such a diffusion, the excitatory affective traces and the subsequent affective character. It is enough to glance at any of the curves previously given—whether they are curves of the affective reactions of students during examination, or of criminals awaiting trial, or the reactions connected with suggestions given during hypnosis—in all these we see one and the same picture: the stimulus evokes a certain reactive process; this reactive process passes over soon in a diffused manner into the motor area, producing marked deformations of the motor curve which can be seen in the whole series of the pressures—sometimes organised, sometimes disorganised, but filling up the whole latent period.

In all these cases, the centrally originating excitation produced by the affective traces and connected with the preparedness to the reaction (the attempt to find the associative response, the choice of the necessary association) is directly connected with the motor system. In this way the reactive process in the affective person is sharply differentiated from the structure of the normal reaction, where often even a very prolonged search for an adequate response arises altogether centrally, not extending into the motor system and not producing any motor symptoms. Such a separation of the preliminary process from the extension into the motor system is one of the most interesting peculiarities of the normal reactive process. Precisely this makes us think that several organised mechanisms, some "functional barrier" restrain here the previous excitation from entering into the motor system. What is the result of the mechanism of this barrier is the question which we shall take up again later: [1] now we are limited to the fact that it exerts an influence in every normal reaction and that it is weakened in the affective state. We find it, therefore, very useful to describe the properties of the affective neurodynamics in the terms of a decreased "funtional barrier" and of the excitation connected with a direct transference into the motor area.

Two factors create especially favourable circumstances for the manifestation of the affective symptoms which we have described. The general affective excitation is produced every time that a stimulus impinges with any potent trace in the psyche of the subject, and the motor setting which is called out in the subject by the conditions of our experiment. Therefore, it is obvious why the symptoms of the diffuse excitation are able to permeate so easily into the system of movements recorded, and our material contains a number of cases of motor disturbances, many of which are built upon precisely this scheme of the uninhibited "barrier" of the impulses.

The most marked and constant pictures of similar disturbances are found in states of neurosis—in those cases in which the affective processes from sporadic reactions become permanent forms of the behaviour of the personality. The actual involuntary impulses, filling up the latent period of the reactions, may be considered especially pathognomonic of hysterical states, in which the marked excitability and the weakness of the "functional barrier" evidently play the deciding rôle.

In Figure 46 several examples of the affective reactions in neurasthenics are given and all of these are arranged according to one type. The beginning central process seen in the adequate reaction produces a considerable delay of the latent period, and the impulses merging over into the motor system fill in this interval with sharply defined reactions, stratified one upon the other.

The picture is usually complicated still more by a series of secondary symptoms which the subject tries to inhibit, and to prevent going over into the motor system, the result is a sharp conflict in the motor area. Subsequently, we have an acute patho-

[1] For details of this see especially Chapter XI.

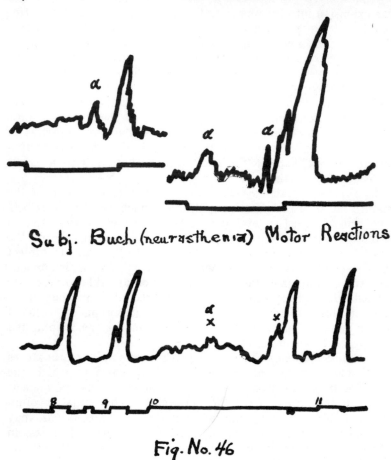

Fig. No. 46

TYPICAL CASE OF THE ACCOMPANYING MOTOR CHANGES IN NEURASTHENIA

logical tremor appearing here as the equivalent of the inhibited excitation. The curves in Figure 46 illustrate this typical relation. Frequently the motor disruption appearing here reinforces the inhibition, and the inhibition evokes the disturbed tremor in the whole curve. Now we see the conflict again and the delay of the adequate reaction, in the source of the symptoms characteristic of affect (as we shall point out further on) as well as in the source of the affect itself.

The lowering of the "functional barrier" during the state of affect and neurosis becomes in this instance especially "energetic." This fact, which we shall refer to again in the description of our method—the fact of the motor reflection of the hidden, inhibited, speech associations—is manifested very sharply just here, in the affective state. Now we are able to see how every thought in the brain, every manifestation in the test-reaction immediately provokes organised movements of the accompanying system and reflects the unexpressed speech associations. We see this symptom in a marked degree in criminals, and in them it becomes especially tragic: the association coming into their minds frequently is of a compromising character, and for this reason it brings about inhibitions; however, the motor reaction of the hand appears the first thing, and one of the most marked of such inhibited associative links in the "crucial" cases here is this obvious compromising symptom.

The inhibition of the "attempt to react" is distinguished by its form from the spontaneous impulses which we have described. Usually they are completely organised according to their character, and are differentiated from the internal inhibitability, which is shown in their connections with the central intellectual processes; in view of this they have lost their impulsiveness of form, but this peculiarity is apparent in the lowering of the barrier and the ease with which the excitation passes over into the motor area. This last characteristic is the subject of our analysis.

4. THE LAW OF THE MOBILISATION OF THE INADEQUATE MASSES OF EXCITATION

THE property which until now we have attributed to the affective neurodynamics is, in substance, a negative one. We limit this statement by the fact that the affective states are distinguished by a lowering of the ability to isolate excitation from the motor area, by the diffused quality of the excitation; but these factors are insufficient to explain the disturbed neurodynamical affect. We must show further whence arise those acute ruptures of the excitation, that excessive expenditure of energy which we observe in the motor storm during the affective reactions.

To explain the positive nature of the affect and to show with sufficient finality what are the sources of this energy supplied to the affect means the solution of this riddle. We do not intend to do this in the present pages; this would mean the changing of our problem to a much broader and purely physiological one. We should like only to draw some general conclusions from the empirical facts in the investigations.

There is no question about the fact that every affective stimulus mobilises inadequately a great mass of excitation. The specificity in the structure of the affect consists precisely in that the activated mass of excitation is so great that the reaction given by the subject is not able to dominate this excitation, and the latter spreads over into the furthermost processes, destroying their normal course.

The affective focus, as a rule, is never limited by the frontiers of the given reaction; almost always every affective process starts off the whole stream of disturbances, which are not infrequently manifested most acutely after the reaction to the given stimulus. The more acutely the focus is irritated by the given stimulus, the greater the probability is that we may expect that the evoked excitation will not be responded to, but that we will obtain a very marked neurodynamical perseveration.[1]

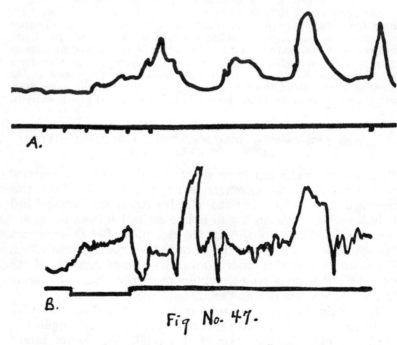

Fig No. 47.

A. SUBJECT FIL. (MURDERER) 27. CLOTHING 7.0″—"WELL BOOTS...I DO NOT KNOW." 28. BUTTER—2.4″—MILK.
B.   MO-OWA.   THE REACTION TIME IS INDICATED BY THE HEAVY LINE. 59. DAMP—3.6″—MORPHIA.

In Figure 47 we give two examples of an acute affective perseveration. The first of these delays comes from the record of the experiments on a criminal.[2] The acutely affective stimulus ("clothing"—burned by the subject after he had committed the murder) immediately provokes in him motor excitation, which,

[1] Perseveration = senseless repetition of an idea, phrase or act.—*Translator.*
[2] The details of this are given in Chapter II, Section 5, of this book.

however, does not subside after the response, and during the course of the whole period we see many spontaneous pressures, appearing evidently as fragments of the excitation not neutralised in the reaction; this same phenomenon in a labile nervous system gives us a more distinctive picture. As is our custom, we search in such a case for the neurosis.

In Figure 47B we have the reaction of a hysteric in whom the stimulus has a marked affective character. To the word *mokrui* (damp) she responds with the reaction "morphia." This evidently not only did not neutralise the process of excitation in this patient, but it secondarily started off a new affective complex; the subject M. was a morphine addict who strove energetically to overcome this vice and also to conceal it. As a result we see a rupture of the excitation, a motor storm, manifesting itself with an acuteness unprecedented for even this patient.

The neurodynamical perseveration is one of the most stable symptoms of the affective reaction; its mechanism is this: the stimulus evokes inadequately a large mass of energy in which the speech stimulus is incapable of producing a reaction. The facts we have brought forth show that back of this phenomenon of the succeeding motor excitation there may be concealed mechanisms of various complexities. Most often the affective stimulus calls out such a quantity of excitation that it cannot be responded to by the subject in a single verbal reaction. The subsequent disturbances observed in this case are the fragments of the process; in other cases the subject starts off a new affective wave having its own reactions; the excitation characterised by perseveration is here of a secondary nature and it becomes very extensive, particularly in view of the absence of any adequate discharge for this wave.

The affective tantrum arises here, as formerly, in those cases where any strong excitation does not find its adequate reaction and leads to inhibition. We come again to the mechanism of the conflict at the source of the affect.

5. THE PROBLEM OF THE RECIPROCITIES OF THE EXPRESSIVE SYSTEMS

WE shall discuss here another problem having to do with a new phase of the mechanics of the affective processes—the reciprocal relations of the expressive systems.

In our method we make use of several expressive systems,

hoping to find therein those symptoms relating to the affective processes of interest to us. As we generally employ the language stimulus we have recorded the speech reaction, accompanying this with an active reaction of the right hand and the simultaneous passive curve of the left hand. Sometimes as a supplement and control we combine this with a record of the respiration.

Notwithstanding the fact that two fundamentally fixed lines were applied to two homologous, synthetic extremities, the psychological significance of both of these curves was completely different. During the time that the pressure of the right hand was actively associated with the speech reaction, making up, so to speak, a unified structure, the passive curve of the left han represented functionally, as it were, a peripheral stratum in which the conflicting processes occurred.

Naturally from such a structure of the expressive symptoms we might expect a maximal reflection of the affective process in the one which was actively connected with the conflict in the speech area. With this in view we devised our method, hoping to obtain in the passive curve of the left hand, only some reflections of those active processes which occurred in the right.

However, does the transference of the disturbance to a passive system disclose any psychologically interesting laws, or can we expect here a more or less accidental picture, when the reflection of the active storm appears now here, now there, in the general neurodynamical setting?

The elements of the motor connections are already contained in every normal movement. Figure 48 gives a typical section of the curve of the synkinesis.[1]

This fact, of itself interesting to many physiologists, will serve us as the subject of special analysis. We would sooner accept it as a primary fact and turn to the question of what occurs during synkinesis, when the active curve of the right hand begins to show marked affective symptoms.

It is impossible to think that the increased excitation in the active hand gives us an increased synkinesis; this follows from all the laws connected with the problem of the reciprocal relations between the expressive systems. The observations show, however, that the matter is somewhat different and more complicated.

The facts make us think that not only synkinesis, but a much more complicated reciprocity is at the basis of the extended

[1] Synkinesis = association of a volitional with an involuntary movement. —*Translator*.

associations of the excitatory process manifesting itself in the active system during affect. We never see, as a rule, during the affective states a marked positive synkinesis, occurring simultaneously with the disturbances manifested in the active system and appearing simply as their physiological echo. The marked affective synkinesis, undoubtedly plays a rôle here, but it does not arise from such positive accompanying movements.

Almost all the affective synkineses we are dealing with are not so much of a positive and associative character as they are

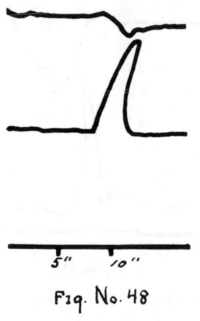

5"   10"

Fig. No. 48

compensatory and interfering. They usually appear where the activity of the functioning system is inhibited or diminished and are not so much synkinesis as they are a transference of the disturbance arising in the neurodynamical system.

In Figure 49 we give such an example of the coupling up of the affect; it is typical for almost all of our cases. The stimulus is presented to the subject, producing in him a marked affective reaction; the affect is reflected here at first in the system of the active hand producing a series of corresponding symptoms; after this, when the right hand has become quiet, we see a definite transference to the left hand, and the left-hand system, until this time passive, enters into a state of acute excitation.

We obtain the impression that the excitation, not finding for itself a path in the activity of the right hand, becomes connected with the free left hand and produces the disturbance there, where until the present there was no disturbance.

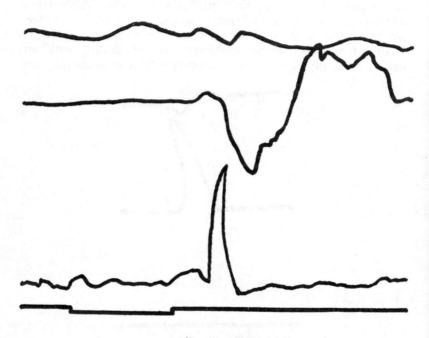

Fig. No. 49

SUBJECT KAR.   CHERVONETS [I.E. 10 RUBLES]—5.5"—DIRTY

Experimentally we are able to verify our supposition concerning the compensatory basis of this transference. In order to do this we must create a situation so that the increasing affect should occur simultaneously with the inhibited activity of the right hand; precisely here we might expect compensation of this limited rupture in the disturbance of the left hand and a transference of the excitation of the free passive system.

The experiment which we submit here is taken from a series which we have chosen from the second part of our investigations. To the subject under hypnotic influence we suggest that after awakening she think fixedly of two words, "red" and "blue" but that she will not be able to utter them. After awakening she was instructed to associate freely, accompanying each word with an active pressure of the right hand.

As expected, after several reactions the store of responses became exhausted, and she continuously approached that compulsive group of reactions which were at the tip of her tongue, but to pronounce which she was unable. There was created an acute affect connected with the impossibility of continuing the series begun. Here we obtained favourable conditions for the observation of how the beginning excitation gradually is transferred to another system, which until this time had been passive. The other system now becomes involved in the activity.

Figure 50 shows us the whole process fairly obviously and with its consequences. At precisely that moment when the tension ceases to be discharged into the functioning activity of the right hand, there begins a transference of the excitation into the left hand; it steadily increases and finally overflows into an acute excitation of the left hand—until now rather quiet. The compensating character of the transference in this case is fairly obvious.

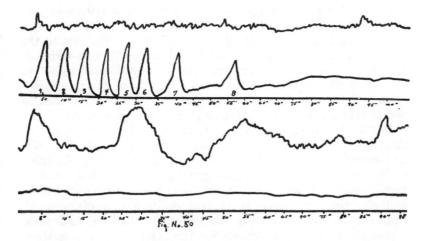

Fig. No. 50

SUBJECT KAR. THE TRANSFERENCE OF EXCITATION TO THE LEFT HAND DURING THE ASSOCIATION OF COLOURS (AFTER SUGGESTION)

1. YELLOW; 2. ORANGE; 3. GREY; 4. VIOLET; 5. GREEN; 6. GREY; 7. YELLOW; 8. BROWN...."I DO NOT KNOW ANY MORE."

A series of facts, brought forward by contemporary psychoneurologists, lead us to believe that under certain conditions the first of which is during inhibition of a voluntary activity, a tension of other systems may occur. And even more—one may conclude that many of the vegetative symptoms of affect have precisely such a secondary origin and are connected with the transference of excitation from the central nervous system to the autonomic. The interesting researches of Mysischev[1] were probably the first attempt to establish the reciprocal relations of the

[1] Mysischev: *The Reciprocal Relations of the Vegetative and Somatic Reactions*, Psychoneurological Science in the U. S. S. R. Report of the First All-Union Congress on Human Behaviour.

whole series of the most important expressive systems during the disruption of human behaviour.

The analysis of the reciprocal expressive systems indicate to us that the neurologically constant mechanisms (synkinesis) can under definite conditions obey other more powerful and more complicated laws, not of a static but of a functional nature. This analysis, however, brings us to several new problems connected with the dynamics of the affective processes and with the active relations of the personality to this dynamics.

6. THE DYNAMICS OF THE AFFECTIVE SYMPTOMS

WE have been considering the personality as a parade-ground where these various processes occur. In addition to this, though, it has a certain active setting, according to its relations to the affective reactions, and these settings can condition a series of symptoms which would remain otherwise incomprehensible to us. We should supplement the mechanics of the affective symptoms by looking on them from the point of view of those changes which take place in the active setting of the personality.

In all of our experiments we meet with the same situation: the subject is not especially inclined to express his affect openly, and every time during its manifestations he strives, according to his relation to the affect, to put up a certain defence reaction. Sometimes this reaction is strengthened by very definite motives: the criminal is in such a position that every manifestation is connected with the affective situation, and these traces are, therefore, dangerous for him. Thus we can understand our subject very well, when he applies all of his energy to suppress the compromising reaction coming into his mind and attempts to conceal the manifestation of the affective symptoms.

Owing to this active reaction of the personality to its affect, the process takes on a much more complicated character, it is reinforced from the side of the personality by a kind of "secondary elaboration," and we often obtain a product so distorted by the active strategy of the personality that its analysis may be far from easy.

Precisely this active character of the reactions of the personality to its affective processes means very interesting changes have occurred in the mechanics of the symptoms which we have studied, and allows us to approach to the analysis of several new mechanisms.

The active setting of the personality, according to its relations to the affective processes entering into the personality, can be expressed in two fundamental forms: the first, the attempt to suppress the manifestation of the affect, and secondly, the attempt to pass over it along other paths, as far as possible. These two forms of reaction constitute the basic means at the disposal of the strategical personality, which it usually manifests during the situations which we have been studying.

We shall examine them in detail.

In the course of all our investigations we have very rarely met with subjects who do not attempt to suppress, to inhibit the experimental affect called out in them. But we also have rarely seen in our cases people who were successful in doing this, or cases where the suppressed affect did not manifest itself by some objective symptoms.

We have a large number of experiments in which the suppressed affective traces are not of serious importance for the subject. With the criminals we come directly in collision with the most violent attempts to inhibit the symptoms of the affect; but even here this is extremely difficult.

Two circumstances make the complete suppression of the symptoms, so that no traces are left, almost impossible: first, the fact that all our experiments are measured by several expressive symptoms, and secondly that the experiment has to do with a whole series of successive reactions, following one on the other. The active inhibition of the affective symptoms always produces tensions, and it is quite natural that these tensions must be expressed either in one of the simultaneously recorded motor systems, or, if these paths are closed, by the course of the subsequent reactive processes. The active confusion of the personality does not remove by these means the existing symptoms, but it only introduces into them some modifications.

We have registered simultaneously three reactive systems: speech, the active reaction of the right hand, and the passive curve of the closed left hand. In these three indicators we have, properly speaking, the representations of three different strata of activity. It is evident that the chief attention of our subject is concentrated on the avoidance of the manifestations of the affect in the speech area (to avoid the compromising associations, etc.). In direct proximation to the chief system of activity is the functioning right hand, connected with the speech process and reflecting the neurodynamical changes arising in this basic system; the passive left hand, not entering into the system of activity, remains on the outside, and constitutes a reservoir into which flows the fundamental changes of the active processes. In such a structure of the expressive symptoms we might expect that the inhibition of the affective symptoms actively manifested by the personality would be reflected primarily in the systems directly connected with this activity; we see the inhibition of the compromising speech reaction, and even perhaps the inhibition of the disturbance manifested in the functioning activity of the right hand. However, precisely in that moment when the excitation in the active system is inhibited we may expect in all probability the transference of the suppressed excitation to another system at the periphery of attention, and this we register in the movements of the left hand. We might expect the manifestation of the symptoms precisely in this system, especially because of its position (the hand hanging in the air, having only the fingers around the apparatus). We made it very sensitive to every change in the system of excitation, and we increased the probabilities in a high degree so that the tension would increase precisely in this direction.

We have every reason to expect, on the other hand, that the changed tension, coming about as a result of the suppressed affect, is manifested in the successive series of reactions; precisely in these cases we have the most favourable circumstances for perseveration, which was shown here not only as a reverberation of the existing storm, but as an acute rupture of the inhibited post-excitation.

The process of suppression, as we observe it, usually flows according to this scheme: one of the stimuli which we give the subject provokes in him an acute affective trace connected with the reaction and surrounded by an affective colouring; the subject suppresses this reaction and attempts to replace it by some indifferent answer; he subtitutes it by the first word coming into his mind which naturally is either some extrasignalising reaction to a stimulus of the surrounding medium, or a perseveration connected with his previous reactions. We obtain a "senseless answer" which on closer examination is either an extrasignalising response or perseveration, or finally, a simple echolalic repetition of the former stimulus.

C. G. Jung first described these associations in his classical work as signs of complex reactions; in further investigations they have been treated exhaustively.[1] Here we should like to

---

[1] C. G. Jung: *Diagnostische Associationsstudien* I-II, 1910. See also O. Lipmann: *Die Spuren der interessbetoten Erlebenisse*, 1911.

make note of the fact that these symptoms of the affective reaction, these primitive responses, occur simultaneously as aids of
the personality to bear the affective reaction, to put up a defence
against it, to control the appearance of the affect. We have shown
above that this attempt is partly successful; in the majority
of cases, however, the affective disturbances are not sustained,
but they pass over into other less-controlled systems, or else
provoke more severe consequent disturbances. The affect en-
dured by the subject, nevertheless, conditions a series of interesting symptoms. We shall illustrate these by appropriate cases.

Among our experimental criminals there was one who was threatened
with a severe punishment if the investigation established the fact of his
guilt. The subject "Drob." was suspected of the murder of his fiancée;
the girl was killed by a blunt instrument, the corpse was tied by wires
to a cast-iron wheel and thrown into the water, from whence after
some time the body was removed. "Drob." denied all participation in the
murder; when cross-questioned about the details he said nothing. When
brought in for the experiment he conducted himself with great assurance
and was highly discreet. Not one of the crucial reactions (to such
stimuli as "wheel," "wheel-barrow," "wire," "weight," etc.) gave responses
connected with the affective situation; the majority of them were of an
extrasignalising character. In the responses to crucial words the subject
gave ordinary reactions, entirely unconnected with him, and simply chosen
from the surroundings or from a previously existing associative series,
for example,

21. wheel-barrow—2.4"—oilcloth (extrasignalising)
40. wheel—2.2"—wheel (echolalia)
41. wire—1.6"—wire (echolalia)
43. weight—1.8"—weight (echolalia)

These primitive reactions, usually not met with in the subject, appear
every time that we touch upon the situation connected with the crime.
If we chose a list of all the words we gave provoking the primitive extrasignalising or stereotyped echolalic answers, they would nearly always
stand in direct relation to the situation of the crime. The accompanying
motor system gives us a situation, which, at first glance, is fairly calm
in all the cases. However, a closer analysis reveals an interesting picture.
Figure 51 gives us some of these reactions. Only in the first of the crucial
ones do we see a more marked excitation in the right hand; in general
the active pressures in the critical instances differ from the others only
a little. The symptoms, however, indicated in the specific excitation connected with these reactions take place in a less controlled passive system,
and we see how each critical stimulus (Figures 20, 30, 40, 41) is accompanied by an acute disturbance in the left hand, shown by an increase
of two or two-and-a-half times the usual synkinesis. This is repeated during the course of the whole experiment with great constancy, and it
can be only interpreted as an original linking-up of the connection with
the suppression of the direct manifestation of the affect.

The further analysis of the facts obtained in this subject show that
during the continued suppression the affective symptoms can be directed

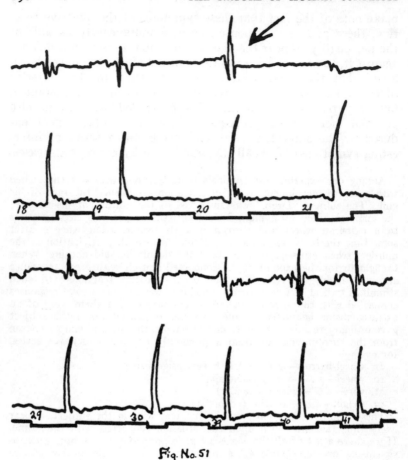

Fig. No. 51

SUBJECT "DROB"

18. foot—2.0"—I
19. paper—2.4"—family
20. *wheel-barrow*—2.6"—oilcloth
21. can—2.0"—my

29. plate—2.0"—knife
30. *tied*—1.6"—chair (extrasignal-ising)
39. plank—1.8"—pen
40. *wheel*—2.2"—I (extrasignalis-ing)
41. *wire*—1.6"—wire (persevera-tion)

even away from the accessory (passive) system; but then they appear with great acuteness in the subsequent part of the experiment, for only the portion of continuous inhibition was given. Here in Figure 52 is an example of such a case.

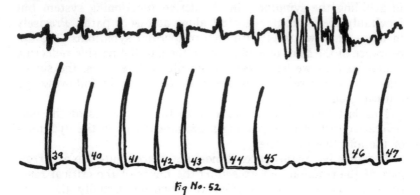

Fig No. 52

SUBJECT "DROB"

39. plank—1.8"—pen
40. *wheel*—2.2"—wheel
41. *wire*—1.6"—wire
42. forest—1.4"—forest
43. *weight*—1.8"—weight

44. nails—1.6"—nails
45. slave—1.4"slave
46. ————2.6"—silk
47. teeth—1.4"—teeth

Two of the tests with the crucial stimuli in the repetition of the experiment produce echolalia and the portion of the associated stupor which is expressed in the echolalic series of six reactions. We are inclined to think that we deal here more with the process than with the symptoms; actually all of these reactions give perfectly normal motor expressions. However, immediately after this participation we gave an increased interval and obtained an acute discharge (the experiment is the same in the passive system of the left hand), at once the equivalent of the affect which is accompanied by the inhibition we have investigated.

The conclusions we arrive at are of unquestionable interest for the study of the affective dynamics. The character of the affective symptoms certainly depends upon the nature of those reactions with which the subject responds to the given stimulus.

A completely frank reproduced affective situation in our experiments gives a definite series of symptoms; its reproduction connected with the conflict is in a large degree different from the original, and finally the suppression of the affective complex, the strife to put a defence against it, not to exhibit it, is a new alteration of the affective neurodynamics.

In the facts of our analysis we discussed only the symptoms connected with this latter situation. The lack of reactivity of the affective complex in the critical associative function, the suppression of the compromising response and its substitution by a neutral, confused one, does undoubtedly aid the subject

NOTION OF
OBLIGAT-
ORY DIS-
CHARGE

in avoiding the symptoms in the active functioning system but inevitably they become manifest along accessory paths. Precisely in these cases we meet with two primordial symptoms: the appearance of the signs of excitation in the parallel passive reflecting system and, as we have seen in the illustrative cases, the subsequent discharge reflected in the reactions directly following the critical group.

This last fact brings us directly to the mechanics of the perseverative disturbance, playing a prominent rôle in the dynamics of the affective processes.

The affective disturbances almost never are limited to a narrow part of the reaction, not exceeding the limits of the critical reactions connected with the affective situation. Usually they are spread far beyond these limits, and the material which we have had the opportunity to analyse gives us confidence in speaking of such an irradiation of the affective process.

Almost every experiment brings forth evidence of such a consequent disturbance of activity; the figures of the delayed reactive time which we have already given and the repetition of the motor disturbances in the cases of the post-critical reactions bear witness to the leading rôle played by the mechanism of perseveration in the dynamics of the affective reactions. The above-described laws of the affective mechanics show the presence of the large amount of the excitation remaining over from every affective reaction.

However, the character and limits of the perseverative disturbances are far from being equal in the different types of reactions in the subject. The frank repetition of the affect, as a rule, in the verbal reaction gives several, unreacted-to, affective complexes, and it is accompanied by only a comparatively insignificant perseveration having the character of a trace influence. On the other hand, those cases where the response of the subject is inhibitory but the affective reaction is suppressed give the maximal perseverated result which has the quality of a compensating discharge. The majority of cases of acute spontaneous impulses and the catalytic action of the stimuli has a bearing exactly here, and they are observed just after the frank reaction to the affective complex was suppressed.

The experiments repeated several times with one and the same subject make it possible to follow very easily the influence of the suppressed frank response to the subsequent course of the process. Often we meet with cases in which in one series of reactions to the given crucial word-stimulus there was ob-

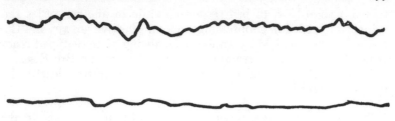

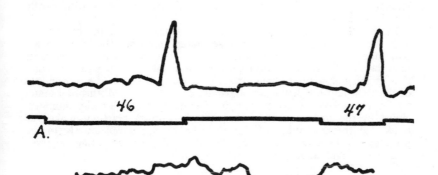

A.

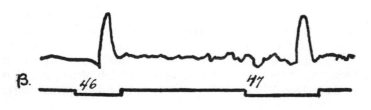

B.

Fig. No. 53

SUBJECT "ST."

46. to drag—4.8"—to drag   1.4" dinner (perseveration)
47. tongue—2.1"—mouth   5.0" tongue—meat

tained a sharply disturbed response, while in another series the subject succeeded in suppressing such an affective answer and the confusion was marked by an extrasignalising of stereotyped reactions. The consequent reaction varies widely in the two cases.

In Figure 53 we have a case which illustrates clearly the described mechanism.

The subject "St." was accused of the murder of a woman. In the first series of stimuli he was given the word "to drag," directly connected with the situation of the crime; his reaction is markedly delayed and there is considerable disturbance. For the ensuing motor curve there remain only slight traces, and the following reaction occurs with hardly any disturbances.

In the second experiment the stimulus is again given to the subject. This time he escapes from the perseverated response; the crucial reaction takes a normal neurodynamic course, but immediately afterwards there begins considerable disturbance in the respiration, and the presentation of the following stimulus produces a sharp break in the movements of the right and left hands accompanied by a clear cut disturbed character of the speech reaction. The indifferent character of the stimulus, giving in the first experiment a perfectly normal reaction, makes us think that the mechanism of this disturbance is referred exactly to the pathological discharges we have described—the compensating suppression of the frank affect during the critical stimulus.

The mechanism of the perseveration makes clear to us the neurodynamical mechanism, and we begin to see the conditions under which it occurs. When we make a detailed analysis of it we are able to differentiate in the phenomenon of the perseverated excitation two entirely separate forms, one based on the influence of the traces, and the other on the discharges as a result of the inhibition.

We investigated the symptoms of the affective processes in several cases; their study leads us to a description of several mechanisms characteristic of the disorganisation of human behaviour. In the course of all these researches we have become convinced that the destruction of human behaviour, as we observe it during acute affect, does not, by any means, represent an accidental, chaotic play of excitation and inhibition, but that behind the external chaos it is possible to discover several fairly constant laws.

We have come to the conclusion that affective states provoke in the psychophysiological picture of behaviour exceedingly serious modifications which often lead to a change of the very *structure of the reactive processes.*

The basic laws that we have established for affect give us the impression that the complicated organised structure of the reactive processes characteristic of the normal person are replaced here by a primitive diffusion. If in the normal state every excitatory process is reinforced until its linking-up with the motor area by some inhibition and central elaboration, then during affective states it manifests a tendency to pass over directly into the motor terminals, to extend into the motor area without being previously isolated from it. If anything is a specific quality of the neurodynamic affective processes, then it is precisely such a diffused structure of the functional barrier connected with the mobilisation of considerable masses of excitation inadequate for the stimulus. The separate symptoms of the affective processes, are, as it seems to us, derivatives of just this fundamental change. We have established here a law which seems to us very important. We came upon it in our experimentation as a result of natural affective disturbances.

Two serious questions arise here: First, what are those conditions that can produce a disturbance of the "functional barrier" and a transformation into a diffused structure of the reactive processes? What connections in the affect of the mechanism evoke these deep alterations in the behaviour of the personality and in its neurodynamics?

And on the other hand: Secondly, what are the results of the mechanism itself of the "functional barrier" and of that organisation of the reactions which are disrupted in the affect; when does it arise and under what conditions?

We come to a host of questions leading us from the affect in all of its concrete connections and details to a series of special questions of neurodynamics.

These we shall occupy ourselves with in the following parts of our investigation.

PART TWO

PSYCHOPHYSIOLOGY
OF THE CONFLICTING PROCESSES

CHAPTER VI

EXPERIMENTS WITH ARTIFICIAL
CONFLICTS

---

1. CONFLICT AND DISORGANISATION OF BEHAVIOUR

THE ANALYSIS of the material dealt with in the first part of the investigation convinces us that one of the fundamental mechanisms of the disorganisation of human behaviour is the mechanism of *conflict*.

Experiments have shown us that each time any active process increases, it augments the conflict and we obtain an acute discharge of the affective state which leads to disorganisation of behaviour and the destruction of the reactive process. Where there was no such internal conflict (we do not have such a case in the analysis of trauma) [1]—we usually do not find such active psychophysiological disturbances of the behaviour playing the deciding rôle in the acute affect.

Our material brings us face to face with a number of considerations which we will now summarise. Every activity represents by itself a complete act, a certain dynamic structure. This structure inevitably spreads to its limits, and the excitation which has been set in motion necessarily manifests the tendency to terminate in the motor system, finding its adequate motor expression in that reaction which we ordinarily record in the subject. If this dynamic structure discloses in one or another of its systems a fairly strong conflict, obstructing its adequate motor completion, the whole reactive system is disorganised; the excitation, not finding its organised exit, becomes spread out, destroying the activity of all the chief systems of behaviour. Precisely the presence of the conflict in our cases allowed us to analyse

---

[1] See Chapter IV, Section 4.

the disorganised behaviour and to establish some characteristics of its activity.

Our investigations with the affect, however, cannot be considered sufficient for the decision of the question concerning the structure and laws of the disorganisation of behaviour. The material outlines the problems, gives us certain data, but does not in any way solve them. A satisfactory and complete understanding of the process can be arrived at only by the path of a special investigation of those factors which lead to the destruction of human behaviour. If until this time we have followed along the path of the analysis of the complicated elaboration of complexes, then we should now go along the path of the synthesis of those same processes from the separate conditions, which the experimenter can vary according to his judgment. We have before us the problem of artificially creating a model of affective disorganisation, not operating once with any natural emotional tendencies, but producing it experimentally with the psychological mechanisms which in themselves are not connected with any affect or emotion.

Our problem is here analogous to the chemist's who takes a number of chemical processes and proceeds from them to known operations, synthetically obtaining new qualities. Precisely by such a path, not easy but still passable, we hope to obtain a clear conception of those conditions which produce a disorganisation of human behaviour, of those principles by virtue of which it is repaired, and of those forms which it takes. The problem before which we stand in this part of our investigation consists in the following: we will artificially produce in the activity we are studying definite and completely isolated conflicts, and attempt to show under what conditions these lead to a wide-spread disorganisation of human behaviour, to a model of artificial affect, of experimental neuroses. Such an artificially created model of the processes we have studied we are able to control and understand.

We are not the first of those who have artificially created disorganisations of human behaviour. A large number of facts pertaining to this problem has been contributed by contemporary physiologists, as well as by psychologists.

I. P. Pavlov was the first investigator who, with the help of exceedingly bold workers, succeeded experimentally in creating neuroses with experimental animals. Working with conditioned reflexes in dogs, Pavlòv came to the conclusion that every time an elaborated reflex came into conflict with the unconditioned reflex, the behaviour of the dog markedly changed. In the experiments of Erofeeva, the conditioned reflex was elaborated to an electrical stimulus. In this case it was sufficient that the conditioned food reflex collides energetically with an unconditioned defence reflex, in order to obtain an acute disorganisation in the behaviour of the dog: the dog began to bark, to become angry, and he manifested a marked irradiation of excitation. The experimenter is a witness of an artificially produced state which corresponds closely to the state of affect. Further experiments showed that, in order to obtain an acute rupture of the diffused excitation, it was necessary only to bring into collision two opposite conditioned reflexes; the conditioned reflex was elaborated to a circle, and then a differentiated inhibitory one to an ellipse—after this Shenger-Krestovnikova obtained a rupture in the "affect" when she brought before the dog a figure halfway between the ellipse and the circle. A similar result was seen in the experiment of Parfenov when he brought about the collision of a conditioned reflex with a conditioned inhibition, using as a differentiated inhibition a certain frequency of the metronome and giving this simultaneously with another frequency of the metronome which was connected with the excitation. The conflict of the two opposite tendencies inevitably produces here an acute disruption of excitation and of disorganisation of behaviour, which sometimes takes the form of a continuous, artificially produced neurosis.[1]

Although, in the experiments with the collision of the conditioned reflexes in animals, it is fairly easy to obtain acute forms of artificial affect, it is much more difficult to get those results in human experiments.

The most successful attempts to produce experimental conflict psychologically are seen in the experiments of M. Ach. He formed some fairly complicated habits, and when he had obtained a stable, perseverative tendency, he brought this into collision with another tendency determined by new stimuli or instruction. The result here was a confusion which, however, was overcome by a certain voluntary act. The tendency of the conflict in the experiments of Ach was too fluctuating and imperative to produce an acute affect; on the other hand, the author brings out facts of general interest having to do with the study of voluntary mechanisms rather than with the study of the mechanism of affect. However, in these cases it has been verified that if the "will" is dominated by the conflict of the tendency, then the conflict is potentially capable of producing an interesting disorganisation of behaviour, and only an insufficient activity of the tendency studied by Ach is the cause of the fact that this process was not called on sufficiently.

K. Lewin, in our opinion, has been one of the most prominent psychologists to elucidate this question of the artificial production of affect and of the experimental disorganisation of behaviour. The method of his procedure—the introduction of an emotional setting into the experience of a human, the interest of the subject in the experiment—helped him to obtain an artificial disruption of the affect of considerable strength. And in his experiments it is only rarely that the affect elaborated experimentally passes over into an actual living experience, and the subject begins to feel success in the experiment, just as he would feel success in life, in a very broad sense of the word.

Here the fundamental conception of Lewin is very close to ours.

---

[1] I. P. Pavlov—*Lectures on Conditioned Reflexes*, Chapters 17-20.

Every elaborated excitation manifests a tendency to a direct discharge (*unmittelbare Entladung*); obviously precisely the inhibition of this tendency, connected with a certain conflict, can produce an acute disruption of the affect and a series of new phenomena not hitherto observed. The closer the action is to realisation, the greater the affective disruption that can be provoked by its inhibition; the inhibition in this situation which is conditionally characterised, as the *Beinahe Entladung* naturally calls out the maximal disruption of the affect.

The experiments with the inhibition of the imperative process lead to confused activity, motor inquietude, and, finally, the complete disorganisation of behaviour, whether they are called out by external, artificial inhibition (interrupted activity—Ovsyankina, Isko), or the impossibility to find the decision of the problem (Dembo). In all these cases, the conflict appearing in a definite phase of activity leads to special forms of the disturbance of the ordinarily organised behaviour.

In our experiments we abandoned the plan of creating experimental conflicts in the same situation in which we usually observed the symptoms of affective disturbances. But this stimulated us to preserve the system of the accompanying intellectual motor acts ordinarily used in our experiments, and to call out certain conflicts in the intellectual system in order to investigate certain changes in the structure of the accompanying motor processes.

Such a system of experiments we introduced here not only with a desire to obtain results similar to those which we saw in the experiments with the acute natural affects; introducing the conflict into the definite leading system, the active system of speech, we obtained a destruction in that process upon which depends the whole structure of the act, and in particular the structure of the reflecting motor system. On the other hand we have, thanks to the complexity of the speech process, the possibility of producing the most varying fluctuations in the conflicts we have experimentally inserted into the psyches; without difficulty we can make the conflict greater or less, put it into the domain of the understanding or make it destroy the activity. In short, owing to this method, we have the freedom of experimentation which is a necessary condition of all worth-while experiments.

We begin with the basic forms of the conflicting processes, having described the mechanisms arising here, hence passing over to the study of the dynamics of the conflicting processes.

We choose two main types of cases in which the acute conflict may arise in the beginning activity; we conditionally name these the *conflict of the setting* and the *conflict of the defection*.

In the first of these, the conflict proceeds from two mutually exclusive tendencies; the experiments of Pavlov are constructed on this principle; the classical example with the situation of the Buridanov ass is the best example of such a conflict. The conflict of the setting can be obtained in any situation of choice, producing in the subject vacillations in the choice between definite possibilities; the more these latter balance each other, the more chances there are for an acute and dominating conflict. If, however, in this case the conflict is evoked in the sphere of purpose, then there is no special difficulty in transferring it to the sphere of activity. In order to do this, it is necessary to use the means employed by Ach, and having elaborated a definite, stable tendency, then to bring it into collision with another belonging to an opposing setting. The conflict of this kind is connected with the fluctuation here, as we can readily see, and daily experiments lead us to think that exactly here we may succeed in elaborating the mechanism of the affect.

The second of the cases is connected with the phenomenon of defection in the person in the face of some complicated fairly important problem. As in the case we have just described, this conflict reveals a very serious and deep-lying process, often constituting the basis of neuroses, and created in the experiment by a situation in which the subject's assurance of his ability to decide the problems comes into collision with his defection in the actual solution. In real life we might expect similarly to provoke a series of processes conditioned by the affective disorganisation of behaviour.

We shall not take up here the other possible cases, but shall begin with the analysis of the facts obtained in the experiment with these two kinds of conflicts.

2. EXPERIMENTS WITH CONFLICT OF THE SETTING

A. Preliminary trials

In our attempt to evoke a conflict of the setting from the very first we proceeded along a simpler path. In order to cause disorganisation in human behaviour we decided it would be sufficient to perform in the human an experiment similar to Pavlov's in the animal, in which he brings together two opposite reflexes or two motor activities.

We did several preliminary experiments in which the instruction about moving the hand upward was connected with one signal, and, vice versa, the instruction to move the hand downward was connected with another signal. Having elaborated these reactions, we gave stimuli to the subject at intervals (for example, after the stimuli "red" and "yellow" colors, and the intermediate colors, etc.), and we obtained almost unchanging negative results. Instead of the expected confusion and disorganisation of the reactive process, the subject reacts in another way; in lieu of the impulsive pressure he forms a link in the behaviour with speech, and begins to reason out the inhibition of his reaction and finally gives some organised response (for example, subsequently, making both movements or perhaps none). The difficulty here caused a reconstruction of the reactive process, but the inclusion of speech made it possible to overcome this difficulty by some organised path. Simple experiments on animals cannot be applied directly to the human, manifesting, as he does, more complicated means of adaptability, and the problem to produce the disintegration of behaviour with the help of a simple setting of conflict is not nearly so easy as we at first thought it would be. Obviously it should be necessary to create a more automatic setting which might not be immediately disrupted by the inclusion of the higher psychological mechanisms, that would allow us to obtain an active conflict sufficiently strong to produce a perceptible disturbance in the subject's neurodynamics.

We attempted to use automatic motor acts to produce this conflict by giving to the subject a definite speed of rhythmical motor reactions and then suddenly trying to change this rate when we gave a signal.

However, in these experiments it is not possible to see complete success. Notwithstanding a fairly considerable automatisation of the process, normal adult subjects master this problem very well, and at the moment of transference we found in these subjects not much disturbance. As might be expected, the transfer from a slow tempo to a quick one produced only a removal of the inhibitory delays and the realisation was accompanied rather easily; the opposite process of a sudden transfer from a quick to a slow tempo was much more difficult and was often connected with a continuation of the old quick tempo and with a certain struggle. However, considerable destruction of the behaviour could be observed in this situation only in subjects having a hyperexcitability of the nervous system and with considerable lowering of the mechanisms; [1] the regulation in our normal subjects is so well developed that the given situation is dominated by it without special difficulty.

[1] See Chapter IX.

Obviously the process of simple motor exchange of tempos is too labile, and one must use additional means to obstruct the transfer from one tempo to another. We can elucidate this problem in a fairly simple way. In order to do this it is sufficient to carry the conflict of tempo from the sphere of simple motor reactions to that of speech, and propose to the subject with maximal abruptness to change the tempo, not of simple rapping but of a complicated associative process, the tempo of which shows a much higher degree of inertia and which tolerates the changes with great difficulty.

We let the subject associate freely and rhythmically, saying every word that comes into his mind and accompanying each word by a pressure; according to the analysis suddenly presented to him the subject should quickly make the transfer to a different tempo. In this series the changing rhythms carry the disturbance in the movement of associative series, already having not an automatic character, but a differentiating definite structure and a much greater intensity; the trial to change abruptly the accepted tempo meets here a greater resistance, and inevitably causes a cleavage of the whole structure of the associative process.

The results which we obtain show that we have chosen the proper method. The marked disturbance of the tempo of a certain process, characterised by a definite structure and inertia, creates a perceptible conflict, which is reflected in the accompanying motor sphere in the form of a sharp disturbance similar in type to that obtained in the investigation of the affective and complex processes.

The instruction to change to a slow tempo produced a collision of the prepared response with a conditioned signal of inhibition, and the completely adequate and normal curves then commence to show a disorganisation, characterised by a tremor.

In our normal subjects we obtain such a result only in the case where the exchange of tempos was carried over into the structural, associated process; and we almost never obtain an acute conflict when such an exchange was brought about in the automatic process of simple rhythmical pressures.

Figure 54 shows that in the automatic peripheral process the subject quickly masters the transfer, but in the complicated structural activity he has much more difficulty and there results an acute expression of conflict. At first we obtain symptoms usually characterising those in the associative series of affects (loss of regularity in the form of the movement, the dispersed

tremor, the signs of acute excitation) by the production of purely
artificial, formal factors, not connected with the contents of the
reaction.

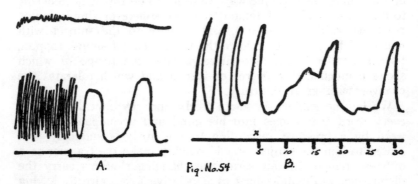

A.   Fig. No. 54   B.

EXCHANGE OF TEMPOS AND THE ACCOMPANYING REACTION

A. Subject R., exchange of tempos during tapping.
B. Subject Ands., exchange of tempos in a chain series. X = slow.

It is important to observe that the disturbance produced by the sudden transference is reflected in profound changes of the structure of the
current process, and the perceptible disturbance of the associative series
shows that the conflict led to a considerable rupture of a more complicated psychological process. It would seem that the simple delayed
associations do not represent any serious obstruction; in reality, however, the inhibition of the motor manifestation of the prepared reaction
inevitably leads to *a rupture of the internal structure of the reactive
process*.

The same "flattening" of the associative series which we usually saw
during affective states appears here every time that we suddenly inhibit
by a signal the tempo of association which the subject has accepted.
As a rule we obtain in these cases an interruption in the series, returning
to the former links and a considerable "flattening" of the associative
connections. Here is a typical case:

Subject B: theatre, bell—corridor— . . . curtain—music—organ—satis-
faction—bad humour—buffet—money (*slowly*)—bell—applause—return
—tram—work . . .

Subject Sol: ladder—window—whistle—scream—fall—(*slowly*) whistle
—passage—university.

In both of the given cases the delayed associative series produces disorganisation and a return to one of the former links; the further series
is considerably disturbed. We are inclined to see the explanation of this
in the fact that the last conflict in direct approximation to the motor
sphere (the inhibition of the preparation of the enunciation of the
word) *conditions the disturbance of the whole central structure of the
process*. We undoubtedly have here one of the most important mechanisms
lying at the basis of the affect, and the inclusion in the conflict of

the complicated intellectual process makes us feel that we are on the right path.

Intentionally we do not speak here about the cases in which our stimulus provokes a linking up to the tempo as quickly as possible. Naturally here we obtained a disturbance incomparably more acute, but these experiments already proceed from those conflicts of tempos, and we shall discuss them especially when we come to speak of the conflict of defection.

B. Experiments with the Conflict of the Language Setting

Before us was the problem of including the conflict of the setting in the process connected with the complicated structural activity, at the same time observing the basic rule of leaving completely unchanged everything connected with the contents of the process we were studying. We decided to try to provoke a conflict by the exchange of the formal settings, leaving unaltered the direct contents of the process. The presence of the change in the contents was expected as a result of the arranged conflict of the mechanisms.

Usually *the system of languages* is very suitable for this problem. One and the same presentation, preserving the identity of the contents, is reflected in the various languages by very different words; speaking in a certain language, the person creates a definite setting, which, during the transfer to another language, loses the marked changes in the forms; but as far as concerns the motor innervations, the expressed contents remain completely untouched. It should be sufficient to bring into collision such language settings in order to evoke a conflict of two very complicated structural systems and to have the possibility of investigating the results which this conflict might call out in the neurodynamics of the subject. This is the procedure we followed in our experimentation.

We took the subjects who knew two languages equally well, and told them that in the series of experiments to be performed, words from both of these languages would be represented. In every case the subject had to answer by the first word thought of, but in the same language as that of the given stimulus.

Our experiment included, consequently, the conditions of the conflict, but this conflict was not connected with the contents of the presented word, but exclusively with that sudden and unexpected exchange of the language setting which occurs in the natural setting and with a comparatively slow tempo, but it appeared exceedingly perplexing in the setting of the experiment in which the subject was given the problem of not inhibiting the responses and answering as quickly as possible by the first word thought of.

We introduced two parallel series in our experiments in order to be sure that the relations we obtained were not connected with ignorance of the foreign language to which the subject must make this transfer but exclusively with the factor of the sudden change of the setting. In the first of these, five foreign words were scattered among twenty-five Russian ones; in the second, the relation was reversed, and twenty-five foreign words were dispersed among five Russian ones.

In order from the very beginning to create a certain basic setting the first eleven word-stimuli were the basic language for the given series; the crucial words requiring transfer to the other language occupied in both series the nos. 12, 17, 24, 26, 29.

Here is a list of both series which we used:

Series A.

1 night (R)[1]	10 bell (R)	18 spectacles (R)	26 Wasser
2 hut (R)	11 hand (R)	19 flag (R)	(l'ordre)
3 lamp (R)	12 Farbe (la me)	20 oar (R)	27 ring (R)
4 fire (R)	13 stick (R)	21 rock (R)	28 earth (R)
5 rope (R)	14 wine (R)	22 image (R)	29 Hund
6 sour (R)	15 bridge (R)	23 roof (R)	(la chaise)
7 pool (R)	16 beam (R)	24 Feder (la	30 switch (R)
8 glass (R)	17 Beispiel (l'ex-	plume)	
9 flowers (R)	emple)	25 frame (R)	

Series B.—German-Russian

1 Monat	9 Leben	17 boat (R)	25 Sommer
2 Himmel	10 Strasse	18 Storch	26 sand (R)
3 Haus	11 Blume	19 Hof	27 Wasser
4 Licht	12 nail (R)	20 Schwester	28 Brille
5 Hase	13 Löwe	21 Winter	29 cat (R)
6 Kopf	14 Heft	22 Feuer	30 Hosen
7 Nachbar	15 Stroh	23 Vogel	
8 Trommel	16 Herde	24 camel (R)	

Series C.—French-Russian

1 l'ombre	9 casser	17 boat (R)	25 la salle
2 le chemin	10 l'argent	18 l'encre	26 sand (R)
3 la neige	11 le livre	19 aller	27 le forest
4 le chien	12 nail (R)	20 la cune	28 le fusil
5 le pain	13 le ciel	21 la vache	29 cat (R)
6 la femme	14 la chaise	22 la tasse	30 la lettre
7 le sac	15 le grain	23 la manche	
8 le chat	16 la viande	24 camel (R)	

[1] (R) indicates that the word was given in Russian, not English.

This list shows that the stimuli themselves were about equally difficult, and, obviously, did not meet with any special obstruction.

In this series we used thirteen adult normal subjects, knowing both languages well. In contradistinction from those whom we were studying in the first part of our investigations, these were people who were in contact with the psychological laboratory, and from whom, consequently, we would naturally expect considerably more organised and confident reactions, in view of their acquaintanceship with the experiment.

The results obtained here proved that our method is correct. One problem is quickly transferred to another language setting after the setting to one language had been created; it called out a considerable conflict and introduced a series of very interesting and serious disturbances in the associative process and in the corresponding motor activity. These symptoms produced by only one acute conflict of the setting were very similar to those which we have seen in the affective and complex reactions, and we think that we were successful in separating in an artificial way that mechanism which plays an important rôle in the psychophysiology of the affect.

Even the first, most general analysis shows that the sudden transfer to another language is combined with a very great destructive process:

TABLE 23

Series A

	Reactive Time			Motor Reactions	
	M (median)	Am	Am—M (average variation)	Normal	Disturbances
Stimuli	1.7″	1.7″	0	96.3%	3.7%
Critical Stimuli	2.6″	2.69″	+0.09″	59.1%	40.9%
Post-critical Stimuli	2.1″	2.04″	—0.06″	78.2%	21.8%

Series B

Stimuli	1.85″	2.18″	+0.33″	92.5%	7.5%
Critical Stimuli	2.2″	2.87″	+0.67″	63.3%	36.7%
Post-critical Stimuli	2.2″	2.35″	+0.15″	71.6%	29.4%

Table 23 shows that the crucial reactions (to the stimuli requiring a sudden transfer) take place with a marked slowing and considerable disturbance in the accompanying motor system. These disturbances are referred not to the difficulty of associating in a foreign language, but exclusively to the position of the given stimuli in the series of stimuli in the other language and to that conflict which is called out by the necessity of transferring from one setting to another. This is shown very clearly in our second control series where the Russian word, occurring among the foreign, calls out a much more inhibited reaction than it would with the more difficult stimuli in the remaining series—at first view a paradoxical situation. One transfer to a new setting and the removal of the former setting is evidently sufficient to cause acute neurodynamic disturbances. It is interesting that the usual result (of course, somewhat weakened) is called out by the negative transfer: the stimuli of the fundamental series occur much more slowly and with many more disturbances if they follow after the word given in the foreign language and, consequently, require a reverse transfer.

One fact deserves our special attention: the disturbance in the accompanying motor reaction is met with in our series almost exclusively in the cases connected in one way or another with the conflict of the settings; if they are encountered hardly at all in the serial reactions of our experiment, then their number is increased to 40% in the foreign words suddenly given, and 20-30% in the post-critical cases. This proves that the inhibition of the new language setting is accompanied by a conflict.

A careful analysis reveals the mechanism of the processes. The sudden inclusion of the new language setting produces a shock in the subject, which is expressed in two forms; it may disturb the receptory activity or cause a conflict in the motor system. Both cases show us the mechanism of the affective reaction.

1. The receptory failure is due to the fact that the subject, during the sudden change of setting, is unable to understand the word presented, although in its normal context it is readily comprehensible. We see here how much the reaction of the word depends upon its context, and what a disorganised process may arise when this context is altered. In the more marked cases there is complete inhibition of word reception during the acute conflict; and the subject complains when the twelfth word is given (the first one in the foreign language) that he does not hear it, although it is pronounced as clearly as the others. Thus:

Subject Mil. (series A) 12. fire—I did not hear it ...
Subject Bir. (series A) 29. la chaise—I did not hear it
Subject Kar. (series A) 12. Farbe—Ach! that's German
Subject Svav. (series A) 12. Farbe—fargei? What is that?

Here we see a mechanism of great interest. The understanding of the word is possible only in the usual language setting; a foreign context makes its perception difficult, or the word inaudible or changes its sound, as in the last example.

In the light of these experiments there are clear to us two facts:
The first of these is the case of the affective and hysterical reception connected with the confused understanding of the presented words. In our former experiments we met with many short examples when the subject was not capable of receiving the word as it appeared only in connection with some affective experience. Thus it often seemed that the subject did not hear those words in the experiment offered him when they related to the performance of a crime, to a traumatic situation, to an affective complex. During many years of work we have hardly met a case of impaired reception outside of such affective complexes, and we fully confirm Jung's statement that the "not hearing" is one of the affective symptoms. We think, however, that the simple simulation or desire not to hear explains this fact not at all, and that behind these facts are concealed the mechanism which we mentioned in this experiment. Evidently the word entering into the affective or complex situation in many cases can actually become isolated from the rest of the psychical structure of the experiments, which presupposes a definite transfer to it calling out the conflict connected with this transfer. The perverted reception, and sometimes even the "unheard" become now fully possible.
The second fact to which we turn is connected with the cases of amnesia described in the literature (Halbwachs), in a considerable part of the experiment during the sharp change of the surrounding context; the described cases of loss of memory during the transfer to an entirely new setting only confirm that dependence of reception upon the context and that conflict of transference which we could establish.

In the cases we have chosen, the produced conflict leads to a disturbance of the receiving system. Much more often, however, we meet with other results than those called out by the conflict. These we shall describe separately:
2. *Cases of Effector Disturbances* are usually connected with the fact that in the subject from the beginning of the experiment there is already created a setting to react to a definite language, and during a sudden transfer to another language this setting is not easily removed. Frequently the subject manifests a tendency to prolong the response to the accepted language; suddenly the transfer collides with this tendency, and at the same time there is brought out a conflict in the linguistic motor system.

Often the subject is not capable of controlling his former setting and we have very accelerated reactions in this series to the
critical word with its simple transfer to the basic language series
(or the associative response to the basic language series)—often
entirely unexpected by the subject:

Subject L. (series A): 12. la rue—1.4″—street
                       17. l'exemple—5.8″—characteristic, ex-
                           ample

Subject Kor. (series A): 12 Beispiel—2.4″—example

This tendency appears very clearly in the defects of the opposite transference, where, after the critical word is given, the
problem is again connected with the basic language of the experiment, for example:

Subject Rub. (series A): 30. branch—1.4″—Schnabel
             (series B): 27. le fôret—5.0″—die Forelle

or the irradiation extends even into the parts of the experiment
which were free from the crucial stimuli, disturbing the adequate
courses of the reactions:

Subject Shub. (series A): 15. bridge—2.0″—Brücke

Subject Rub. (series A): 15. bridge—3.0″—pont de marechal

All this shows that in our experiment we evoke a considerable
perseverative tendency which the subject is not always able to
manage. The attempts to overcome this produce an acute conflict, and here we have a series of symptoms of disorganisation
of the associative process, bringing us again to the mechanism
of the affective disturbances. The subject is rarely able to correct
altogether the intense perseverative setting; usually the normal
response is given only after the removal of the former perseverative response which comes into the mind of the subject first. As
a result of such a conflict we have a complicated reaction, the
open speech link of which is the structure for the preliminary
removed, first, impulsive answer:

Subject Eoch. (series A): 15.—bridge—6.0″—m ... m ... distress (I wanted to say Brücke).

Subject Er. (series B): 24.—la plume—4.6″—p ... poisson I
wanted to say "pero" [Russian for feather].

The structure of these reactions appears to us fairly clearly.
From the analysis of the whole process the senseless character
of the reactive response is comprehensible: owing to the conflict
of the setting in the subject there is manifested a definite perseverative tendency to the translation of the word given here;
this tendency is extinguished, but the speech response is given
not as an association to the presented stimulus, but as a substitu-

tion of the extinguished translation; more often it is connected with the replacing link by means of the sound connection (Subject Er. feather—poisson. Subject Shp.; 20 oar—Ruder—roo—ka [this is the Russian word for hand]. Subject Poch;—bridge—bridge—Brücke), sometimes given as the result of perseveration. In all these cases the lowered character of the association is accompanied by considerable motor disturbance, which convinces us that the process is the result of a conflict.

The more typical of these motor disturbances reflect the complete conflicting structure of the process here. In Figure 55 we see the graphic equivalents of two of our recent reactions:

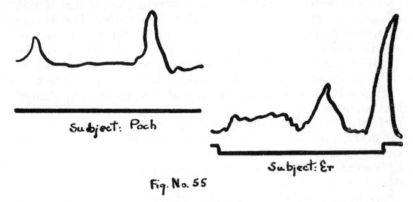

Subject: Poch

Subject: Er

Fig. No. 55

THE DISTURBED REACTIVE PROCESS DURING THE CONFLICT OF THE SETTING

SUBJECT POCH.: BRIDGE—6.0"—M.M.—DISTRESS (I WANTED TO SAY BRÜCKE)

SUBJECT ER.: LA PLUME 4.6"—P...POISSON (I WANTED TO SAY *pero*—RUSSIAN == FEATHER)

We see at a glance that the last reaction expressed in the speech response is a result of a fairly complicated and intensive conflict, connected with the dislodged perseverative link; the accompanying motor changes show that all this process does not have an undisturbed course by any means, and that the conflict actually is the basis of such "flattening" speech responses similar to those we have met already in the experiments with the affective signalisation.

In the case given of the accompanying motor reaction, the whole structure of the reaction comes out in full: the manifestations of the intervening link, its dislodgement, and the matching of the final speech reaction. However, it would be a mistake to think that the conflict does not arise from any other processes than the complexity of the structure of the reaction. The experiment confirms that the conflict provokes deep neurodynamic changes, analogous to that which we have already described in the study of affects.

We shall stop to consider only two of these mechanisms: the appearance of the impulsive reactions and of the perseverated excitation.

The conflict which we bring out very often causes in the subject a considerable shock of the higher speech processes, which are accompanied by a rupture of the "functional barrier" and the emancipation of the motor area from its connected organised process. A series of cases that we observed showed that during the acute conflict the inhibition of the speech reaction is connected with the fact that the excitation is directly transferred to the motor sphere, and the impulsive pressure, later the inhibitory, gives us a picture completely analogous to that which we have observed during the reactions in the state of affect.

Figure 56 shows typical examples of such an emancipation of the motor area from the complicated cortical processes; it is perfectly obvious that the speech response, having collided with the obstacle, could not be restrained in the accompanying motor sphere as it was restrained in the chief speech area, and such a disorganisation of the reactive process is a necessary consequence of the conflict.

One of the chief mechanisms characteristic of the neurodynamic affective state is created in the artificial experiment and genetically connected with the mechanism of the conflict.

The disturbances which we have obtained by this artificial path manifest not only the symptoms proceeding from the affect, but they reveal the analogous dynamics. The disorganisation connected with the conflict is not concentrated on the crucial reaction, and if we look carefully at the structure of the neurodynamic process, which conceals the accompanying motor reactions, we see that every conflict produced by us leaves after it certain traces, and these are continued for some time; only gradually they become extinguished and are activated by the presentation of the following stimulus. We approach here the mechanism of perseveration exactly as we did in the case of the natural affective complexes, and we are able to see its neurodynamic basis behind this empirically described phenomenon.

In reality the conflict introduced into the psyche of the subject does not leave the neurodynamics in a complete state of rest after the reaction to the conflicting stimulus is given; the

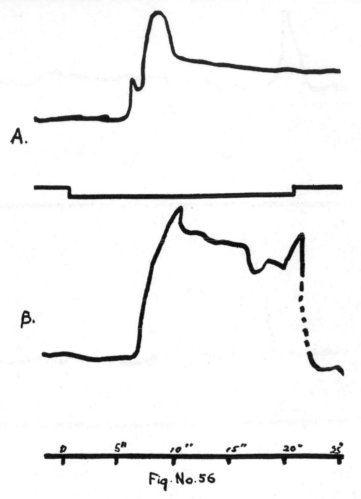

Fig. No. 56

THE DISTURBANCE OF THE FUNCTIONAL BARRIER DURING THE CONFLICT
OF THE SETTING

A. SUBJECT ZAB.: KATZE—WHO IN THE DEVIL KNOWS THAT
B. SUBJECT LEON.: KATZE—5.0″—DAS . . . D . . . THE DEVIL! DER HUND![1]

accompanying motor reactions almost always give us a sharp
increase of the tremor after the conflicting reaction. Once more
this shows that the conflict provoked a certain excitation which
was not neutral for the given response. Figure 57 shows curves

[1] All of the responses in these experiments given in English are translations
from the Russian.

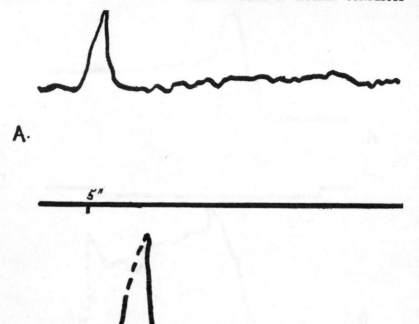

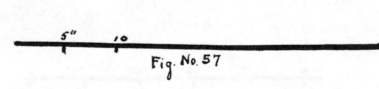

Fig. No. 57

THE SUBSEQUENT EXCITATION DURING CONFLICTING REACTIONS

A. SUBJECT SVAV. 17   B. RUB. 12

proving that after the evoked conflicting reaction of the obstacle
the neurodynamics loses for some time its regular and organised
form of work.

These results bring us squarely up to that fact which was
described by many authors, and the neurodynamical mechanism
of which for so long a time we were unable to study directly.
We knew that in the associative series there was often a disturbance not only of the crucial reaction but also of the subsequent one; in the present experiments, having produced the

conflicting process in the subject, we obtained the same results artificially. What neurodynamical processes, however, are at the basis of this process? The adduced facts allow us to arrive at its decision. The experiment proves that the excitation begun during the conflict is not only continued for some time after the conflicting reaction, but it influences the next reaction to a certain degree. The subsequent stimulus falls already on an excitatory soil prepared for disorganisation, and we often see here the emancipation of the motor area from the control of the higher cortical apparatus, the tendency of a direct transfer of the excitation to the motor sphere. This is evidence of the weakened participation of the higher psychological system and of the return of the reactive process to the primitive diffused state.

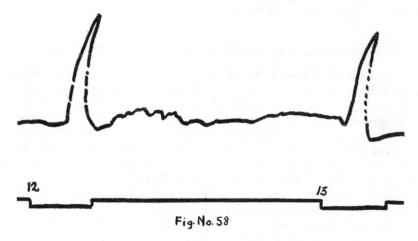

Fig. No. 58

THE MOTOR SYMPTOMS OF THE PERSEVERATIVE EXCITATION

SUBJECT LEON. (SERIES B)

Figure 58 brings us to the mechanism of this process. We see clearly that in the latent period the subject shows some inquietude marked by the increased tremor of the hand; with this is connected the impulsive character of the following reactions, the excitation after the crucial reaction is somewhat calmer, but the readiness of the subject to give the impulsive response remains, and the presented stimulus calls out the motor reaction which is already not coordinated with the speech response; this is shown by the premature, impulsive pressure. We obtained the structure of a process completely analogous to that which we have already observed in the natural setting (see Figure 27). With such a structure of the neurodynamics, of course, there are connected considerable defects, and the course of the associated reactions as well as the mechanism of the perseveration become much clearer.

We shall not take up here a question which might be fully studied in our series, but which would take us far afield of the chief problems of this book. The collision of two language settings permitted us to study experimentally that interesting question which is connected with the psychological picture of linguistics. Our experiments could be compared with pidgin English. The changed forms which we obtain here allow us to establish experimentally the basic lines along which proceed the perversions of a language during collisions of it with another language. The separate cases furnish us beautiful examples of those abbreviations and combinations resulting in a conflicting structure of language which we see so frequently in children and in bi-lingual peoples.

3. EXPERIMENTS WITH THE CONFLICT OF DEFECTION

THE experiments with the conflict of the setting permits us artificially to create a skeleton of the affective reactions and synthetically to obtain a series of symptoms characteristic of its neurodynamics. The experiments with the conflict of defection make it possible to take the next step in this direction and enable us to give a reasonable explanation of the series of new mechanisms characterising the "synthetic model of affect." We can speak of the conflict of defection in those cases in which the subject suddenly becomes unable to complete any complicated problem which he had considered possible.

In order to produce the conflict of defection the collision of these two basic conditions is necessary: the activity which the person is taking up should from the beginning tax his ability, and he should actually begin to try to realise the problem; on the other hand, it should reach beyond the difficult, exceeding the limits of his capabilities, and the attempts which he began must meet with an insurmountable obstacle. Precisely in the result of such a collision the attempt toward activity and the impossibility to attain it, of hope and of weakness, inevitably brings about a certain state, characterised by confusion, affective and disorganised behaviour.

The conflict of the setting led us directly to the problem of affect; then the conflict of defection should be directly connected with the problem of neurosis. There is not a single neuropathologist who would not point to social or biological defections of the subject as the basis of the entire series of psychoneuroses. Alfred Adler constructed around this conflict a whole system which greatly aided us in the comprehension of neurotic mechanisms; the conflict of defection in the presence of an impossibility to compensate meets here a fundamental mechanism, giving birth to a pathological affect and bringing about a prolonged neurosis.

The above neuropathologist confirms our opinion of the considerable rôle played by this conflict. Having investigated it in the experimental setting we can obtain a fairly well reflected disorganisation of behaviour.

In order to obtain synthetically in the subject a similar conflict, far more is necessary than to give him a problem so difficult that it exceeds his ability. Such a situation may bring about a refusal of the attempt to solve it; but then there is not always a conflict. We should produce in the subject assurance that the proposed problem is capable of solution to encourage his active essays directed to the decision of the problem, and afterwards, bring these trials to a difficult obstruction, before which he is impotent. Precisely such a setting toward "success," arranged in the face of a serious impediment, constitutes the condition necessary to obtain the desired conflict.

Some of the experimental applications in the work of K. Lewin furnish excellent examples of the means which may be used in such tests. The experiments of T. Dembo called out probably the most acute and stable affects of all those known in psychological research. The scheme according to which they were arranged was precisely one of deceptive setting toward success. It was proposed to the subject to accomplish a definite action: for example, to get some flowers lying in a chair, not going beyond the limits of a certain area marked out on the floor. The experiment was done in such a way that the subject was assured of success, and after he had successfully solved the problem by two successive ways, it was proposed to substitute the solution by still a third method; the situation, however, was incapable of solution by this method, but the previous accomplishments created in the subject a setting towards success, which met with an unsurpassable obstruction. The result of this conflict leads to an affective discharge, and Lewin, describing these experiments, notes the especial acuteness of the affect provoked.

Very clear results of the collision of the setting for success in the unattained problem were seen in another series of experiments done also under the direction of Lewin. To a child it was proposed that he get a confection, separated from him by some distance, but which he could not reach with his hand. The greater the setting toward success was, the more marked was the activity of the child and also the appearance of the affect during failure. The activity and consequent disorganisation of behaviour assumed especially clear-cut forms when the confection was brought so near to the child that he could almost touch it with his hands, and the impossibility to get it collided with the acute setting toward success. Such a *Beinahe Situation* was very advantageous in producing the sharp conflict of defection and in obtaining so definite a disorganisation of behaviour.

All these results furnished us the scheme with which it was possible to obtain such an interesting conflict; we arranged several series in which the intensity of the response collided with the impossibility of attainment.

A. *Experiments with Limited Associations*

We employed a very simple method to obtain the structure of the described process, not fundamentally changing the scheme of the experiment which we had applied to all of our investigations. We proposed to the subject a series of words to which it was necessary to answer by limited associations according to the scheme "whole-part." Together with a comparatively easy answer for such a word, we brought about in the subject the setting for success, and then unexpectedly connected up in the series of stimuli such words which made it either impossible or very difficult. These words, presented separately, might be met with refusal on the part of the subject; in a series of fairly easy stimuli, however, they bring about attempts to find the corresponding answers, and these always produce that conflict which we sought. In a series of fifteen students (age fifteen to thirty-five) we used the following list of stimuli:

1 house	7 court	13 dress	19 *salt*
2 forest	8 family	14 leg	20 boat
3 knife	9 garden	15 letter	21 mouth
4 chair	10 story	16 boat	22 *flour*
5 steppe	11 *moon*	17 *chest*	23 spectacles
6 mountain	12 stick	18 hat	24 *pain*
			25 package

An analogous series was used in thirty neurotics; the results of this control series coincided throughout with the first, and will be considered in another context. As a control our first series was used twice; for the first time the instruction was given to react to any part as a whole (series A), and for the second time it was complicated by the prohibition to repeat again answers already given in the first series (series B).

A detailed psychological analysis shows us that the conflict here differs from the conflict of the setting not only by the concrete conditions of the experiment but in the structure itself. Whilst the typical part of that conflict was the collision of the language setting and the inhibition of the prepared answers (often in the tendency described by us to translation, etc.), in the conflict of defection all the main points are contained precisely in the prepared answer. We can say that the conflict came into being much earlier here, and is contained not in the withholding of the prepared answer but in the inhibiting intention, colliding with the absence of the adequate reaction.

If in the first case the conflict is most often manifested in the speech and motor spheres, then in the given case we usually have a conflict of the active quests, meeting the impediment, and the absence of a ready decision of the prepared speech impulses is most often characteristic for this series.

Precisely this conflict of excited activity with the impossibility of finding an adequate reaction is typical for the given process; only where this activity is present, have we the actual conflict and the actual appearance of some of the affective traces; in those cases in which the subject refuses to try, as in an impossible problem, there is no conflict, and the neurodynamics of the subject remains undisturbed. Only when there is a possible path of activity can we get a conflicting process; without this activity we may get a trauma but not a conflict. This activity may have a more or less definite form, it may be reflected in a general intention or in a special impulse, but the actual conflict is possible only in the field of excitation, met with in the motor sphere.

This position is fully reflected in the structure of the accompanying motor processes. Figure 59 illustrates these two cases.

We present to the subject two provocative stimuli, which is not an easy problem. In both cases, after some time, the subject refuses; he says he does not know which word is an adequate answer in the given case. However, the psychological picture of refusal is in the two cases very different. Our first subject immediately decides that it is impossible to choose a part to the word "flour," and he makes no attempts; the second, on the contrary, thinks that he has a fully adequate answer to the word "moon," and only after unsuccessful trials to find it does he refuse. The structure of both processes differs widely. In the first case we do not have any signs of a conflict; the subject refuses to decide, not making an attempt to find a word, and the perfectly calm motor system indicates that we have no proper conflict here. The structure of the reactive process in another of our subjects is entirely different; already after 1.5" the accompanying motor curve shows considerable excitation, beginning with frequent active intentions, not reaching, however, any considerable development and going over after its restraint into a diffused tremor. The structure of the reactive process is here, thanks to the accompanying motor reactions, fairly clear: the beginning activity collides with the absence of the adequate reaction; the intention is inhibited, not having found an adequate exit. Precisely this consequence of the conflict spreads over into the irradiated excitation which is expressed in the tremulous, disturbed curve.

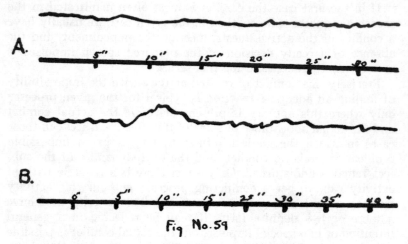

Fig No. 59

THE ACCOMPANYING MOTOR REFUSAL DURING LIMITED ASSOCIATION

A. SUBJECT KOG. 22. FLOUR—6.8″—I DO NOT KNOW
B. SUBJECT GEN. 11. MOON—15.0″—I DO NOT KNOW WHAT

The disorganisation of the behaviour is the consequence of an inhibited adequate exit of activity; a comparison of the two cases confirms us in the view that the affect can come only from a conflict arising in the active sphere. Again by the synthetic path, we approach one of the most important proofs connected with the mechanics of the disorganisation of human behaviour.

A closer examination shows us that the disturbance obtained in this case actually brings about the mechanism of conflict in the intentional sphere. In most of the acute cases we see this and also the character of the speech process; not every time, however, does a difficult stimulus produce in the subject a direct and calm refusal, coming after an interval; much oftener we obtain a direct excitation of the speech apparatus, the subject repeats the word given him, pronounces it clearly, gives many evidences of its confused phases, and, meeting with an obstruction in the decision of the problem "in his mind," he tries to decide it by words directed to the difficulty, and there is a disorganisation of the speech process itself.

Subject M. 24 pain—20.0"—well ... pain ... well ... I simply do not understand.

Subject Usp. flour—15.0"—well I don't know, I do not know, I will not do the reaction.

All such examples show us that the process is characterised here by the production of activity and a direct transfer of excitation to the speech sphere. The difficulty, the transfer to the setting of success, does not give an organised intellectual decision of the problem, and the consequent influence of the decision in the speech reaction, but directly connects with the speech, and gives to all of the processes a diffused, inhibitory character.

All these symptoms of diffused excitation of the speech apparatus stand out with especial clearness in those cases in which we use subjects for the experiment having an insufficient vocabulary for verbal thinking. We conducted this series of experiments with workers from one of the Moscow factories, and we obtained very acute symptoms in the speech as well as the motor excitability when it was given an unexpected difficult stimulus:

Subject Zak: trough—12.0"—trough ... what to say ... I do not know ... how can I answer ... round or flat ... well ... flat

Subject Bush: pitch-fork—4.6"—pitch-fork ... how pitch-fork ... what shall I call it ... fork

Subject Sluish: circle—6.8"—circle ... what to say ... I do not know what to say for a circle ... I do not know

In all these cases the disturbed neurodynamic processes appear very clearly. The intention to answer, meeting with an impossibility to give a ready reaction produces usually a diffused, disturbed neurodynamics. This disturbance is more intense the more stable this intention and the less mobile the intellectual speech system of the subject which must find an exit from the conflict created. As a rule we rarely meet here with those ready attempts to react which were so sharply expressed in the experiments with the conflict of the setting; on the contrary, the dispersed motor excitation, appearing after the inhibited intention, is a typical scheme of the conflict of defection.

Figure 60 gives us an example of such a disturbance of the curve obtained in a subject with defection of verbal culture, in whom a difficult problem produced an acute conflicting state.

The conflict of defection met with in a subject who finds it

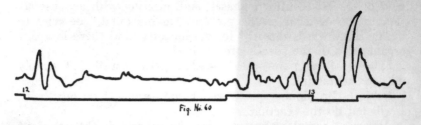

Fig. No. 60

CONFLICT OF DEFECTION; NEURODYNAMIC SYMPTOMS; LIMITED ASSOCIATION

SUBJECT SLUISH (LABOURER): 12. BUTTER—12.5″—BUTTER; 13. TROOPS —3.0″—RED ARMY

impossible to give an adequate reaction, produces a marked dispersion of excitation in the neurodynamic apparatus; the impossibility of an adequate reaction inevitably leads to some transfer of the excitation to another motor system, similar to that which we described in the investigation of the symptoms of the affective state. Generally such transfers and such prolonged forms of the neurodynamic disorganisation are not met with in the conflict of the setting, where after some fluctuations the subject gave an adequate reaction. On the contrary, here we encounter a whole series of such cases, and they bring us to the important mechanisms of the disorganisation of behaviour.

In Figure 61 we present several typical cases of similar motor disturbances. They are all constructed according to one scheme, and they allow us to investigate the inclusion in the mechanics of this form of disturbance.

In all these cases we see that the disturbance having begun with the right hand, very quickly extends over to the left passive hand, and is there reflected with marked intensity. In all of them the disorganisation shows a marked tendency to come toward the end of the latent period, and is connected thus with the moment of final refusal from the adequate reaction. Here we have the right to think that the symptoms observed are the neurodynamic equivalent of the refusal from the adequate reaction, and they point to that unorganised flow of excitation which appears every time that the adequate reaction is delayed, or fails altogether. Precisely these disturbances bring out anew the whole complex of symptoms which we described in the experiments dealing with the affective processes, and make comprehensible those mechanisms having an affective discharge.

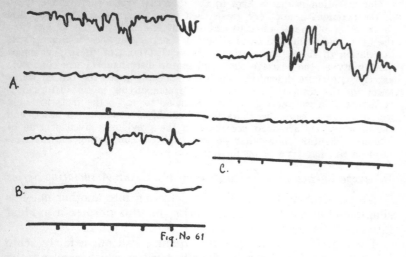

DISTURBANCE OF THE ACCOMPANYING REACTION AT THE END OF
THE LATENT PERIOD

A. SUBJECT KOG.: POLKA—12.0″—WELL, WHAT TO SAY . . . I DO NOT KNOW
B. SUBJECT KOG.: CHEST—24.0″—I DO NOT KNOW
C. SUBJECT LEON.: PAIN—9.6″—REFUSAL

The series of experiments, the analysis of which we only touched upon, do not show an obvious statistical relation, because the reaction of the conflict of defection can be called out not only by words we present as crucial, but, indeed, by others, having a personal difficulty for the subject. Therefore we give only a short statistical summary of the characteristics of this material in Table 24.

TABLE 24

	Reaction Time		Motor Reactions	
	Median	d variation	normal	disturbances
Average in the experiment	1.8″	1.0″	72%	28%
Stimulus "moon"	3.2″	0.7″	47%	53%
"chest"	3.6″	1.2″	40%	60%
"salt"	4.0″	1.1″	40%	60%
"flour"	3.0″	4.0″	54%	46%
"pain"	6.0″	3.6″	34%	76%

Our attention is drawn here to the fact that when the average speed of the reactions is not very great, then its variation ($1.0'' = 52\%$) and the number of motor disturbances sharply differentiate this series from the usual one of limited associations. A summary of these characteristics in relation to the separate stimuli shows that both of these phenomena (instability of the reactive time and motor disturbances) are connected exactly with those difficulties which the suddenly presented crucial words mean for the subject. The number of accompanying motor disturbances is increased in the individual cases from 60 to 70%; the fact that only a few of them have the character of inhibited attempts to react, and the majority are arranged according to the previously given scheme of inhibited intention shows that we were right in considering the manifestation a peculiar type of conflicting processes.

B. *Experiments with Exhaustion of the Chain Associative Series*

We can prolong this conflict of defection into another not less simple and attainable situation, using for this purpose a gradual fatigue of the associative series.

The associative series can very quickly call out a fairly acute affective tone if we limit its definite borders which appear to be quickly exhausted. In that case where the exhaustion of the limited series attacks the subject himself very quickly we obtain in a marked degree the same conflict of intention with the absence of the adequate reaction. The accompanying motor reactions bear witness to the presence of a considerable dispersed excitation, approaching in its type to the excitation observed in the acute affective series.

Here is a short series in which the subject is given as a problem the recitation of a list of the names of different kinds of fish (or birds), pressing the pneumatic bulb during each reaction. We chose these because for the average subject who is not a specialist and for the person living in the city these categories are fairly simple but are extremely quickly exhausted.

We used about twenty subjects, and in a large number of them it was possible to see the origin of the conflict in a fairly well-marked way. This conflict was reflected as an acute disturbance of the structure of the intervals of the chain series on the one hand, and by the sharp disorganisation of the accompanying motor reactions on the other hand.

Figure 62 shows the ordinates of the intervals between the separate reactions of the chain series characterising the associative series obtained in our subjects. A single glance is sufficient to establish the fact of what we have before us—of course not the process of gradually increasing inhibition and not the process of the limited refusal of the reactions. The conflicting character is seen here from the alternating, sharply marked portions; the accompanying motor reactions of these series which we give in Figure 63 indicate that behind these disorganised intervals is the same conflict of the mobilised activity, colliding with the defection.

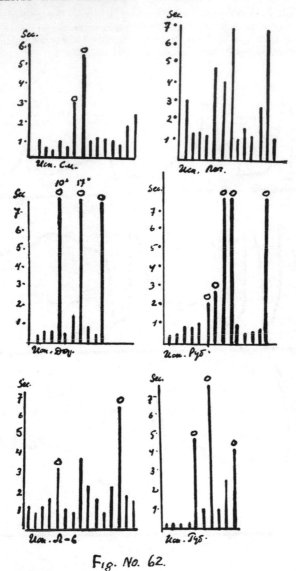

Fig. No. 62.

INTERVALS OF THE LIMITED CHAIN SERIES (FISH)

o = THE MOTOR DISTURBANCES

The separate delayed impulses, the scattered excitation, having lost the regular well-marked movement of discoordination, characterise that process which we have just described in our experiments with the conflict during limited associations, only carrying it from the unified reactions to a chain process, separated by considerable intervals of time. Here we again come to a synthetic origin of the model of the phenomenon which we have seen so many times under natural conditions.

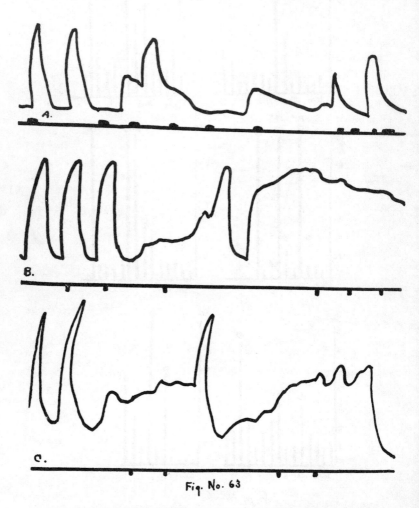

Fig. No. 63

THE ACCOMPANYING MOTOR REACTIONS OF THE CHAIN SERIES

A. SUBJECT DET.   B. SUBJECT SM.   C. SUBJECT GUB.

4. THE CONFLICTING PROCESSES AND THE AFFECTIVE SYMPTOMS

HERE we have a similar experiment, possessing, however, an artificial character, and we have performed it only because it does not fall within an affective field, but it makes use of the most simple intellectual processes, to create the skeleton of those symptoms which we are accustomed to see during the affective and complex reactions.

During these experiments we have tried to observe the objective symptoms of the acute affects as well as those natural affective traces, complexes, which exist in every subject, and may by a careful examination become manifest.

Following in the steps of other authors, we thought that the symptoms obtained by us during the reactive and chain associations—that these symptoms of the accompanying disturbances can be attributed to the affective character of the process we are studying. We established several general laws for that disorganisation of behaviour which the affect provokes, and we shall discuss them in order to understand those concrete mechanisms which explain the affective influence in the associative series. Here we met with many difficulties and disagreements. Some of the authors studying the affective process averred that the disturbance provoked by the affect in the intellectual activity was conditioned by an "affective emptiness" (*affective Leerheit*). The affect first of all overcomes the higher associative processes and the created inhibitory association is the stimulus for the most extreme course of the affective processes. Other authors showed that in the affective characteristic—in the process of the conscious inhibition, of the conscious delay of any prepared reactions, and in the conflicts of the conscious delays with the subconscious striving to express the affective tendency—they saw the basis of those disturbances which the affect produced in the behaviour of a person.

All these disputes left little hope for a complete solution; primarily because none of them brought forth really objective arguments. The futility of the discussions consisted in this: trying to explain the definite laws, the authors preferred to operate with subjective material, turning away from the objective psychophysiological generalisations.

The application of the method, reflected in the objective structure of the psychological processes, made it possible to examine these disputes more closely. The attempts synthetically to create the usual symptoms of the affective series gave us the possibility of establishing more exactly those of the laws which most frequently lie at the basis of the disorganising activity of the affect and of the complexes.

Carrying the experiments over to the most simple intellectual processes, we established that, at all events, two types of conflicts can create the same symptoms which usually are the result of the affects and the affective traces; these two types of conflicts were most closely connected with the two types of mechanisms.

The first of these was the conflict of the setting, which most often provoked the delay of the prepared but inadequate reaction. The structure of the process connected with it was usually characterised by those delayed, but perfectly formed, "attempts to react," examples of which we brought out above in the corresponding analysis. The second of these conflicts we observed has been described as the *conflict of defection;* the processes connected with it are characterised by a delay of the general intention during the absence of the adequate reaction, of the general defection of the subject in the face of the problem set before him. The conflict of the setting towards success, with the absence or exhaustion of the adequate responsive forms, provoked here in the accompanying motor sphere the phenomenon of delay of the general intentional activity, with the subsequent irradiation of excitation, extending usually over a considerable area and into other expressive symptoms. In both of the cases the fundamental fact was the delayed activity. In the first of these cases, this delay of activity came about after the activity had been formulated and prepared as a motor-expressed answer; but in the second, the intention was only reinforced by the inhibition, as the former was not formulated as a prepared reaction.

The analysis of the artificially obtained symptoms compared with those facts resulting from the analysis of the natural affects and complexes confirmed our belief that the mechanism of the similar conflict and withholding of the activity is the chief mechanism of the affective processes, and that precisely with it are connected those symptoms which are the characteristic signs of the presence of the affective process.

If we analyse our resulting symptoms, in the cases of the natural affective complexes, then we have no difficulty in confirming our conclusion and in establishing that one or another of the cases we observed corresponds in its mechanisms to one of the described types of conflict. The associated motor method makes it possible for us to establish the presence of the affective process, and not only this, but it enables us to show to what type of conflict it corresponds in its structure.

In Figure 64 we have such a case illustrating our analysis. The first two curves are characterised by the "attempts to react," and are fairly well formulated, but restrained. In their structure they approach more closely to the first type of conflicts which we have described, and we may expect that in the given case some fairly well-formulated speech reaction was inhibited by another more adequate one.

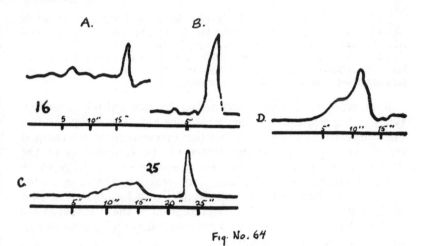

Fig. No. 64

VARIOUS STRUCTURES OF THE ACCOMPANYING SYMPTOMS

A. SUBJECT GL.—CUPBOARD—3.6"—BUREAU
B. SUBJECT L.—GIVEN—1.8"—ENEMY
C. SUBJECT ER.—SQUARE—5.0"—KUDRINSKY SQUARE
D. SUBJECT ER.—ROUGH—2.8"—FINE

The protocol of the experiment confirms this supposition. In both cases we actually have a displacement of the already prepared speech reaction:

Subject Gl.—cupboard—3.6"—room ("I wanted to say a definite word, but it did not seem to be the right one and so I chose another one.")
Subject L.—given—1.8"—enemy ("I recalled the name of an acquaintance and I wanted to give his family name but it seemed to me unsuitable and I gave that of the first one coming into my mind.")

The experiments with the criminal, those with the suggested complexes, those with hysterical patients, furnish us with similar cases, all characterised by the displacement of the prepared word corresponding to the most complicated emotional setting. The structural symptoms, similar to those just described, are characteristic of all these cases.

Two successive curves in Figure 64 (C and D) in their type correspond closely to that case in which the excitation of the intention collides with the absence of the adequate reaction, and the conflict appears connected with the delay of the already formulated activity. The analysis of the curves in the protocol confirm this view:

Subject Er.—square—5.0″—Kudrinsky Square ("I recalled the whole picture of a very emotional meeting on this square, and I did not know what to say, and then I decided to say 'Kudrinsky.'")

Subject Er.—rough—2.8″—fine ("Oi, there is so much here! I remembered an acquaintance, he was always very rough. There are many unpleasant things connected with this memory.")

Both types of reaction correspond to two entirely different types of the affective process, which are conditioned by the fact that the delay in the adequate reaction proceeds from two unequal causes, and from a varying degree of the formulation of the delayed reaction. If the first case presupposes the delay of an already prepared and fully conscious reaction, then the second deals with an intended one, still insufficiently formulated in view of the primitive diffused affective reception or the isolation of the affective experiment from the main part of consciousness—unattainable for quick verbalisation.

In every case we closely approach to the structure of the affective processes and to the characteristics of its fundamental types.

CHAPTER VII

EXPERIMENTS WITH ARTIFICIAL NEUROSES

---

1. THE PROBLEM OF THE STABLE EXPERIMENTAL CONFLICT

THE EXPERIMENTS which we have just described have shown us by what means it is possible to provoke definite conflicting processes, and by the help of them artificially to obtain certain concentrated symptoms of disorganised behaviour.

The methods applied by us, however, could provoke only temporary excitatory processes, of a comparatively light and transient character. We obtained an artificial model of a process analogous to a slight actual affect, but we were still far from the experimental production of the stable affective disturbance, from the production of an artificial model of neurosis.

Several fundamental characteristics stood between us and such a stable, well marked destruction of behaviour. First, the conflicts of ours arose within the borders of a very *limited system,* and usually they *did not extend into the entire personality.* The experiment did not arise from beyond the borders of this series of very artificial operations, and the failure in the experiment was of a partial character, not originating in the failure of the given experiment but with the failure of the personality. Such an extension of the system in which the conflict might arise should have been explained by our first researches, if there had been before us the question of obtaining a more stable and more intense disorganisation of behaviour.

Contemporary experimental psychology attempted to proceed along just this path; and we must look on the experiments of K. Lewin as very successful because they effaced the borders of the serious, vital acts and of artificial acts obtained in the experiment, and not the fairly serious relation provoked on the part of the subject. The problem of "the serious experiment" in which "the failure in the experiment begins with the failure in life" was extended by Lewin in a series of experiments, and he, perhaps, was the first in experimental psychology who succeeded in artificially producing changes, not limited by the rôle of the experiment, but making contact with the personality itself.[1]

The first factor which complicated our attempts to obtain stable experimental disturbances in the behaviour of the personality is very closely related to that which we have just discussed. It consists in this: that we practically never obtained a fairly imperative system of activity, the delay or limitation of which actually should have produced an acute reaction on the part of the personality. We tried to attain to this imperativeness by artificially creating in the subject a setting to the reactivity in a special system (the conflict of the settings), or we attempted to create in it assurance through the possible solution of a laborious and sometimes insoluble problem (conflict of defection); we used extensively the automatism of behaviour, the automatisms creating here one or another collision and delay. However, by these means we did not succeed in reaching a complete imperativeness of those tendencies in the area of which we provoked the conflict, and this fact, that many of our subjects were well able to adjust themselves to or correct the difficulties set before them, indicated that we attained only limited results. These results told us, first of all, that the disturbances we obtained were not of a stable and intensive character, and before us arose the problem of the artificial production of a process closely related to the stable affect. We undertook to produce synthetically a complete model of a stable neurosis, just as we had constructed a model of unified affective disturbances experimentally. We took a model of neurosis because in it are found those properties of a stable conflict, of a prolonged affective disorganisation of behaviour, the study of which we took as our problem.

All the difficulties which we have referred to might be successfully removed by the help of the hypnotic method. In hypnosis we can count on obtaining a conflict of fair stability and intensity, not approaching the artificial origin of automatisms and, hardly, the artificial limitations of the experiment. Then, that which we obtained in the usual experiment by the aid of a prolonged elaboration of an automatism and its consequent limitation may be obtained in the hypnotic state by a direct suggestion. In the suggestion we have in our hands a measure by the help of which we may provoke a tendency of undisputed imperativeness; these

[1] See K. Lewin: *Die Entwicklung der experimentelle Willenspsychologie und Psychotherapie,* 1929.

tendencies called out by the suggestion are able to create stable states prolonged for a rather extended period and not requiring special external stimuli for their reinforcement.

Both of these factors are very favourable for the production of imperative forms of activity by means of the hypnotic method, which should involve the whole personality, and which should be spontaneous and very prolonged.

The hypnotic method opens up for us some very interesting possibilities, capable of helping us in the experimental setting to obtain those stable conflicts which are limited in their influence by the artificially provoked model of neurosis.

We may suggest to the subject in a hypnotic state some importunate tendency, rather obligatory for him and of an artificial and foreign character which remains in his subconsciousness; and we create opportunities for the study of the dynamics of exceedingly imperative forms of activity, built on the type of almost irresistible urges.

Wishing to study the dynamics of conflicts, we may easily cause a collision between our suggested activity and the natural setting of the personality; we may investigate the states in which the personality orients himself to the suggested intrusion as to something extraneous, and this conflict conditions the deep-lying neurodynamic changes. We may further oppose the activity produced in the hypnotic state by the subsequent instructions given in the waking state, excluding the free manifestation of the former activity; then we have a collision of activities characterised by compulsion or tension with a subconscious motive.

Finally, we can introduce into the psyche of the subject the entire conflicting process by suggesting during hypnosis two equally obligatory and opposed tendencies: for example, having made the subject incapable of expressing something imperative for him.

In all these cases we are able artificially to produce a model of compulsion and to oppose it by some psychological measure, beginning with a natural reaction of the personality and ending with a motor delay called out in a state of hypnosis. It is obvious that for the artificial creation of acute processes of disorganised human behaviour, and for a study of its laws, the situation of the hypnotic experiment offers many favourable opportunities. By means of this procedure—the production of exceedingly imperative and stable tendencies through the hypnotic application—we decided to construct a situation as similar as possible to the type of some of the neurotic processes.

In our method we created artificial states of tensions in order, from the beginning, to conceal the neurodynamical basis of the natural reactions of the personalities to these states, and then, by a succession of measures having inhibited the desires, to obtain a stable conflict of maximal strength, closely related in its structure to the more acute neurotic states. We changed the psychological systems entering into the conflict, and "removed" the conflict we were studying, in order to approach certain general laws connected with the disorganised behaviour, to which we shall return later.

The material which we will discuss here was obtained in 1926 and 1927 in a series of experiments carried on with the collaboration of V. I. Zabrezhnev and Varshava. About twenty subjects, who were fairly easily hypnotised, were the objects of our investigation in the various experiments. With many of them we performed quite a number of séances.

Here especially it would be unwise to use a simple statistical elaboration of the material; here, more than anywhere else, is applicable the clinical method of analysing the results. The fact brought out in the experiment is not a statistical entity, but a phenomenon which sometimes permits us to draw conclusions leading to general laws, and therefore of primary importance.[1] Precisely this position prompts us sometimes to analyse the separate parts of the experiments in which we see the reflections of the general laws.

2. EXPERIMENTS WITH ARTIFICIAL TENSIONS OR COMPULSIONS

Our first problem was exceedingly simple. It consisted in the production of a definite tension during the hypnotic state and its investigation when it appears in the further behaviour of the subject.

In contrast to the former investigations and descriptions, we introduced a state of tension into a strictly limited situation of our experiment and followed the alterations in the structure of the psychological and neurodynamical processes which we had called out. Precisely such an analysis of psychological character and neurodynamic structure of the compulsive state should give us the opportunity of an experimental approach to the question of how tension introduced into the psychobiological functions acts on the general course of the psychical processes, what specific reactions of the personality it calls out, and what forms of the compulsion can be differentiated.

The methodological path along which we might go was very

[1] See K. Lewin: *Gesetz und Experiments in der Psychologie*, Symposium, 1927.

simple; in the hypnotic state we created a definite tendency toward a constant origin of one or another complex; on awakening the subject, we let him associate freely, and then we observed how this group of tensions, the origin of which was not known to the subject, determined the course and structure of his associative process.

It appeared to us that our similar experiments might, under specific conditions and analysis, explain some purely psychiatric questions and directly aid in the elaboration of the problem, as yet so poorly understood, concerning the structure of the states having to do with compulsions and tensions.

In our laboratory, we have already considered the question of the structural analysis of the associative processes in the normal person. A. N. Leontyev has shown that every emotional complex creates a certain tendency to reproduce itself in a chain of associations. We are tempted to approach to this well-known fact by an objective analysis, and we explained that in different subjects the chain of associations dominates the various objective structures, and that this structure depends upon the relation of the subject to the affective traces. These exhibit the tendency again and again to become manifest tensions in the associative series. Already the experiments directly lead to the problem of the structure of the compulsive processes; the present investigation, having artificially produced states of tension, may bear a very direct relation to them.

In reality, the theoretical interest and practical problems require a similar description of the paths by which the states of tension determine the given structure of the thought of the personality. This question is closely connected with how the personality is related to its own compulsions, whether it accepts them without a conflict and whether it willingly submits to their course, or whether its thinking is elaborated as the result of the conflict with the idea of compulsion, its attempt at removal and repression. In both cases the structure of the thinking process as well as its result are, of course, different. The experimental study of the states of tension and their reflection in the intellectual process undoubtedly aid us in coming to a solution of the questions concerning the structure of every normal, intellectual process. However, each intellectual act has its own voluntary structure, built on the mechanisms of a certain afteraction, of a certain tension; such an urge is inherent in every intellectual problem, every unfinished action. An intellectual process through its energetic components, represents a certain domination of tensions and their expression in the decision of the problem in hand.

As we apply ourselves to the experiments dealing with the study of the states of tension, two questions arise before us: we should like to have the exact facts of how far we had succeeded in actually obtaining the imperative urge; and, on the other hand, of how the personality orients himself to the suggested tendency. If the first problem is under our control, then the second may lead directly to the study of those specific conflicts which, in the final analysis, give birth to every neurosis, and lead to the pathological reaction of the personality to every tendency foreign to it.

Our experiments here were performed upon ten subjects, students from twenty-two to twenty-eight, in whom a fairly deep state of hypnosis could be obtained.

To our hynotised subjects we suggested that after awakening they would have the desire to think of the names of different birds. After the suggestion we awakened them and registered a series of free chain associations, telling them to say any word that they thought of. This series was compared with the free associations obtained in the subject during a normal state before any suggestion was given. Finally, in several cases, as control, we caused the suggested tension to collide with the instruction to associate in another direction: for example, to give without interruption names of fish, trees, etc. The control experiments served in the same way as those in which we told the subject to compose definite short stories on some given theme and then observed how the suggested tendency blended into an alloyage with the consciously built-up, logical structure.

The results of our experiments were fairly convincing. Almost all of our subjects began their post-hypnotic series with the names of birds; all without exception showed the tendency to associate with the tension, if not in the first then in the second or third links of the free associative series. The data given in Table 25 indicates that from ten to a hundred per cent of all the speech reactions are related to the suggested compulsion.

TABLE 25

Subject	1	2	3	4	5	6	7	8	9	10
% of reactions from the suggested tendency	12%	75%	70%	10%	100%	71%	60%	25%	20%	20%

In the majority of subjects the compulsion is very stable, the subject begins to reproduce in the associative series the compulsive group, not understanding why he does this, or trying to rationalise this fact with the explanation given.

Here is an example which at once illustrates the stability of the compulsive reaction in a typical subject:

Subject Kar. gives, after the suggestion, the following series of free associations: winter, jack-daw, sparrow, eagle, kite, rooster, nightingale, wood, blackbird, falcon, raven, road, siskin dove.

After ten minutes we asked again for a free associative series and this is what we obtain:

Forest, wood, bird, goose, duck, sparrow, crow, jack-daw, tom-tit, garden, summer, sparrow.

The compulsive group is fairly stable, although the subject is completely ignorant of the actual motives compelling her to associate in the given way. According to her own account she tried to explain the series of associations and we can see now the urge series is justified by a whole system of confabulations and of "recollections."

(This is her account of the second associative series): "I remembered when I lived in the city of A. the nightingales sang so beautifully, and I listened to them every evening..."

The suggested tension enters here into the structure of the personality's experiences, and the spontaneous fabulations prove that what we suggested is accepted here as an actual product of great interest.

The suggested compulsion is very stable and we can easily verify this by making the subject construct short tales on a given theme. In all these tales the group becomes implicated in the warp and woof of the story, artfully woven into its very structure.

1. Suggested theme, "square":
   Subject: "The first thought that came into my mind was: on the square they feed the doves."
2. Suggested theme, "summer":
   Subject: "Gathering mushrooms, raspberries, darnel.... It was pleasant to look at the sunset, to listen to the birds singing, to come back home and go to sleep."
3. Suggested theme, "snow":
   Subject: "It is a winter evening; there's snow on the street; now I must go out to-day; it will be fine if it is snowing in the forest; a raven croaks; a very sad memory comes before me."
4. Suggested theme, "factory":
   Subject: "I do not know what to say. It seems to me very strange to-day how the birds pursue me. Well, here in our village was a factory, and near it stood a house. There we met, played, and from the fields came the songs of nightingales."

All these experiments showed that, notwithstanding the instructions to avoid the theme of the suggested tendency, the subject continues to reproduce the group of compulsions, weaving it into the structure of his elaborated imagery; in the beginning the compulsive character is gradually repeated in the groups unconsciously; later appear symptoms showing that we have something extraneous (Table 3). Quickly and unexpectedly there is a change of mood: "It will be fine if it is snowing," and "the forest; the raven croaks—a very sad memory comes to me." In the last example, the theme is very far removed from that of the compulsion, but the tension finally breaks through, and the subject says that he does not know why birds pursue him.

This example shows that the group of compulsions can determine the intellectual series and the course of its associations, although the subject may not be conscious of it. This fact explains why the number of words relating to the suggested compulsive group may not be large, though, at the same time, the whole associative series is constructed under the influence of the group of compulsions.

Here is a typical example:

Subject Ner. gives an associative series including only twenty per cent of words referred to the compulsive group:
Dinner — *chicken* — setting — club — tram — flat — *crow* — grain — *pigeon* — dog — chain — table — bureau — milk — cottage — Yesenin — nuts — death — funeral — *sparrow* — street — police — square.

At first the compulsive character of the series is hardly noticeable; however, it becomes very clear when we analyse the account the subject gives of his own associative series:

"Now I am hungry, and I recall that chicken is very good for dinner; then I begin to think about the club and its social life, about my apartment, and returning home; in the courtyard there are many crows, and in the association, I remember Strastnaya Square, where there are pigeons which are fed with grain; next I think about the funeral of Yesenin and its setting as I saw it there."

The separate words taken from the compulsive series are not accidental inclusions in the freely flowing associative current; they are reversed points, its chief elements, and the whole associative process—not noticed by the subject—is precisely arranged according to these separate details, behind which is concealed the suggested tension.

The picture which we have just described is very similar to the picture of the manifestation of the affective complex in the free associative series. There, as well as here, we have a certain degree of tension; there as well as here it often appears in the frank origin of the elements connected with the complex situation, but the whole series is arranged with evident manifestations only in the definite compulsive reactions. A considerable difference is seen in that the whole series conveying the complex is of a conflicting character, while in our material we do not yet see this conflict.

This series convinces us of the stability of the suggested tension. However, it by no means always flows without obstructions, by no means does the personality always accept the suggested tendency as its own tendency not requiring special inhibition. We have observed many cases in which the suggested group remains unconnected with the rest of the associative series, when it appears there as a foreign body—and then the personality begins to struggle with it, tries not to discharge it, but to inhibit it as something unconnected, foreign, onerous. In such cases the matter was changed into a completely perceptible conflict, and this was clearly reflected in the associative series.

This reminds us of two typical structures of behaviour, described by Jaensch under the term *integrated* and *disintegrated* structure of the psychical life. The first of these is characterised by this: the personality refers to the eidetic [visual] image arising before it and dominating a certain part of the compulsion (and from the material of the image these types were described).... Such an individual is inclined to observe his eidetic images with interest, as they appear to him as an integrated part of his personality, he tends to connect with them his own creative power, and to evaluate them as products of his own free fancies.

The behaviour of the second type belongs to another group. It assumes its eidetic images as somewhat foreign, not integrated with the whole personality; they are aliens; he fears them, looking upon them as something extraneous overwhelming the picture. This, under certain conditions, can be reflected in the whole fabric of his psychical life.

We shall return to the subject in whom the suggestive compulsion entered into the conflict with the setting of the personality and produced a considerable disorganisation of the psychological processes.

Subject Zhel in the hypnotic state is given an analogous suggestion. After awakening we register in this subject a series of free associative reactions, and we obtain a picture sharply differing from all those examples with which we have operated before:

house — tram — *magpie* — divan — pillow — university — plank — mirror — *chicken* — lamp — I do not know —...samovar — cup — *nightingale* — flowers — leaves — water — grass — I do not remember —...book—conduit.

An external analysis of this series shows very clearly how fundamentally it differs from those we analysed above. The separate parts of this series are characterised by this peculiarity: the rapid and unorganised exchange sharply differentiates this series from the chain associations usually occurring in the given subject. The words relating to the suggested compulsion series enter into the general associative current, as a foreign ingredient; often they punctuate the series, which afterwards continues on (plank —mirror—*chicken*—lamb—...); one gets the impression that the subject herself fights against the suggested group, and the whole series acquires a peculiarly disorganised character. The account given by the subject testifies to the fact that we have produced here a process characterised by a conflict and confusion:

"It was difficult for me to remember any word...I do not know why —sometimes there came into my head individual words entirely disconnected with what I was speaking of...here magpie comes whence I do not know. It is not connected with anything that I was talking about."

Before us we have a process of an entirely different structure. While in those cases with which we began our discussion, the compulsive group was accepted by the personality and was distributed through the whole series, here the suggestions are accepted by the personality as something foreign, are inhibited, and precisely in this field there arises an acute conflict, causing confusion and inhibiting the normal course of the psychological processes.

Before us are two types of reaction of the personality of a group of tensions introduced into the psyche, and two types of the compulsive state created by us in the experimental setting. It is perfectly natural that both types of the psychological processes should be characterised by entirely different neurodynamics. Though in the first case we have no reason to expect a conflicting character of the process nor any marked disorganisation of behaviour, in the second instance the suggested compulsion should inevitably produce a certain affect, and attempts to remove it will result in a considerable disorganisation of behaviour.

We can easily verify this by turning our attention to the study of the structure of the integral chain associative series and to the character of the accompanying motor reactions.

From previous works coming from this laboratory [1] we know that the structure of the integral chain associative series very delicately reflects its psychological peculiarities, and that each affect or affective complex is manifested here in marked inhibitory separate intervals and disorganisation of their structure. We shall choose, therefore, the structure of the associative series introduced above, in which the suggested compulsion becomes so intimately

[1] A. N. Leontyev, *The Structural Analysis of the Chain Associative Series*, Russian-German Medical Journal, 1927.

entangled in the system of the subject's association (v. Subject
Ner.) and we compare it with the structure of the series. As an
example of the latter, we shall take the series of subject Ip.,
showing an acutely disrupted character, and ending by a refusal to continue the associations:

raven — stork — goose — duck — store — poverty — word — time —
Mary Pickford — red — beyond the sea — *they flew — storks* — I do
not want to say anything more... (Why do I tremble! I am shaking so
that even my hands tremble!)

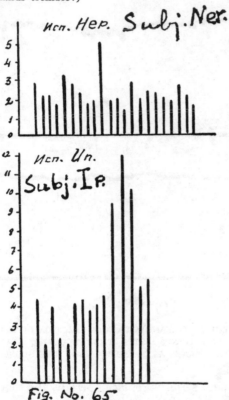

INTERVALS OF CHAIN SERIES DURING THE INHIBITION
OF THE COMPULSION

If we compare the structure of the intervals of both of these
series, then we see how much more sharply the conflicting character of the latter is reflected in it. Figure 65 shows that the
regular and only slightly varying character of the successive in-

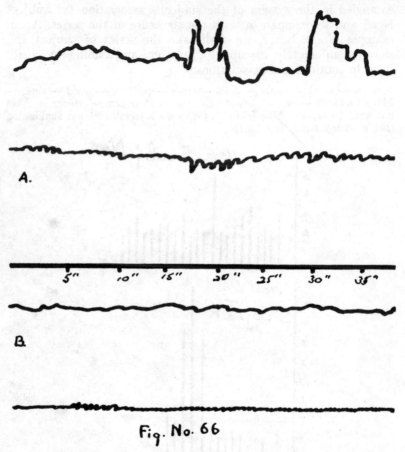

Fig. No. 66

SUBJECT IP. THE ACCOMPANYING MOTOR REACTION OF THE CHAIN SERIES:
A. TREMOR OF THE HANDS AFTER THE SUGGESTED STATE OF TENSION;
B. TREMOR OF THE HANDS AFTER REMOVAL OF THE SUGGESTION.

tervals of the first series is replaced here by the sharply increasing
inhibition, which markedly differentiates the second series from
the normal associative process. The conflict of the compulsion
with the setting of the personality produces here an acute disorganisation of the structure of the associative series, bringing it
nearer in type to the structure of the acute affective processes.

The fact that the signs of acute inhibition and finally the
refusal to react are the results of a very intense conflict is beautifully shown by an analysis of the accompanying motor activity.

At the places where the subject refuses to make further answers, from the accompanying motor curves (See Figure 66) we see the acute tremor of the right hand, and the transfer to the left hand with a picture of the irradiated excitation by extension into the individual motor systems, present every time that our activity collides with an impassable obstruction.

Comparing these curves with the static curve of both hands, which we get after removing the suggested compulsion (Figure 66, Curve B), we are convinced that this diffuse excitation was produced only by that conflict which was connected with the inhibited suggested compulsion. We succeeded in creating a model of the compulsive state which further evoked independently those conflicts from which usually develops the neurotic tendency, and completey destroyed the normal course of the neurodynamic processes.

If we examine the accompanying motor reactions in all these cases where we see before us a conflict of the suggested compulsion with the general setting of the personality, the fundamental neurodynamic changes connected with this conflict stand out before us in strong relief. In the experiments with the exhaustion of the limited series of associations,[1] we frequently saw cases where the subject was able to correct in a limited way the difficulties met with, by refusing attempts to make further associations to the given theme; but now during the compulsive character of these associations this is not possible, and we see before us a conflict of considerable intensity. Figure 67 shows that here the conflict extends over into the marked disorganisation of all the neurodynamic processes, and the analysis of the character of similar disturbances permits us to form a conjecture as to the structure of the processes having a place here.

In all of the cases where the suggestion provokes a compulsive series quickly becoming exhausted, as, for example, in the curve A of the subject Cher. (eagle—pigeon—what more—cock—nightingale—I do not know what next—eagle—crow—pigeon—guinea—kite—), or when the experiment led to a conflict between this tendency and the decision to association to another theme (as, for example, in Curve B of subject Zver.), we obtained a considerable disturbance, making the structure of the series distinctly pathological. Both of these instances make it possible to understand better those deep neurodynamic disturbances which are produced by the very intense conflict, and

[1] See Chapter VI, section 3.

at the same time, to approach experimentally the psychological structure of the state of compulsion.

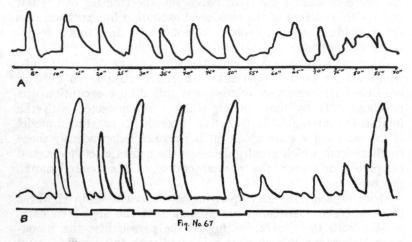

ACCOMPANYING MOTOR REACTIONS DURING SUGGESTION

A. SUBJECT CHER.   B. SUBJECT ZBER.

We can make the conflict we have chosen very much more intense, if after the suggested tendency we resist by excluding it through instructions given when the subject is awake. In a series of control experiments, having suggested the tendency to name birds, in the post-hypnotic state we told the subject to recite a list of fish or trees. After this we saw an acute exacerbation of the conflict. The results were very significant; although often, in more than sixty per cent of the cases, the instructions given in the waking state became dominant, and the subject began to give relatively regular associative series, yet this was attained always with considerable difficulty, and both the character of the speech reactions (as we see in subject Ip., sturgeon—*crow*...ach a crow is not a fish...*duck—sparrow*—what kind of a fish is this!...*titmouse*—carp...), as well as the accompanying motor reactions always indicates an extremely severe disturbance associated with such a process.

This type of conflict usually is accompanied by the presence of definitely elaborated impulses, which are then inhibited (Curve B in Figure 67 illustrates such an experiment), and this also assures the experimenter of the possibility to look in on the processes playing their part in the structure before him.

The experiments with the suggested tendency plainly show that the state of compulsion easily provokes a conflict with the fundamental setting of the personality; even though having been deprived of the affective contents, they easily provoke a spread of the excitation and affects, which is manifested precisely in the attempts to overcome these tendencies by inhibition. The more imperative the excitement and the tension, the more foreign its setting for the subject, the greater the disturbance of behaviour we may expect as a result of the collision with the regulating systems of the personality.

3. EXPERIMENTS WITH INHIBITED COMPULSIONS

IN the clinical practise of medicine it has been frequently observed that the more acute attacks of fear are obtained when we try to prevent the patient with the neurosis of fear from completing his compulsive activity.[1] This fact leads us to believe that just here in the more acute forms of conflict, arising from the arrest of the compulsive tendency, we are able to approach more closely to the mechanism of the affect.

After this, as we have said, we can easily describe the process of the affective disruption; some fairly powerful (and usually connected with the subcortical apparatus) system of activity falls under the sway of the inhibition. The conflict arising is the more intense the more imperative the arrested tendency and the more categorical the inhibition; the tension produced in the neurodynamic system strives to escape along the path of inadequate innervation, the adequate exit being closed, and there is thus created the symptoms of an intense diffuse excitation, characteristic of the affect.

This very general scheme, however, is necessary in testing the experimental material, and we may make a decided step in the solution of this problem, if we are able to create artificially such an attack of affect, and to produce it in such a situation that it would be maximally favourable for the exact study of the mechanisms appearing here.

We can easily obtain a model of an acute affective seizure if we add to the suggestion in the hypnotic state some compulsive tendency, some categorical suggestion making impossible the realisation of the compulsion. For this it is most satisfactory to create a type closely resembling motor aphasia as a model; we may suggest thinking of certain words, accompanying this with the suggested impossibility to pronounce them; thus we are able to produce a state of acute conflict, and we have a case where we can follow up the mechanisms appearing here.

[1] S. Freud: *Lectures on the Introduction to Psychoanalysis*, Volume II, page 192.

In the following series, we proceeded by this method: in order to concentrate the affect, we limited our suggestion to only two definite words, which would continually arise in the thoughts of the subject and which he would not be able to speak. Our suggested instruction was this:

"When you come into the experimental room and sit before the apparatus, you will want to repeat two words—red and blue, red and blue. However, you will not be able to speak them, although they will continue to be present in your thoughts."

In order to test the stability of the suggested inhibition we arranged special control experiments in which we first proposed to the subject to repeat after us separate words. Among these were the suggested inhibitory ones. Secondly, we asked the subject to answer questions naming the colour of some object shown him or brought to mind. Our chief experiment consisted in giving the subject an opportunity to associate freely, repeating successively all the words given him, or, in order to concentrate the conflict more markedly, enumerating individual names of colours, thus narrowing the circle of reactions and creating conditions for the more acute manifestations of the inhibitory tendency. Out of the ten subjects tested in this series, seven gave extremely marked conflicting reactions, disclosing the possibility for the study of the actual conflict in its most intense form; in the other three, we saw a somewhat different picture, showing how, during the transfer to the circuitous route, the subject was capable of mastering the present conflict.

We began by testing the stability of the suggestion we had given. It is very simple to do this, having made the subject repeat a list of words.

Figure 68 gives typical results of the experiment thus arranged. The subject readily repeats the individual words (white—white, black—black), but he refuses to repeat the word "red," inhibited by the suggestion; the accompanying motor system shows that in this case the inhibition set in after the intention had begun; the form of the curve disturbed by the tremor indicates that the excitation inhibited here was resisted, but it conditioned a certain disturbance in the motor activity of the subject.

This disorganisation stands out clearly, when from the simple and senseless repetition of words we pass over to the reasoned activity, which, however, cannot manifest itself, colliding, as it does, with the obstacle due to the suggestion in the hypnotic

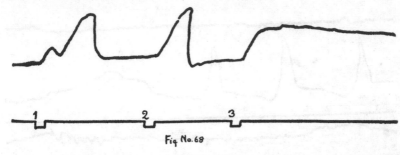

Fig No. 68

THE REPETITION OF WORDS AFTER A SUGGESTED INHIBITORY TENDENCY:
1. WHITE—WHITE; 2. BLACK—BLACK; 3. RED—(REFUSES TO ANSWER)

state. When we propose to the subject to repeat after us given words, and he cannot do this, we produce in him a state of perplexity; when we ask him to define the colour of things and he is not able to carry out such a simple request—there arises in him a state of affect; by including the suggested inhibition in the system of thought-out activity, we can produce an affect of much greater intensity.

In Figure 69 are the results of two experiments done on subject Kar.; in the first of these we propose to the subject to define the colour of definite objects, conducting the experiment after the suggestion of the inhibited tendency; the second time the same experiment is performed, directly after removing the inhibitory suggestion. The protocol shows that while the definitely "neutral" colours come out without any symptoms of delay (1. grass—1.2" —green, 2. snow—1.6"—white, 3. sand—1.4"—yellow), then the words presented touching on the crucial response produced not only considerable inhibition (4. blood—14."—blood is what colour ... bright red), but characteristic of these cases is the inhibition of the intention; the conflict is of an especially acute form when in the succeeding reaction (5. sun—8.4"—it is hard to say) approximates the usual speech motor expression connected with the inhibitory compulsive link (sun—red). After removing our suggestion, all the corresponding reactions proceed without the slightest inhibition, and do not manifest any disturbance in the neurodynamic process.

After this, the disconnected facts become obvious: the free associations succeeding the suggestion of the inhibited compulsion cannot pass through in an organised way, and their structure shows fundamental changes. Already the simple analysis of the temporary structure of the chain associative series proves how

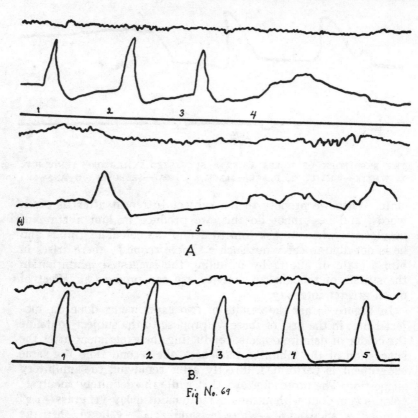

DURING THE SUGGESTED INHIBITORY TENDENCY

A

1. GRASS—1.2″—GREEN; 2. SNOW—1.6″—WHITE; 3. SAND—1.4″—YELLOW;
4. BLOOD—14.8″—WHAT COLOUR IS BLOOD? . . . BRIGHT RED! 5. SUN—8.4″
—IT IS HARD TO SAY

B. SAME AS A., AFTER REMOVING THE SUGGESTION

B

1. GRASS—2.4″—GREEN; 2. SNOW—1.0″—WHITE; 3. SAND—1.2″—YELLOW;
4. BLOOD—1.4″—RED; 5. CROW—1.0″—GREY

sharply behaviour is disorganised under the influence of the suggested conflict of the inhibitory tendency.

Figure 70 gives typical examples of such a marked influence
of the suggested conflict. If the associative series in a normal

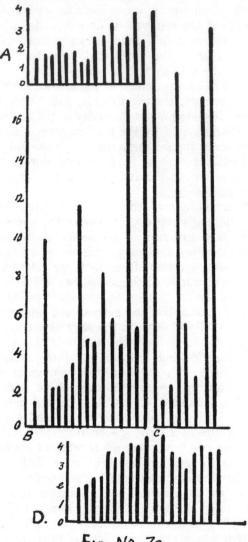

Fig. No. 70

THE GRAPHIC INTERVALS OF THE CHAIN OF ASSOCIATIVE SERIES

SUBJECT IP.: FREE ASSOCIATIVE SERIES BEFORE THE SUGGESTION; WINTER—AUTUMN—EVENING—TO WALK—IT IS POSSIBLE—CINEMATOGRAPH—DARK COLOUR—AUTUMN—ALWAYS—COLD—BREATH—HYPNOSIS ...

FREE SERIES AFTER THE SUGGESTION: 1. SPRING; 2. PORTFOLIO; 3. DIVAN; 4. CHAIR; 5. CARPET; 6. BED; 7. LENIN; 7a. WELL, I CAN NOT SAY; 8. MIRROR; 9. WHITE; 10. BLACK; 11. TABLE; 12. SHELVES; 13. BOOKS ... I CANNOT SAY ... FAIRLY ...; 14. DRESS; 15. NECKTIE—WELL, WHAT MORE TO SAY ...; 16. OMITTED ...; 17. CLOCK; 18. AGAIN OMITTED ... I WILL NOT SAY THIS WORD ... WELL, EVERYTHING ...

state is characterised by an inconsiderable variation and by a regular structure of the intervals (Curve A), then after the suggested conflict the intervals take on an actutely disorganised character, increasing in the individual cases to 12-15", in the course of which the subject vainly searches for an adequate reaction (Curve B). The problem to name successively separate colours further complicates the process, and Curve C gives an acute inhibition, breaking down the series in the seventh reaction. This process, characterised by the marked formal disorganisation of the reaction series immediately changes, when only we remove the suggested conflict; Curve B shows that during the removal of the suggestion the associative series begins anew to take a completely normal course.

The speech composition of these series completes this picture, indicating by the undisturbed character in the normal series the intensely conflicting structure of the series given after the suggestion of the inhibitory tendency, and the return to the normal after removing the suggestion. These facts are indeed very typical.

The conflicting character of the series obtained is quite obvious. The inhibition of the compulsion we produced called out a series of considerable disturbances, and gave all the fundamental symptoms which we usually observe in the most severe cases of affect. The subject begins the series with the words arising in the context of her first series, but immediately there ensue the extra-signalising reactions (2-3-4), then the naming of the colours (9), finally the attempt to say the compulsive word (7A), and the refusal. The inhibited compulsion creates here a marked limitation of the activity, producing at the end a complete inhibition and rupture of all the speech reactions; well known to everyone studying affect and neurosis is refusal from the reaction; *Sperrung* (blocking) was obtained here in an artificial way. Such a conflicting characteristic distinguishes and limits the series; the enumeration of the colours are here persistent trials by one or another path to give the compulsive reaction, "red" and "blue," and the subject begins to choose colours close to them, in order to create confusion where the direct path is unattainable.

1. Violet; 2. deep blue; 3. green; 4. well, the colour of my dress, I can't say the colour...; 5. black; 6. yellow; 7. greyish; 8. again I can't tell, I don't know the word; 9. brown; 10. again I've forgotten the colour, I do not know, I've forgotten the colour, but I should know; 11. rose...; 12. I don't know any more.

Only after removal of the conflicting structure of the series do we have a normal course of the associative processes:

winter — always — snow — frozen — Chita — aunt — letter — square
— apartment — revolution — force — Riga — science — love — hap-
piness — corner — choir — mother.

From the artificial neurosis and the disrupted structure of the
associations, we return to the normal course of the associative
series, and the normal structure of the intervals, indicating that
the conflict and the disorganisation called out by it remained
delayed.

By inhibiting the suggested tendency we produce an acute disorganisation of behaviour; it is shown in the following—the associative processes and their rhythm, as well as their content,
become acutely disturbed; the ability to give the unified con-

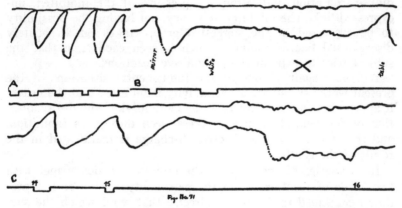

SUBJECT IP. ASSOCIATIONS DURING INHIBITED TENDENCIES

A. FREE ASSOCIATIONS IN THE NORMAL.

B. AND C. FREE ASSOCIATIONS AFTER THE SUGGESTION OF THE INHIBITED
TENDENCY.

nected series of associations within the limits of the more or less
complete intellectual structure is sharply disturbed, the conflict
is primarily reflected in the appearance of extrasignalising primitive reactions, acute inhibitions, giving to the series a markedly
disorganised character.

It is obvious that behind these there must be concealed serious
disturbances in the neurodynamical process, and the accompanying motor system reveals them. From the analysis of the associated motor reactions we see that each approximation to the
inhibited group of tendencies gives acute symptoms of diffuse
excitations, of the characteristic disorganisation of the neurodynamic process under the influence of the delayed intent.

Figure 71 is a graphic protocol of the experiment which we

have just analysed. Throughout, it discloses the dynamics of that process we are discussing. The neurodynamics of this experiment differs widely from that which is characteristic of the normal experiment (Curve A). Having begun with fairly normal associated pressures, during the approach to the inhibited link (9. white ... curve B), the subject gives the signs of the conflict arising here. The curve shows considerable and continuous tension, and it is accompanied by a sharp tremor, indicating that the adequate exit of the intention did not remain inhibited. Such a phenomenon is seen every time that the associated series approaches the inhibited group; thus the section "14. dress—15. necktie ... red!" gives an acute disorganisation of behaviour and diffuse excitation, indicating the pressure of the inhibited, unexpressed link. The inhibited tendency, not having the possibility to be expressed in the suggested group, takes on an acutely disorganised neurodynamics, which is seen each time that the subject tries to explain the compulsive reactions.

We come again to one of the fundamental situations of the present work: the stronger the activity manifested and the nearer it approaches to the motor end, the more marked the disorganisation of the neurodynamical process, seen during its inhibition, and the more acute the affective discharge is manifested in the result of the conflict.

In our series of experiments the inhibited tendency met with two kinds of reactions from the personality; sometimes it produced continued trials to say directly that word which the suggestion introduced into the reaction; at other times the subject chose numerous diverse paths, attempting to avoid the inhibited tendency by numerous confused acts. Two forms of reaction to the suggested tendency constitute the two fundamental forms of behaviour in the compulsion artificially produced by us in the laboratory; they conceal entirely different neurodynamical mechanisms.

During all of our work we never saw a more marked affect than that which appeared when the subject tried directly to explain the suggested tendency causing the conflict. The disorganisation of behaviour during such attempts takes on very acute forms.

We shall give a typical example. To subject Cher. we give our usual suggestion and obtain an associative series characterised by continued attempts to give the suggested but inhibited word. This series and its motor equivalent is shown in Figure 72.

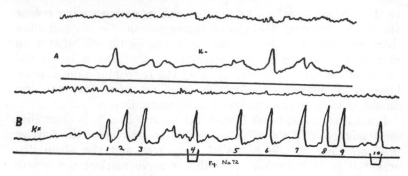

SUBJECT CHER.: MOVEMENTS DURING DIRECT ATTEMPTS TO GIVE THE PROHIBITED COMPULSIVE WORD.
A. FIRST SERIES OF FREE ASSOCIATIONS.
B. CHAIN ASSOCIATIVE SERIES.

Blue ... *blue* ...; 1. lion; 2. chicken; 3. table ... for K[1] (Experimenter: "say it in French"); 4. *rouge;* 5. *blue*; 6. rose; 7. yellow; 8. cow; 9. lion; 10. *red;* 11. *red;* 12. *blue;* 13. *k*[1] ... orova (cow); 14. lion; 15. *K* ...; 16. *blue;* 17. red; 18. *blue;* 19. white; 20. yellow; 21. horse; 22. *red;* 23. *blue* ... I do not know what to say further (glancing aside); 24. chair; 25. table ... I do not know any more ...

Before us is the compulsive tendency, manifested with the usual stability. It is true that the inhibition extends only to one part of the tendency, spreading to the word "red"; however, exactly in this direction is mobilised the whole activity of the subject. Each attempt to overturn this barrier leads only to the enunciation of the initial letter of the inhibited word and the acute disturbance of the excitation. To this is connected the general disorganisation of behaviour characterising the following section of the protocol:

During the proposition to react to all the words coming into the mind, the subject begins spasmodically to try to say something, then leaning on the back of the chair he removes his hands from the apparatus. At the request of the experimenter to spell the word he makes another confused attempt to pronounce it. The face becomes red, the eyes tearful, the pulse is markedly increased, the respiration irregular, the brow knit—in all the behaviour are the signs of an acute attack of affect.

The picture of the acute disturbance of behaviour is not confined to the attempts to say directly the compulsive word, and the subject quickly connects up the attempts with its alliteration

[1] K is the initial letter of the Russian word *krasny,* meaning red.—*Translator.*

(8. *k* . . . *orova* (cow) . . . 13. *k* . . . *orova*) or with a similar colour
(6. rose); however the motor disorganisation is considerably
shortened only after the decision to pronounce the inhibited word
in French (4), and further attempts to give the word in the
course of the series (10, 11, 17, 22); the remaining urge evokes,
however, a number of extrasignalising reactions (24, 25) and
finally, it leads to the absolute refusal to continue.

From this protocol and from other similar ones it is clear that
the tendency with the direct attempts to overthrow the barrier
produces only the discharge of the affect and the acute disorganisation of behaviour, and this is more marked the nearer
these inhibited attempts approach to the motor terminal.

This is what makes us turn our attention especially to those
cases where such direct attempts are confused with the surrounding paths by virtue of which the subject tries to avoid the given
conflict.

The analysis of all the protocols shows us that we actually
obtain a state very similar in its type to the compulsive neurosis.
Having produced artificially a compulsive but inhibited tendency
we could observe not only attempts to the direct explanation of
our instructions but attempts to make a substitution for the inhibited compulsive tendency. In such substitutions our subjects
show considerable stability, and from all our experiments we
did not have a single protocol in which such a tendency to substitution was not manifested.

The significance of this problem for our researches impels us to point
out here the basic types of these substitutions as they appear in our
subjects. We shall give them in their whole extent, ranging from the
closest to the tendency to react directly on the compulsion up to the
most complicated forms of intellectual substitutions.

1. The closest of the above cases of direct attempts is the substitution of the inhibited words by alliterations. This form of substitution may
be termed secondary; the subject tries here to pronounce the compulsive
word, but being unsuccessful, gives another word with the same initial
letter.

Thus subject Ak. gives us a series, with attempts to change the reaction from the word "blue" (*siniy*) by alliterations: machine—snake
(*smeya*)—*s* . . . hay (*seno*)—Africa—*s* . . . I do not know what to say
. . . city—house—*s* . . . sit (*sizhu*) . . .—pine (*sosna*)—earth—wane—grief
—*s* . . .—oak—Siberia—Asia—*s* . . . pig (*svinya*).

In the response the subject indicates that there was continually coming
into his mind words beginning with "s," but he was unable to explain
the cause of this.

2. Substitution by reactions such as extrasignalising or stereotypy
are seen in our experiments very often. In this case the subject tries to
get rid of the created tension by a simple removal of the surrounding

things or by a stereotyped repetition of certain words producing this.

Subject Zer. gives us such a series with a stereotyped repetition of the separate words and the transfer to primitive reactions:

City — village — forest — *village* — beasts — colours — *beasts* — hares — *city* — university — *first* — *second* — *third* — *fourth* — *fifth* — *sixth* — ... s ... table — chair — sofa — divan. ...

All known forms of substitution, from stereotyped reactions to alliteration and transfer to extrasignalising forms, appear in this series, thus providing a primitive exit for the created tension.

3. A much more interesting form is represented by the substitution of inhibitions close to the inhibited group. Thus in the prohibited compulsive reactions, "red," "blue," our subjects substitute similar colours, repeating the words, "rose," "deep blue," "violet," etc., trying to express the prohibited colours in other terms:

Subject Kar. (removal of colours): deep blue—green—*rose*—black—*violet*—greyish. ...

Subject Bas. (removal of colours: inhibited red) brown—green—yellow—raspberry ... (subject bites the gums, and opens the eyes wide) I forgot ... how is it I do not think ... *rose*—white—carmine—*orange* ... violet. ...

This scheme of substituting similarities is often met with, and gives a picture constantly appearing in neurotic compulsions. We have had many opportunities to observe it in other situations: thus in the suggestion to name birds, one of our subjects gives a substitution series showing the same mechanism:

Subject Zhil. house—tram—divan—*chicken*—lamps—straw—I do not know ... *nightingale*—flowers ... pencil ... *butterfly* ... The last reaction illustrates this rule.

4. The last form of substitution is more complicated. In this case there is not direct use of the prohibited word by one similar to it, but the subject chooses some image which runs through the whole associative series, so that here it becomes difficult to notice the direct appearance of the suggested tendency.

Here is such an example:

After the suggested inhibitory compulsive group "red-blue," Subject Bas. gives this free associative series:

Plank—pencil—armchair—*handkerchief*—lamp—old man—tram—stable—yellow—garden—wall—fire—*handkerchief*.

We cannot immediately see in this series anything of the suggested tendency besides the repetition of the word "handkerchief." The account of the subject reveals, however, the connection of this series with the suggested compulsive tendency.

"I was always thinking of our red Turkish handkerchief."

The structure of the series is now clear to us. The direct manifestation of the inhibited compulsive links are substituted here by a fixation of a certain image, which begins to replace the inhibited group and becomes the compulsion.

cf Freud's symbolic interpretation of symptom

These examples have been given in order to show that the reaction obtained mobilises the whole personality of the subject and permeates the series, sometimes being very complicated, and in

its structure approaching the model of the compulsive neuroses.
A careful study enables us to draw important conclusions from
the analysis of these states, leading to the existing mechanisms
of affect and to the neurotic destruction of behaviour.

We arranged the given material in the order of the known
movement of the subject's inhibitory activity: if in the first instance we saw attempts which almost never went to their motor
terminations and were inhibited after the subject had begun to
say the forbidden word, then in the further cases this conflict
was still more displaced from the motor sphere, the activity remains further removed from it and the entire difficulty is transferred from the motor apparatus to the connecting: our subjects
discard the attempt to break through the motor dam and they
begin to seek new connections, new speech exits, new replacing
images. The last examples which we have given refer especially
to this form of exit: the subject does not try to pass over to the
direct motor innervations; instead of this he directs all of his
strength toward the discovery of an adequate intellectual exit
to replace the prohibited path by a new one. The conflict is displaced from the motor sphere to the connecting one, and the
substitution begins to have here an entirely new character; from
the senseless substitution by alliterations, which are only trials
to pronounce, as it were, the beginning of the word, the subject
goes over to a rational replacement of the name of the forbidden
colour by others—instead of red, rose, carmine, violet,—or to the
arrangement of the replaced image—"red handkerchief": these
replaced images help to determine the subsequent associative
series, replacing the peripheral conflict by a central reconstructed
series. Without doubt, here we dealt with two very different compulsive states, and it is very important for us that we had two
special structures of the neurodynamic processes.

The movement of the inhibition from the motor system to the
connecting, coupling-up one relieves the personality from the open
conflict and avoids that affective rupture which is inevitable in
the presence of inhibition of the already formulated compulsive
activity. All our material makes it possible to draw such a conclusion. Our subject almost always discards the direct attempts
to utter the forbidden word, and passes over to its central replacement because this saves him from the acute neurodynamic
disturbance.

In Figure 73, we give the neurodynamics of two cases; in the
first of these the excitatory compulsive activity should reach to
its motor terminal, and thanks to the suggested prohibition, the

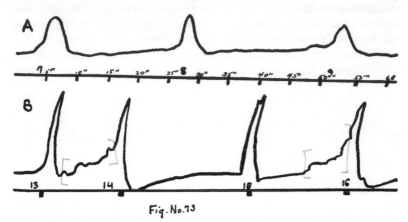

Fig. No. 73

A. SUBJECT BAS.: FREE ASSOCIATION AFTER THE SUGGESTION OF THE IN-
HIBITED TENDENCY. 7. WHITE; 8. *carmine;* 9. ORANGE.
B. SUBJECT ANT.: FREE ASSOCIATION AFTER SUGGESTION OF THE INHIBITED
TENDENCY; 13. CAPTAIN; 14. *k...k...*I DO NOT KNOW ANY MORE;
15. CAKES [*keks*]; 16. *klopit.*

conflict was produced in the speech sphere, with typical replacement by alliteration.

The observations obtained after the suggested compulsive, but
inhibited word, *"kamen"* (stone) gave us a series with a typical
motor conflict:

Subject Ant.... 1. iron; 2. mountain; 5. spring; 8. sweet; 9. autumn;
10. *kapusta* (cabbage); 11. *kisly* (sour); 12. *kartofel* (potato)...; 13.
kapitan (captain); 14. *k...k...*; 15. *k...keks* (cake); 16. *klo...*

The accompanying movements of this series point to strenuous
attempts to react, to inhibition and to considerable disorganisation of behaviour, similar to that which we saw in the above case
of Subject Cher. (Figure 72.)

The series characterised by a central replacement pursues an
entirely different course; Curve B represents the accompanying
movements of that portion of the series of Subject Bas., which
go exactly along the line of the substitution of the prohibited
colours by those similar to them:

6. *rose* 7. white 8. carmine 9. orange ...

We see that the central exit of the prohibited link is not accompanied by any remarkable motor disturbances, and that the
chief outflow of activity, which is registered by the accompanying movements, remains undisturbed and does not show any conflicts. The substitution of the peripheral conflict by the central,

connecting conflict, displaced from the motor system into the central one, carries with it considerable alteration in the course of the neurodynamical processes.

We come here to important questions of the structure of the conflicts, and these we shall take up in the following chapter.

CHAPTER VIII

THE STRUCTURE OF THE CONFLICTING PROCESSES

1. THE STRUCTURE OF THE CONFLICTS AND THE MECHANISATION OF THE DISORGANISED BEHAVIOUR

W E HAVE come to the very important questions concerning the structure of the disorganisation of human behaviour, and the location of the conflicting process.

All the experiments which we have discussed until now bring us to the conclusion that the mechanism of the conflict plays the chief rôle in the disorganisation of human behaviour, and that the delay in the excitatory system of activity may easily call out the affect and lead to a disturbance of behaviour. But now we can ask ourselves: where must the conflict arise in order that the behaviour may be disorganised maximally? At what moment, in what stage of the arising activity, does the operative conflict have a maximal chance to cause a rupture of the organised behaviour?

Before us is the most important question of the structure of the conflicting act itself and of the mechanics of its influence. This we are able to solve only by special experiments, dealing with the movements of the conflicting process, and with the artificial approach of the conflict to various stages of human activity.

Our former experiments give some clues to the solution. The experiments with the natural affect and with the artificial conflicts convince us that the disorganisation of behaviour arises only in the case where some fairly strong system of activity is subjected to inhibition; control cases showed that when a more difficult problem is given the subject, the conflict and the disorganisation of the neurodynamic processes connected with it come about only if the subject attempts to decide the problem and the obstacles inhibit these trials through several levels of the

267

beginning activity.[1] The cases of simple refusals to attempt the problem, without a mobilisation of the activity, seldom cause a conflict or any kind of disturbance.

However, we have far from sufficient evidence to enable us to define the limit of activity of those disturbances giving rise to the conflict in the behaviour. In our experiments we have seen cases which indicate at a glance that the structure and intensiveness of the disorganisation of behaviour take very unequal forms in dependence upon what limits the activity we have called out reaches, and at which levels it becomes inhibited.

We can distinguish in our material at least three fundamental instances, characterised by very different structures of the conflict and giving entirely different states of affect.

First, the excited activity of the subject may almost reach the final reaction; it may assume a concrete character, prepared for expression, and be inhibited only in the last moment at the very end of the motor act.

In this case we have to do with inhibition in the diverted motor system, and we may speak of a conflict during direct confusion in the system, *Beinahe-Entladung*. Examples of such conflicts were seen in our experiments with the "conflict of the setting," in which the word prepared for utterance suddenly appears unfit for the reaction and contradictory instructions. Similar experiments in dogs in more acute forms have been demonstrated by us in the cases of inhibited compulsion, where the subject collides with the marked obstruction during direct trials to establish the compulsive speech reaction. (See Subject Cher. Figure 72, and Subject Ant., Figure 73 A.)

Second, there is an entirely different structure in those cases where the general intention of the subject is not formulated as a reactive possibility. In these cases the beginning activity conditions only a general tension and flows over into the tonic innervations, not finding for itself, however, adequate conditioned reactions. Such cases are seen in the *conflict of defection*, such a mechanism is often met in the acute affective reactions which are characterised by the rupture and disturbance in the regularity of the speech activity, and, hence, in the decreasing possibly adequate reactions.

Third, in this case the characteristic feature is that the conflict moves from the effector system into the linking or *coupling-up* system, which has to do with making connections; the subject

---

[1] See control experiments with the *conflict of defections;* Chapter VI, and Figure 59.

does not mobilise his direct activity in order to attempt immediately to overcome the difficult problem. For the direct motor
attempts he substitutes intellectual detours, and his reaction is
characterised by the fact that the entire conflict and all the difficulties connected with it, play a rôle in the central, linking-up
apparatus. Such a process is often seen in experiments with inhibited tension. This will be the subject of our following investigations.[1]

All these forms of conflict cause very unequal disturbances in
the flow of the neurodynamic processes. The maximum disturbance in behaviour was produced by the conflict of the first
order; its traces gave rise to strong inhibitions, although there
were no perceptible signs of disorganised motor reactions. We
became convinced that the closer the conflict moves towards a
motor termination, the more active and acute are the resulting
forms of the disorganised neurodynamic process. On the contrary,
the conflict transferred from the motor sphere into the connecting
system becomes isolated, so to speak, from direct manifestation
and from any direct influence on the disorganisation of behaviour.

This statement is one of the most convincing and fundamental
conclusions which we arrive at in this stage of our investigation.
It suggests many additional questions about the structure of the
reactive processes, to which we shall give our detailed attention in
the third part of this work. Obviously, the inequality of the affect
is called out not only by the proximity of the first forms of the
conflicts to the motor sphere and the complete separation from
it of the conflicts in the connecting system, but it is clear that
between both systems there exists a great functional difference,
and that on the frontier between them there are several "barriers"
obstructing the reflection in the motor system of any conflict
originating in the connecting system.

We shall try, however, to describe the more detailed facts
confirming this view in order to consider the following conclusions.

The experiments we have performed, in a certain sense, force
us along the path of further investigation: the obtained facts
call to our mind neuropathological phenomena connected with
the confusion of the intellectual processes and speech. This
makes us think that in the control cases we may be able to
find many further facts necessary for the establishment of the
mechanisms interesting us. Many processes which we have observed in the experimental conflicts bring us strikingly close to

[1] See Chapter VII, Section 3, and Figures 71, 73-8.

the phenomena of aphasia. It is true that everything we have seen so far can be thought of as a series of phenomena reminding us of aphasia only in their separate neurodynamic manifestations; but in the given investigation our conflicts play the deciding rôle, depending upon their proximity to it.

The described forms of conflict have their extremes in two types of disorganised behaviour, which correspond most closely to aphasia of the motor and sensory amnestic types. In a typical model of concentrated motor aphasia we see what we have just referred to in the case of the artificial tension with the inhibited result. These cases give us, as a rule, a maximal destruction of behaviour. The reverse type—the conflict reminding us of amnestic aphasia—we most often see in the conflict of defection, where the subject is not able to choose or "remember" the words suitable for the occasion. Finally, experiments with the conflict of the setting show, in the cases already described, overcoming of the obstacle of the unexpected word given in another language, and it dominates the process according to the structure of the remembered sensory aphasiac phenomena. The neurodynamics of these cases are entirely different from those that we see in the open motor conflict, and we may now consider this question: what kind of neurodynamic changes are seen in the displacement of the conflicting processes?

2. EXPERIMENTS WITH CONFLICTS OF APHASIA

APHASIA is an ideal disease for the study of these problems. Not giving any constant disturbance of the neurodynamics, and often accompanied by few changes in the practical behaviour of the patient, aphasia enables us to observe the acute forms of conflict just as the patient is returning to his normal speech activity. The conflict during the motor paraphasia and during the cases of amnestic aphasia often has an acutely expressed character "of the conflict at the motor termination"; the patient understands the word that he wants to say, sometimes pronounces the first letter but is not able to utter the word, owing to the inhibition during its final formation and pronunciation. This is why it is possible to observe in the general behaviour, and excitability, an acute disorganisation of the neurodynamics, evidently depending upon the actual speech conflict.

First, in aphasia it is possible to observe exact fixation of the natural conflicts which are manifested here in an unusually well-defined and isolated form.

However, along with this there is a second possibility, also of a purely experimental character. We can try to move the conflict in the aphasiac, carrying it from the motor sphere to the receptory-connecting area. We can arrange the experiment so that the patient meets with the obstacle not during the reaction to the word, but during the reception and elaboration of the proffered stimulus and the search for an adequate reaction. Those changes in the neurodynamic processes which we have obtained in this case will be especially instructive because they take place in a motor conflict belonging to the subject, depriving his behaviour of its usual organisation.

We shall begin with an analysis of those changes which occur in the behaviour of the aphasiac with the speech conflict. Out of a series of ten cases of amnestic aphasia, upon which we performed our experiments, we shall limit our discussion to only those of them showing fairly uniform results.

We shall describe those cases of amnestic aphasia upon which most of our experiments were done:

Patient A. Kut., 20 years old, a peasant boy having finished a country school. Eight months before the experiment there was a marked disturbance of speech, beginning with complete dumbness, and then gradually passing over into a clearly expressed disturbance of the amnestic type. It was easy for him to speak entire phrases and sentences, but very difficult to say single words. He could readily count up to 8, but he laboured considerably in repeating the figures backwards.

Patient Pal., 56 years old, housewife. An analogous picture of aphasia but in a more severe form. She is able to speak several phrases, but finds it difficult to pronounce the separate words.

Patient Alt., 52 years, housewife. She shows the same symptoms as the above except in a more marked degree.

Patient Avt., 47 years, an engineer, highly educated. Aphasia of the amnestic type. He converses freely, complains that his memory is weak, that he forgets many words. There is great difficulty in naming objects.

Patient Gen., 54 years, showing serious aphasiac symptoms. He can hardly talk connectedly; he says parts of phrases, he often unexpectedly utters an entirely different word from the one he desires to say. There is marked retardation in naming objects and in repeating words.

Patient Yak., 55 years. Amnestic aphasia with forgetting of separate expressions and words, but preservation of the ability to make connected conversation.

We limit ourselves to only a few patients; the material especially connected with aphasia, we have discussed elsewhere.[1] As the starting point for our analysis we shall take the patient Kut., according to Head, an especially interesting case of aphasia, where at an early age all of the conflicts of interest to us have a much more energetic tonus.

[1] Lebedinsky und Luria: *Die Methode der abbildenden Motorik und ihre Anwendung an die Nerwenklinik.* Archiv f. Psychiatrie, Bd. 87, 1929.

We can establish our analysis on the basis of the general neurodynamics underlying the aphasiac conflict. A series of control experiments were made to determine the simplest neurodynamic processes outside of the speech activities.

The experiment with the simple reaction shows that the motor system of the aphasiac beyond the speech activity presents hardly any deviation from the normal. A series of special disturbances in the structure of the reactive processes will be discussed later. Figure 74 illustrates the simple reactions of Subject K. to sound signals. Besides a slight tremor of the right hand and an intense one of the left, we do not meet here with any perceptible declination from the normal; these symptoms of increased motor labileness are seen, as a rule, in normal subjects.

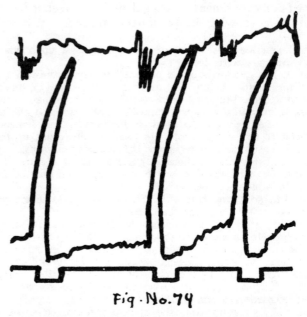

Fig · No. 74

SUBJECT K. SIMPLE REACTION TO SOUND SIGNALS.

Tapping also gives in this subject, as well as in many other cases of paraphasia, practically normal results.

Entirely analogous facts are obtained during the inclusion of a simple activity connected with the apparatus of articulation. We began by asking the patient to repeat definite sounds or syllables, while he simultaneously presses with the right hand;

we investigated first not the speech but the primitive vocal activity.

The results may be seen in Figure 75. This figure contains a section of the experiment in which we tell the subject to repeat after us the sound "a" accompanied by pressing the bulb; in part B he should similarly repeat exactly the syllable "va." In both cases the process occurs without perceptible difficulty, and the neurodynamics reflected in the motor curves indicate that the simple vocal reactions are not yet connected with the conflict which we are accustomed to observe in aphasiacs.

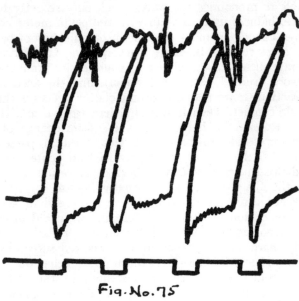

Fig. No. 75

SUBJECT K. REPETITIONS OF THE SYLLABLE "VA."

The first manifestation of the aphasiac conflict connected with the simple vocal activity is seen not during its activity, but at the time of the first conflict of the setting, which comes out very clearly in this subject in the experiments with the simple exchange of vocal coordination.

Every one of the several repetitions by the aphasiac of the vocal reactions creates in him a definite habitual setting; and when after the enunciation several times of the syllable "ma" we propose to the aphasiac to say the hardly less easy syllable "pa," he comes upon a definite obstruction as a consequence of the articulative setting we have created to the syllable "ma."

Thus there is evoked a more primitive one of the aphasiac conflicts, which is nothing else than the conflict of the setting manifested with great facility. In Figure 75 we give the motor picture of this conflict, clearly indicating that the inhibition of the active setting brought about by us in the actual motor terminal produces an acute motor excitation, and for a considerable period of time disorganises the behaviour. One can easily understand that this disorganisation attains its maximum when we pass over to the pronunciation of words difficult to the subject. This fact, that after the setting which we have created, the subject is not able to pronounce the word which only recently he could pronounce, induces us to conjoin with the acute motor conflict a still deeper affective conflict, and the disorganisation of behaviour in these cases reaches its most marked form. In Figure 77 we demonstrate such a case: Subject K. could easily pronounce after us the word "ruiba" (Russian for fish), and the accompanying motor reaction shows that this pronunciation occurs without any perceptible conflict. Then it was sufficient to give him the word "loshad" (Russian for horse), and the sudden change of setting made it impossible to pronounce this word, a perseverative tendency with the former word produced an acute motor conflict, and this caused a considerable disorganisation of behaviour with all the symptoms of an unusually intense spread of excitation. When after several minutes we succeeded in getting an adequate repetition of the word "loshad," we could observe the reverse phenomenon; the sudden transfer "ruiba" created an extremely sharp conflict, resulting in a marked spreading of the excitation and a complete disorganisation of behaviour.

If the conflict of the setting appeared in the aphasiac in marked degree, then no less marked was the phenomenon of the conflict of defection, connected, however, with the inability to name the given word, though well known to the subject. As in that case, we had here a clear example of the "conflict at the motor end," and Figure 78 shows that it was inevitably accompanied by an intense peripheral excitation and complete disintegration of the organised form of behaviour.

We have repeatedly seen that our conflict produces not only active motor disturbances (that would naturally follow from the fact of the active speech tendency which accompanies the motor reaction), but those mechanisms of the transfer of the motor excitation which we have already had an opportunity to observe in the study of affects and conflicts. These cases of transfer were obtained very easily when the movement of the right hand was not accompanied by the speech reaction;

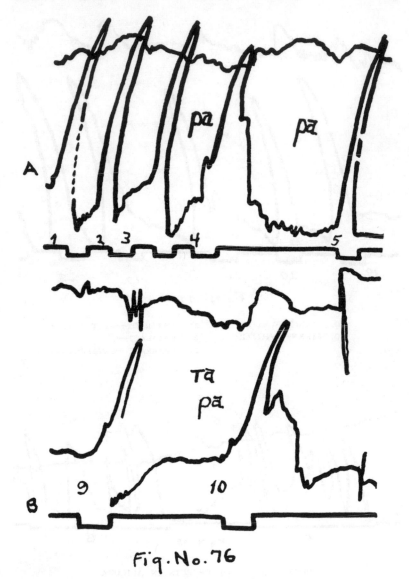

Fig. No. 76

SUBJECT K. REPETITION OF WORDS 1, 2, 3.—NA, MA; 4. PA—P . . .; 5. PA—
PA; 9, PA—PA; 10, RA—PA.

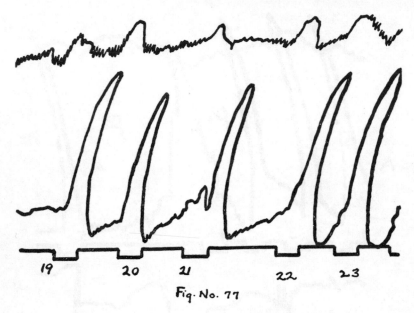

Fig. No. 77

19.	LINEN—WHITER	21.	CATARACT—SLEY
20.	LINEN—WHITER	22.	CATARACT—SLEY
		23.	CATARACT—CATARACT

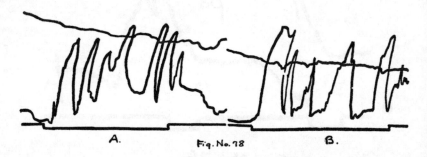

A.   Fig. No. 78   B.

IDENTIFICATION OF OBJECTS IN APHASIA

A. SUBJECT K.: WHAT IS THIS? (HOLDING UP THE HAND)—I DO NOT KNOW.

B. WHAT IS THIS? (HOLDING UP A FINGER)—I DO NOT KNOW. IS IT A TOE?—NO. IS IT A FINGER?—YES.

the mechanisms of the reflection of the affective processes in the passive expressive systems—described by many authors, beginning with R. Sommer and ending with O. Löwenstein and his school—were obtained here in the actual conflict of the aphasiac.

Such a case is shown in Figure 79. In Part A of this figure, we have an example of how the repetition of the word "krupa" (Russian for grits) after the setting created to the word "ruka" (Russian for hand) is reflected in the active accompanying motor system. Curve B of the same figure demonstrates a similar obstruction in the passive motor systems. At the same time that we get typical discoordinations in the first case, produced by the increasing changes reflected by the active functions of the right hand, in the passive motor systems these conditions caused marked phenomena of transferred and considerable tremor of the left hand.

In all these cases the conflict we produced continued through to the motor termination; the subject well knew what he should say, but the confusion of aphasia made this impossible, destroying the reaction during the very act of enunciation. The extremely active disturbances which are observed here, we are inclined to ascribe to the fact that the conflict arises in direct proximity to the motor area, and that precisely here, more than in any other case, we see inhibition during the *Beinahe-Entladung, i.e.,* during the more active moment of the reactive process.

After we have been convinced of the exceedingly well defined manifestation of the conflict, distributed in direct approximation to the motor area, we turn with great interest to the experiments on the "displacement" of the conflict. Our problem here consists in transferring the obstruction from the motor part of the process to the receptory, or the connecting area, and to investigate the neurodynamic changes occurring with such a movement of the conflict. We should consequently produce in the subject a tendency to decide the problem given him (not inhibiting his answer from the very first), according to his capabilities in the receptory-connecting system.

We can determine this by a very simple experiment. We show the aphasiac various pictures and instruct him to name the objects portrayed. In certain cases we can make the pictures easily understood, but we may make difficult the process of naming them in its motor part; in other cases, we may put obstacles in the path of the receptory process by giving pictures which are not clear in their outlines, or which are unfamiliar to the subject. In both cases he is asked to name the object and to accompany the naming with the pressure of the bulb.

Many experiments make it clear that the conflict moved into the receptory area exhibits the same phenomena of excitation

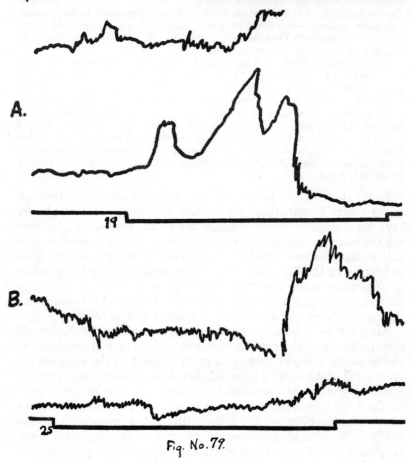

Fig. No. 79.

REFLECTION OF THE APHASIAC DIFFICULTIES IN THE ACTIVE AND PASSIVE
MOTOR SYSTEMS

SUBJECT K.—19. (AFTER REPETITION OF "RUKA") "KRUPA"—RUT—RUKA
—NO; 24. (UNDER THE SAME CONDITIONS, BUT WITH REGISTRATION OF
THE PASSIVE TREMOR IN BOTH HANDS) KRUPA—KRU—MA—RUKA—RU—

and disorganisation of behaviour which were characteristic of
the cases of motor conflict.

In Figure 80 two such examples are shown. In Part A of this
picture is given the reaction of Subject Alt. to a picture containing a word difficult to pronounce ("paravoz"—Russian for
locomotive); the motor symptoms of this reaction are illustrated by the sharp disturbance of excitation analogous to cases
which we have already seen (Reaction 12). Reaction 13 is en-

tirely different; here we show the subject a sketch of a bird's head, drawn very badly; the subject tries to understand this picture but finally refuses to answer. We bring out a completely analogous process in Subject Avt. (Curve B of Figure 80) presenting to him this time an easily named picture (Reaction 7), and then one incomprehensible for him—a rhinoceros—which he tries to identify as a pig or a bear, not reaching any final decision, however.

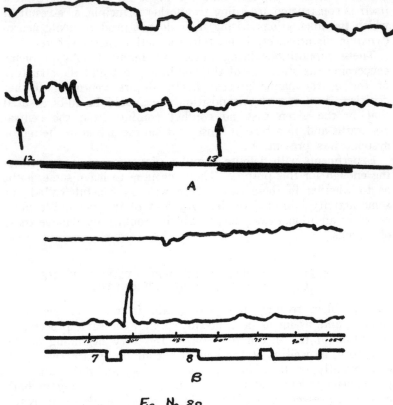

Fig. No. 80

NAMING OF PICTURES IN APHASIA

A

SUBJECT ALT.—12. MOTOR CONFLICT; 13. RECEPTORY CONFLICT.

B

SUBJECT AVT.—7. EASILY UNDERSTOOD PICTURES; 8. INCOMPREHENSIBLE PICTURE (SENSORY CONFLICT).

In both of the cases we see the same neurodynamic picture; the displacement of the conflict into the receptory part of the process has been completely deprived of the neurodynamic disturbances which were so active during the conflict arising in direct approximation to the motor terminal.

In our opinion, the receptory-connecting process is separated from the motor sphere by some kind of "barrier," impenetrable to the conflict arising in the prepared central process; on the other hand, it is possible that the prepared connecting system itself is constructed according to another principle, as a result of which the fluctuations arising in it do not produce acute neurodynamic disturbances, at least in the active motor sphere.

These suppositions bring before us many serious problems concerning the structure of the conflicting act and the structure of the neurodynamic process itself. Before venturing further criticism, however, of this position, we should be fully assured that in the given case no conflict coming from the central apparatus and, in a certain sense, not having arisen in the motor system, was present.

Experiments with definite complex pictures were not convincing enough for this purpose. They continue to leave some doubt as to whether in these cases there was, in general, called out some activity inhibited in the very first of its stages. We must resort to additional experiments which should fully remove these objections.

3. EXPERIMENTS WITH THE DISPLACEMENT OF THE CONFLICTS IN SPEECH DIFFICULTIES

OUR problem requires that we obtain in one and the same subject, and, as far as possible, in one and the same process, an inhibition of the speech reaction at the very beginning of the receptory, as well as at the end of the motor, phase; we must, consequently, try to create a model of sensory and motor aphasiac phenomena in one and the same subject, guaranteeing in both cases the presence of excitation in its active tendency to react, and, when possible, obtaining the movement of the conflicts during the course of the experiment.

For the solution of this problem, we chose a very simple approach. In order to create speech conflicts of the most varied structures, with general preservation of the intellectual processes, it was sufficient to perform associative language experiments in a subject who was far from being proficient in the given language. With such experiments in the foreign language we could reckon on obtaining an acute conflict of defection, produced by a collision of the setting to the associative response and the insufficiency in the speech inventory. We could surely expect here that the structures of the conflicts which we had produced were far from being equal. In certain cases the conflict was the result of the fact that the subject was not able to remember the name of the given word in the foreign language, and the prepared reactive image did not find its motor formulation. We shall deal with the process which, in its structure, is similar to amnestic aphasia. Other cases will be characterised by the fact that the word in the foreign language presented to the subject is not understood by him; precisely at this point we may count on finding a marked fluctuation connected with attempts to comprehend it, and the process which results will in this case have all the characteristics of the receptory conflict. We do not see anything reminding us of the model of aphasia of the sensory type.

We do not know of any experiments devoted to the investigation of the associative activity in people not thoroughly understanding the language in which they are required to associate. Classical psychology always required a complete knowledge of the language, and only under these conditions did it consider possible the study of the associative processes. The study of the speech reactions, however, in a foreign, badly understood language, is full of possibilities. Creating a fertile soil for the reception of conflicting and affective processes, a similar experiment makes it possible to study a series of structures of the speech and associative processes which were concealed and not manifest in the usual experiments, and stand out clearly only in such a "pathological experiment."

By such a method we performed experiments on 15 subjects. They were all students having some knowledge of the foreign language, but were not proficient in it. All of them were given 25 word-stimuli in succession in the foreign language, and they had to give associative reactions in the same language.

The behaviour itself of the subject is proof that we have here a well-defined affective reaction to a situation connected with a major conflict. At first the subject averred that the test with him would not be successful, and only after repeated assurances did he come into the experiment. The extreme tension and then the perturbation and confusion which accompanied the experiment created a general atmosphere very irritating to the subject, but exceedingly favourable for the study of the conflicts under consideration.

The character of the speech reactions we obtained in this experiment is, obviously, very different from that which we have seen in the general, normal, associative experiment.

TABLE 26

Subject	Language	Reaction	mV
1 Bog.	French	6.0″	2.0″
2 K.	English	4.3″	7.7″
3 Kog.	English	2.2″	0.5″
4 Kaul.	German	3.2″	1.4″
5 Lur.	English	3.0″	0.8″
6 Mor. N.	English	2.8″	1.0″
7 Mor. T.	German	2.2″	0.9″
8 Mor. T.	English	2.2″	0.5″
9 Sad.	English	5.0″	3.5″
10 Shav.	German	2.8″	1.2″
11 Shav.	German	2.8″	0.4″
12 Er.	English	3.0″	0.6″
13 Er.	English	3.4″	1.8″
14 Ud.	French	4.2″	2.4″
15 Cher.	French	3.2″	1.2″
Average		3.6″	1.8″

The confusion of the subject appears not only in his behaviour, but in the character of the associative processes themselves. Table 26 gives a summary of the reactive times obtained in this experiment. A great delay is accompanied here by extreme variations, averaging 50%. From these we may see the extremely chaotic and disorganised character of the series. The curves of distribution of the reactive time have in the different subjects a varying and irregular character (see the curve in Figure 81), and they show that the standard forms of reaction have been entirely lost here, and they are by no means typical of the higher automatisms. Finally, the speech reactions were sharply decreased, and not at all comparable with those which we usually obtain in the associative experiment on adult subjects.

Table 27 shows that 60% of the primitive inadequate speech reactions are given by those figures which reflect the difficulty and, partly, the impossibility of the subjects attaining to the conditions laid down by us in our instructions.

All of this shows the conflicting character of the picture, and gives us reason to expect great disturbances in the neurodynamic processes.

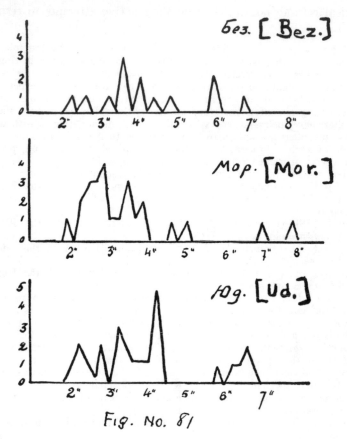

Fig. No. 81

CURVES OF DISTRIBUTION DURING THE REACTIONS TO A FOREIGN LANGUAGE

TABLE 27

Refusals	Extra-signallisation	Sound and Speech Movements	Adequate Associations	Special Forms (translation compounding, etc.)
10.5%	16.5%	23.0%	40.2%	9.8%

The facts obtained in this series are characterised, however, by a marked peculiarity: the subject always manifests here considerable activity, and we almost never meet with cases in which the given word produces immediately a definite and categorical refusal, not anticipating their active attempts to respond to it.

One may think that a chief rôle in this act is played by the following circumstance: that with the transfer to the foreign language in thinking there is always resurrected those mechanisms of syncretism [1] which in the verbal thinking in the native language had been already experienced in childhood. All of our experiments confirm this view. The subject, when experiencing an unfamiliar word or one with which he is only slightly familiar, nevertheless attempts to think it out, assimilating it with words whose meanings are known to him, or trying to guess its meaning. As a result of such a process, we have a very peculiar association, proving how deeply ingrained syncretism is in our thought.

Here are several such typical syncretistic responses:

Subject K. (English) ball—evening [assimilation with the Russian word "ball' equivalent to the English word "ball" in the sense of a formal dance].

Subject Sl. (German) *Lippe—Baum* [assimilation with the Russian word *lipa,* meaning a lime tree].

Subject Ud. (French) *la vache—laver* [assimilation with the German word *waschen*].

Subject Er. (English) letter—summer [assimilation with the Russian word *leto* meaning summer].

It is evident that, during such a syncretistic tendency to reactions, very capricious forms of responses occur, in which the conflict is reflected in the very structure of the speech response. The involvement of the assimilation and of another more familiar language creates for such a conflict an unusually rich soil and brings about the movement of this conflict to the speech termination of the reaction. Here are typical examples of such conflicting structures of the speech responses, representing some mechanisms of the verbal new elaborations.

Subject K. (English) ink—inkkerchief (instead of inkstand; through the elaboration hand—handkerchief).

Subject Mor. (German) *Vogel—Springling* (combining springen and *Sperling*).

Subject Vil. (German) *Vogel—der Ers* (combining the German "Nest" and the Russian *aist* meaning "stork").

Subject Mor. (English) stone—stoner (according to the formation *kamen—kamentschik,* Russian words for "stone" and "brick-layer" respectively).

The examples we have given show very clearly that we can easily obtain in this series conflicts arising in the speech termination of the reaction. The instance of the strongly inhibited reactions proves that we can with equal success produce conflicts in the receptory area.

Here are examples of conflicts of both types:

[1] Syncretism is a term introduced by Claparède and Piaget to indicate a primitive mechanism of thinking whereby the conclusion is reached without sufficient basis by the external appearance of the object. See *Amer. Jour. of Psychology,* Jan. 1932, p. 123.—*Translator.*

A. *Receptory conflict:*
Subject Bod. (French) *le ciel*—16.0"—*le ciel, le ciel,* I do not know what this is.

Subject K. (English) town—5.8"—town, town...Ah! village! (I thought this was a very difficult word, but then I remembered and it seemed funny to me.)

Subject K. (English) see [1]—14.0"—a verb?—Ach! oh no! moon! (I was thinking that this was a verb, then I remembered that it is the sea.)

In all these cases the conflict is connected with the reception of the given word-stimulus; it causes in the subject a confused conception, then begins the attempt to assimilate, to understand this word; connected with the reception of the word-stimulus, there may be a very real conflict, but after this, when it is overcome, the answer is given by the subject easily.

B. *The effector conflict* is characterised by the converse of the above: the perception of the given word takes place fairly easily, the obstacle is overcome by a search for the adequate word response; a deficient vocabulary will make this process an especially conflicting one. Here are some examples:

Subject Vil. (German) *Morgen*—nothing comes of it. ("I recalled dawn, then came morning, many thoughts, but I could not find the proper word.")

Subject Bod. (French) *la cloche*—I do not know... ("I thought of: foot, church bells").

Subject K. (English) nose—19.0"—Oi, *nichevo.*[2]... ("I wanted to say some part of the face, and then I thought of many words but none of them seemed suitable, then I decided not to answer.")

The conflicting character of both of these parts are indisputable; therefore we may confidently expect a fairly marked neurodynamic change accompanying these conflicting processes. The results confirm our supposition. As much as 82% of all the accompanying motor reactions occur in this series with considerable disturbances. As is shown in Table 28 (we submit only 10 cases and their registered accompanying reactions), this quantity drops sometimes to 40-60%; in some cases all 100% of the accompanying reactions are disrupted.

It is obvious, however, that in the various structures of the

---

[1] In choosing between "c," "sea," and "see" we have used the last to represent phonetically the word given by the person performing the test.—*Translator.*

[2] *Nichevo* is a word very commonly used throughout Russia, having no equivalent in English, usually indicative of a negative passivity, but having a range of meanings from nothing, "no," "all right," through *comme ci comme ça* to a fatalistic "it doesn't matter," "it can't be helped."—*Translator.*

TABLE 28

No.	Subject	Total Motor Disturbances	Diffuse Passive Disturbances	Active Disturbance
1	Bod.	100%	70%	30%
2	Pog.	44%	44%	
3	Kaul.	12%	8%	4%
4	Lur.	24%	20%	4%
5	Mor. N.	12%	8%	4%
6	Mor. T.	28%	12%	16%
7	Slav.	44%	36%	8%
8	Er.	20%	12%	8%
9	Ud.	68%	40%	28%
Average		32%	22.2%	9.8%

conflicting processes we may expect equal arrangements of the neurodynamic disturbances. Actually all of the motor disruptions met with in this series fall into two groups; in some of the cases we observe disturbances in the latent period, having the character of a passive, diffused disorganisation (such disturbances make up about 22% of our series). Other cases are connected with acute disturbances of the active type, which may be considered as inhibition of the individual, more or less formulated, impulses; and these make up about 10% of all the cases, and they usually are the more marked forms of the disorganised behaviour. We can easily understand how the latter forms of disturbances are most often connected with the conflict situated in the motor sphere, while the first is characterised by more general confusion, arising in the receptory conflict.

The analysis of the structure of the accompanying motor responses allows us to conclude further: the neurodynamics of the receptory conflict, as our graphic protocol shows, are distinguished not only by their peculiar structure, but by their qualitatively and quantitatively lessened disturbance in comparison with the neurodynamics of the conflicts arising directly in the motor sphere. AND AS EXPRESSED MOTORICALLY IN TREMOR

In Figure 82 there are several examples of such a receptory conflict, and they occur with the same structure of the motor reactions as those we have already seen in the effector conflicts.

Three of our curves are distinguished by one general structure. The conflict arising in the receptory area does not pass over to the direct active innervation of the motor reactions;

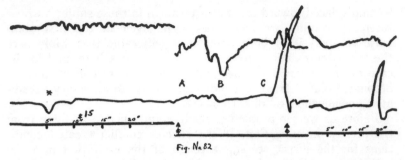

Fig. No 82

THE RECEPTORY CONFLICT IN EXPERIMENTS WITH FOREIGN LANGUAGES

A. SUBJECT SL.—*Kreide*—4.8″—I DON'T KNOW WHAT THIS IS.
B. BED.—*le gateau*—6.3″—*le lo* (SOUND).
C. ER.—LOVE—4.6″—HOW? I DON'T KNOW WHAT IT IS.

it conditions several passive, diffuse fluctuations in the right hand, and as a rule, brings about a transfer of the excitation to the left hand, thus extending into the passive motor system. All of the disturbances produced here are not of an acute active character, and we again get the impression that the conflict, removed from the motor sphere, manifests a less acute structural form. In effect, if we actually compare this picture with the motor symptoms obtained during the actual speech conflict, the structural differences are considerable.

In Figure 83 we have examples of how the conflict behaves

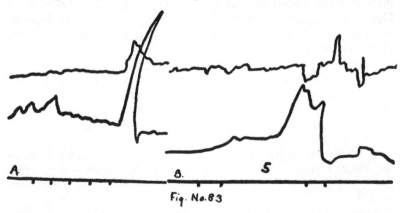

Fig. No. 83

THE EFFECTOR CONFLICT DURING THE REACTION TO A FOREIGN LANGUAGE

A. SUBJECT BOD.—*L'école*—6.0″—*l'école . . . le mâitre* (I WANTED TO SAY TEACHER).

B. SUBJECT ER.—HEART—8.2″—*nichevo* (I THOUGHT OF THE GERMAN WORD *Haare*).

when displaced toward the motor terminal in those subjects whose receptory conflict we have just seen. Even in the first comparative analysis of both cases it is noticeable that while here the excitation extends directly into the motor sphere, and in the case of the removal of the conflict into the receptory field, it becomes isolated from it, conditioning only an accessory, irradiated phenomenon of disturbance.

Before us we see problems which we are unable to solve from the present investigation. If the effector conflict created conditions for the direct seeping through of the excitation into the active motor area and produced marked disorganisation of the active behaviour, then the conflict, forced into the receptory-connecting sphere, can evoke certain changes in the neurodynamics of the organism. A series of observations leads us to believe, however, that the excitation caused by the conflict, having been separated from the active motor area, finds other paths of expression, extending primarily into the passive motor field and into the vegetative processes. We are fully assured that a detailed analysis would reveal during the receptory conflict considerable vegetative changes, and this should make it possible to reach an evaluation from the new aspect of the mechanics of the disorganisation of human behaviour.

The experiments with the displaced conflicts enable us to reach a conclusion which has been already noted in the examination of the affective processes: the disorganisation of the active behaviour is connected with the conflicting process, and depends upon the inhibition of some significant part of the given process of the (leading) activity. This disorganisation is the more acute the closer the conflict comes to the motor sphere.

The maximal and most acute forms of the disorganisation of active behaviour occur in those cases where the conflict arises directly in the motor termination, inhibiting the action already completely prepared for expression (*Beinahe Entladung*).

The displacement of the conflict into the receptory-connecting area in the majority of cases (in the cultured adult) isolates the conflict from direct influence upon the active motor reactions, and the conflict in this instance ceases to produce a serious pathological disorganisation of behaviour.

Analysing those extremely acute forms into which the effector conflict flows, we begin to understand how the conflict displaced from the motor area plays the deciding rôle in the preservation of the personality from that disruption which might threaten it if all of the conflicts went over directly into the motor apparatus. For this reason, among the mechanisms causing the domination of the actual affect, the leading rôle should unquestionably be taken by the mechanism of the displacement of the conflict, isolating it from the motor sphere.

What is the significance of the conflict's becoming isolated from the motor function—from the effector sphere—and displaced into the receptory-connecting area? How do we explain the fact, that having been displaced to that point, the conflict ceases to go over directly into the active motor area and to disorganise the active behaviour?

We are inclined to see the answer to this problem in the fact that the receptory-connecting system, on the one hand, and the effector, on the other, play functionally unequal rôles in the activity of the organism, and they dominate unequivalent structures. Having special functions according to the previous elaboration of the activity, this first system in the cultured adult is isolated from the motor area in such a way that the excitation beginning in it does not go over directly into the motor apparatus, but is transferred to it only when the elaborated process is completed.

This division of all the activities into two strictly separated phases is characteristic of the behaviour of every adult, so that in normal behaviour one receives the impression that between the two phases there is some "barrier," obstructing the direct transfer of excitation to the motor area and allowing the organism to prepare itself for activity, in order that it may then, by the organised motor act, complete the prepared connection.

Because the connecting apparatus is so extremely labile and has such a wealth of functional possibilities, and the motor apparatus is comparatively simple, is perhaps the reason why every conflict occurring in the motor area, disrupts the normal motor activity, while the same conflict displaced toward the receptory-connecting terminal, is successfully utilised by the complex psychological mechanisms, and remains isolated from a detrimental influence on the behaviour.

4. STRUCTURE OF THE CONFLICTING PROCESSES AND THE PROBLEM OF THE NEURODYNAMIC TYPE

In our analysis so far we have ventured an opinion concerning those individual differences which are characteristic of the behaviour of various subjects. However, such differences play an important rôle in the formulation of the reactions to the given conditions of our experiments. When one and the same set of circumstances, evoking, for example, a given psychological mechanism, produce, however, different neurodynamic reactions, we have a right to speak of individual variations in the neurodynamics of our subjects, and to refer the data precisely to this.

We shall return to the example which gives us an opportunity directly to analyse the mechanisms lying at the basis of the individual differences of the neurodynamic apparatus.

Figure 84 gives two reactions in two subjects. Both reactions occurred under the conditions of the conflict of defection during the experiment with limited associations. The two are almost equal in their psychological structures; in each of the subjects the stimulus meets with a certain obstacle, and after considerable inhibition, the subject responds by giving some word.

However, the structures of the neurodynamic processes lying at the basis of each of these reactions, differ essentially one from the other. Although in the first subject the associative obstruction does not produce any perceptible neurodynamic disturbance, the reactive process of the second is distinguished by the signs of intense excitation, sharp disorganisation of the motor system, occurring throughout the latent period, and transferred even to the left, passive hand. The introduction of the difficulty does not cause loss of equilibrium in the first subject, but in the second subject it gives rise to a marked disorganisation of behaviour. According to the facts, we have here two subjects characterised by different degrees of labileness of neurodynamics, and in these subjects the proximity of the intensity of the excitation produces entirely unequal neurodynamic reactions. We might call these two types of nervous systems the stable and labile, and expect that these differences would be manifested not only in the separate reactions but in the whole behaviour.

Both pictures of the reactive processes in these two subjects confirm the hypothesis that the differences we observed were not accidental. Below is a summary of the characteristic reactions in the experiment with limited associations:

	Subject K.	Subject Is.
Weak motor disturbances	7.5%	35%
Isolated motor disturbances in the left hand	2.5%	2.5%
Marked motor disturbances	—	5%
Total motor disturbances	10%	40%

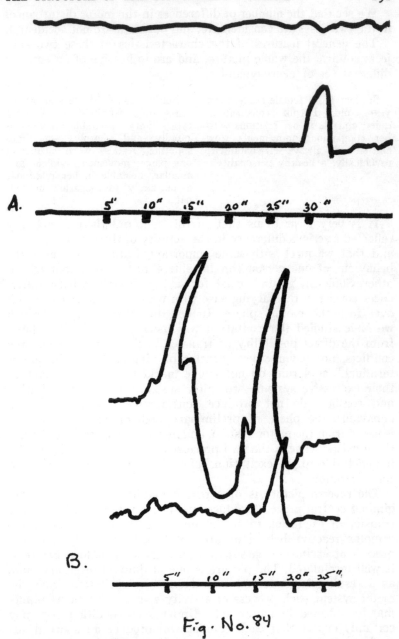

Fig. No. 84

INDIVIDUAL DIFFERENCES IN THE REACTIVE PROCESS
A. SUBJECT K.—TALE—7.2″—WELL, WORD
B. SUBJECT IS.—DRESS—4.0″—BUTTON

We see that the number of differences in the motor disturbances in the two cases are considerable, and our data are not accidental.

The general features of the characteristics of these two subjects confirm the whole picture, and are indicative of an entirely different set of neurodynamics.

Subject K., a female student, 25 years old, Pycnik constitution, quiet, equable in her relations with her companions, movements slow and smooth, always self-contained; psychically, a healthy personality.

Subject Is., a female student, 24 years old, definitely an asthenic type, very excitable, converses rapidly and sharply, sometimes shouting, restless when sitting in one place, movements violent and angular, unstable in her relations; a markedly psychopathic individual.

It is very clear to us that in this material there is actually reflected a serious difference in the activity of the nervous system, and that we meet with some important features by which the behaviour of one person can be differentiated from that of another. Sufficient grounds exist for saying that these basic differences consist in the varying ease with which the excitation passes over into the motor sphere. In certain of the subjects which we have studied the excitation was usually fairly well isolated from the direct possibility of transfer to the motor system; the conflicts, not having the character of "inhibition at the motor terminal," as a rule, do not evoke marked motor disturbances; their expressive systems are fairly stable, the central excitation and conflicts do not produce considerable disorganisation of behaviour, the phase of preliminary elaboration is fairly well isolated from the motor system, and as we have already indicated, there exists between the two processes, it seems, a stable barrier impenetrable to the excitation before it is sufficiently elaborated for a reaction.

The reverse picture is of a reactive-labile type; only the beginning central process produces in such a subject an immediate transfer of excitation to the motor system; both phases of the complex reactive behaviour are not timed accurately, and the process of excitation passes over into motor reactions before it is well formulated. The picture is one of diffused reactions; and, as a result of the defection, isolating the excitation from the motor system, each process of activity goes too far, being immediately reflected in motor acts. Under such conditions we may certainly expect that each conflict will produce an acute disorganisation of behaviour.

We can expect here that the pathological material is an extreme instance of such a mechanism. We return, therefore, to those diseases in which we may expect marked flaws in the structure of the reactive process.

As an example of the stable structure of the reactive processes we shall refer to cases of *pseudobulbar paralysis*. We might use other material, such as the neurodynamics of schizoid patients, but pseudobulbar paralysis is of particular interest for us on account of certain of its aspects; in spite of the forced movements, having an emotional character (the forced laugh and grimacing) called out by any acute tension, these patients usually manifest considerable emotional stability, and behind these compulsive movements, there is not usually concealed any perceptible psychological affect. All these facts make us turn with considerable interest to those phenomena which the given patients show us during attempts to introduce in their activity the conflict.

That which we see in similar patients shows the absence in their symptomatology of marked motor excitation even in the cases of the more energetic intellectual conflicts. As a rule, the given patients do not manifest a tendency to impulsive mobilisation of energy and to a direct transfer of it to the motor sphere. Although in the experiments with artificial conflicts the results are markedly different from those with normal people, showing an average labileness of the nervous system, the variations usually consist in this, that the conflict is almost never expressed in the motor system, and as a result, the curves have a stable, uniform character.

While bringing out a certain difficulty in these subjects, we, however, do not stimulate directly the current of the activity which is transferred to the motor sphere and which produces the usual motor disturbances seen in our cases. Even during considerable conflict the motor curve remains inactive, inexpressive. It appears that these illnesses are sharply differentiated from normal subjects in one respect: usually there exists between the receptory-connecting system and the motor system a "functional barrier" obstructing the direct transfer of the excitation to the motor sphere, but we have here a rupture, so to speak, between the two systems of activity, and those severe conflicts which may arise in the first of them is not transferred at all to the motor area. Our customary descriptions of dementia—the stupidity of these patients, the stereotyped character of their "expressive" movements—is proof that various central experiences are not reflected adequately here in the motor system, and that we actually have good reasons to describe this group of diseases as typical, even though pathological, cases of that which we have called the stable type of neurodynamics.

Patient M with pseudobulbar paralysis usually gives very stable, stereotyped and inexpressive motor reactions. In this experiment with the conflict of defection in which the problem is to give limited associative responses (whole-part) it was frequently above the threshold of capability for the subject. In these cases we naturally obtain an inhibition of the reactions, a marked increase of the latent period, symptoms of an inner intellectual fluctuation, reflected even in the speech; yet an absolutely undisturbed and inexpressive motor curve, not reflecting in any degree the central conflict in progress.

At the basis of the extreme cases of the stable type lies the rupture between the coupling-up (connecting) activity and the motor expression, as a result of which the neutral excitation is not adequately reflected in the motor system.

We have cited pseudobulbar paralysis because it is characterised by an unusually obvious rupture between the emotional activity and the pseudo-emotional expressive symptoms. It is equally propitious, however, for our results if we take a case of Parkinson's disease: in this the incoordination of both systems is well marked. In severe types of Parkinson's disease the motor expression of the conflict is complicated by an intense immobility and rigidity; in the lighter forms, where the external motor reactions are not markedly interfered with, and the rigidity does not complicate the motor manifestation of the neurodynamic conflicts, we may see a very stable, and almost unchanged picture of the motor reactions. Here the mechanism which we have indicated leads to the appearance of the more stable, stereotyped forms of neurodynamics.

The reverse picture might be looked for in the case where both stages of the reactive process—the receptory-connecting and the effector—are so closely bound together that the differentiated structure of the neurodynamic apparatus takes the place of the diffused. We have spoken of the acutely reactive labile type in those instances in which every excitation, even in the beginning of its stages, is directly transferred to the motor system, and where the "functional barrier" is so weak that the excitation isolated from the motor sphere is not obtainable. In those cases we may expect maximal impulsiveness—because the motor course of the excitation is poorly inhibited—and a maximal expression because each central change is easily reflected in the motor innervation—finally, we may expect a maximal affectiveness, a

maximal tendency to respond to each conflict of the disorganisation of behaviour—because the conflict is not capable of being
isolated from the motor sphere and limited to the receptory-
connecting area.

In functional neuroses we have such cases, particularly in
hysteria and *neurasthenia.*

Experiment shows that these diseases are characterised by a
well-marked reactivity to every difficulty, to every conflict, and
by complete inability to keep the excitations isolated from the
motor sphere. Any problem produces here a current of activity,
diffusedly spreading over into the motor area, and a conflict
arising in the receptory-connecting system immediately causes
an intense motor disorganisation.

We had an opportunity to make a series of systematic observations on the behaviour of patients with nervous diseases under
the conditions of experimental conflict. About twenty-five subjects
(neurasthenia and hysteria) were investigated by the method of
associations; what we obtained here was the exact opposite of
the material described before with the stable type of neurodynamics.

Figure 86 gives us the comparative figures of the experiments
with limited associations, performed on three patients with a
well-defined form of neurasthenia. All these facts are characterised by a certain structure, making this material highly con-
clusive, and showing us the fundamental neurodynamic mechanism of the functional neurosis.

The reactions obtained are as follows. As a rule, the first reactions, not causing any difficulty or obstruction, flow over into
the speech and into the motor relations normally:

Subject Buch.	Subject Prok.	Subject Chist.
5. table—4.2″—feet	6. hand—1.6″—finger	2. ship—6.0″—ship
6. ship—3.4″—pipe	7. bureau—2.4″—drawer	3. forest—8.0″—well,
7. forest—3.2″—fir	8. cart—3.2″—wheel	knot . . . etc.
8. gun—3.6″—	9. train—3.0″—locomotive	

The difficulty introduced, however, calls out an acute disorganisation of the speech and motor activity. During the marked
excitation of these patients the presentation of the difficulty acts
as a shock, producing a conflict and at once being transferred
to the acute inhibition of the whole associative activity, connected

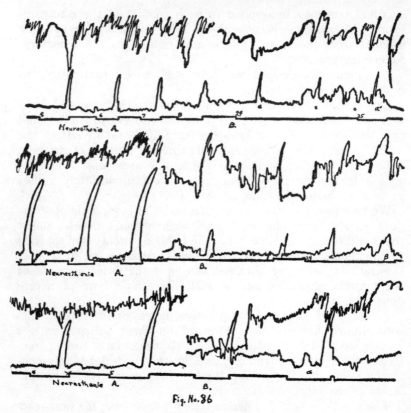

Fig. No. 86

NEURASTHENIC REACTIONS

A: SUBJECT BUCH.   B: SUBJECT BROK.   C: SUBJECT CHIST.

with a complete inability to respond adequately to the given word.

Those examples of marked obstruction, corresponding to the great speech excitation which we observed in our subjects show that the conflict primarily ruptures all the normal associative activity changing the attempt to make an adequate answer into a process of acute disorganisation:

Subject Buch.

19. samovar—6.0"—well, what must I say ... well, pipe, I do not know.

24. glass—12.0"—glass ... just glass ... what part to say I do not know.

Subject Prok.

12. notebook—7.0"—1...1... covers ... leaf ... I want to say so much at once ... ruler, sheet ... I do not know what to say.

13. butter—14.4"—what kind of butter ... I do not know ... Russian butter or creamery butter.

Subject Chist.

12. notebook—9.2"—Oi, I do not know what to answer!

15. stairs—6.6"—well, I do not know ... well, stoop.

21. fire—6.0"—fire, well, what more ... I cannot say.

23. troops—5.8"—troops ... well, battling.

Here we have nicely defined examples of the coupling-up conflicts connected with the attempts to give adequate answers, as well as the effector responses, the chief obstructions in which give rise to the necessity of choosing the adequate reaction from among several thought of.

After what has been said above, it is clear that we find here considerable disorganisation of motor behaviour. Our attention is directed to those cases in which the coupling-up character of the conflict leaves no doubt that the conflict was well removed from the motor sphere. An analysis of these cases gives very characteristic results: the coupling-up conflict was here almost indistinguishable from the motor conflict; both cases produced an acute neurodynamical excitation and an acute disorganisation of the motor curve.

The figure demonstrated above illustrates this. The reaction in which the difficulty occurs in the absence of the suitable answer (Curve A of Reaction 24, Curve B of Reaction 13, Curve C of Reactions 21 and 23) produce, however, a direct transfer of the excitation to the motor sphere. This is manifested by the fact that the latent period is completed by sharp impulses freed from the speech response, and by the subsequent irradiated excitation which disorganises the whole behaviour and goes beyond the limits of the given reaction.

Sometimes these emancipated, direct impulses (a, a) take the form of acute, completely uninhibited reactions, following just after the stimulation. They show very convincingly that the reactive process here takes on a diffuse character, and this excitation immediately and directly extends over into the motor sphere.

The diffuse character of the reaction, taking its course in the area of its general excitation, stands out in bold relief if we compare it with those which we usually obtain in the analogous experiment with subjects having a nervous system of average labileness, and not exceeding the normal limits. The coupling-up conflict, connected with the absence of the adequate response, inevitably is expressed here in several motor symptoms, but these motor symptoms (explained by the analogy of the excitation leaking over into the motor area) are of incomparably lesser intensity and they are overcome by the inhibition much more easily.

In Figure 87 we have a protocol of an analogous experiment performed in the same clinical setting on two subjects who came to the ambulatory for fatigue, headache, etc., but who had no symptoms of a functional neurosis. The curves obtained show that there is no definite deformity of the structure of the reactive process, no definitely obstructed, diffused transfer of the excitation to the motor sphere, no acute disturbance of the functional barrier, and these subjects, according to the data of the experiments, cannot be classified with the acute neurotics.

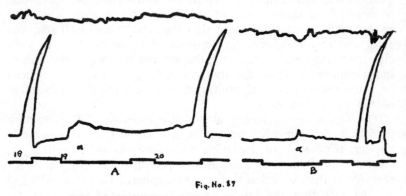

Fig. No. 87

THE COUPLING-UP CONFLICT IN NORMAL SUBJECTS

A. SUBJECT RUIH.
    18. CAP—1.8"—FIELD
    19. SALT—7.0"—I DO NOT KNOW.
    20. SPOON—4.6"—HANDLE

B. SUBJECT SLUTZ.
    24. PAIN—5.6"—I DO NOT KNOW.
    25. PACKAGE—2.4"—PAPER

The group of neurotic subjects is sharply differentiated from the normal by the diffused structure of the reactive process, by the direct transfer of the excitation to the motor sphere, and by the inability to keep the conflict isolated from the motor area. These impulsive reactions take place in our subjects on the basis of the general excitability; each conflict manifests a tendency to mobilise the inadequate mass of excitation so that the response given by the subject is not capable of neutralising them, and we see an acutely expressed subsequent disorganisation of behaviour (see for example Figure 86, Curve A, Reaction 24), differing in the whole following interval and disturbing the course of the next reaction. The conflict introduced into the psyche is changed into a diffused disturbance of the neurodynamic processes, and we have a picture exactly analogous to that analysis with which we concluded the first part of our investigations, dealing with the psychophysiology of the natural affects.

TABLE 29

No.	Subject	Diagnosis	Reaction time	mV	% of motor disturbances
1	Ler.	Neurasthenia	1.8"	0.8"	20%
2	Roz.	"	1.6"	0.6"	20%
3	Cher.	"	2.2"	0.4"	64%
4	Buch.	"	3.8"	1.0"	60%
5	Mir.	"	3.8"	1.2"	32%
6	Naum.	"	2.4"	0.6"	44%
7	Chist.	"	4.4"	1.6"	24%
8	Prok.	"	5.2"	1.8"	40%
		Average	3.1"	1.0"	38%

The list given in Table 29 shows that the similar disturbances are not exceptional, and that the reactions of the majority of subjects with a functional neurosis which we have studied (neurasthenia) give a large number of markedly disturbed and fairly unstable results.

We have performed numerous experiments on hysterical patients. In spite of the complicated nature of the material we can at least state that the same laws hold in hysteria. It is true that in this material we see etiologically different groups of hysterical patients, having almost nothing in common.

Hysteria is a psychogenic disease, concealing in its past a conflict or a trauma, and it is sharply distinguished from diseases having at their basis a constitutional labileness of the nervous system, a great excitability of the sub-cortical and vegetative systems and a defective isolation from the activity of the cortex. The classical forms of hysteria, however, undoubtedly result from a convergence of both causes, when an acute trauma or conflict falls on the soil of an excitable and labile nervous system. And precisely in these cases we always witness those phenomena, the analysis of which we have just completed: the diffused character of the reaction and the inability to isolate the conflict from the motor sphere is as characteristic for hysteria as it is for the other acutely expressed functional neuroses.

A comparative analysis of the material resulting from the structure of the conflicting processes makes it possible for us thus to approach the problem of the typological differences in the activity of the nervous system, not putting at the basis of the typological divisions any new symptoms but examining these qualitative variations as a result of the degree of organisation of the structure of the reactive processes, of the degree of isolation of the arising excitation from its motor termination.

The experiments with the movements of the conflicts show that the typological differences in the neurodynamics consist primarily in the unequal influence of such shifts, and if during the satisfactory differentiation of the neurodynamic apparatus only one shift of the conflict into the receptory connecting sphere almost isolates it from the motor system, then in the labile nervous system—and especially in the diffused structure of behaviour the extreme cases of which we see in neuroses—such a shift ceases to play its rôle, and the conflict freely passes over into the motor sphere, at the same time disorganising the behaviour.

We have arrived at the fundamental neurodynamic mechanism lying at the basis of the neurosis. The inability to isolate the conflict from the motor sphere and destruction of the "functional barrier" situated between the connecting and the motor activity is one of the chief psychophysiological mechanisms, and from this soil there may quickly spring a neurosis. During its presence any conflict might easily pass over into an affective state, and we have those exceedingly acute disturbances in behaviour which we have studied—producing them artificially or observing them in the neurotic cases.

The analysis of the structure of the conflicting processes brings us to the recognition of the great rôle which the structure of the reactive process and the differentiation of its separate parts plays in the pathogenesis and therapy of human behaviour. Therefore, in the third part of our investigation, we shall try to give detailed experiments which will make this structure more comprehensible and show the origin of the diffusion noted by us here as well as the mechanisms, with the help of which the connecting apparatus acquires in the normal human adult the specific ability to separate the excitation from the direct transfer to the motor sphere.

CHAPTER IX

THE DYNAMIC ANALYSIS OF THE CONFLICTING PROCESSES

1. THE PROBLEM OF THE STRATIFIED ANALYSIS OF THE CONFLICTING PROCESSES

WHAT we have been occupied with to this point has been at most but a momentary view of those mechanisms which characterised the conflict and its influence on the behaviour of the personality. The manifestations of the mechanisms which we have described are characteristic of the conflict itself, but only very slightly of the personality. From this point of view they are but partial trials taken from separate divisions of the systems, the exact significance of which in the whole system of the personality remains unknown to us. In order to draw fairly complete conclusions concerning the personality from the investigation of the conflicting processes we must proceed by the method of the stratified analysis of the conflicts, by the method of the dynamic sections which might characterise as well as influence the conflict in the various stages of human behaviour.

Having noted the chief mechanisms of the disorganisation of human behaviour under the influence of the conflicting processes we may ask ourselves the question: at what level of behaviour does the conflict begin to produce in a given personality the destruction of the organised behaviour?

Precisely such a form of the question, and not the data obtained in the separate partial experiments, can provide us with a dynamic delineation of the personality, and make possible a more exact and more complete evaluation of the character of its neurodynamic processes.

We are undoubtedly justified in speaking of the presence of certain strata of organisation in the behaviour of every personality; whilst the more primitive of them are already regulated at the earlier stages of their development, the more complex and difficult ones are also more labile even in the very complex human organism. The estimation of the labileness of the personality's neurodynamics can arise not only in proportion to the ability of the conflict going on within it to remain outside the motor sphere (seeping through into it disturbs the behaviour)— but also depending upon in which stratum of behaviour the conflict necessarily begins to produce its destruction, its disorganisation.

Several examples will help us to make the exposition of the question more complete. We cannot state whether the behaviour of the very young is completely unorganised: it appears clearly organised if we observe it in the primitive stratum, for example, in the act of sucking, and disorganised if we pass over into the more complicated strata having to do with the activity of the cortical apparatus. An analogous picture can be seen in the behaviour of the adult, only the disorganisation of the behaviour is here shifted to a much more complicated stratum of behaviour, being under the influence of entirely other factors and therefore characterised by qualitatively different structure. Previously, during the analysis of the affective processes, we convinced ourselves that in the whole series of cases the simplest movements are completely attainable to the subject and have their course without any considerable disturbances, whilst the inclusion of the more complicated, and chiefly of the higher associative processes, inevitably produce a rupture and severe disorganisation of behaviour.

Before us looms up the problem of how to find that level of complexity at which the neurodynamics of the process of the given subject readily begins to foster the disturbances, and at which the conflict introduced into the behaviour of the subject ceases to dominate the organised setting. Such a problem is really considerably more complicated than it would seem and therefore it requires a series of preliminary methodological exactions which guarantee that we are planning its solution in the right way.

The matter consists in this: the process of the development of neurodynamic functions is by no means as simple and gradual a process of elementary growth of organisation as we might think. In reality the position is certainly concluded in the fact that the organisation of the activity constantly attains to a higher and higher stratum of behaviour, reaching over by degrees immediately beyond the instinctive reflex acts into the strata of habits and the stratum of the more complicated coordination, and, finally, terminating with the intellectual and speech functions.

Actually the process of development has here a complicated, and so to speak, a dialectic character, changing the leading factors in their various stages, and correspondingly altering the qualitative regularity. In the young child everything connected with the primitive instinctive activity and partially with the habits may have somewhat of an organised character, while at the same time the given problem connected with the speech problem of behaviour represents great difficulties, and readily disorganises the process—but in the adult the state of affairs is markedly changed, and often even reversed. All the elementary functions of behaviour in which speech plays a part are more stable and organised, and the exclusion of its participation makes the behaviour much more labile. This is satisfactorily explained by the fact that the inclusion of the speech fundamentally changes the principles of the organisation of the behaviour; it alters the natural forms of the gradual organisation "from below," the cultured forms of behaviour "from above." Then that which previously was the more complicated and difficult stratum of behaviour, appears now not only the more stable layer, but indeed the system playing the organised rôle in its relation to other strata of behaviour.

The alluring picture of the simply complicated systems, with the subsequent study of their labileness, makes more intricate the direct character of the process of development, and our analysis necessarily must take into account the dialectics, estimating at each stage of the development the new context of the given phenomena, the new forms and principles according to the organisations, proceeding from the analysis of the new leading factors, and consequently the new structure of the given phenomena.

All this leads us to recognise that we are only at the very beginning of that path which can conduct us to the satisfactory study of the degree of the neurodynamical labileness of the personality. This problem presupposes a prolonged investigation of those actual correlations existing between the different functional systems and that structure characterising the behaviour at the various stages of development. Therefore, from the very beginning we should limit our problem only to the discovery of those most general paths which are able to lead to the study of the dynamics of the conflicts on the ground of the common neurodynamical distinctions of the given personality.

For the dynamical stratified analysis of the conflicting processes we shall choose the same pathological material which was the subject of our analysis in the preceding chapter. Many circumstances impel us to do this. The material of the neuropathic individuals gives us much that is very favourable for our problem; the facts connected with the analysis of the conflicting processes in neurotics bear witness to this.

The most important factors appear to us as follows: during the study of the conflicting processes in the normal subjects we should each time artificially refer the known conflict to the system being studied by us. But here we are able to investigate the spontaneous, conflicting phenomena, arising in the different systems of activity, thanks to the fact that the neurotic subject is far from always capable of controlling his neurodynamical processes. The nervous system of such a subject, as a rule, is much more sensitive and excitable; precisely owing to this, the comparatively weakly regulated mechanisms are not here capable of coping with the excitation arising frequently, even in the fairly primitive stages of activity. Thus in the functions of the psychoneurotic there are manifest conflicts where, in normal subjects with a fairly regulated behaviour, there are none. The very structure of the neurodynamical processes allows us to change in this case our approach, our method. At the same time in order to introduce artificially conflicts into the activity of the subject, and then to observe how this introduced conflict alters the whole behaviour, we can present to our subject problems of successive degrees of difficulty and observe how he is able to handle them. That level of difficulty of neurodynamical problems at which the subject is not able to control the excitation and reacts by a disturbance of behaviour will serve us in defining the limits of one system of activity—an index of the labileness of the behaviour.

THRESHOLD FOR DISORGANIZATION AS MEASURE OF I.D.'s.

The simplest example shows us in which comparatively primitive strata, presenting no difficulties whatever for the normal subject, the behaviour of the neurotic acquires a conflicting character. The increased excitability of the neurotic with the neurodynamical tendency characteristic of all excitation to reach directly to the motor terminal create a considerable conflict even during the simplest necessity to inhibit its beginning activity.

Figure 88 gives an example of such a conflict arising in the comparatively primitive system of motor activity. Our subject, a neurotic boy of ten, is given as a problem to tap rhythmically on a pneumatic plate; the instructions state that the sound signal given in the process of the rhythmical tapping will serve as a stimulus for the immediate cessation of the reaction. In the normal subject this instruction does not give rise to any difficulty and the problem is easily performed. The specific structure of the reactive processes in the neurotic makes this problem very difficult. The stimulus given the subject is not immediately accepted by him, but it is directly transferred to the motor sphere, producing not the expected inhibition but an acute impulsive rupture of the motor activity. It is obvious that during such a direct action of the stimulus, its inhibiting rôle is complicated by a reverse excitation of its influence, and the simple act of restraining the motor activity is an intricate conflicting process, presupposing the acquisition of a direct impulsive tendency.

Such a conflicting structure of the process can be seen even in the more primitive strata of the activity in the neurotic subject. From the degree of labileness of its neurodynamics and from the masses of excitation which every stimulus mobilises within it, depends upon in which stratum its behaviour acquires a conflicting character; the development and strength of its regulating mechanisms will depend upon whether it is able to dominate these conflicts, and in each stratum we may seek to obtain disorganisation of its behaviour.

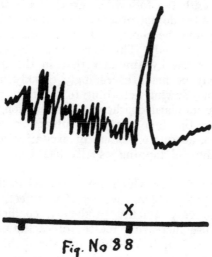

Fig. No 88

THE STIMULATING INFLUENCE OF THE INHIBITORY AGENT

SUBJECT GR. P.   X = SIGNAL FOR THE PRESSURE

The subsequent study of the organisation of behaviour at the separate levels makes it possible to trace very readily the dynamical development of the conflicting processes.

2. EXPERIMENTS WITH SPONTANEOUS ORIGIN OF CONFLICTS

THOSE features characteristic of the neurodynamics of our patients, which we have described above, make us think that even the comparatively simple actions, easily flowing into the normal, call out here a spontaneous appearance of the conflicting process. The conflict is a result of the fact that the mobilisation of the inadequate masses of energy meets here with an insufficiency of the motor apparatus which is incapable of dominating these excitations seen in life and of neutralising them in the motor reactions. This process creates from the most primitive reactions of the neurotic an activity characteristic of the conflict and quickly ending with a complete disorganisation of the entire behaviour.

We shall begin here to give a number of complexes, elementary in their character, but under extreme degrees of labileness in the nervous system, producing an acute disorganisation of behaviour.

1. We begin with the following: experiments with the simple rhythmical pressures do not produce any difficulty for the normal adult, and they may be considered among the most elementary of the processes we study. This very simple aspect of the reactions is characterised by the fact that in the normal subject, interruptions may be made exceedingly quickly in the series of automatic actions, flowing according to a certain motor formula, and reflecting a standard character. These actions are primarily characterised by the fact that the subject at once begins to mobilise definite, adequate, masses of excitation and the normal curve and rhythmical tapping usually has a very regular character.

It is just these factors which are disturbed in the reactions of the neurotic. The problems we set the subject, to give rhythmical pressures, very quickly produce a conflict; the subject begins to mobilise increasing masses of excitation; the general excitability forces him to do this, and the mobilised masses of excitation are inadequate, they destroy the elaborated cortical automatisms, obstruct the delicate phenomena, and in place of the regular rhythmical pressures we have an irregular disorganised curve.

In the more acute cases the simple series of rhythmical pressures enable us to distinguish the neurotic subject with marked excitability and weak cortical regularity from the normal person.

Figure 89 shows both types of cases. The normal subject gives here a very regular series of motor reactions; the neurotic, irregularity in the excitability, and inequality in the tensity of the pressures, delaying the delicate phenomena and destroying the rhythm. The difference between the two types of reactions is brought out clearly if we express the stability of each series in the curve of distribution of intensity in the individual reactive links accompanying the respective series.

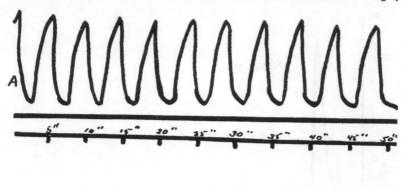

Fig. No 89

RHYTHMICAL PRESSURES

A. NORMAL SUBJECT
B. SUBJECT BUH.: NEURASTHENIA GRAVIS

In Figure 90 we have the comparative curves of intensity of the rhythmic reactions of the normal and of the neurasthenic. We consider their reactions symptomatic. They show that the organised active process led by the higher cortical automatisms to the maximal degree of regularity is here destroyed, and it loses all of its organisation. Here these reactions remain regular in their form but the disorganisation is reflected chiefly in the disturbed rhythm and intensity of the curves, i.e., in the loss of that standard character which distinguishes this process in the normal. We may think that, as a result of the diffused character of the neurodynamic processes and the very easy mobilisation of the inadequate masses of excitation in our neurotic subjects, there may be already formed at this level of behaviour an acute conflict connected with the loss of the "motor formula" characteristic of it and a destruction of those "reaction patterns," which are so easily elaborated in the normal.

A considerable part of the rhythmical reactions observed in our neurotic subjects were characterised by a certain degree of disorganisation of the forms of behaviour. This was usually ex-

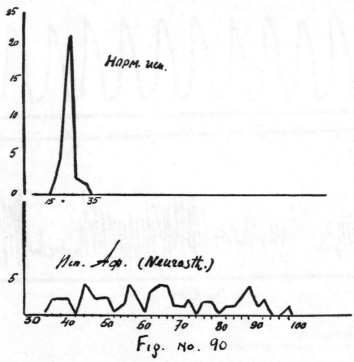

CURVE OF DISTRIBUTION OF INTENSITY OF THE REACTIONS DURING
RHYTHMICAL TAPPING

A. NORMAL SUBJECT
B. SUBJECT AF. (NEURASTHENIA)

pressed in the unequal form and it reflected the intense degree
of labileness of the nervous system in the personality under consideration; a great excitability and diminished strength of the
cortical regularity inevitably led to a destruction of the behaviour
even at this stage.

We had an opportunity to prove experimentally that the deviation of
the cortical regularity increases the picture of destruction observed here,
while this regularity leads to the organisation of the system of behaviour.
In Figure 91, we have two kinds of reactive movements of a hysterical
patient. The first of these was registered while the patient was in his usual
state; the second immediately after an acute attack of hysteria. In the
intervals between the two experiments the patient exhibited the typical
symptoms of the attacks of *grande hysterie*.

These classical movements which we saw here (fine movements of the
hands and fingers, etc.) were convincing evidence that the regulating rôle
of the cortex ceased to connect up with the motor system and that the
movements reverted to those of a primitive and, as it were, sub-cortical

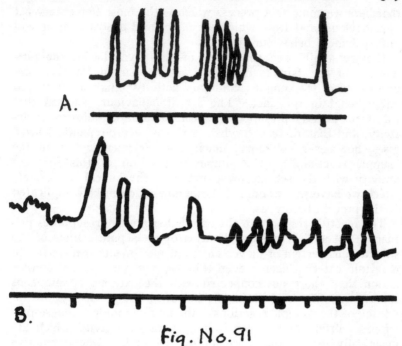

Fig. No. 91

REACTION TO THE SIGNAL OF PATIENT MOZH.

A. BEFORE THE ATTACK OF HYSTERIA
B. IMMEDIATELY AFTER THE ATTACK OF HYSTERIA

type. The following experiment done twenty minutes after the attack, led us to believe that the higher cortical regularity was certainly in abeyance; after the attack the character of the reactions was sharply changed; instead of the standard movements proceeding according to the elaborated motor formula, with every mobilisation of the adequate masses of energy, we see here deautomatised reactions, which have lost the motor formula and have been deprived of the property of intensity as well as form.

2. The experiments with rhythmical movements demonstrating the presence of the simple reactive movements in the conflicting reactive process even at the most elementary level of the neurodynamics leads us directly to the following series, which appears even more elementary but which actually is considerably more complex and difficult.

The experiments with a simple reaction to a signal were considered by a whole generation of psychologists as the most simple and elementary of all psychophysiological experiments. It seems that here we come to a process which is the most elementary act of behaviour, and from which we may build a structure of voluntary human behaviour.

History annihilated the hopes of the psychologist, the phenomena of the "simple reaction" was not suited for the comprehension of the complex voluntary activity; analysis destroyed naïve belief in this fact. "The act of behaviour" showed that this form already presupposed a considerable complexity of activity, and that there is a whole series of neurodynamical processes, howsoever voluntary, much more "elementary" than the "simple reaction."[1] The simple comparison of this form of activity with the scheme of spontaneous rhythmical movements which we have just examined shows how much more complicated is the process before us.

The reactive response to the external stimulus presupposes primarily, not an internal coordination of the separate links of the spontaneous system of movements, but movements transferred to a certain external agent; even this one is a much more complex action than those not connected with the external spontaneous movements. The second factor, however, shows clearly the intricacy of the "simple reactions"; the unified motor response presupposes origin of this act from systems of activity which are genetically earlier and more unified. Occurring among reactive processes of a diffused character, this origin postulates an obstructing, inhibiting tendency to the spread of motor excitation, which is characteristic for primitive forms of activity and which should be included in the "simple reactions."

It is clear that with the increased tendency of our neurotics to the mobilisation of excitation and the decreased activity of the higher regulative mechanisms such a problem becomes very difficult, and the simple reaction develops into a conflicting process. It will be of advantage for us to point out the dynamics of this process in the subsequent number of examples taken from the protocols of our experiments on neurotic patients.

Figure 92 gives a typical example, showing that the process of gradually acquired domination of excitation is here very evident: subject Roz. in response to an auditory signal readily gives a sharp pressure, but he is not able at once to inhibit the excitation arising, and many of the subsequent extinguished waves prove that he overcame these only after some time. These phenomena, seen here in very definite forms, were present in one or another degree in all of our neurotics. The experiments with

[1] This will be discussed in detail in Chapter X, sections 2 and 3.

simple reactions, as a rule, were accompanied by many impulses, additional pressures, often unexpected even for the subject himself. In these extra pressures we see an emancipation of the excitation from the regulative mechanisms and sometimes strenuous efforts to master them again; the conflict in the reactions of the choice created for the neurotic is chiefly a conflict of the inadequate excitation, emancipating it from the higher regulation, a conflict with the attempt of the regulating processes to inhibit it, to produce organisation in the given reactions.

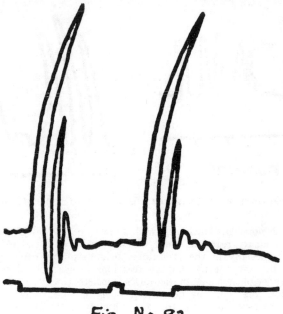

Fig. No. 92

SIMPLE REACTIONS OF SUBJECT ROZ. (NEURASTHENIA) TO EXTERNAL
STIMULI

Figure 93 gives such typical examples of the emancipation of the motor impulses from the regulating processes, and the conflicts connected with this appearance in the neurotics. The deformity of the curves during the attempts to inhibit the extra impulses, and the disorganised behaviour connected with this is comprehensible from the conflicting character of the reactive processes in the neurotic.

The fact that the manifestation of the conflicts of the motor reactions in the neurotics causes a return of those elements which were characteristic for the neurodynamics will occupy our attention now. We can easily obtain analogous phenomena in those neurotics in whom these symptoms did not appear clearly in the usual experiment. We substantiate that which German investigators call *Einjagen;* by increasing the speed of the stimuli and creating in our subject an acute motor setting, and telling him to respond as quickly as possible in his movements, we obtain very easily extra pressures, proving that the excitation has been separated from the influence of the cortical regulation.

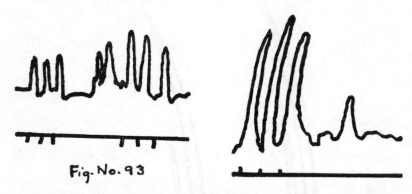

Fig. No. 93

SIMPLE REACTIONS WITH EXTRA IMPULSES IN TWO SUBJECTS OF HYSTERIA

Those phenomena, which are well known to psychologists under the term "preliminary reactions" and which may be observed in every subject, and especially in the excitatory, belong to this category. A great difference between the preliminary reactions in the normal subjects and the analogous phenomena in neurotics consists chiefly in the fact that this process creates in the neurotic a fairly intense conflict which in a labile nervous system may for a certain time destroy the organised character of his behaviour, while the normal subject easily masters the preliminary impulses, and his behaviour does not suffer as a result of this conflict.

3. The experiments described indicate the method by which we may make more difficult the reactive process and create in our subject a conflict of considerable intensity. This method means that we introduce into the experiment with the neurotic those conditions requiring an increased inhibition of the direct impulses and the mastery of the primitive diffuse reactive process. We see, therefore, subsequent difficulties in the experiments with the delayed movements.

We propose to our subject that he respond to the presented

signal by a slow motor reaction; but at the same time we bring about such conditions that the reactive movements themselves—in both of their parts, the active and passive—are fairly slow. The subject found it necessary to bring in an inhibiting regulation in the system of movements; he acquired a natural tendency to this. In order to produce a direct disturbance of excitation in the impulsive motor response, he must give instead of this movement one differing from the ordinary regularity in all of its movements, and having an equable, inhibited character.

In the normal organisation of behaviour, such a problem, obviously, does not represent any serious difficulty, and the subject copes with it successfully; but naturally for the neurodynamics of the neurotic patient suffering from an increased excitability and a lowered ability to regulate, this is a problem of great difficulty and it produces a sharp conflict. Thanks to the diffuse structure of the reactive processes the neurotic stands here before a constant conflict; the instructions produce attempts which are not capable of overcoming the primitive impulses, and even those subjects first described by us, in whom the changes in behaviour did not deviate from the normal, show marked symptoms of disorganisation.

We have the material of about twenty-five clinically verified cases of neurotic patients; in hardly a single case could we observe a completely normal and fairly well-organised delayed movement. We obtain here, as a rule, either complete inability to delay the movements, or an application of such inhibition to only one part of the reactive movement (inhibition either at one end or an interval), and the curve as a whole shows a lack of organisation and coordination. The complete regulation of the movements and control of the equalised delayed reactions are not to be seen anywhere in this material. The fact, however, is very evident, that the attempts to dominate these impulsive reactions and to master the problem produces acute conflicts in our neurotics leading to the disorganisation of the whole behaviour. This disturbance is reflected in the curve of the disorganisation of the delayed pressure, the marked impulses having a general inhibited curve giving it a sawtooth appearance; in the most acute cases, there is a complete disorganisation of behaviour with a failure of the reactions to all of the parts of the separate chaotic pressures. The experiment with the delayed reactions made it possible to divide our subjects into a series of groups, characteristic of the different degrees of destruction, and, consequently, of the grades of labileness of the nervous system.

In Figure 94 we shall give a table of the separate stages of destruction of the neurodynamical processes in a given situation.

The picture of the conflict during the delayed reactions is shown to us in its full panorama; we see here that the problem is easily

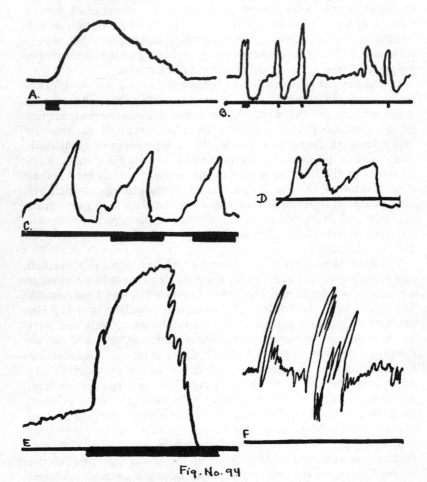

Fig. No. 94

DELAYED REACTIONS IN NEUROTICS

A. EXPERIMENT WITH A NORMAL SUBJECT
B. INABILITY OF DELAYED PRESSURE (HYSTERIA)
C. PARTIAL DELAY (HYSTERIA)
D. DISORGANISATION OF THE STRUCTURE OF THE PRESSURE (HYSTERIA)
E. COMPLETE DESTRUCTION OF THE BEHAVIOUR (NEURASTHENIA)
F. COMPLETE DESTRUCTION OF BEHAVIOUR (HYSTERIA)

accomplished by the normal subject (Curve A); often it is impossible for the neurotic, who although thinking that he is making a delayed pressure, is in reality giving rapid and uninhibited reactions (B); the attempts to inhibit are frequently not capable of extending equally over the whole process, and influence only one of its parts (C); finally the attempts to delay the movements lead to a conflict and the complete destruction of the behaviour (D, E, F).

The experiments with the delayed movements produce numerous and considerable conflicts, and their registration makes possible the establishment of that level at which the behaviour of the subject begins to show disturbances. Although in normal subjects we only occasionally encounter the signs of the extension to the disorganisation of behaviour at this level; in neurotic labileness this level of behaviour in most cases produces considerable conflict, and is often accompanied by marked phenomena of disorganisation.

4. In the case just described, we require the subject to inhibit his reaction during the process of movement; however, we may successfully produce a spontaneous conflict by putting the subject in such a situation that he must delay the direct motor impulse and give it only after some prepared process will have been finished. This can be done by the aid of a simple associative reaction, the concluding part of which is accompanied by a motor pressure.

In this instance we return to that method which has been applied as the basic one in the whole of our investigations. Creating in the subject a central associative process, by that means we evoke a certain central excitation, under normal conditions independent and isolated from the excitation of the motor system; connecting this excitation with speech, under ordinary circumstances we include a factor which has an organising influence on the neurodynamic reactions and does not at all disturb their equilibrium.

The state of affairs is entirely different from that of the neurotic. With extreme excitability and great labileness of the nervous system, the tension produced by us in a central apparatus may manifest a tendency to flow directly into the motor area, producing in it certain traces of excitation and disorganising the normal motor curve. Under these circumstances the inclusion of the speech is not a strong enough agent for the organisation of the neurodynamic process; often in the presence of the irradiation, the speech is hardly capable of playing any organising rôle and the central tension directly causes a destruction in the accompanying motor process.

Such cases we have already seen. We shall consider here only certain examples showing how the markedly labile neurodynamics manifests a tendency to the direct destruction of the central tension in the motor process. Subject Maz. was a hysterical patient with typical hysterical attacks and symptoms. In Figure 95 we show a series of her reactions; from the data of Curve A it is seen that the spontaneous rhythmical reactions do not represent for her any great difficulty and are not accompanied by conflicting processes. Therefore the phenomena obtained during her associative reactions are the more characteristic. It was nec-

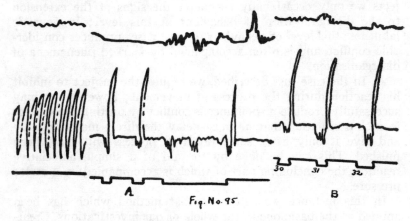

A.   B.

Fig. No. 95

SUBJECT MAZ. (HYSTERIA)

A. RHYTHMICAL REACTIONS
B. ASSOCIATIVE REACTIONS WITH THE ACCOMPANYING PRESSURES

essary for us to produce in her considerable central tension and it immediately gave rise to an acute motor disturbance, and the accompanying curve shows that the whole latent period is filled with the disruption of the excitation, which the subject was not able to overcome. We have such phenomena in all the associative reactions, without exception, regardless of their difficulty; in the presence of great central obstructions this process becomes more marked, but we can see the chief mechanisms of such obstructions in any given case. The central tension is directly transferred to the motor area and it produces those disturbances in the latent period which we see here.

This mechanism furnishes the basis of those disturbances in

the latent period of the associative reaction with which we have become acquainted in detail above. In order that the motor movements accompanying the associative process should be markedly disturbed in the neurotic patient, it is by no means necessary that the reaction be connected with the affective contents; it is sufficient for it to produce a certain central tension which the neurotic patient cannot keep isolated from the motor area in the presence of the weakened regulating processes in the diffuse character of the reaction. This is why in numerous instances we observed normal reactions in the primitive stratum of behaviour, and a complete failure of the reactive processes at a more complicated level.

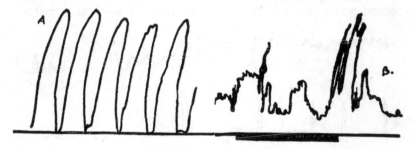

Fig. No. 96

STRATIFIED ANALYSIS OF THE REACTIVE PROCESSES IN PATIENT PROK.
(NEURASTHENIA GRAVIS)

A. THE RHYTHMICAL PRESSURES
B. ASSOCIATIVE REACTIONS AND ACCOMPANYING PRESSURES

The typical illustration of this is given in Figure 96. With the normal rhythmical pressures it is sufficient for us to introduce in this subject an increased central tension connected with the associative problem, in order that it completely disorganise the neurodynamical process, making the accompanying reaction actually unrecognisable.

5. Further experiments proceed along certain paths of the complex central processes and additional difficulties introduced into them. If at the level of the simple associative processes we do not obtain in some of our patients a disorganisation of behaviour, then the introduction into the central process of several additional difficulties, increasing the tension there, inevitably leads to a disorganisation of the neurodynamics and to a manifestation of the symptoms of the diffused excitation in all of the

behaviour. The tendency of the transfer of the central tension to the motor disturbance is seen here very clearly, and this is shown by all the experiments we have performed on neurotics, including the additional difficulties introduced into the central activity.

We shall limit ourselves here to only one citation which again proves that the behaviour may be completely normal at one level, but markedly disorganised at another level, which latter represents great difficulties.

Consequently we arranged two series of experiments with our neurotic patients, equivalent in the situation but different in complexity. In the first of these, we propose to the subject to give simple judgments on the presentation of words; in the second series, we ask him to make these definitions senseless,

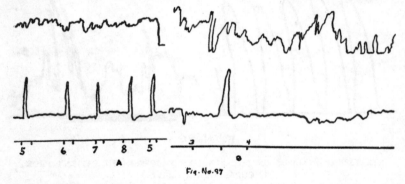

Fig. No. 97

NORMAL AND COMPLEX REACTIONS IN A HYSTERICAL PATIENT

A. SIMPLE REACTIONS: 5. GRAMOPHONE—TO PLAY; 6. LITTLE BALL—FAIR; 7. BIRD—FLOOR

B. ABSURD REACTIONS: 3. BUTCHER—I WENT; 4. BOY—I DO NOT KNOW

answering to each given word in an absurd manner. The experiment showed that to follow these instructions was not so easy; the subject must deviate from the usual experiment and give the opposite kind of answers, but according to a purely verbal and logical plan. For a person with defective verbal culture and with concrete thoughts such a problem was very difficult, and within the limits of the same structure of the answer it was possible to introduce into the neurodynamics a marked central tension.

The results were very definite. Although the signs of the conflict were absent in the normal experiment, in a complex control series they were clearly expressed, and the behaviour became acutely disorganised. Figure 97 presents such an example, taken from an experiment on a hysterical patient not showing any symptoms of disturbances in the comparatively easier stages of the reactive processes. Here we see entirely normal reactions with simple judgments, and marked disorganisation (passing over to the passive system of the left hand) in the presence of a complex central process.

The necessity of restraining the central tension, created under these conditions from a direct participation in the motor system leads here to a sharp conflict with a diffused structure of the re-active processes, and conditions a failure of the behaviour, falling at one or another level, depending upon the degree of labileness of our subject's nervous system.

3. EXPERIMENTAL CONFLICTS

IF in the neurotic subjects which we have been dealing with in this chapter, even the simple reactive processes are connected with spontaneous manifestation of conflicts, then the séances dealing with the experimental introduction of conflicting proc-esses show that conflicts connected with even the most primitive levels of behaviour may cause acute disturbances. If in the neurotic we actually observe considerable excitation connected with free access of all the excitation with the motor area, and a markedly lowered regulating ability, then it will not be sur-prising that our subject is frequently unable to cope with a conflict even of a very primitive type.

We have performed control series of experiments with experi-mental conflicts, analogous to those described above, on neurotic patients. A consideration of them takes us back to former mate-rial, and we therefore will not go into details concerning them; following up the problem of this chapter we shall deal with only two variations of a single conflict, investigated by us at different levels of behaviour.

1. We shall return at first to the simple *conflict of accelera-tion*. We have already noted that the normal subject handles pretty well simple problems of change from one reactive speed to another. When in the experiment with the simple rhythmical tapping we propose to the subject at a given signal that he quickly decrease his velocity, he overcomes the inertia and makes the transfer readily.

In neurotic subjects we may expect other results. If in the transfer from a slow speed to a rapid one in the simple motor experiments there is no perceptible difficulty, then in the experiment where at our signal the subject must, on the contrary, alter the velocity from rapid to slow, we place before him two obstacles: on the one hand, the speed he has adopted acquires a certain, and sometimes very considerable inertia; with a weak regulating apparatus he is not able to master this inertia, and after the signal for the alteration the subject continues to give numerous pressures, often occurring without noticeable inhibition. On the other hand, an additional complication comes in here: the slow movements of themselves represent for the diffuse neurodynamics of our subject a considerable difficulty; and it is comprehensible why we should obtain acute conflicts here.

The data of our investigations prove that the given experiment acquires those features characteristic of the conflict at its lower level. Some of the neurotics, especially those who at the more stable reactive processes, have not yet given marked disturbances here; but in others we have seen a great disorganisation of behaviour.

Figure 98 gives a section of the curves showing the mechanism of the failure of the reactive process in the given case. It is easily seen that the mechanism of the conflict here consists in this: that the speed adopted by the subject can not be immediately inhibited, and in the attempts to change this to a slower velocity, the original speed is continued as a perseveration, heaping up on the slow reaction and destroying its form.

This phenomenon convinces us that we have here a conflicting process with which the regulative apparatus can successfully cope in only a few of our subjects. We are led to believe that if in this process there is created much inertia, causing a great tension, we can, without changing the method, produce many disturbances.

2. We proceed along the same path, transferring the experiment to another stratum of behaviour, including in it the speech mechanisms. We introduce in neurotic material those experiments with the conflict of acceleration in a chain associative series, as was done in the normal subject in our former examinations. The subject is required to recite consecutively all the words coming into his mind, accompanying each with a pressure. At the given signal he must quickly change to another velocity, having begun to associate either with a maximal rate or, vice versa, as slowly as possible.

Experiments thus performed have led to the establishment of both symptoms which we have seen in less marked degree in

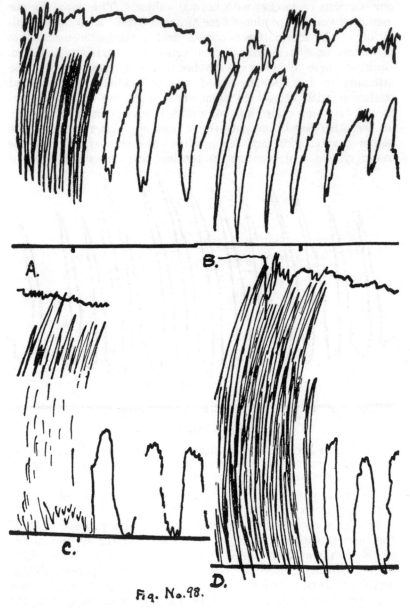

Fig. No. 98.

CONFLICT OF ACCELERATION IN EXPERIMENTS WITH NEUROTICS

A. SUBJECT FROL. (NEURASTHENIA)   C. SUBJECT US. (NEURASTHENIA)
B. SUBJECT PROK. (NEURASTHENIA)   D. SUBJECT AF. (NEURASTHENIA)

our previous researches with normal subjects. The signal for the
increased velocity produces here simultaneously a complete inhibition of the associative processes and a marked emancipation
of the motor system from the influence of a cortical regulation.
Both of these symptoms were brought out very clearly. The
attempts to increase the speed resulted chiefly in a marked
confusion with refusal to associate ("I cannot think of anything," "nothing comes into my mind, I can not think further") ;
on the other hand, one may think precisely this rupture of the
higher psychological activity produces the emancipation of the
motor system, and, creating the tension, was directly transferred

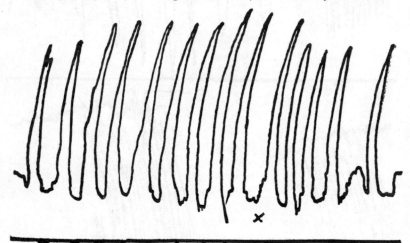

Fig. No. 99

CONFLICT OF ACCELERATION IN THE CHAIN ASSOCIATIVE SERIES; EXPERI-
MENTS WITH NEUROTICS. X—SIGNAL FOR THE SPEED OF THE ASSOCIATIONS
(ALL THE PRESSURES AFTER X ARE EXTRA ONES).

to the motor area, producing there disturbances not coordinated
with the speech function.

In Figure 99 we show an example of such a process. Both of
the cases prove that the attempts to transfer the subject immediately to the maximal speed of association result in an inhibition
of the associative processes connected with the hyperexcitability,
and the marked transfer of the tension to the emancipated motor
reaction. Under these conditions the attempts to inhibit the
emancipated motor system and to pass over to a state of organised behaviour readily call out a conflict and disorganisation
of the reactive process.

Cases illustrating the process of such failure will not be given here; but in all of our neurotic subjects we have seen this process.

All the neurotics give us such a reaction of disorganisation, more or less clearly marked in this experiment, and we are convinced that the experiments showing instability of the reactive process at the lower levels, show them also in a certain form when they are complicated by new difficulties and displaced toward more intricate levels of the psychophysiological processes.

4. TYPOLOGICAL SIGNIFICANCE OF THE STRATIFIED ANALYSIS

BECAUSE we consider the stratified analysis essential for a typological study of personality, we have dwelt on the facts at such length in this chapter. What we have discussed here shows that the general characters of the typological differences, the referring of our subjects to the stable or labile groups of nervous systems, requires changing the concrete characteristic of that tendency which we consider fundamental for the formulation of the neurodynamic peculiarities. All the previous analyses showed that such tendencies, lying at the bottom of the individual differences, are the unequal ability to inhibit the beginning excitation, separating it from the motor sphere; in other words, at the basis of our classifying personalities into one or another group we consider an unequal diffuseness in the activity of their nervous system, the unequal rôle which it plays in the regulation of the beginning excitation. The further the excitation reaches, directly striving to extend to its motor termination, the less the subject is able to inhibit the conflicts arising and the difficulties resulting from isolation from the motor sphere, and the more right we have to speak of the given subject as the neurodynamically labile type. The more developed in him the regulative processes, the greater his ability to prevent the excitation from reaching the motor termination, restraining it by some "functional barrier" and supporting it until the transfer to the motor system by some previous elaboration, the more justification we have to speak of the subject as the neurodynamically stable type, and the fewer the chances of an actual disorganisation of the reaction resulting from conflicts.

The question arises whether to change the external description of the type by the study of the dynamic mechanisms which form it. Without such an indication of the dynamical mechanism we would not have an actual scientific typology; a weakness of all contemporary typology is that it is too much occupied with a description of the individual differences, and too little with the individual peculiarities of the dynamical changes of some of the leading mechanisms. This analysis of the destruction of the organised behaviour during special conflicting processes lays the foundation for such a differential analysis, at the basis of which is the study of the definite leading mechanisms.

This is the path along which we intend to go, availing ourselves of an important methodological possibility. Studying the degree of organisation of behaviour at different levels, substantiating the influence of the conflict on the failure of the reactive process in the stratified analysis, we approached the possibility of expressing the individual differences in several dynamical units, discarding the absolute reference of the subjects to one or another statistical "type." Establishing that in the different subjects the disturbances of behaviour are clearly expressed only at a definite level of activity, we are able to describe the labileness of his behaviour in special stages, using successfully categorical measures with categorical qualities, and thus making our individual analysis dynamic. On the other hand, studying the structure of the peculiarities of that process in the presence of which the behaviour manifests an acute disturbance, we are in a position to substantiate the analysis of the conditions of this disturbance, and to speak of the functional peculiarities of that decree of labileness with which we are dealing.

Experiments performed on neurotic patients prove that the detailed analysis is the only path to a scientific approach toward the individual differences, and that only in the categorical measures and qualities can we express the individual peculiarities of the neurodynamics in the subjects studied by us.

In our comparative typological analysis we must each time decide two questions: in what degree is the labileness of the neurodynamics manifested in a given subject, and, secondly, what structure characterises the usual failure of the behaviour? The answer to the first question provides a dynamical analysis of the reactions of our subject at the definite levels of his behaviour; the second problem is decided by a study of the following: what qualities have the disturbances, in what stage is it, what are its reciprocal parts in the disorganisation of the somatic and vegetative systems, is the inhibited and deformed setting of the subject passive or active, intentional or formulative. The detailed analysis of the personality, obviously, cannot be reckoned previously; we have touched only on some sides of this work; some have been dealt with in our experiments in detail; other questions (for example, reciprocal relations of the somatic and vegetative reactions in the disorganisation of behaviour) have not been taken up at all; [1] the whole dynamical analysis of the typological differences is the task of the future, and we shall here express only a few generalities relating to this problem.

We shall illustrate the detailed analysis of the individual variations by only two cases of hysteria. Before us are two patients; both having a confirmed diagnosis of hysteria. Both of them had hysterical attacks, and both had a very labile and sensitive nervous system. However, there are some marked clinical differences in them:

Patient Mor., 29 years old, female, factory labourer. She came to the doctor complaining of pain in the region of the heart, disability of the hands, and systematic attacks. At first the attacks appeared to be convulsions, and then when she saw another woman having seizures with loss of consciousness and shrieking, her attacks assumed the same form. Forgetful, confused, intensely excitable, inability to restrain herself; sharply increased reflexes; skin hyperæsthesia.

Patient Mozh., female, 43 years old, cashier in shop. Complains of pain in the region of the heart and convulsive seizures. During these, consciousness is not lost and she can control herself for some time. In general she is very restrained; she does not relate her experiences frankly; never cries; she is very emotional and sensitive, however. The chief conflict is connected with a change to a new job which she does not like and in which she feels incapable. Tremor of the fingers, increased tendon reflexes, dermatographia.

The marked differences in the characteristics lead us to believe that a careful analysis of the neurodynamical systems in both cases will show us considerable differences in the degree of diffuseness of excitation as well as in the structure of their distribution in the neurodynamics of the subjects. While in the first subject we can presuppose a great primitiveness and diffusion of the reactive processes, with a more open manifestation of the excitation in the motor system, the properties of the second indicate that the general excitability and predisposition to acute conflicts is inhibited here, the patient tries to restrain herself at a certain stage of organisation, but this she can accomplish only on a certain psychical level; in view of this character of the psychophysiological processes we may expect here an intense concentration of the disturbances beginning to be manifested only at a certain level of complexity of the psychological processes.

The stratified analysis of the neurodynamics of both of the subjects confirm our suppositions. In each case we obtain very different results in degree as well as in the structure of the labileness of the neurodynamical processes observed. Figure 100 summarises these. Analysing the reactive processes in the first of our subjects, we see that she cannot deal with even the first of our experiments; indeed, in the simple rhythmical tapping the marked excitation begins to participate, which is a symptom of a strong tendency to mobilise the excitation and sometimes is not able to master the reactive process.

This excitation is very marked in the experiments with the simple reactions to a signal, and even at the level of the slowed movements,

---

[1] In the works of V. N. Myasnischtheva this is discussed. See his *Reciprocal Relations of the Vegetative and Somatic Reactions*, Psychoneurological Science in the U.S.S.R., Leningrad, 1930.

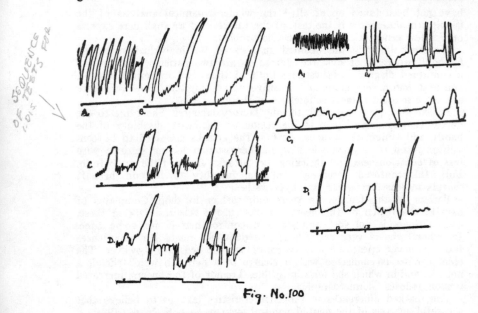

SEQUENCE OF TESTS FOR LOIS

Fig. No.100

STRATIFIED ANALYSIS OF THE NEURODYNAMICAL PROCESSES IN TWO
PATIENTS WITH HYSTERIA

SUBJECT MOR.: A. RHYTHMICAL PRESSURES; B. REACTION TO A SIGNAL;
C. SLOW PRESSURES; D. ASSOCIATIVE REACTIONS
SUBJECT MOZH.: AI. RHYTHMICAL PRESSURES; B2. REACTIONS TO A SIG-
NAL; CI. SLOW PRESSURES; DI. ASSOCIATIVE REACTIONS

the neurodynamics of the subject is disturbed; she cannot solve the
problem, and as a result of the trial to make an organised slow reaction
there is a wide-spread disorganisation of behaviour. The introduction
of the speech reactions and consequently the excitation of the additional
central foci finally disorganises the behaviour, and the chaotic motor
disturbances bear witness to the tension introduced into the psyche of
the patient.

The reactive processes of subject Mozh. give us an entirely different
picture of the dynamic disruptions. In the simpler stratum of reactions—
in the simple rhythmical tapping—we do not observe any abnormality.
Only very slight variations differentiate this level of behaviour from
the usual neurodynamic picture. But already in the experiments with
simple reactions to a signal there is a marked change. Characteristic for
our patient were the concurrent impulsive pressures, not connected with
the signals, and even after the inhibition, which showed very clearly
the increased tendency of the excitation to pass over into activity, the
augmented inertia of the excitation, and, on the other hand, the perceptible weakness of the regulating system. The transfer to the slow movements did not disorganise this subject, although the impulsive character
of the reactions is well manifested here; the patient remained fairly calm

even in the experiments with the associative answers. However, we meet here with a sudden and intense disorganisation of behaviour. When the subject is given a word producing a considerable difficulty, the reaction to it serves to relieve the neurodynamics from a contact with the marked disorganisation of the motor reactions. This occurs, with the corresponding differences, even in cases of complex reactions and of decidedly intellectual difficulties. At this level of activity the neurodynamics manifests its insufficiency, and the disturbance of the behaviour proves that we have here a level of behaviour critical for the subject.

The differences in these two cases consist in the degree of the neurodynamical labileness, but this not all. The varying activity of the conflict, its fluctuating extent of irradiation, and finally the varying participation of the motor system in the conflict create a structure specific for each case, and compel us to think here of different structures of the hysterical processes.

We are convinced that under the general term "hysteria" there are included very divergent neurodynamical processes. The detailed investigation of the neurodynamics helps us to unveil the exact picture of those disturbances which are thrown together under the usual name of hysteria, and to describe exactly those differences, and finally to classify them into groups.

The analysis given leads us to believe that a careful study of the mechanism of the individual differences is incomparably more complete and concrete than the general usual description of the external peculiarities. The study of the conflicting processes constitute the fundamental mechanism of the disorganisation of human behaviour, and brings to light very important facts.

However, we cannot yet state that the processes we are studying are entirely comprehensible. They will be clear only if we are able to understand the processes in all of their dynamics, but this places before us two final problems of maximal complexity, but also of a decisive nature in the investigation of the disorganisation and organisation of human behaviour.

The first of these problems has to do with the cortical disorganisation and organisation of behaviour. Having seen the mechanics of the conflicting processes and their influence on the destruction of behaviour, we are convinced that the laws of this disorganisation will be fully comprehensible when we are able to give their genetic analysis, approaching their study by the historical method. Only by a careful investigation of those successive stages through which the organised behaviour in the transition from child to adult passes, can we thoroughly understand in what degree the facts observed by us in the affective and conflicting processes originate only at some more primitive stages of development of the neurodynamical processes—and how we stand here before those varied inclusions which can help to make the process of destruction only partially an approach to the given levels, never allowing them to coincide. The genetic analysis of organised human behaviour makes it possible to evaluate the observed laws and to put each one of them in its respective place in that complex system which represents the behaviour of the human.

On the other hand, before us stands another tremendous problem. We cannot represent human behaviour simply as an arena in which affects and conflicts play. The human does not only experience a failure of his behaviour, but he tries to master it, to control it. We have studied the mechanisms of destruction, but we stand before the no less important problem of the investigation of the mechanisms of organisation. The separate descriptions of the laws we have given are comprehensible for us only when we consider in some details those means which the human applies in overcoming his behaviour, and those stages through which this mastery of behaviour passes.

If all of our efforts have been so far directed to the analysis of the conditions causing the destruction and disorganisation of behaviour, then now we must return resolutely to the consideration of the factors and means of overcoming this disorganisation and of controlling human behaviour.

In addition to the problem of the neurodynamics of neuroses there is the problem of the psychological basis of therapy. This should be studied by the same experimental methods which we have used already in the investigation of the disorganisation of human behaviour. We have no more hope to solve the problem of the psychological basis and neurodynamical mechanisms of the mastery of behaviour and therapy than we have that our investigation will give a fundamental and exhaustive foundation for the understanding of disorganisation and neuroses. We believe, however, that only experiments dedicated to the genetic analysis of the organised forms of behaviour and the experimental study of their control can give us a foundation upon which we may make a contribution to the contemporary growth of knowledge.

We recognise that we become acquainted with phenomena only by understanding them. The third part of our investigation will be devoted to the attempt to control these processes experimentally.

PART THREE

THE GENESIS OF THE
REACTIVE PROCESSES AND THE
PSYCHOPHYSIOLOGY
OF THE CONTROL OF BEHAVIOUR

CHAPTER X

DEVELOPMENT OF THE REACTIVE PROCESSES

1. PROBLEMS

THAT AFFECT basically changes the structure of the reactive processes, destroying the organised behaviour, and converting the reactive process into a diffused one, has been shown already. Experimental tests proved that such a change of structure of the reactive processes occurs each time the behaviour becomes conflicting in its nature; the collision of the opposing tendencies breaks down the "functional barrier" and transforms the reaction into a diffused state of excitation.

We have analysed the mechanisms of the disorganisation in human behaviour; before us now is the problem of the genesis of the organised forms of its activity.

In what way does the disturbance of the psychophysiological mechanisms during the failures of the normal, regulating behaviour occur? Does the affect create in the neurosis new forms of behaviour, or does it only throw the individual back on some old mechanisms?

The world literature of the last few decades has shown a marked tendency to accept the second point of view, supporting arguments that the destruction of human behaviour only makes the individual revert backward through many generations, so that the affect returns to ancient phases of behaviour and the neurosis regresses toward an archaic stage of development.

Darwin considered affect as a vital primitive sort of behaviour, and in each symptom of affect he saw the origin of the primordial, archaic forms of reaction.

This, in addition to the findings of comparative anatomy, strengthened the view that affect, considered neurologically, represents a transfer from the cortical type of excitation to that which is connected with the subcortical ganglia; these form the ancient parts of the brain and are the seat of the archaic types of processes.

This shows how confused were the attempts to express the qualitative peculiarities of these states in the terms of regression to the previous phases; this approach makes use of its own intrinsic system of dynamics; but is it really more satisfactory for the investigator than when he tries to reveal the new and incomprehensible phenomena as only a stage of the former genetic path?

The genetic approach and its desire to comprehend the forms of the vital activity as phases of development is without doubt one of the most daring scientific adventures and contains within it the golden kernels of dialectics. However, precisely this obliges us to refer very cautiously to those increases which are connected with the attempts to see in the newly elaborated disturbance only a simple return to the primitive paths. Without doubt the disturbance, cutting off the more complex higher forms of the regulating capacities, is manifested chiefly in the stratum of the primitive, previously experienced forms of behaviour; we are fully justified in presupposing that the disorganised behaviour occurs, not along accidental, *ad hoc* intricate paths, but it usurps the rôle of the lower functions which were already formed. But it is also certain that these higher mechanisms will not be complete, but that they remain in the new form of behaviour as a partial aspect, just as in the normal behaviour the archaic, primitive forms of reaction preserve their partial aspect, having collided on the level of the first plan. We may suppose that the process studied by us will occur not so much according to the scheme of the simple regression, as to the scheme of the reversion, in which the archaic and higher elaborations changed places, so to speak, because in the newly destroyed form of behaviour these latter continue to play a certain perverted rôle. This is why in every destruction we must necessarily expect a return to some of the former stages of development, but these manifestations of the reappearing, archaic forms will naturally be different in people of different cultural states, different types and different individual peculiarities.

In our investigations we must not, consequently, look for a simple regression of behaviour, disorganised by affect or conflict so that it represents a primitive phase of development; there arises the important problem of studying these former stages of development in order to understand those characteristic mechanisms forming the skeleton of those higher regulations of human behaviour which have been destroyed.

A certain path seems to us to be the correct one in the solution of this problem; desiring to answer the question, exactly which neurodynamical mechanisms of affect revert to the former phases of development, we must first take up the ontogenesis of the reactive processes and turn our attention to the study of the neurodynamical properties of childhood. From this investigation we may properly expect the establishment of many qualitative peculiarities of the reactions typical in the early stages of growth; having already investigated these, we may conclude from the factors in the failure of human behaviour (which we have already studied), that the neurodynamics of the person reverts to a former, early stage.

We decided to take up two questions which one must solve experimentally:

1. Does the reaction of the child differ in its structure from the reaction of the adult, and does it have in any degree that quality of diffusiveness which we saw in the conflict and in the state of affect?

2. If the "functional barrier," the lowering of which we established during affect, conflict, and neurosis, is indeed lowered in the young child, then under what conditions is it destroyed and to what mechanisms does it belong?

The first question relates to the development of the reactive processes; the second is connected with the problem of control of the behaviour. In the ensuing chapters we shall attempt to solve them experimentally.

In regard to the latter subject, we shall concern ourselves with our own work, and, as well, with that of our collaborators. Some of these researches were done in the Institute of Experimental Psychology, some in the Psychological Laboratory of the Communistic Academy, and finally, the investigations on nervous diseases in the laboratory of the clinic of nervous diseases at the First Moscow University. From the researches of our collaborators we have used chiefly those of Lebedensky, performed in our laboratory over a number of years, whose monograph on the development of the regulating processes will appear shortly.

This exposition is constructed, as is a clinical one, dealing with separate typical cases and omitting all statistics, which the reader will find partly in other of our papers, and partly in the above-mentioned researches of Lebedensky. In our opinion the described phases and tendencies of development are able to give us a better analysis than volumes of statistically elaborated material.

The main proposition, which seems to us proven by a series of our experiments, is as follows: the reactive processes of the human complete the development, which by no means consists in the gradual combinations of the earlier given mechanisms, but, on the contrary, their development is distinguished by the conflicting characteristics passing over into qualitatively new phases, included in the new regulated mechanisms, and the reactions of the young child differ fundamentally in their structure from those of the adult.

These properties of the reactive processes in the child remind us of the mechanisms which we have already discussed. They refer to two situations, mentioned previously in this book: (1) every act of behaviour in the young child has a direct character, and the excitation arising manifests a tendency, not to be restrained, but to proceed to its motor termination; and (2) every reaction exhibits the ability to carry along in the active process an inadequately large mass of excitation.

We may state that diffusion and impulsiveness are fundamental features of the reactive processes of the young child. These characteristics explain the very special peculiarities in the behaviour, thinking, and personality of the child; they reveal to us the genetic roots of those neurodynamical deformities which are found in the disorganisation of human behaviour in the states of affect, conflict, and neurosis.

We shall examine successively several groups of experiments performed by us on children. In these we shall try to discover the development of the organised forms of behaviour at the different (in their complexity) neurodynamical stages, exactly as we have previously attempted to give a stratified analysis of the disturbances of the neurodynamical processes. We shall be well satisfied if, parallel with the examination of the functional peculiarities of the reactive processes at an early age, we shall succeed in observing some of their psychological mechanisms.

2. EXPERIMENTS WITH RHYTHMICAL REACTIONS

IN the mechanisms of the affective and conflicting processes we have already observed the fact that the neurodynamics shows symptoms of disorganisation, as a rule, only at a definite level of complexity of the reactive processes. In a number of reactive processes, differing in their complexities according to the age, the simple rhythmical pressures were preeminent; even in the more affectively excitatory subjects they occurred usually in a fairly well-organised way, and with the mobilisation of very large masses of excitation (which was generally met with in some of our neurotics) in order that the rhythmical reactions be destroyed.

We decided to begin our genetic investigation with this very simple neurodynamical process, in order that we might begin as low as possible on the genetic ladder.

Our experiments with the simple rhythmical reactions were conducted in children beginning at two and a half years of age and concluding with those of school age. The experiments made possible the establishment of certain peculiarities of the neurodynamical processes in the child, which serve as a foundation for further investigations.

The technique of the experiment was very simple: the child was seated in front of a pneumatic apparatus, and he was told to make rhythmical pressures at any speed he desired.

In older children this constituted the whole procedure; but in the very young ones (those too small to attend school), we reinforced the method by certain measures to ensure their observance of the instructions and their participation in the experiment. One of these was "the paired experiment," in which the child at first watched another child several years older running through the experiment; after this the younger one began to imitate him. This method gave excellent results. In certain cases we introduced the element of play, being careful, however, that this did not disturb the basic fundamental setting of the experiment itself.

The instructions to make rhythmical movements, generally following one another rather rapidly, presupposes a fairly high development of the cortical processes; only with a fairly well-organised action of the motor cortex, with development of the higher cortical automatisms, could we reckon on obtaining an accurate picture of similar rhythmical pressures.

Precisely these factors are absent in the young child, and what we see there is evidence of a series of specific peculiarities, properties of the neurodynamics at the given age. We intentionally do not discuss here the fact that slight movements are still not well developed at that age with which we begin our analysis. We are much more interested in those neurodynamical properties which we can trace in the activity of those, as yet fairly well-developed, systems. Such an examination makes it possible to draw certain conclusions concerning the neurodynamical basis of this lack of development.

The first thing that strikes us in this material is that each beginning cortical process readily passes over in the young child to the subcortical mechanisms, rapidly depriving this process of its pure cortical character and involving intricate diffused processes. To trace these was not very difficult. The younger the child, the more clearly do we observe these processes.

In Figure 101 we submit a case, one of the earliest of the experimental, psychological investigations of neurodynamics known to us: the curve of this figure is taken from an experiment performed on a little girl two years and three months old.

The curves in the preceding figure bring out two fundamental properties: the subject begins with rather regular pressures, after two reactions tonic components appear, which then extend through the succeeding reactions; on the other hand, the reactions themselves become irregular, losing their organised character. These two factors are extremely characteristic of the early neurodynamics, and give us a basis on which we can trace the development of the neurodynamic processes; they reveal two chief features of the neurodynamical processes in a very young child. The first of these is the inability to elaborate the higher cortical automatisms; that which is easily accomplished by the adult is impossible for the child. A series of equal, regular pressures readily and automatically given by the adult, evidently requires a very high organisation of the cortex, lacking in the child; that which the adult does automatically, the child performs without that elaboration of the reactive formulæ lying at the basis of this process in the adult; [1] as a result we see unstable and unequal processes, having in some children a very marked form.

Secondly, the characteristics described here are especially typical for the neurodynamics of early childhood; the appearance of marked tonic components proves that the beginning excitation evidently is not restrained in a limited cortical system, but has a diffused character, extending over the whole of the cerebral apparatus, and spreading even into the sub-cortical activity. This introduction into every activity of inadequately large masses of excitation, and at the same time into the sub-cortical excitation, is typical for early childhood and is the foundation upon which is laid the further development of the process.

The tonic phenomena, whose presence we have established, continue for a very long time; as a rule, they are always seen in children up to seven years old, and begin then only to drop out as the higher cortical processes become better developed (see Curves B and C, Figure 101). Indeed in adults we may easily

[1] See M. O. Gurevitch, *Psychomotorika*, Moscow, 1930.

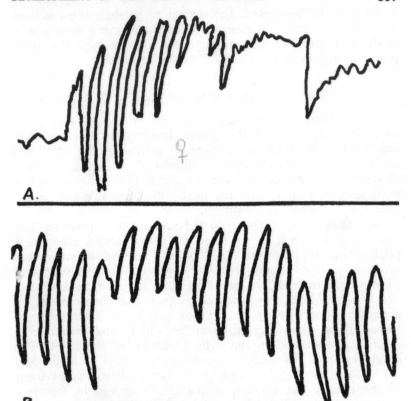

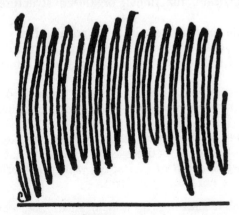

Fig. No. 101. C.

RHYTHMICAL REACTIONS IN YOUNG CHILDREN

A. TWO YEARS AND THREE MONTHS OF AGE; B. FIVE YEARS OLD; C. SEVEN
YEARS OLD.

evoke them by instructing the subject to produce the reactions at a maximal speed; in neurotics these phenomena have a definitely expressed form, showing more prominently the tonic phenomena than do the more excitatory subjects.

3. EXPERIMENTS WITH SIMPLE REACTIONS TO A SIGNAL

WE might think that the simple reaction to a signal is such an elementary process that the genetic investigation cannot show any perceptible difference between its course in the adult and in the child. Authors who have considered psychology as a science of reactions have silently taken for granted that this process is maximally elementary and maximally unchangeable during the course of the whole development.

Nevertheless, experiments do not confirm this premise. The reaction to a signal, as we know it in the human adult, is a product of very complex development, an elaboration which arises on the basis of other, considerably more primitive processes. "The simple reaction" in young children differs from the reaction of adults in having another structure, and characterised by a marked specificity of the diffused excitation, a weakness of those higher regulating mechanisms which are undoubtedly a basic phenomenon in the neurodynamics of the adult. The development of the reactive processes from child to adult does not by any means take place by the quantitative improvement of the process but through a qualitative change in structure overcoming primordial diffusiveness and passing over into a new, controlling, intricate, functional, organised structure of the reaction.

Those simple movements which we speak of as "simple reactions" of the adult are, really, very late formations, built up on the basis of the suppressed, diffused system of the primitive impulses.

In our investigation we used children from two and a half years to about seven or eight; the picture obtained was very similar in all the children.[1]

The reactions to the signal in the young child (usually four or five years old, but sometimes older) showed that *each signal mobilised a large amount of excitation,* which the cortical activity of the child was not able to control.

---

[1] We used thirty children from the work of M. C. Lebedinsky to which we have added material from eighty-five other children. The similarity of the results made it possible for us to limit ourselves to this number of subjects.

Each stimulus produces in the young child many movements, spread out over a large part of the experiment and only gradually becoming inhibited. In the youngest of the children the signs of such a control of the successive developing impulses, yet not entirely perceptible, has the character of a continuous, chaotic, "spontaneous" activity, not at all regulated by the stimulus. Figure 102A gives a section of the protocol of an experiment done with a child two years and three months of age, the rhythmical reactions of which have been given above.

This figure shows that the spontaneous pressures are hardly at all connected with the external signal, but, on the other hand, may even be inhibited by this signal. Nevertheless, the extra impulses not connected with the signal are not inhibited and continue to act spontaneously. Such a picture is characteristic, as a rule, for a child of two to two and a half years old, in which under the conditions of the experiment it is still very difficult to bring about a differentiation from the general excitation of the organised reaction.

In children from three to three and a half years we meet with another picture, a typical example of which is given in Figure 102B: the separate pressures begin to be readily coordinated with the signal, but the child is not able to inhibit the succeeding excitation, and the free interval following the signal is usually filled by one or several extra pressures. Here for the first time is formulated the fact which is very characteristic for the neurodynamics of the early stages of development; the child is not capable of restraining the spontaneous impulse taking place within him, and the cortical regulating apparatus is delayed, the inhibition is reflected not in active pressures, but in the passive parts of the additional pressures. Typical for such a case is Reaction 19 in Figure 102B. The impulsiveness makes its way through the pent-up regulating apparatus, the beginning excitation manifests a tendency to pass directly to its motor termination, but the regulating restraint is delayed and occurs not before the final impulse, but after. The specific structure of the reactive process is conditioned to this, with the direct transfer of excitation to the motor sphere; as we shall see, this is characteristic for other more intricate aspects of the activity of the child.

All the further development of the reactive processes consists primarily in the development of this ability to restrain the remaining impulses and

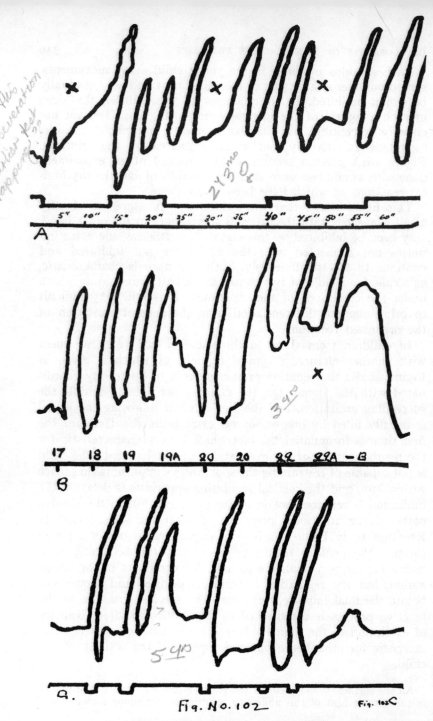

Could this be perseveration of earlier test of tapping?

2y3mo Ob

5" 10" 15" 20" 25" 30" 35" 40" 45" 50" 55" 60"

A

3y0

17 18 19 19A 20 20 22 22A — B

B

5y0

C.

Fig. No. 102   Fig. 102 C

REACTIONS TO A SIGNAL IN CHILDREN

A. TWO YEARS AND THREE MONTHS; B. THREE YEARS; C. FIVE YEARS.

to overcome the amount of excitation caused by the stimulus. M. C. Lebedinsky introduced the term "coefficient of inhibition" for this process.

$$K = \frac{h_1}{h_2} \times \frac{d_2}{d_1}$$

where h_1 and $h_2 =$ the intensity of the adequate and inadequate pressures, and d_1 and d_2 correspond to the breadth of their base. Detailed analysis indicated that this coefficient adequately reflects the dynamics of the regulating processes and indicates their extension in the development of the child; as a rule this coefficient is reflected in its comparatively small size in young children, reaching its maximum about the age of seven, and disappearing in adults, for they do not give any inadequate extra pressures.

This does not hold, however, for every adult. Ordinarily it is sufficient only to increase the cortical load, by increasing the number of successive signals, in order to obtain in any subject an inadequate impulse, occurring notwithstanding the sudden curtailment of the giving of the signals. This phenomenon was described by some physiologists (Zeliony), and then it was used as a test for automatism and voluntary control in a system of psychological investigation (Rossolimo).[1] The experiments show without doubt that the similar, remaining, impulsive reactions are clearly seen where the general neurodynamical tonus of the excitation is increased, and the complicated regulating mechanisms are weakened. The neurotic subjects in this experiment approach closely to the scheme of the early neurodynamic reactions, preserving the specificity for the given stage of development of the neurodynamics.

A certain phenomenon demands our attention: if the reactions of the young child were not accustomed to the external stimulus, and were deprived of the restraining extra impulses of inhibition, then they were fairly normal and regular in form. Only with the development of the child and with the appearance of the restrained extra impulses, do the reactions begin to have an irregular, disturbed character. This fact shows that at the basis of the ability to give a unified reaction to the signal there lies genetically the conflicting process, included in the necessity to overcome the extra, impulsive reactions and to control those inadequate large amounts of excitation, which, thanks to the diffused character of the child's neurodynamics, enter into the action every time that the stimulus is presented.

If in the adult the simple reaction begins again to have a regular form, then this occurs only because next to the development of the cortical regulations there appears the ability to mobilise for the reactions an adequate quantity of excitation. This requires, moreover, the inclusion of specific, new mecha-

[1] Rossolimo, *Psychological Profiles. A Plan of the Investigation of Children*, 1910. *The Basis of Psychomechanisms*, 1927.

isms, and, as we shall see further on, they are actually included in the reactive processes of the human adult.

We should like to note only one fact characteristic of the diffused structure of the reactive processes ín the young child. If the reactive movements of the child have the direct character and are the immediate continuation of that excitation which was produced in the subject by the stimulus, then it follows as a matter of course that the augmentation of the stimulus should cause a direct increase of the motor result.

Such an effect is generally seen in the child. His movements customarily reflect directly the intensiveness of the given stimulus; the strengthening of the stimulus brings about the marked reactive impulse, the stimulus having a certain normal intensity, passes over into a state of shock and exhibits a disturbed motor reaction.

Such a reflection of the intensity of the signal is not generally seen in adult normal subjects. The increase of the strength of the signal does not always cause a corresponding increase of the intensity of the motor reaction, and this is evidence that the structure of the reactive process is different in the adult from what it is in the child. We come to the conclusion that between the stimulus and the reaction in the adult lies a certain regulating mechanism which causes a corresponding transfer of excitation to the motor path, but does not admit to the motor system the whole quantity of excitation which was produced by the stimulus. We are led to believe that the psychological reactions of the normal adult control a special organisation, differing from the simple reflex and from the diffused reaction of the child.

It is interesting that precisely such a separation of the motor result from the direct connection with the excitation evoked by the stimulus is lost in the neurotic. Here we obtain a definite change of the motor reactions in response to the increased intensity of the stimulus, and the picture of the direct reflection in the motor reactions of the receptory excitation appears in a clearer form.

The analysis of the simple reactions to a signal confirms our belief that the reactive processes in the early stages of development are sharply differentiated by their diffuse structure: the beginning excitation mobilises immediately a considerable (and inadequate) amount of energy, which the cortical apparatus cannot control; hence the extra impulses, following adequate reactions, usually observed in the reactions of children; the development of the regular reactive movements requires primarily a restraint of these inadequate impulses, and is thus based on the conflict of the cortical regulations with the primitive, diffused excitation; the whole development of the neurodynamics consists in the creation of a "functional barrier" separating the excitation from the direct transfer to the motor system and to the elaboration of those standard forms of reactions in the presence of which the subject is able to mobilise accurately the amount of excitation required by the situation.

4. EXPERIMENTS WITH DELAYED MOVEMENTS

THE diffused character of the early neurodynamics stands out in strong relief in those cases where we study the processes requiring a very intensive regulation of the excitation.

We can take two such cases: the first, when the movement itself must be completed with maximal delay; second, when the delay must be carried forward, preceding the movement, and when the movement itself must be finished only after the preliminary delay and production of the definite coupling-up effect.

The first conditions are fulfilled in the study of the delayed instructions of movement; the second, in the experiments with the complex reactions connected with the situation of choice.

We begin with the investigation of the delayed movements; in many cases this experiment seems to be decisive.

Many considerations impel us to the study of the development of the regulating processes precisely in the delayed movements. The higher regulations appearing in the control of behaviour should not be studied in the manifestation of the maximal activity: every small child is already capable of such a direct activity. Our path must be exactly the opposite, and the appearance of the regulating possibilities should be studied in the reverse process—in the delay of the direct impulses, in the delayed movements.

The instructions which we applied in these cases were very simple: we gave a signal to the subject and proposed that in his response he delay the movement of pressure as much as possible; we did not limit the exact speed of this movement, but we required that it be delayed maximally.

The analysis of the results obtained indicated that the development of the reactive processes occurs in very specific stages, and this brings us back to the fact of the chief differences in structure of the reactive processes in the adult and child.

The problem is to make the delayed movements for the normal adult so that they do not present any difficulty, and thus we obtain a typical curve with uniformly inhibited peaks and intervals; the curve has the customary regular cupola form. Examples of such typical curves have been given above; from the very first, the inhibited process begins to be organised with the giving of the signal and occurs without interrupting any impulses or losing its uniformly inhibited character. The curve obtained is until this stage simple and regular, so that we can hardly discern with what difficulty this movement is performed, and at what level of development the corresponding cortical processes take place.

Nevertheless the experiments with the child show us this.

For a child of six or seven years, any organised delayed movement is, as a rule, entirely impossible. In a number of experiments we have seen beyond doubt that the young child, three or four years old, is not capable of delaying its movements, and the reactions which the child gives in this experiment differ only slightly from those which we obtained from him during the usual instructions. Evidently the impulsiveness of the child's reactive systems is so powerful that to inhibit them is almost impossible for him.[1]

The fact that the difficulty that we meet here in the child is connected with defects of the regulating systems and with the tendency of every excitation to be directly linked up to the motor system is well illustrated by the cases where we strive to attain in the child the maximally delayed reaction. Under these conditions all the curves we have seen of the child's reactions show the presence of a definite conflict. Our instructions are not complied with by the child because in him those mechanisms are absent which might control the direct motor impulses, converting them into regulating, delayed movements. Therefore "the delayed movements" in the child are converted into a series of impulses occurring in the motor area and of an inhibitory nature; the defect of the regulating apparatus consists in this: the organised and constant inhibited movements are substituted by interrupted processes, and these are characterised by impulses which do not differ in rapidity from the usual movements, and they are accompanied by very late inhibitions, incapable of restraining the excitation to such a prolonged interval of time. Therefore they are broken up and new impulses, in their turn, also become inhibited. Every time we tried to produce in a young child a delayed pressure we saw a process having a definite conflicting character. Figure 103 shows typical examples of such curves recorded in children from four to five and seven to eight years of age. The last (Curves C and D) show a step forward in comparison with that disorganisation which was always brought about by the delayed instructions

---

[1] It should be stated that for the adult the problem of mobilising his speed and increasing it to the maximum is much easier than the reverse—to restrain his normal speed and make it much slower. Many special researches have shown that the latter is much more difficult.

in very young children (Curves A and B); then these defects in organisation were especially marked again in neurotic children (Curves E and F).

We performed this series of experiments in order to show

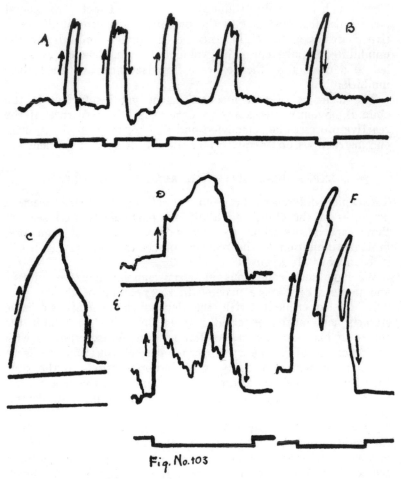

Fig. No. 103

DELAYED MOVEMENTS IN CHILDREN

A. FOUR YEARS OLD
B. FOUR AND A HALF YEARS OLD
C. SEVEN YEARS OLD
D. NINE YEARS OLD
E. EIGHT YEARS OLD (FUNCTIONAL NEUROSIS)
F. TEN YEARS OLD (TRAUMATIC HYSTERIA)

the phenomena characteristic of the reactive processes in the child. Notwithstanding the definite instructions about the delayed movements, the component movements in the child were actually unchanged, and the impulsiveness, at least in the early stages of development, were not capable of being regulated. That which was easily attainable for the adult met with several neurodynamical obstacles in the primitive structure of the reactive processes in the child, and we can understand why in the uninhibited impulsiveness the problem of giving delayed pressures led to a conflict of the separate impulses and abolished their inhibition.

The inclusion of new mechanisms as yet insufficient in the child is obviously necessary in order that the structure of the reactive processes be remodeled and that we may obtain through our instructions an adequately organised, delayed movement.

5. EXPERIMENTS WITH THE REACTIONS OF CHOICE

THE chief differences between the structure of the reactive processes of the child and adult are particularly well seen in those experiments which presuppose the presence of some preliminary inhibition of the reactive processes, and only then can it be adequately realised.

We have such conditions in every complex reactive process, and perhaps even more marked in the reaction of choice.

In the experiments with the delayed movements we have studied how much the child is able uniformly to inhibit the course of his motor processes, but now in the experiments with the reactions of choice we turn to another question: to what extent is he capable of delaying his motor reactions, at the same time isolating the excitation from a transfer to the motor area, in order to make this connection only after an adequate central preparation.

This question is psychologically much more important than the question of the uniformity of delay of some motor process; however, the speech proceeds here not simply according to a temporal delay of some reactions, but according to that specific structure of the neurodynamic processes which are necessary conditions for the origin of the higher forms of intellectual behaviour. All intellectual behaviour, nevertheless, is possible only in that case when the decision of the problems will be deferred for a time. The problem is temporarily isolated from the motor sphere and from the seat of those preliminary internal trials which are not immediately reflected in the motor system; here exists the mechanism of the intellect.

Does the structure of the reactive processes in the young child furnish a neurodynamical foundation for these complex forms of behaviour?

The experiments with the comparative study of the behaviour of the child and adult in the situation of the intricate reactions of choice answer this question for us; they show all the principal differences characterising the reactive processes in both cases.

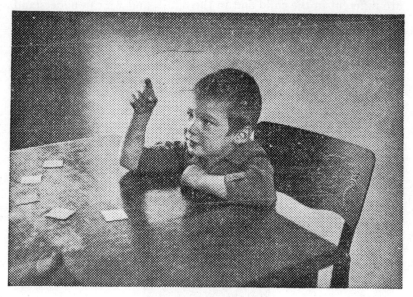

FIG. 104

SITUATION OF THE EXPERIMENT WITH THE REACTIONS OF CHOICE

The method which we have employed is as follows: the hand of the subject with extended index finger is placed at an angle of 60 degrees to the surface of the table; on the table there is an arc containing four or five coloured cards, arranged for a choice. After explaining the apparatus to the subject, we tell him to choose a definite colour or a letter and that when a certain stimulus is given he must quickly indicate the chosen card. This is repeated several times, after which the stimulus is presented and the corresponding reaction is recorded. The situation of a simple experiment, suitable for clinical observation is given in Figure 104.

In the exact experiments we used a complicated registration of the process: to the extended finger of the subject there is fastened a small light, and the trajectory of the movements are recorded; the card itself is changed by a special apparatus constructed in our laboratory, and the pressure is registered on the revolving drum.

Besides our experiments, we include some very interesting material from those of P. S. Lubimov at the Institute of Experimental Psychology. There are only some technical differences between his and our methods. The subject's hand lies on the key A during the giving of the stimulus; the subject should change his hand to key B, 50 cm. from the first; at the same time the summated process is registered; the projectory of the movement is recorded cyclographically; the intensity of the pressure to key B (connected with the dynamoscope of Lubimov) is also recorded....

The reactions of choice with which we are concerned here are different in the child and in the adult, and we can understand the principal differences of structure of the reactive processes in both cases if we compare the typical results obtained in the adult with those in the young child.

The reactive process of the normal adult is characterised primarily by the fact that it shows two definite phases: these may be termed the phase of preparation and the phase of fulfilment.

The stimulus presented to the adult does not evoke in him a direct, delayed movement; for some time the hand remains quiet; there arise several preliminary, prepared processes, which terminate by a definite decision after this excitation is transferred to the motor system, making a simple realisation of the connection. Our cyclographic chart records this structure fairly clearly; Figure 105 shows us this process in all of its details.

FIG. 105

CYCLOGRAM OF THE REACTION OF CHOICE IN THE NORMAL ADULT

Two things here require our attention: the unusually simple character of the movement and the marked process. And this is easily understood. Our subject attempts a reactive process by such a differentiation: beginning from the given stimulus the excitation is not transferred directly to the motor area; it appears cut off, as it were, by a certain barrier not going outside of the limits of the central activity.... The first period of the reactive process is connected with such a linking-up activity, transferring the excitation to the regular path and elaborating some preliminary formulæ of movement; during this time the excitation is not yet separated from the motor system, and the motor system is inactive. After this, when the connection is made, the excitation immediately is coupled up to the motor system, and there appear rapid and definite movements because in this movement there are no components of choice but there are only simple accomplishments occurring before a preliminary act.[1]

Therefore the movement itself in the presence of such a structure of the reaction does not fundamentally differ from any given movement during a simple reaction or even during an elementary reflex. The complex "intellectual" component is absent here; it was carried over into the prepared stage, and even further (it is immaterial whether the soldiers obey an order which was a result of the complex work of the whole soviet, i.e., committee, or the decision of a commander, their strides will be equal in both cases).

The explanation of the structure of the reactive process brings us to a scheme differing somewhat from the usual, the scheme of the reactive arc. The given stimulus evokes in the system a certain excitation; reaching the central apparatus, it, however, is not connected directly to the motor system, but is restrained by some "functional barrier," and after the definite preliminary elaboration as a result of which there comes about a linking-up to the motor system, and the motor reactions do not show the traces of that "overloading" characteristic of the preliminary central process.

Such a splitting of the reactive process into two phases with a definite process of choice from the motor system has a distinct biological significance. The complex choice must be carried out by an apparatus specially fitted for this; such an apparatus is the cortex, with its intricate and labile system of making connections. It would be unfortunate indeed if this choice and these connections might occur only within the limits of the motor system; every regular movement would then be broken and its organisation destroyed.

There is nothing new, properly speaking, in our scheme; we simply find in the higher stages of behaviour the principles corresponding to those which Sherrington has described as a principle of the "general motor field." In these works is given the general neurological setting for such a system of preliminary connections; it remains for us to find an explanation of those complex psychological mechanisms which fulfil this rôle in the complicated actions of behaviour which we are studying.

[1] The details of the structure of the reaction of choice have been described by many authors. H. Luederitz (*Beitrag zur experimentellen Untersuchung der Wahleorg.*, Gottingen, 1929) showed that the process of choice is not connected in the human adult with the manifest activity.

Although if such a "paired" or "doubled-phased" structure of the reactive processes may be seen in the adult, the reaction of choice in the young child occurs differently. Placed in the situation of the experiment, the child of six or seven years (in younger children it is difficult to obtain an actual reaction of choice, it being substituted by impulsive pressures on any key of the apparatus closest), we usually see a picture differing strikingly in its structure.

In contradistinction to the adult, the stimulus presented to the child provokes in him a delayed motor reaction, beginning at once after the signal and long before the definite connection was prepared. The first, preliminary phase, showing in the cyclogram as a sharply expressed delay of the movement, is entirely absent here, and the excitation is characterised by an open, diffuse structure. It is plain why the movement itself should present certain other signs. No traces remain of the positive and quick movements of the adult; in the diffuse structure of the process the movement is not realised earlier than the preliminary connections, but occurs in the very process of choice; having included the motor system too soon, the child wavers between the separate stimuli and produces uncertain movements which are continued for some time and only later they reach one of their final points.

We should not limit ourselves here to the peculiarities of the forms of the reactive movements of the child; it is much more important that they differ from the reactive movements of the adult in function. We have already seen that the reactive movements of the adult are lacking in any "intellectual" components, that they are simple, fulfilled realisations in the central system of connections, and in their structure they are exceedingly similar to all the other more primitive movements, as for example, the movements during a simple reaction or in a reflex. In this relation the reactive movements of a young child differ markedly from those of an adult; the function of choice occurs here not in the transfer of the excitation to the motor region, but in a diffused extension into it; the hand likewise executes here the problem of choice as in the central part of the system, and the tragedy of the decision takes place on an open stage.

It is sufficient to examine a cyclographic record of a typical reactive process in a child of five years (see Figure 106) in order to be convinced that the hand does not simply execute a prepared connection, but it is a participant in the complicated problem of choice which was before realised in the preliminary, preceding motor connections. The reactive process of the child is of a distinctly diffused nature; during the absence or weakness of the "functional barrier" the beginning excitation, not being inhibited, passes through into the motor region, and the movements are direct.

The diffused character of the process and the absence of the "functional barrier," separating the excitation from a direct transfer to the motor region, leads us to postulate the existence here of some other structure of the reactions and that there will be adequate for it another scheme, displacing the direct character of the process. The excitation, having begun in the receptory system, does not meet any obstacle here but spreads directly to the motor sphere, extending over into it and producing numerous impulsive movements, frequently having all the signs of the conflict. In this scheme of the reactive process there is absent that intricacy which is present in the former scheme; this is

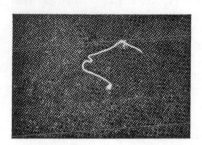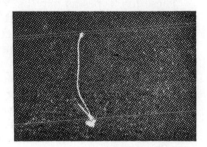

FIG. 106

CYCLOGRAM OF THE REACTION OF CHOICE IN THE CHILD

inevitably distinguished by a small degree of differentiation and there should lie at its basis much more primitive processes.

We are justified in presupposing two specific foundations of this process of behaviour. On the one hand, we should indicate the fact that there is extensive irradiation inherent in the neurodynamics of the child and noted by many investigators working with the reflex activity in the young.[1] On the other hand, the decisive factor which we should recognise is that in the reactive process of the child there are not included any higher, regulating systems opposing the process and obstructing the direct transfer of excitation to the motor system.

In passing from the diffused structure of the reactive process in the child to its complicated, functional organisation in the adult, we might expect the repression of the primary irradiation, which in all probability should be brought about by the inclusion in the process of the complex mechanisms playing a specific, organised rôle and not participating in it earlier.

[1] See Schtchelovanov: *Genetic Reflexology and Pedagogy of the Young*, 1929. Ivanov-Smolensky: *Investigations of the Higher Nervous Activity of the Child*, Moscow, 1930.

We shall support our opinion by statistical material borrowed from the work of P. S. Lubimov. This investigator studied cyclographically the form of the reactive movements in subjects of various ages and different phases of mental development. With the cyclogram he recorded the trajectory path during a simple motor reaction, and secondly the reaction of choice.

The forms of the movements are classified by him in five groups:
1. Simple, rapid movements
2. Delayed, but regular movements
3. Movements with arrestment before the actual instant of choice
4. Movements with delay of the motor attempts before the choice
5. Movements characterising the general irradiation of the impulses, and the diffused and chaotic structure (uncertain strokes without signs of restraining the impulses).

These five types as may be seen here, are distinguished by the degree of the organisation of the process, and we may postulate the existence of different structural reactions underlying them; the first type of rapid and regular movements, with preliminary inhibition, usually corresponds to that case in which the movements simply execute the prepared and preliminary stages of making connections, not being complicated by any intellectual components; the second is already characterised by some spreading of the inhibition, although organised, into the motor region, indicating that the movements are complicated by the carrying out of the problem; this appears strikingly in the third type— the arrestment of the movement before the reaction—characterised by the extended disturbance of this process, which in the first case—the regular decision of the problem—was preliminary and internal; finally, the fourth and fifth types are very definite pictures of the diffused structure of the reactions, where the very process of choice occurs not in the central but in the motor system, and the motor area itself plays not a complementary but a diffused rôle in the whole reactive process.

These forms of movement are far from equally distributed among the subjects of different ages and degrees of development. Table 30 shows the distribution.

The results which we obtain from the analysis of this table are very clear. Whilst in the retarded child ten years old, with a mental age of six years, even the simple reactions were distinguished by some leaking of the inhibition into the movement, and the reaction of choice in 50% of the cases gave a picture of diffuse movements (with a complete absence of the reactions occurring in the first group), but the behaviour of the normal

TABLE 30

	Type of Reactive Movements				
	I	II	III	IV	V
Oligophrenia, 10 years	55 2%	54.5%	30%	8%	5.5%
Simple reactions	48 —	123%	20%	17.5%	50%
Reactions of choice, normal child, 10 years	39 61%	39%	—	—	—
Normal adult, simple reactions	66 88%	12%	—	—	—
Reactions of choice	63 89%	8%	3%	—	—

adult gives a picture exactly the reverse of this. About 90% of all the reactions are definite, quick movements; these movements are equal in the case of the simple reaction as well as in the reaction of choice; the complex problem of choice does not displace here the structure of the movement toward diffusion, does not change the picture of the motor curve. Our data convincingly prove that the complicated reactive process here is almost never reflected in the reactive movement itself and that all the qualities peculiar to the transfer from the simple reactive process to the complex one were completed in the period before the beginning of the movement. The presence of the inhibition preceding the realisation of the movements points to a specific "functional barrier" characteristic of the reactive process of the adult and practically absent in the young child.

TABLE 31

Subject, Group	A	B	C	
Oligophrenia, 10-12 years	+40%	+46%	+65%	—
Normal Children, 10-11 years	+ 7%	+ 6%	+ 9%	+ 6%
Adults	— 1%	— 5%	+ 3%	+ 2%

Changes of Movement during the Reaction of Choice Compared with the Simple Reactions.

This situation—that the movement itself of the adult remains almost unchanged in the case of the reaction of choice as well as in the simple reaction, while in the child in both cases it is very different—is well demonstrated by the coefficient expressing the augmentation of the period of movements bringing about the reaction of choice in comparison with the periods of movement in the simple reactive process. Table 31 gives us such a résumé, again taken from the work of Lubimov.

These figures clearly show that, in the oligophrenics (partly as in young children, the figures of which are not given here), the movements of the complex reactions have a less simple and prolonged character, occupying 40-60% more of the period than the movements during the simple reactions; but in adults we do not find a perceptible difference in the two cases, and the changes are very slight, and not exceeding the limits of probable error, sometimes negative, sometimes positive. This again shows how incorrect it would be to seek in the adult for specific peculiarities of the complex reactive process of the movement itself, and makes us think that the movement plays here only a rôle of completing that connection which was already prepared earlier and which was separated from the movement by the "functional barrier," allowing the excitation to pass over into the motor sphere only at the termination of this preliminary process.

This convinces us that the development of the reactive processes is not by any means a simple process of a gradual growth of complexity, of a continuous improvement in coordination; the path from the reactions of the child to the reactive processes of the adult leads through deep internal changes through a qualitative rebuilding of the whole structure of the neurodynamical acts, through a replacement of one primitive structure by another much more complicated and functionally different organisation.

This functional organisation of the reactive processes in the adult, according to all the data, is distinguished by the inclusion of the complicated mechanisms restraining the direct transfer of excitation to the motor region, regularly bringing to pass the intricate connections in order to carry over the excitation at the given instance. Undifferentiated and diffused from the beginning, the reactive process divides into two definite phases: the phase of preparation with the periodic isolation of excitation from the motor area, and the phase of realisation, bringing about by means of movements the connections prepared in the central apparatus.

Such a structure of the reactive process does not appear at birth, and does not grow by a gradual development; on the contrary, it matures by virtue of the repression of that primitive type of activity of the nervous system which is manifested in the tendency of every excitation to proceed to its motor terminus and is accomplished by a direct reaction. Precisely because the reactions of the adult are constructed on the basis of the repressed natural laws of activity of the nervous system, we may think that in its foundation lies the involved processes having a specific character, which must be the subject of a special investigation.

If the "functional barrier" and the regulating mechanisms of the reactive processes appear at a comparatively late age, then we may look for their origin from those conditions amongst which the child develops, and from those mechanisms created in him under the influence of the connections with these conditions. The problem of the organisation of the complex forms of behaviour should follow for us the problem of the genetic analysis of the forms of its disorganisation. This will occupy our attention in the following chapters.

6. THE PSYCHOLOGICAL PECULIARITIES CONNECTED WITH THE DIFFUSE STRUCTURE OF THE CHILD'S NEURODYNAMICS

IT would be entirely incorrect if we were to limit our analysis to the comparatively simple, artificial psychophysiological processes taken especially for experimentation.

Many facts convince us that the diffused character of each excitatory process is a basic factor characterising a primitive degree of development of the neurodynamic apparatus, and that all its growth in the main consists in the repression of this primary diffusion.

In his very illuminating researches, K. Lewin showed that every tension (*Spannung*) arising in the neurodynamical system of the young manifests a tendency slowly to pass over to motor innervation. This fact, however, was especially characteristic: every neurodynamical tension produced here not a corresponding movement of some one organ, but a diffuse reaction of all the systems as a whole. Photographs taken by K. Lewin showed that infants a few months old cling with the whole body, but not with one or another organ, to a toy or food given them, and that the excitation provoked by the stimulus manifests a tendency to spread diffusely over the whole system.

Embryological data indicate that this observation is not accidental, and that in the earlier stages of development we may postulate still more general and diffused reactions. The experiments of Coghill, presented before the Ninth International Congress of Psychologists [1] show

[1] G. E. Coghill: *The Genetic Interrelation of Instinctive Behaviour and Reflexes—Individuation versus Integration of Human Behaviour*, Proceedings of the Ninth International Congress of Psychology, 1929.

that the more early forms of reaction in the amblystoma are diffused reactions of the whole body, and that the component isolated reflexes are separated only rather late from the more integrated motor units; his experiments on the movements of the human embryo showed that the winking reflex is substituted by a diffuse motor reaction of the whole organism; experiments with irritation of the oral palate gave analogous results, showing that the isolated reflex movements from these organs appeared only at the moment of birth.

This diffused character of the neurodynamical processes—already repressed in the primitive stages of the neurodynamics in the first months of life—for a long time remains characteristic for the behaviour of the child, and the tendency to the direct discharge of excitation to its immediate transfer to the motor sphere may be seen even in children of pre-school age and in those a little older.

Our experiments prove that this diffusion is a specific feature of the structure in the reactive processes of the child, and it is expressed more clearly as we use a more complicated situation for the child.

However, it would not be correct to think that this structure characterises only the child's "voluntary activity," not being reflected in the other aspects of its behaviour. The experiments and observations indicate that the matter here is otherwise, and that all the actual factors in the behaviour of the child are characterised to a greater or lesser degree by an analogous structure.

Special experiments done in our laboratory brought out the fact that such a diffusion and tendency of the direct transfer to the motor area is highly characteristic for the emotional acts of the child. In experiments performed together with our collaborator, A. V. Zaporozhets, we proposed to the child to draw phrases having a neutral and emotional content, and containing elements of activity, movements (as for example, a boy running, a malicious teacher, war, etc.), and we registered the motor activity which he expended on the drawing in both cases. It is seen in the experiment that while the neutral, indifferent pictures are characterised by a comparatively small expenditure of energy, the picture having some emotional, active element is accompanied by a sharp motor excitation; the emotional image was expressed not only in the separate signs in the drawing, but also in the "emotional" character of the lines connected with the fact that the given emotional image was directly transferred to the motor system, producing there an active motor discharge.

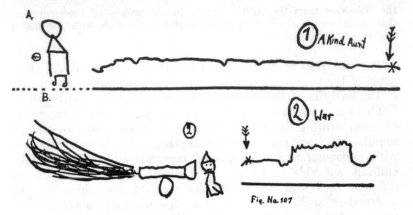

DRAWINGS OF A CHILD WITH THEIR MOTOR EQUIVALENTS

VANYA STARIKOV, NOV. 2, 1929, AGE 6 YEARS

A. "A KIND AUNT" (DRAWING AND MOTOR EQUIVALENT)
B. "WAR" (DRAWING AND MOTOR EQUIVALENT)

Figure 107 gives such an example. To a child six years old, there is given a problem to draw "A Kind Aunt," and then "War." Their motor equivalents are recorded alongside of the drawings (the drawings are on a special pneumatic stand, and every pressure of the pencil is registered on the kymograph). The record shows that the second drawing is much more emotional, and is distinguished by its neurodynamics: the motor equivalent exhibits here intense motor discharges, entirely lacking in the first drawing.

Such an affect of the direct transfer of the emotional-motor image to the motor system is observed only at a definite age, and in older children the motor equivalent of the drawing with the emotional content does not differ perceptibly from the motor equivalent of the drawing containing an indifferent image.[1]

It is interesting that this peculiarity was noticed by E. R. Jaensch[2] for the more primitive psychological processes. In his researches with eidetic images he shows that in experiencing active eidetic images the subject maintains a certain muscular tension; this tension is a fact very closely connected with the eidetic image; the artificial muscular tension can in these cases provoke a blending of the eidetic image. In the more complicated development of the psychological structures, during

[1] The details of this we shall describe in a special research having to do with graphic signs in the child.
[2] E. R. Jaensch, *Ueber die Aufbau der Wahrnehmungswelt*, 2 Aufl. 1927, S. 197-198.

the transition from the eidetic images to the images of representation, this result is not obtained, and the direct connection with the motor system ceases to play a rôle.

The weakness of the "functional barrier" and the direct character of the psychological processes stands out especially clearly in the analysis of the natural forms of the child's behaviour. There is a marked tendency of the young child, incapable of concentrating for a long time on a given thing, to change impulsively from one object to another. This is evidence that with a comparative weakness of the "functional barrier" the child is not able to restrain the stimulating influence of the different factors of the surroundings acting upon him. Coming under their spell, he finds it necessary to react to them every time, and this transfer from one stimulus to another is absent only in those cases where there is present some very strong dominant which replaces for a time all of the other stimuli.

It has been shown by K. Lewin that the behaviour of the young child is characterised by the tendency to a direct discharge of the tension created, and that a whole group of actions in the child are explained by this peculiarity. Therefore the series of the forms of behaviour established by Lewin, leading to the created tension, is especially clear in children. Such processes, as the active return to the interrupted action, the direct transfer from one object to another, the blending of the action during a prohibition—all of these phenomena are observed in a child in very marked forms.[1]

With greater clarity, however, the direct and impulsive character of the child's behaviour is expressed in his thinking. While in the old psychology we met with only a few, and always partial, descriptions of the child's thinking, emphasising his concreteness and subjectivity, in recent works, especially those of J. Piaget, we have a fairly complete and clear picture of the child's thinking. In our problems there has not entered in any degree a description of the peculiarities of this primitive thinking. For us it is important to note only this: that many of its characteristics give foundation to the belief that the structure of the intellectual process in the child actually differs from that which we are accustomed to see in the adult. The child's thinking is described as being constructed according to the type of *Kurzschluss;* as a rule he cannot restrain himself from a direct and impulsive judgment, which is not a result of deliberation but

[1] K. Lewin: *Die Entwichlung der Experimentellen Willens Psychologie und Psychotherapie,* 1929.

of a direct "short connection." From such a direct character of the judgment there is created a primitive child logic, described by Claparède, Stern and Piaget.

However, this is much clearer in the practical thinking of the child. That impulsive character which distinguishes the behaviour of the young child does not justify us in speaking of his decision of practical situations as an intellectual decision. The direct quality of the reactions and the ignorant application of instruments, the clumsy means of controlling his own behaviour, which appears in the absence of a working setting in the young child and in his play behaviour—all this is evidence of the dominating tendency, directly opposed to the complex organised behaviour. Every experiment which we perform on a child of three or four years (for example, bringing him into a situation analogous to Köhler's experiments with anthropoids) is verification that the intellectual act is preceded by the long period of primitive direct trials; these trials are very conservative and stable and only the gradual inhibition of errors on the one hand, and the inclusion of the higher regulating forms of behaviour on the other, lead to the development of more involved intellectual forms of behaviour.[1]

These features are connected in their origin from two facts: on the one hand, that direct character of the reactive processes, the tendency of all excitation immediately to be associated with activity, as we have described above; on the other hand, the higher psychological mechanisms, particularly that of speech, which have not yet begun to play in the child that regulating rôle taken later in adolescents and adults. In the young child speech is not a perfect means of making judgments and planning, and the loss of this preliminary stage gives to the intellectual processes of the child the primitive form, not less diffuse than that which we have noted in the more simple reactive processes.

The direct impulsiveness, already disappearing in the simplest reactive processes at the beginning of the school age, still remains in the most intricate intellectual operations for a very long time, and even in many adults a very complex intellectual situation may provoke an unexpected return to the most primitive childish form of pre-intellectual behaviour.

[1] A. R. Luria, *The Development of the Child's Thinking. Nature and Marxism*, 1929. L. C. Vuigotsky and Luria, *Studies in the History of Behaviour*, Moscow, 1930.

7. PROBLEMS OF THE NEURODYNAMICAL AGE AND TYPE

UNTIL now we have discussed the diffusion of the reactive processes of the child, relating to all children in general; but such a disposition of the problem must needs be further modified.

Obviously every child shows a diffusive structure of the reactive processes as we have already said, but the behaviour of everyone is not characterised by the same primitiveness and directness. During his development the child passes through very important stages, each of which is distinguished by conspicuous features. This is in direct opposition to the view that the phases of development have a single general basis. The reactive process under consideration undergoes development as do all the other processes, and the peculiarities of the structure which we have noted appear to be only tendencies influencing the neurodynamics of the young child.

Pedagogues studying the development of the child in all its details have always attempted to elaborate some index which might be characteristic of any given stage. The view that the actual age is an indicator, characterising the whole complex of the corresponding qualities by definite degrees, was quickly abandoned by pedagogues because the development proceeded disproportionately in the different systems. Therefore the summary actual age in a more detailed analysis was substituted by another more concrete indicator.

The first concept which was usually applied in pedagogy might be termed the morphological age of the child. This indicator includes several indices characterising the structural development of the child's organism and defining his age according to the phase of development of the morphological signs; the index of the circumference of the chest to the height, the index of the bony growth, the index of proportion belong in this group.

Together with this group of indices there is another one usually employed in pedagogy. While the first attempts to condition the more stable morphological signs, the second reflects these signs in a more fluctuating way; the indices of the mental age take into account how much the child differs from his actual, morphological age in his intellectual development.

These two indices can hardly exhaust the whole range of indicators of the child's development, but, on the contrary, between these two important indices there is a considerable gap.

In effect, if the index of the intellectual development is

markedly labile and dependent upon surrounding influences from the material given the child in school from inculcated habits, then this index cannot tell us the degree of the development of the neurodynamical processes lying at the basis of the child's behaviour. On the other hand, the index of the morphological age is distinguished by definite statistics, and for one and the same morphological characteristics there may exist entirely unequal dynamical properties of the behaviour in different cases. The morphological age, as a matter of fact, tells us no more than the mental age of the child about the fundamental dynamical forms of behaviour.[1]

This is not the place to define in detail the conditions which this index must fulfil; but we shall briefly point out the problem. The changing stages of the child's neurodynamical development have, of course, as much significance as the changes of its morphological and mental character. The index of the neurodynamical development should indicate what are the features of its reactive process, and how far the child represses that primary diffusion of the excitation which characterises the activity of the primitive nervous apparatus.

If the behaviour of the young child is characterised by this, that the mobilisation of the adequate amounts of excitation to the given stimulus is absent, and the child as a rule mobilises inadequate masses of energy, which it is unable to organise, considerably exceeding the necessary limits, if the behaviour manifest a tendency of every arising excitation directly to pass to the motor termination, to express itself in the immediate reaction —then in the repressing of these qualities, in the growth of the regulating processes, in the creation and reinforcement of the "functional barrier" and the gradual organisation of behaviour— precisely in these processes there may be primarily expressed the gradual development of the neurodynamics, precisely in the correlated coefficients is reflected the neurodynamics of the age.

By virtue of such a character, obviously, the neurodynamics of the age is actually the psychophysiological coefficient. In the first stages of development, it must differentiate the process of repression of the diffused, irradiated excitation, and its first

---

[1] There is no doubt, however, that there is a close relation between both of these and the neurodynamics; investigations of the relations between the neurodynamics and constitution have shown this. The connection of the intellectual developments with the neurodynamics has not been so thoroughly worked out, but it is of no less significance. We are able to establish very important relations between the level of the cultural development and the neurodynamical peculiarities of behaviour.

steps lie wholly within the confines of these physiological processes of development, which are studied in the terms of irradiation and concentration of excitation, development and establishment of differentiation, etc. In its final stage it will be connected with the more complex processes of control of its behaviour, or in other words, with such an organisation of the neurodynamical apparatus, with which the overcoming of the primitive neurodynamical process was possible and the subordination of its more complex forms of regulation arising as a result of the cultural development. Thanks to this, that the problem of the organisation of behaviour rests in the final stage with the problem of control of the behaviour, the question concerning the neurodynamical age ceases to be a question of biology and becomes one of the cultural elaboration on biological grounds, i.e., in the final analysis, a problem of psychophysiology.

We do not intend to indicate now those paths by which the investigator can establish the neurodynamical age; the elaboration of a standard method of investigation is a problem for the future. However, much has already been done toward this, and the material available to the investigator gives a general outline of these paths. There is no doubt that the facts obtained with the help of the physiological methods of investigation of the higher activity of the nervous system lie at the basis of the neurodynamical characteristics of the child; and the degree of irradiation, generalisation, and the concentration of the nervous excitation will be one of the important indices of the neurodynamical age. The researches of Schtchlovanov with young children and those of Ivanov-Smolensky with older children are valuable contributions.

Over this foundation there should be erected a second tier of applicable methods, which, together with the first, constitute the neurodynamical development of the child. This second tier should concern itself with the "voluntary" activity and decide the problem of its control. This we are occupied with at present. The investigations should certainly include a whole system of experiments to decide the question of control of behaviour by a series of problems increasing in complexity and by the inclusion of the more intricate mechanisms. The coefficient expressing the neurodynamical age might be explained from the investigations of the repression of the primitive diffusion and the growth of the regulating behaviour in successive, complex systems, where at one end of the series there is the action, the organised control attainable by the child several months old, and at the other end should be sections of the behaviour in which the impulsiveness and diffusion are repressed only in the fully developed, neurodynamical relations of the personality.

Fundamental and not simply empirical will be the construction of such a system; it will be possible, however, only in case we explain the nature of the control of the personality by its behaviour and if we explain the character of those mechanisms forming the "functional barrier" and the chief regulating apparatus of the complex functions of the behaviour.

Together with the question of the neurodynamical age is that of the neurodynamical type. Speaking of the degree of diffusion of the reactive processes in the child and neglecting the individual characteristics, we would make the same mistake as if we were to shift our attention from the age and to limit ourselves by a summary indicator of the tendency of the child's development.

The question concerning the psychophysiological type is based on many methodological problems and is therefore especially interesting. Its significance in our problem impels us to discuss it here.

In previous studies we have pointed out that our material obtained from different subjects was not equivalent. This forced us to consider the presence among our subjects of an inclination sometimes to one, sometimes to another, method of behaviour; and we spoke of the reactively labile and reactively stable types of neurodynamics.

We were fully justified in describing them in our first approach to the problem of individual differences; however it would be very disadvantageous to be limited by such substitution of the study of dynamics of the accumulating individual qualities by a mere typological label. We shall try to give, however brief, a logical analysis of the concept "type." We are justified in speaking of "type" in those cases where all of the material falls into two or three clearly expressed groups, differing by certain features of the laws governing them. Nevertheless, in our usual psychophysiological investigations we most often do not find any of these above-mentioned features. On the one hand, to the clearly expressed type there belong only a few of our subjects and the distinct typological characteristics are found primarily in the pathological material; the others are usually scattered between these two (generally we encounter such dichotomous phenomena, acquiring now a simple, now a more complex form) between these two branches of our series. If we divide all of our subjects according to the given characteristics, then in place of the expected double curve, we see an irregular one of the converse type; a small number form a sharply expressed unknown type, and the majority belong to the intervening group.

Under such circumstances, to speak of the presence of two or several clearly defined typological groups is very difficult, and it is possible to separate one type from another only approximately. This state of affairs indicates that some very specific combinations of mechanisms, some new qualitative properties arising on the basis of the same laws are necessary before we can make the differentiation into types. To divide people into types—tall and short, stout and thin,—leaving 70% in the intermediate types would be a very useless procedure; the typological grouping is justified only when at the basis of the phenomena there are actually specific combinations of signs which are not only clearly expressed in extreme cases but include the whole mass of the intermediate ones. However, this is not often seen in the material we have studied. The phenomena observed often have an entirely different etiology, and consist of different mechanisms. The classification of our types, according to the purely phenotypical symptoms and not according to their genotypical analysis, runs the risk of making errors, or, at best, remaining at the level of the external description.

It is our belief that in view of the above-discussed conditions, further investigations should change the conception of type to a more dynamic term, substituting the usual analysis by a more dynamic one.

Our analysis is much more vital if we attempt to understand the described types as phases in the ensuing processes. Only in such a substitution of the static analysis by the dynamical analysis can we properly evaluate our material and approach it in the light of an entirely different point of view.

The dialectic analysis gives to typology a new basis and makes possible the inclusion of the individual peculiarities into a single unified process. These individual peculiarities may be externally dissimilar one to the other, but, finding the same mechanism at their basis, we can consider them as different phases of a single dynamical series. The conception of types is replaced here by a conception of tendencies, giving to each stage a quantitative and qualitative characteristic. The division of all the material into two types with many intervening ones, inert and undifferentiated, is substituted by a dynamical analysis of those concrete forms which the given tendency takes at the various stages of its development. The metaphysical division is substituted by a single scientific one, and that which was always most burdensome and confusing for the investigator—the large intermediate group between the pure types—became more interesting for him because he was enabled to proceed along the most important paths leading him to the very existence of the process.

Only with such a dialectic analysis, the simple description of the facts confronting us is changed into a direct investigation of the process, and the typological method from the description becomes a powerful instrument of scientific investigation.

It is obvious that the dynamical analysis of the individual differences makes the study of the processes much more complicated and incomparably more circuitous.

In the process of the typological analysis there is included the whole arsenal of the genetic study of the phenomena; the "type" ceases to be separated from the genesis and begins to be founded on the careful study of those phases through which the personality passed in its development; the typological features now commence to be connected with the genetic characteristics, and the study of the development becomes a most important means of coordinating the qualities of the personality.

The separation of the central principle of development becomes a conditioned typology, and only after the decision of these two questions is the problem itself of the typological analysis possible, and the simple description of the concrete facts is replaced by a genuine scientific investigation.

In order to make concrete the methodological analysis of the typological investigation it is best to cite the material which we have already studied.

Studying the laws and factors of disorganisation of human behaviour we came to the conclusion that in the individual cases this disorganisation is unequal and that at the basis of such differences lies the dissimilar organisation and regulation of the neuropsychical apparatus. This regulation is much more perfect in a state of composure than during affect; it may be artificially destroyed by introducing certain conflicts into the psyche of the personality; it is well marked in neurosis. On the other hand, the regulation of behaviour, its stability in relation to all these circumstances is not the same in all subjects and is different at the various stages of development. A careful analysis convinces us that this degree of regulation of behaviour is fundamental and determines the lines of development of the behaviour as well as the individual peculiarities of the personality. The behaviour appears insufficiently organised in its activity, it easily becomes disintegrated, manifesting a tendency to mobilise in each stimulus an inadequately large amount of excitation which it is incapable of controlling. It is noteworthy that the behaviour of young children belongs here; their neurodynamics is distinguished by these two symptoms. On the other hand, some variations are seen in the pathological behaviour of psychoneurotics, who show hypersensibility, mobilising inadequate amounts of excitation, and defects of that which we call the "functional barrier." Another line of development shows the very opposite symptoms, and in these subjects we see a fair organisation of behaviour, stability of the neurodynamical interrelations to conflicts and traumata, an adequate mobilisation of excitation, and a well-defined isolation of the processes of excitation from a direct transfer to the motor sphere. Among normal adults we have, as a rule, a greater or lesser tendency of the neurodynamics to fall into this group, and within certain limits the behaviour of every normal adult is fairly stable and well regulated.

These two lines of development are of interest to us chiefly from the point of view of methodology. By no means shall we attempt to classify normal subjects in one or another of these groups. Our descriptions represent not stable types, but only tendencies. ... The real problem before us leads to this: the establishment of the degree of manifestation of the regulating behaviour in any given subject at that time, and the description of those qualitative peculiarities which are associated with the degree of regulation of the neurodynamical labileness. The statistical analysis of types is replaced here by a dynamical analysis of the developing peculiarities of the neurodynamics, resulting from the study of the principal characteristics. The distribution of all the subjects into several limited and stable types is substituted by their reciprocal relations with the definite stage of growth of the regulation of behaviour, its increasing participation with the complex psychological systems, and the description of the interrelations of the various stages of the qualitative peculiarities.

We do not presume now to offer either a ready system of methods for the establishment of the typological peculiarities of the neurodynamics, or a finished description of the individual neurodynamic structures. It seems to us that such an investigation of the typological properties of the neurodynamics is a problem for the future, and we are content to limit ourselves to that stratified analysis mentioned above, hoping that a more detailed disposition of its developing peculiarities, the detailed study of the disintegration of behaviour in the various neurodynamical systems, may in time reveal to us the nature and mechanics of the neurodynamical types.

CHAPTER XI

NATURE OF THE FUNCTIONAL BARRIER

---

1. PROBLEMS OF THE FUNCTIONAL BARRIER

W E HAVE shown what rôle the "functional barrier" plays in restraining the excitation from a direct transfer to the motor sphere. Now we must explain its nature. How are we to consider this apparatus? Is it inborn, congenital, only gradually appearing in the process of unnatural growth, or is it a product of education, becoming manifest together with certain new cultural elaborations in the human psychobiology? Must we think of it as a morphologically formed apparatus; or is that which we call the "functional barrier" a functional conception, not concealing any new morphological elaborations and having to do only with the combination of other already present systems, of other structures of the process, of the inclusion in the neurodynamics of behaviour of new and higher culturally psychological relations and of their influence in the course of the reactive processes?

Upon the solution of this question depends the direction of our further researches and the whole path of the investigation.

What should we do here to avoid mistakes in the solution of this problem? Nowhere is a system of concepts so evident on first acquaintance and so mythological in fact as in those chapters of psychology which touch neurology and attempt to proceed from it. Psychologists working in this region feel at home among the most delicate neurological elements as if every nook and cranny were known to them in detail and connected with definite established functions. In such a psychologist every theory influences his concepts: the forming of habits depends upon the connecting synapses; forgetting or sleep, upon their separation; every disturbance in psychobiological activity is linked up with a distinct morphological injury, and each step along the path of development may be expressed in explicit terms of neurological formations.

But the lucidness is often deceptive, the exact and detailed descriptions represent doubtful facts, unproven experimentally, and hardly universally recognised by scientists. The history of the border-lying territory between psychology and neurology for the last few decades is a history of mythology.

To think in terms of things is much easier than to think in terms of processes; in the latter instance the thinking must satisfy complex concepts and interrelations, whilst in the first it operates with evident optical images and mechanised models. Under these conditions one is obviously inclined to a construction based on concreteness.

There is a whole history of the attempts to build psychology on such concrete neurological concepts. These trials have not explained a single element of the nervous apparatus; they have their roots deep in antiquity and terminate with the newest mythology, localising the most intricate psychological processes and finding for them the most "exact" morphological apparatuses and trying to connect the archaic concepts of mental processes with the most recent knowledge concerning the function of the corpus striatum and thalamus. Neither the nerve fibrils nor the plasma have escaped such essays. The synapses particularly have come in for their share of these relations, and, according to some authors, they explain the mechanisms of associations, sleep, hypnosis, forgetting, recollection and almost all the remaining psychological functions.

An excellent criticism of such mythological concepts in contemporary neurology is given by many authors, and especially clearly by Lashley, who has shown that many similar conjectures, explaining empirical facts by quotations from "neurological mechanisms are often worthless and merely an obstacle to the progress of science."[1]

Thus, that on which psychoneurology has often built its entire system of thought is frequently false, only touching on the concrete and numerous cases revealing nothing except a logical concreteness in the form of the structure. This explains the constant tendency of the authors to express opinions concerning the "concrete" and formulated mechanisms to the definite "concrete" structure. An action which is connected with the representation of some morphological apparatus is much more evident and more easily comprehended; functional conceptions are always more difficult and involved, and naïve thinking will for a long time consider "thinking in terms of things" a criterion of accuracy and science.

However, precisely this inclination to a visual conception (it is difficult for us to find another term for it), with the aid of

[1] K. S. Lashley: *Basic Neural Mechanisms in Behaviour,* Psychological Review, 1930.

scientific thinking, quickly becomes one of the most serious obstacles. Nothing is easier than to postulate a morphological apparatus in any functional conception, using the analogies of mechanisms known to us in this simple procedure, which is a product of pure analogy and the application of thought in a certain optical concreteness—to substitute a much more complicated relationship of the phenomena.

In speaking of one or another mechanism of behaviour it is not obligatory for us to presuppose the existence of any special morphological structure. The supposition that the development of psychological functions is necessarily connected with the growth of cortical new formations underlying them is a conjecture hardly tenable; in effect, we know many more complex forms of development connected with new combinations in the use of those same morphological elaborations accompanied by a change in their functional significance; and those modifications which we meet in the development of the behaviour of the child may be referred to these processes of the second type. Does not the inclusion in the social surroundings, the acquisition of speech, the use of instruments, and the transition of the new cultured forms of organisation of the individual behaviour change the structure of the psychophysiological processes just as much as the appearance of some purely morphological alteration of the nervous apparatus? Moreover, in this complicated organisation with which behaviour is connected, these functional changes are often predominant, and we know scores of cases where it was possible to compensate for serious defects in the coarse morphological structure of the nervous apparatus.

But we stand here before another system of conceptions than that which is usually accepted in the morphological approach to the psychophysiological causes. Of course, no scientifically and materialistically minded psychologist could deny that at the basis of any complex psychological phenomenon lies a definite organisation of the cerebral apparatus; nevertheless, not every psychologist-materialist will attempt to ascribe the peculiarity in this organisation to the specific morphological new formations.

The higher forms of behaviour as well as the primitive can be functions of such an exact morphological brain; cultured behaviour does not require a new brain morphology, and the brain of a savage may be morphologically identical with that of a member of the Academy of Sciences; the most intricate psychological elaborations may be comprehended in a plan of functional reconstructions, the use of the same functions in entirely new combinations and the employment of the new and adapted mechanisms of the surroundings.

We are firmly convinced that these mechanisms, which are often far more complicated to understand, are, notwithstanding, more adequate for the explanation of the intricate elaborations of behaviour. From this point of view, we see the origin of those partly mythological images which obsess the naïve investigator.

But where must we look for the mechanisms conditioning the "functional barrier" and creating the differentiation of the complex structure of the reactive processes about which we spoke in the last chapter?

The facts which we find in the scientific literature impel us to turn our attention to the reciprocities of the higher cortical mechanisms with the general sensibility of the nervous apparatus, and to seek for the destruction of the "functional barrier" in the places where the former are weakened or where the sub-cortical mechanisms with the latter are strengthened.

Contemporary neurology, on the basis of the facts which we must undoubtedly use, begins in the conflicting conceptions of the structure of the nervous apparatus. All the authors concur in the opinion that the cortex and the recent elaborations of the brain are in conflict with the older parts and serve the function of the organiser of the primitive impulses connected with the latter parts.

In 1884, Hughlings Jackson outlined the position existing then, showing the influence of the brain on function and structure; the conclusion was that the higher stratum of the nervous apparatus was inhibitory, restraining the primitive reactions of the older cerebral systems; this included the restraining and organising rôle of the morphologically higher strata of the apparatus as well as the analogous rôle of the higher functional systems, creating the complex processes of biological and historical evolution. Jackson and Head, working on aphasia, pointed out the primary organising rôle played by speech on the voluntary and emotional disturbances occurring when these complex functional strata were injured.

This exposition is of vital importance for us—our further discussion is based on it: many experiments show during emotional excitation a marked inhibitory rôle of the cortex. The effect of chloroform and other anesthetics acting on the cortex are too well known to necessitate description. Woodworth and Sherrington described a case in which the appearance of symptoms analogous to those seen in an acute affective state was produced by allowing strong stimuli to act on the sensory area of the cortex; such symptoms were seen in decerebrated cats and in the experiments of Bazett and Penfield.[1]

---

[1] Bazett and Penfield—*A Study of the Sherrington Decerebrate Animal*, Brain, 1922, V. 45. Cited by Ph. Bard, *The Neuro-Humoral Basis of Emotional Reactions*, Murchison's Foundations of Experimental Psychology, 1929, p. 472.

Especially illuminating material comes from the clinic; injury to the paths between the cortex and the sub-cortical ganglia—chiefly the thalamus opticus—produces a sharp increase of the uncontrolled impulsive, emotional movements. In the clinical researches of Wilson,[1] he concludes that the destruction of the cortical control leads to a considerable increase of the sub-cortical activity, which usually holds in check the effect of the cortical systems.

A review of the important data brings one of the authors to the following decision, very important for us: Philip Bard (above quotation, p. 477) concludes that "the sub-cortical processes are at every moment ready to seize the power over the motor reactions, and every time that the cortical restraint is weakened they quickly and vigorously do this."

The above facts outline a definite path in the investigation of the organisation and disorganisation of human behaviour. We may presuppose that there is increased diffuseness of the reactive processes and lowering of the functional barrier where the sensibility of the apparatus is increased and the sub-cortical processes are more active, and, on the other hand, in those cases where the participation of the higher cortical systems in the behaviour is weakened—that the same cortical apparatus is defective. We may assuredly expect that the action of the functional barrier will be closely connected not only in the participation with the newer morphological strata of the cortex, but with the inclusion of those higher functional systems as indicated by Jackson and Head, which could be elaborated only in the most intricate processes of psychological development and which play not only an inhibitory, but also a formative, organising rôle.

Therefore, we should pay particular attention to those cases where the sensibility of the nervous system is increased, and to the others where the cortical regulators are decreased, impairing the higher psychological functions. In both instances we may expect symptoms of a lowered functional barrier and, in a certain degree, a return to a primitive, diffuse structure of the reaction. From a careful analysis of these cases it is possible to state something more concerning the nature of the given mechanisms than we have heretofore known.

2. THE STRUCTURE OF THE REACTIVE PROCESSES IN FUNCTIONAL NEUROSES

WE shall discuss only briefly the structure of the reactive processes in functional neuroses; for the material which has been given in Chapters VIII and IX makes it possible to limit our remarks here to only a few conclusions.

[1] Wilson, *Modern Problems in Neurology*, N. Y., 1929.

That which is most characteristic of the neurodynamics of the functional neurosis has been already described by us as a diffuse structure of the reactions connected with a general increased excitability, on the one hand, and on the other, a decreased ability to restrain the excitation from its direct transfer to the motor sphere. In view of these factors, the patients with functional neuroses exhibited a picture of intense motor conflicts, deeply disorganising their neurodynamics, incapacitating them by an isolation from the motor sphere. We discussed these facts in detail in regard to neurasthenia as well as hysteria. The former, characterised by disorganisation of the behaviour from a weakening of the cortical regulators and a general hyperexcitability, differing from the latter in its etiology, gives, however, a very similar structure of the reactive processes. If we take from the very heterogeneous group of hysterics those of them who have underlying their pathologic condition a constitutional peculiarity of their nervous system, we can often observe a completely analogous neurodynamical influence, although provoked by a different etiology.

Until recently the question of constitutional peculiarities of the nervous system in hysteria was in a state of confusion. However, many of the symptoms lead us to believe that in the cases of the constitutionally conditioned hysteric we primarily have a considerable increase in the functions of the sub-cortical apparatus, accompanying its extreme labileness. The presence of the symptoms of the vegetative neurosis in hysteria, the primitive character of the behaviour often found in these diseases tends to confirm the above view.[1] The lowered threshold, the presence of secondary reactions (Löwenstein) and many related symptoms, the presence of stigmatism, on the other hand, shows the excessive labileness and the excitability of the cortex, which therefore frequently begins to refuse to regulate the increased energetic action of the sub-cortical apparatus.

These facts give a general foundation for the comprehension of the structure of the hysterical reactions. The experimental material confirms and amplifies this picture into a concrete plan.

A simple experiment shows that the hysteric differs in the markedly increased excitability plus the tendency of the excitation to extend directly to the motor sphere. We tell the hysterical patient to put his hand passively on the pneumatic bulb, and inform him that we shall register its tremors, and then suddenly give an auditory stimulus, unexpected by the subject;

[1] C. Gordanesco: *Conception nouvelles sûr l'hysterie,* Bucharest, 1926.

whilst in the normal subject this auditory shock produces only a slight tremor, in the neurotic there is a very conspicuous motor disturbance not comparable to the normal, either in form or intensity. Löwenstein (*Experimentelle Hysterielehre*, 1923) sees in these phenomena the fundamental features of the neuro-dynamics of hysteria, and we have had an opportunity to con-firm this.

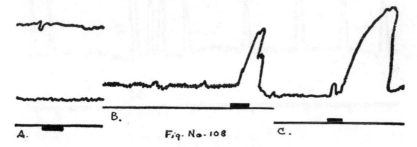

REACTIONS TO AUDITORY SHOCK

A = NORMAL SUBJECT   B AND C = HYSTERICAL PATIENTS

Figure 108 gives the characteristic reactions to shock in the normal subject and in the hysterical patient. It is obvious that the general excitability and the direct extension (already de-scribed by Löwenstein and brought out especially in Curve C) is characteristic of the neurodynamics of the functional illness.

We shall now take up the diffuse direct action of the receptory excitation to the reactive process characterising the behaviour of the hysteric.

The distinguishing feature of the reactions of the normal human adult is the little-known fact that the change of intensity of the stimulus cannot produce a proportional change of the intensity of the reaction; this gives the impression that the connecting, coupling-up system plays only the rôle of including the standard motor response, not placing the motor system in dependence upon the intensity of the given signal.

An entirely different picture is observed in functional neurotics. The stimulus does not play here the rôle of a simple conditioned signal, always including the same mass of motor excitation; but thanks to the diffused character of the reactions produced by the stimulus, the excitation directly seeps over into the motor sphere, and it is evident that during this the motor reactions begin to depend upon the strength of the given signal; the intensive signal directly calls out an intensive reaction which varies with the strength of the process of the excitation produced by the stimulus.

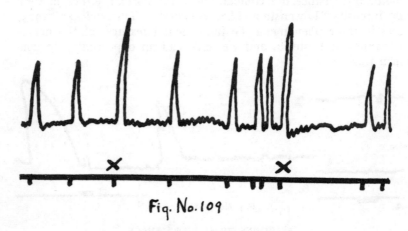

Fig. No. 109

SIMPLE REACTIONS OF HYSTERICAL PATIENTS

X = STRONG SIGNALS

Figure 109 demonstrates such a direct dependence of the reactive movements upon the intensity of the stimulus. Patient Zhuk. (hysteria) reacts by a sharp and impulsive disturbance every time we give her a strong signal, and this is evidence that we have here a qualitatively different structure of the reactions distinguished by the absence of the well-elaborated and standard motor automatisms, brought about by the conditioned stimulus and characterised by the direct passage of the receptory excitation into the motor area.

In this experiment we touch on two phenomena almost pathognomonic of hysteria. Firstly, we are inclined to see here a psychophysiological foundation for the increased suggestibility of the hysteric; the immediate subordination of his motor receptory phenomena are very conspicuous; such a direct tendency of the realisation of the external stimulus in the motor region, we consider one of the most important factors of his suggestibility.

Secondly, there is this very interesting fact: the direct extension of the excitation is dependent not only on the intensity of the given stimulus but also upon the level of the tension, which, until this time, was present in the central system. The centrally arising excitation is unable to isolate itself from the motor sphere just as is the stimulus. Two examples of this are given in Figure 110.

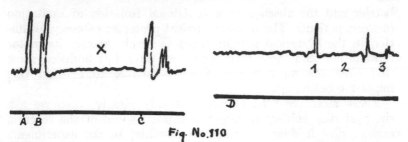

THE INFLUENCE OF THE CENTRAL EXCITATION ON THE MOTOR SYSTEM

A = REACTION TO A NORMAL SIGNAL
B = REACTION TO A STRONG SIGNAL
C = REACTION TO A NORMAL SIGNAL
D = INTENSITY OF MOTOR OVERFLOW

Here we give an example of reactions to a normal and to a strong signal, and then we forewarn the subject that we will give him a strong stimulus, but actually give him the usual, normal one. The tension produced by the expectation, however, causes a marked disturbance, completely deforming the normal reactive process (Curve C). We tell the subject that when we count "three" we will give him a shock, and after this we count but do not give the stimulus. As the experiment shows, the preliminary expectation creates in the subject such a tension that he cannot prevent the motor overflow, and Curve D illustrates the intensity of this phenomenon.

The impulsive and direct character of the neurodynamics of the hysterical patient has in its own changes of structure the same reactive process.

In the experiments with ideo-motor phenomena we have a confirmation of the diffusion of the reactive processes in the hysteric. When every external stimulus provokes in these patients a tendency to a direct extension to the motor system we cannot expect a different effect from the excitation of central origin. The great strength which the ideo-motor phenomena acquire in the hysteric has been adequately described in psychological and medical literature, and has served as a determining factor in the qualification of behaviour as hysterical. Stigmatism and conversion, the symbolic basis of the somatic disturbances, are evidence of the property of the central excitation to pass over into the motor area. Numerous experiments prove that this phenomenon is preserved in many of our patients, and it is not necessary to substantiate this obvious fact by protocols. We again come to the increased sensibility of the nervous apparatus, being manifested in the conditions of the lowered functional barrier and the absence of a functional isolation of excitation in these patients. The neurodynamical processes of every excitation in the hysterical patient tends to reach directly its motor termination, and these facts which we have just adduced show that even the most intense force is unable to restrain this impulsive behaviour.

These facts are brought out especially clearly when we ask the hysterical subject to inhibit his usual speed of the reaction and to slow it down as much as possible. In the experiments with the delayed reactions, described before, the extreme impulsiveness of the hysterics was not able to isolate the excitation from the direct transfer to the motor area; as a rule, the signal produced a slow motor impulse which was then inhibited; instead of the regulated movements, according to the ordinary motor formula, there were secondary trials to control the impulsive reactions, not always successful but always characteristic of the hysteric. A comparative picture of the slow pressures in the normal and hysteric subjects have already been given (Chapter IX, section 3); these data show that the previously elaborated formulæ for the delayed movements play a part here in the secondary delay of the direct motor impulse.

The impulsive character of the reactive processes in hysteria is manifested in the experiments where there is a preliminary organised inhibition of the movements and a transfer of the excitation to the motor sphere only when the corresponding reactions have been prepared by the central, coupling-up processes. In these instances the hysteric is most helpless, and in the experiments with the complicated reactions of choice we obtain a picture similar to that described for the young child. Ordinarily the motor innervation does not await the moment when in the preliminary process the regular choice of the movement will have been made; it begins long before this, and the actual process of choosing is accomplished not prior to the motor reaction, but after it has started; the excitation is too early and it flows without obstruction into the motor area, and in the unfitness for this motor apparatus is the conflict of choice; in the hysteric the movement of choice is complicated by the uncertain impulsive attempts of the usual response. A cinematograph of such cases shows that a stimulus given the subject immediately evokes impulsive movements which are quickly inhibited, and the reactions are terminated with much less assurance than in the normal adult where they are prepared in the preliminary period.

Those profound alterations in the structure of the reactive

process which we have pointed out previously in the analysis of the child's behaviour is equally characteristic for the hysteric. The general increased excitability, not colliding with the stable functional barrier, brings about the diffuseness of the reaction, distinguishing it from the structure of the reactive processes in the normal adult, and creating a specific psychophysiological basis of hysterical behaviour.

That diffuse character of the reactive processes seen in hysteria is reflected in the whole behaviour. The tendency of the excitation to pass over directly into the motor sphere has its counterpart in the thinking of the hysteric, and we are justified in believing that his thinking differs as much as his behaviour from that of the normal subject. Logical judgments cannot play the same rôle here that they do in the normal, but on the contrary, direct conclusions, logical *Kurzschlüsse,* impulsive judgment and primitive elaborations of understanding have a different significance from what they have in the normal subject of the same intellectual level. For many reasons we think that there is such a primitive structure of the hysteric's thinking. Experiments done with Vuigotsky and Eidinov confirm this view.

3. THE STRUCTURE OF THE REACTIVE PROCESSES IN ORGANIC DECREASE OF THE CORTICAL REGULATION: EXPERIMENTS WITH CASES OF MENTAL RETARDATION

EXPERIMENTS on hysterical patients prove that during the increased excitability observed in them the functional barrier is usually destroyed and the reactive process takes on a diffuse character. These facts, which we have twice mentioned in this discussion, were not unexpected; in the existing sensibility of the nervous apparatus and the tendency to mobilise inadequate masses of excitation we obtain naturally those defects in the delay of this excitation; in our conception this is connected with the diffuse structure of the reactive process.

It is not surprising that the diffuse character of the reaction was associated with the increased constitutional lableness of the nervous apparatus; but it is of more interest that the analogous diffusion of the neurodynamics is present in the cases having an entirely different neurodynamical structure. The diffuse character of the reactive processes may be a consequence of the insufficiency of the higher cortical mechanisms equally as well as a result of the increased excitability and sensibility of the sub-cortical and vegetative apparatuses. The externally equivalent symptoms may conceal entirely different etiologies, and therefore a diligent study of the latter may be extremely helpful in the understanding of the interesting mechanisms lying at the basis of the organisation and disorganisation of human behaviour.

If we desire to study the neurodynamical processes analogous to those which we have already considered, but under the conditions of an increased activity of the higher cortical systems, we should make use of the cases where, as a result of the lack of development of the cortex, its higher regulating activity is weakened. Such instances can be found in the more serious forms of mental retardation.

While in hysteria the transfer to the diffuse structure of the reactive process is accompanied by a general increased sensibility of the nervous apparatus, in the experiments with the forms of cortical insufficiency found in oligergasia or imbecility the change in structure of the reactive processes is associated with just the reverse—with a destruction of the higher regulating mechanisms.

At first we might suppose that mental retardation is limited by alterations in the complex intellectual processes and that the existing disturbance there does not get through deeper than the neurodynamical stratum in which the intellect participates and which is insufficient in oligergasia.

However, our supposition is entirely wrong. All of human behaviour is strictly dependent upon the higher cortical mechanisms which we are accustomed to designate as the intellectual processes. Experimentation shows that the simplest acts of behaviour are intimately connected with the most complex cortical processes, that in the activity of the human there are not any strata which cannot be included in the system of the higher cortical regulators, and the structure of the simplest reactive processes is entirely reconstructed, as we can see in those cases where a disturbance of the central nervous system reduced the activity of the higher functions usually considered as purely intellectual.

Increased tendon reflexes have been described for a long time in cases of oligergasia (imbecility, feeblemindedness),[1] supposedly caused by the weakened influence of the cortex on the lower-lying centers owing to undeveloped pyramidal paths.[2]

Many changes are observed in the conditioned reflex activity in oligergasia. Many investigators have shown that while the positive reflexes are elaborated more quickly in the mentally retarded, the differentiations and very weak and unstable.[3] The excitation produced in oligergasia has

---

[1] Dupre et Merklen: Revue Neurol., 1909; Dupre et Gilma, *idem.*, 1910.

[2] For description of motor symptoms in this disease see Gurevitch: *Psychomotorika*, Moscow, 1930, p. 89 (Russian).

[3] V. N. Ossipov, *Speed of Formation of Reflexes in School Children*, Reflexology, 11, 1926 Ilinsky, *Processes of Excitation and Inhibition in Mentally*

considerable inertia, and the facts of perseveration and inability to inhibit the beginning excitation brings the authors to the conclusion that the most characteristic feature in these cases is the disturbance of the regulating nervous processes, and that the defects in the higher cortical systems are manifested clearly in the less complicated strata of reflex activity.

After the facts bearing witness to the great disorganisation of the reflex activity in oligergasia, the serious disintegration characterising the course of the simplest processes, we will not be surprised if specific experiments reveal decisive changes in the structure of simplest reactions, sharply distinguishing them from normal children of the same age.

Our experiments (chiefly the material of M. C. Lebedinsky) convincingly proved that the structure of the reactive processes is disturbed at its very basis and that these fundamental disintegrations bring about the substitution of the differentiated structure of the diffuse reaction, with an acute injury of the functional barrier and with complete inability to restrain the beginning process of excitation, and to isolate it from the direct transfer to the motor sphere. The tendency to a direct discharge characterises the imbecile in all of his acts, and is frequently associated with excessive excitability present in most oligophrenics.

Those phenomena noted during hysteria usually arise from a different basis, with insufficiency of different mechanisms; and those defects in the activity of the functional barrier are connected there with hypersensibility of the nervous apparatus, but here with the failure of the complex regulating parts of the cortex.

The principal laws governing the neurodynamics of oligergasia are brought out in the experiments with simple reactions to a signal. Those peculiarities which we observe here differentiate the imbecile from the normal person.

Our attention is brought first to the picture of the simple reactive movements in oligergasia, the considerably lowered ability to elaborate the higher automatisms and to give reactions characterising the definite standard forms. This defect in the elaboration of the "motor formula" is clearly expressed in the fact that the imbecile gives motor curves distinguished by an excessive variability. Our facts convince us that, in distinction to that picture which we are accustomed to see in the normal subject, the reactions of the oligergastic are not constructed accord-

Retarded Children, Dissertation, 1928. U. Segal, *Elaboration of Conditioned Reflexes and Differentiations in Oligophrenia*, Jour. of Neuropathology of Korsakov, 1927. A. L. Shnirman, *Reciprocal Relations of Positive Reflexes in Oligophrenia*, Reflexology, III, 1930.

ing to a definite model, and they are sharply differentiated one
from the other in the form as well as in the intensiveness of the
movements. It is obvious that these processes are characterised
by unequal mobilisation of the excitation, and that the preliminary elaboration of the stable motor formulae is very much
weakened here. The behaviour of the oligergastic is not disorganised, because it was never organised, and the insufficiency of
the higher regulating cortical functions is in the defects of or-

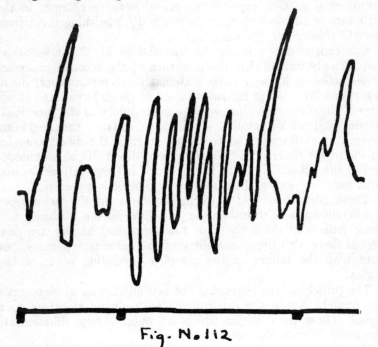

Fig. No. 112

SUBJECT ROS. (10 YRS., IMBECILE)

REACTION TO A SIGNAL

ganisation in the fairly primitive functions. The defects of regulation are much greater along other lines, in the impossibility
for the oligergastic to mobilise adequate amounts of excitation
for each stimulus. As in the very young child, we see here, as
a rule, a mass of excitation considerably greater than can be
used in the reactions, and the additional impulsive pressures
coming after each reaction show that there is a marked weakening of the ability to isolate the excitation from the motor sphere.
  Figure 112 shows the typical section of an experiment with

an imbecile, and that the extra impulses are expressed here much more distinctly than usual. It is characteristic of the neurodynamics of oligergasia that these extra pressures, which manifest in normal children a tendency to inhibition and delay (see Chapter X, section 3) do not have this tendency here. The regulating systems are not involved in these extra pressures, and therefore the coefficient of inhibition in the extra impulses frequently takes on a negative sign. This was shown convincingly by Lebedinsky, and it gives the basis for thinking that in this phenomenon we have a key to the functional understanding of the nervous insufficiency in oligergasia. We think that this insufficiency is brilliantly shown in the general picture of mental retardation, and has at its basis the defects in the regulations of the behaviour proper. The cortex in its higher divisions not only connects a person, with the surroundings, but with the help of the specific psychological mechanisms, plays a rôle of organiser and regulator of its acts. The oligophrenic is able to control certain external situations, it can even decide fairly complicated problems; but it never attempts to control itself, and in this relation the statement of Segen that "the mentally retarded primarily strive with the defects of will" is perfectly correct.

These defects are clearly brought out in experiments in which we attempt to make the oligergastic modify the style of his reactions, and control his behaviour. When we ask him to give delayed reactions this becomes exceedingly difficult and well-nigh impossible for him. The type of curves obtained are characteristic of the structure of the neurodynamical processes of the oligophrenic.

Figure 113 gives the delayed reactions of a normal child and of an imbecile. The chief difference is that the normal child has a certain tonus in the regulating inhibition of its motor process, but the regulating inhibition is entirely lacking in the oligergastic. The movement of the latter shows a direct discharge (*Unmittelbare Entladung*); the subject gives a very delayed impulsive pressure, holds the hand then for some time under tension (hence the plateau in the curve), and again presses directly and impulsively. As a result we do not have a single, regulated movement, but three separate acts, equally impulsive and direct. The imbecile is not able to execute a motor act of any prolonged, organised, cortical process, and it is therefore not surprising that in the further experiments, instead of following our instructions, and producing regulated and organised movements, we get primitive and chaotic ones.

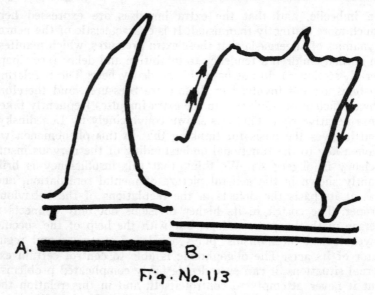

DELAYED REACTIONS IN NORMAL CHILD (A) AND IN IMBECILE (B)

A. KOLYA S. (SEVEN YEARS OLD)   B. IGOR (FOURTEEN YEARS OLD)

Of great interest are those cases in which the oligergastic
attempts to bring about some activity requiring inhibition of its
excitatory process so that it does not reach the motor termination. As in the other instances, we have here to do with the
reactions of choice, demonstrating the weak moments in the
organised activity of the oligophrenic. Here we undoubtedly have
facts which we might observe in young children and in hysterical
subjects, although the mechanism of the disturbances is very dissimilar. In the figures already given from the work of Lubimov
concerning the reactions of choice, we have seen what are the
characteristics of the neurodynamical process: the stimulus provokes a direct motor impulse, not delayed by the absence of
the prepared decision; the child begins the movements earlier
than it realises the choice and precisely because its choice is
determined by the motor process; the curve of the reaction of
choice is reflected in the complicated fluctuations in the motor
cycle, and it clearly indicates the weakness here of that functional
barrier which might delay the movement and transfer the excitation to the motor system only after the preliminary connection is effected.

Figure 114 contains the cyclograms of the reactions of choice in the oligergastic compared with those in the normal child. The diffuse character of the reactive processes in the mentally defective show at once that the higher cortical mechanisms are very *But is all deficiency cortical?* important in the elaboration of the functional barrier. We are convinced from this that the defect of the cortical apparatus produces not only an abatement of the intellectual processes, but profound changes in the very structure of the simplest neuro-dynamical acts.

The behaviour and thinking of the oligophrenic convinces us that the defect of the functional barrier, the tendency of all excitation to discharge immediately, has for the imbecile a special significance. His impulsiveness, his inability to restrain from the fulfilment of every wish, the direct response to each stimulus represents the life of the mentally retarded. The reactions to an intellectual problem before it is solved, the impulsive trials and errors, where judgment is necessary, create that complex of voluntary and intellectual defects which are perhaps most characteristic of the oligergastic. . . . [1]

Our conclusion brings us to a recognition of the significant and deciding rôle of those functions which are connected with the higher parts of the cortical apparatus in the creation of that form of regular motor activity which we see in every human adult and in the work of the functional barrier.

FIG. 114

CYCLOGRAMS ILLUSTRATING CHOICE IN THE NORMAL AND IN THE IMBECILE

4. STRUCTURE OF THE REACTIVE PROCESSES IN THE FUNCTIONAL DISTURBANCE OF THE CORTICAL REGULATORS

HOWEVER, the facts obtained still do not solve the problem. The defect in the structure of the reactive processes in the organised insufficiency of the cortical apparatus, it is true, indicates

[1] For a discussion of the investigations of these symptoms see de Greef's *Essays sur la personalité du debile mental*, Jour. de Psychologie, vol. 24, No. 5, 1927.

a connection between the latter and those higher and specific forms of the organisation of human behaviour, but it does not give any clear answer to the question of the nature of the mechanisms of interest to us. In these instances it may be brought out that the deformities in the reactive processes are connected with the profound neurodynamical changes. We know, however, that the organised disturbances in oligophrenia do not exhaust the systems directly associated with the intellectual activity, and the material is evidence only of the deep changes in the structure of the reactive processes in the presence of a seriously damaged brain.

If we desire to prove that the differentiated structure of the reactions and the presence of the functional barrier is connected with the activity of the higher functional systems, we must consider the series of psychological experiments dealing with the modifications of the reactive processes in the functional inclusion of one or another regulating mechanism.

We attain this by two simple methods: we may use the normal subject while in a condition of extreme fatigue, or we may divert the higher regulators from the reactive function, giving it another load, inducing the subject to change his attention.

The first of these methods is a problem of special investigation, and we shall not therefore consider it in detail; it is necessary only to mention that psychophysiological fatigue is distinguished by the physiological symptoms of fatigue (change of the vegetative activity, decrease of muscle tone, modification in metabolism), but detailed investigations of the activity in fatigue have given too little attention to the important fact that intense cortical fatigue impairs the higher regulators of behaviour. Many facts indicate that activity of the organised functions always suffers during marked fatigue; such a state is usually characterised by the appearance of the uninhibited impulses, and the attention is of an uninterrupted nature. Other symptoms show that the neurodynamics of severe fatigue is associated primarily with a conspicuous lowering of the regulating ability of its replacement by a disorganised impulsive character of the reactive processes.

We made our observations on adults, at 7 to 8 p.m., after the day's work, so that they came to us very fatigued. The experiment with the simple reactions to a signal show a number of extra impulses, which the subject cannot inhibit, and which almost never occurred in another series of experiments with adults in a different setting. Figure 115 illustrates such cases, showing the presence of diffuse unregulated excitation. Elsewhere we

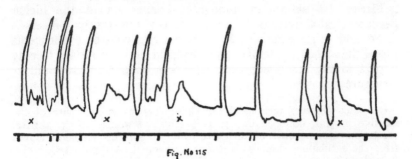

Fig. No 115

SIMPLE REACTIONS OF THE WORKER IN STATE OF FATIGUE

ZAK., THIRTY-EIGHT YEARS OLD, AFTER TEN HOURS' WORK

present control experiments to prove that connected with the serious mental fatigue the weakening of the higher cortical regulators inevitably leads to a diffused structure of the reactive processes.

The relation of the "functional barrier" and the organised character of the complex reactive processes is brought out especially clearly in the experiments with the simple reaction to a signal accompanying the diversion of the subject's attention.

The experiment is done very easily: we violate the rules of our usual laboratory procedure for the study of the reactive processes; instead of isolating the subject from everything which might distract his attention, we do just the opposite—while performing the experiment we converse with him, give him a book to read, and at intervals interrupt him by the auditory signal requiring the motor response.

Such a functional exclusion of the higher cortical mechanisms from participation of the simple reaction evokes a return to the primitive, diffuse type of reactive processes and a sharp lowering of the "functional barrier."

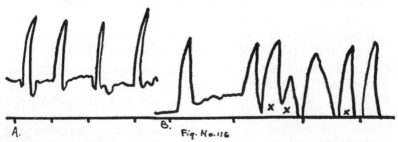

Fig. No. 116

A. NORMAL REACTION

B. REACTION DURING DISTRACTION OF ATTENTION BY CONVERSATION

Figure 116 shows an undoubted connection of the higher psychological activity with the structure of the reactive processes.

To add other examples is unnecessary; control experiments prove that when a complex psychological activity ceases to play a part in the reactive process, it takes on a primitive, diffuse structure.

One fact deserves mention here. Those changes in structure of the reactive process, obtained during a functional lowering of the cortical regulation, may be observed in the transfer to systems farther removed from the regulations dealt with in our experiment. A typical representative of such a system is the left hand; it is much more poorly regulated in the human adult than the right, with which he works and writes, and which, being connected with the greater development of the left hemisphere, is closer to the centers of speech.

In the left hand we may expect a greater diffusion of the reactive processes only if the organised reactions and the ability to restrain the direct transfer of excitation to the motor sphere actually exist, and are more closely connected with the higher psychological regulations.

Our supposition was confirmed; all the experiments with the left hand showed a much greater diffusion of the reactive processes and a poorer development of the functional barrier here than in the right hand. In children where there is some diffusion of the reactive processes, even with the right hand, the experiments brought out with marked lucidity the increased diffusion present in the transfer to the left hand.

Figure 117 gives the results of two experiments employing the simple reaction to a signal, performed on a child. It is clear that the reactions of the left hand show a greater irregularity of the excitatory process than those of the right. In Part A we see only the unified extra pressures, but in Part B these extra pressures acquire an acute character, being scarcely at all regulated by the cortical control.

The results cannot be attributed to the lack of agility and coordination in the left hand. Nor can they be explained by a greater excitation and different laws of neurodynamics in comparison with the right hand. The phenomena spring from a lessened neurodynamical regulation in the left hand, and this is evidently associated with the depressed functional connection with the higher processes of organised behaviour in comparison with the right which plays in behaviour the active, leading rôle.

5. STRUCTURE OF THE REACTIVE PROCESSES WITH INJURY OF THE HIGHER PSYCHOLOGICAL SYSTEMS

OUR experiments showed that we should establish complex, organised reactive processes in association with the higher psychological functions connected with the cortical mechanisms; and from this we concluded that the nature of the functional barrier and the complex organisation is a question not only of methodology concerning the higher stages of the nervous apparatus, but it has to do with the functional systems playing

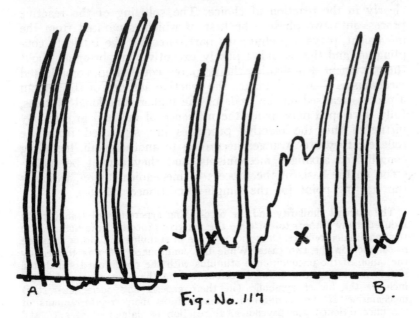

Fig. No. 117

REACTIONS OF THE RIGHT AND LEFT HANDS: A = RIGHT; B = LEFT;
SUBJECT LILYA, TEN YEARS OLD

the part of a regulator in behaviour. By diverting the active
attention, giving the subject some other work to do, we were
able to obtain the same reversion to a primitive, diffused form
of reaction as we had in an organised injury of the higher parts
of the cortex, or during a constitutional hyperexcitability of
the cortical, and especially subcortical, apparatus.

This brings us to the conclusion that in the reactive processes
of the human we do not have the simple phenomena which might
be governed by the laws for the lower reflex mechanisms. Many
considerations confirm us in the opinion that the reactive movements of the adult differ qualitatively from those of reflex activity, that they are constructed not only from *below* out of
the simplest neurodynamical mechanisms, but also from *above*,
according to those laws which govern the activity of the higher
psychological systems.

The analysis of a simple reaction has already shown us that
in the human adult it is connected with an adequate elaboration
of the motor formula, with the inhibition of extra impulsive acts,
with the organised response to a signal. The specific features of
the complex organisation of the reactive process was seen very

clearly in the reaction of choice. The splitting of the reactive process into two phases, the first of which, separated from the movement, plays a preliminary part, effecting the intricate coupling-up, and the second, a purely executive one, bringing about the movement, marshalling the prepared coupled-up, complicated mechanisms [1]—all this makes the reactive activity of the human a process realised on the basis of the higher functional systems, fully developed only under the influence of cultural growth. By virtue of this the reactive processes are separated from the reflexes; they are arranged according to another plan, including complicated auxiliary mechanisms, and they cannot be understood on the basis of the process of mechanical union, which is the starting point for the simple conditioned reflexes.

The external similarity and the astonishing syncretism of thinking has induced many authors to correlate the reactive process of the human with the conditioned reflexes. Only the presence of stimulus and motor response is common in the two cases. While the conditioned reflex is formed by the union of the unconditioned stimulus with the conditioned signal, the simple psychological reaction is elaborated on the basis of speech [2] and includes the higher symbolic (in their genesis and social character) mechanisms. If the conditioned reflex requires many reinforcements of the unconditioned, the psychological reaction is elaborated at once and does not need any support; it does not obey the law of extinction, and on further repetitions it is only more and more strengthened. . . .

There is reason to believe that in the two cases we are dealing with different mechanisms. One of our basic principles—the extraordinary stability of the reactive process once it has been coupled-up—does not require an external reinforcement, and this leads us to the view that in the composition of the reactive process there are present some higher psychological mechanisms supporting and causing the reactive process.

The internal structure of the simple reactions is thus a very complicated one and we should search for the specific mechanisms concealed within it and having to do with its regulation. Undoubtedly these higher mechanisms are connected with the reconstruction of the reactive process; and those profound changes which distinguish the reaction of the adult from that of the child are tied up with the inclusion in the reactive process of the complex regulating mechanisms. Evidently with these there should be associated the stability of the reaction of the adult (absent in the child) as well as the process of control of the

[1] The experiments of Morozova done in our laboratory (*Psychological Development of the Reaction of Choice*).

[2] For an exposition of the opposite view, that words themselves are but conditioned stimuli, one must consult Pavlov and his pupils, particularly Ishlondsky: *Neuropsyche und Hirnrinde*, Bd. 2, Wien, 1931, reviewed in Arch. Neurology and Psychiatry, Dec. 1931.—*Translator*.

direct motor discharge, and that mechanism of the functional barrier which we consider decisive for the complex organised, reactive process.

All these mechanisms should stand in dependence upon the presence of the higher regulating mechanisms organising human behaviour, and during the failure of these mechanisms the behaviour must suffer. Damage to the higher functional mechanisms entails profound changes of the simple reactive processes. This fact serves as a proof of the complicated structure.

For the decision of this question we experiment with an impaired speech activity. Many investigations [1] have separated the speech function from other psychological functions, as something specific. Observations on children showed that the speech ceases to play a purely communicating part, and begins to assume that specific organising rôle which we might term *instrumental*. Precisely in the activity connected with speech we succeeded in observing the transfer from the primitive, diffuse and direct process to the process splitting into two functionally different phases— the phases of preparation and of execution. By virtue of speech, the primitive impulsiveness is overcome, and the direct attempts of adaptation are substituted by the preliminary connection in words; after this comes the motor execution.

The speech and activity connected with it are functions which have played in many processes an organising rôle, and therefore in its pathology we have decided to search for the disturbances of the complex processes.

We return to the investigation of aphasia.

We intentionally started this book with a discussion of cases of aphasia. The instances cited proved that during aphasia there occurs not only a simple dropping out of speech as a communicating function, but this is associated with a disintegration of the whole organised behaviour, and that for the aphasiac there become impossible the acts of behaviour which present no difficulty for the normal person. Simple experiments on aphasia show that the limits of speech are not where we are accustomed to see them, that numerous functions externally having nothing to do with speech are actually verbalised, and after impairment of the speech function, they drop out. The aphasiac easily produces imitative movements, but it is very difficult for him to imitate a person facing him using the homonymous hand, i.e., the one opposite his corresponding hand instead of being on the same side. Such an action as carrying out the instruction, "Raise the right hand when I raise my right," obviously requires the use of the function of language, and is wellnigh impossible in the absence of speech.

[1] Vuigotsky and Luria: *Studies in the History of Behaviour*, Moscow, 1930. Vuigotsky: *Foundations of Thinking and Speech, Nature and Marxism*, 1929, No. 1. Luria: *Development of the Child's Thinking, Ibid.*, No. 2.

Our experiments brought out the fact that aphasia is associated with a marked disintegration in the elaboration of intention. The aphasiac is helpless when we give him something necessitating an elaborated purpose; for example the indefinite command to "do something" or "draw something" frequently places before the aphasiac an insuperable difficulty; often in connection with the obstacle in the elaboration of intention the aphasiac is unable to draw any figure, not knowing "with what to begin"; the failure of speech leads to complete helplessness in those strata of behaviour where we properly do not suspect the participation of language.

The failure of the higher regulating systems is inevitably connected with the intensifying of the primitive reactions, which in the governing action of speech is suppressed and replaced by the higher forms of adaptation. In the aphasiac the reasoning power (by virtue of which a definite act is completed) frequently suffers; by way of compensation there occurs an involuntary and sometimes impulsive subordination of that usual optical structure in which it happens.

Here is an example to illustrate how difficult it is for the aphasiac to execute an organised action arising as a result of the experimentally produced purpose, and how easily the voluntary act is substituted in him by an impulsive one. Patient Chas., 55 years old, with amnestic aphasia; experiment of 30 April 1930. Before the patient was placed a wooden spoon, a pencil, paper. He is asked to repeat the actions made by the experimenter. The latter takes the spoon and with the handle he writes on the paper the figure "5." The patient looks at the experimenter, takes the pencil, and writes "5" on the paper. The ordinarily optically active situation of the pencil-paper provokes in him an indirect tendency which is substituted by the inappropriate operation of the experimenter, but this does not meet with any opposition on the part of the aphasiac.

Experiment of 24, May 1930. As above, the patient is told to repeat the acts of the experimenter. Before him is a box of matches, a wooden spoon, and a candle-stick. The operator scratches the spoon on the box of matches and goes through the motions of lighting the candle. The patient takes the match-box, turns it around, takes out a match, strikes it and lights the candle. The presence of the match-box in the hand, produces the customary cycle of events, not corresponding to the presented image. The senseless performance here is substituted by the appropriate, spontaneous action, the mechanism of which leads to a direct motor sequence of the situation.

All of our experiments with amnestic aphasia show a serious disintegration of behaviour, with a weakening of the regulating mechanisms and a corresponding lack of control of the optical situation, and a direct execution of the motor act. Similar results have been obtained by Grünbaum, Gell and other authors.

Naturally, under these conditions, we may expect that the aphasiacs will exhibit a greatly changed structure of the reactive process and that the functional barrier will be disturbed.

In the experiments with the simple reactions to a signal we did not obtain any remarkable data; the experiments were too simple for our aphasiacs and too automatic, and therefore we saw neither an acute disturbance of the reactive processes nor the presence of extra pressures. The fact that most of our subjects were of the inhibitory type may have had to do with the lack of excitation in the reactions.

Nevertheless, in the serious cases of aphasia there was considerable disturbance in the reactive processes, a sudden weakening of the functional barrier with emancipation of the spontaneous impulses.

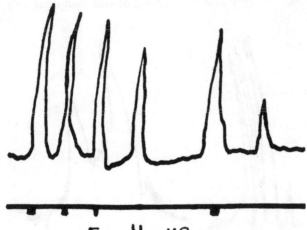

Fig. No. 118

EXPERIMENTS WITH REACTION TO A SIGNAL IN APHASIA (SUBJECT CHAS.)

Figure 118 contains the protocol of such a case. After the adequate, regular and coordinated reactions, there are signs of diffuse excitation and the mobilisation of inadequate masses of energy, and suddenly the inadequate pressures become emancipated from the signals. . . . The absence of the inhibition of the extra pressures usual in such cases distinguishes them from those, as in children, where the regulating systems are weak and included in the action only after a delay. (See Chapter X, section 3.)

A more marked picture of the disturbance of the functional barrier in aphasia can be observed in those cases where in view of the conditions of the experiment the intention in the action was delayed, being temporarily cut off from the motor system. A simple experiment shows us that the regulating psychological functions are disturbed.

The desired situation is obtained when we have the subject make a movement according to a command—counting to three.

For the normal subject to give himself a command by making the definite movement on the count of "three" is very easy. The psychological structure of the process corresponds to our problems: the first figure ("One") creates the intention which the normal restrains until the end of the command.

This simple response is impossible to obtain in severe cases of aphasia. In aphasia with apraxia we often see complete inability to restrain the intention created from a direct transfer to the motor system, and destruction of this comparatively simple process.

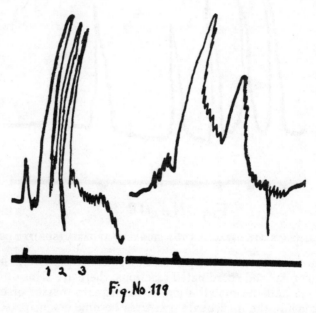

Fig. No. 119

APHASIA: REACTION TO A SIGNAL 1-2-3! (PATIENT CHAS.)

In Figure 119 with the patient Chas. we perform the following experiment: we ask him to count three and then press the pneumatic bulb with his finger, showing him once or twice exactly how to do this. The subject was unable to carry out the instructions; the pressure is given to the first figure of the count and held until the end. The signal creating the intention is for him the signal for the execution of the act, and the attempt to restrain it, to complete this as if it were a simple instruction produces a considerable destruction of the motor curve. The insufficiency of the functional barrier is so great that the subject continues to exhibit a direct transfer of the excitation to the motor sphere.

Such a picture is seen very clearly in those cases where there is at the beginning of the experiment an establishment of certain preliminary connections and then their execution into actions. We repeated the experiments of choice in patients with severe amnestic aphasia, and we were able to establish a transfer to the diffuse type of reaction with the absence of the inhibition of the excitation and its transfer to the motor sphere.

The explanation is not to be found in the failure of the patient to understand; the insufficiency is not marked by the delay and refusal often seen in adults, but by a direct motor excitation of the hand and seeking movements in the air which finally lead to a definite (though not always correct) reaction.

The disappearance of the regulating speech mechanisms in the aphasiac causes a diffuse reaction and the same unregulated impulsiveness seen in the child and in hysteria. . . .

Our view of aphasia differs radically from the ordinary one; we hold that there is a disturbance of will as well as that of intellect, because in the aphasiac the impaired speech produces a disintegration of the elaboration of intention. The patient is not able to separate himself from the immediate surroundings and create that which we call "voluntary intention." The problem to "do something," so indefinitely formulated and requiring an active elaboration of intention provokes a maximal difficulty. On the other hand, the intention is not restrained, and the signal giving rise to it simultaneously calls out the reaction. Therefore the aphasiac falls under the influence of the situation and is not able to master it. With the failure of the regulating and inhibiting functions, every tension created in the personality appears with an insurmountable force. The very clear and stable manifestations of those *Quasi-Bedürfnisse* are met with precisely in aphasiacs, and at almost every turn of their behaviour. This is evidenced by the prominent rôle of perseveration in aphasia; the whole structure of the paraphasiacal disturbance of speech with the jumbled and broken words can be explained from this point of view. We have noted during the play and drawing of the aphasiac the *Quasi-Bedürfnisse* described by Lewin to be especially uncontrollable.

We come to the conclusion that speech is a preeminent factor in behaviour, and that the investigation of the neurodynamical activity of the human with an impaired function of speech is a problem of great interest for our analysis.

6. THE NATURE OF THE FUNCTIONAL BARRIER AND THE STRUCTURE OF THE REACTIVE PROCESSES

We may briefly summarise our views concerning the nature of the functional barrier and the structure of the reactive processes.

The reactive process as we know it in the normal adult human is a complicated elaboration, in structure not having anything in common with those impulsive reactions which we observed in the child or the reflex activity of animals. The chief difference of the reactive process from those forms of activity in the child and animals is that in the former the direct character of the motor discharge is controlled and it is a process in which the same cortical mechanisms act under the conditions of the complex functional inclusion.

It is thus incorrect to say that the stimulus directly provokes the reaction. The psychological act differs from the reflex movement in that the former is always along an intricate, circuitous path.

The outstanding feature of this indirect character of the reactive process is the fact that the tendency of every natural reflex act to discharge its excitation directly is controlled in the complex reactive process; there is created, as we know, between the excitation and the motor sphere a functional barrier which restrains this transfer of the excitation and permits it only after the preliminary connections have been completed. This functional barrier is destroyed during affect and during conflict, and these states show that the reactive process becomes diffused, and the excitation is able to pass over into the motor area. This condition is intensified by the fact that in affect and neuroses there is a tendency to mobilisation of inadequate masses of excitation and the personality loses the power of organising higher forms of behaviour.

In studying the genesis of the reactive movements, we see that the functional barrier does not exist in the early years of childhood, but is elaborated rather late. Experimentation shows that it appears about the time of the development in the child of the active organisation of speech, and that it is absent in cases of serious mental retardation. All this connects the functional barrier with the higher psychological mechanisms, and the data of aphasia place it in direct relation to speech and symbolic mechanisms, the falling out of which produces a diffused reaction.

This leads us to believe that in the functional barrier we have not a natural mechanism but one of cultural origin, and that we may connect it with any purely morphological elaboration in the cortical system, but not with a conception of the unlinking or weakening of the synapses between the central activity and the motor area, but with a functional inclusion in the reactive process of the intricate psychological systems having a general regulating character.

The inclusion in the reactive process of the systems of internal speech or the analogous systems of the auxiliary stimuli is, we think, fully adequate for the explanation of the mechanism of the functional barrier. It indicates that the reactive process is a complicated psychological one; it reveals those possible forces that restrain the excitation from a direct discharge and leads to the understanding of the mechanism of the establishment of the psychological reactions.

As a result of such an explanation of the reactive process two factors arise. The first has to do with the stability of the reaction; this we have mentioned previously. Psychologists are accustomed to study a reaction, post mortem, as it were; they neglect the scores of reactions during the formative period, and wait until it is fully formed, thereby losing the most interesting part of it: how the reactive movements are elaborated, how external reinforcement ceases to be necessary, etc. The presence of the internal stimulation of the reactive process, especially evident in the first stages of its development before the establishment of the constant automatisms, leads us to the adequate decision of this problem. Considering the reaction not as a mechanical habit but as a mnemonic-technical act, realised by the inclusion of the complex psychological mechanisms, we are enabled to throw some light on the nature of the psychological reactions.

The second factor concerns the explanation of the mechanism of the failure of the reactions during the process of conflict. It would be strange, indeed, if the comparatively slight intellectual disturbance produced by our conflict in the speech function could cause such a serious destruction of the motor habits and upset the regular course of the reactive processes. ...

However, the matter is seen in a new light if we postulate that in the structure of the reaction there is included as a regulating factor the higher psychological processes, particularly that of speech. From this point of view it becomes clear that every, even slight, disturbance in the regulating system inevitably brings about a considerable disintegration in the regulating systems connected with it. The ready appearance of motor disturbances in cases of affect beginning in the intellectual sphere becomes comprehensible.

The reactive process gains a tremendous advantage by the inclusion in it of the regulating functional system, thereby becoming more plastic and independent of the mechanical conditions; but at the same time this makes it dependent upon accidents which may occur in this regulating system, and the case of the failure of speech, the affective disorganisation of the intellectual processes shows us how deep may be the disintegration provoked by the damaging of these higher regulating systems.

The reactive process of the human adult cannot be explained as a mechanical habit; it is constructed not only from below, but from above, it includes within itself the regulating systems of a higher psychological order.

These systems are disturbed during affect and conflict, but they may also aid the human in overcoming the disorganisation. We come now to the study of the problem of the control of behaviour and the mechanics of this process. With extreme caution we approach the question which has served as a touchstone for all psychological theory, upon which have been focused the dreams of idealistic philosophy and of scientific materialism; with the help of some experiments we shall attempt to point out those mechanisms which appear to us to lie at the basis of the psychological control of human behaviour.

CHAPTER XII

THE CONTROL OF BEHAVIOUR

1. PROBLEMS

THE study of the mechanisms through which the human is able to control his behaviour brings us directly to the problem of *will*. One may state without fear of contradiction that no other psychological question has a history so fraught with errors; the actual history of the study of will is a history of mistakes, and the inventory of the contemporary psychological conceptions concerning will is a cemetery of fallacies, of loosely put questions and trivial investigations.

The history of the study of will consists in the battle of two main conceptions, different in their postulates but equally false. Some investigators, those belonging to the idealistic camp, considered will as a phenomenon of spontaneity specific for the human; they saw the decision of this problem in the investigation of that active tension by virtue of which the human is able to alter his behaviour, set himself purposes and energetically and voluntarily to accomplish them. In the opinion of these authors such a will distinguishes the human from the animal, and while the latter controls only his reactivity, the human manifests an active, spontaneous, and consequently voluntary behaviour; it does not appear at once, existing in embryo in the child, being disturbed in mental diseases, and fully developed in the normal adult.[1]

While the first group of psychologists considered will as a momentous problem in human behaviour and the study of it as a problem of psychological science, the second group took the opposite position. The psychologists, considering themselves positivists, or even materialists, supposed that the "will" force

---

[1] See Ch. Bühler, *Zwei Grundtypen der Lebensprozessen*, Ztschft. f. Psychologie, Bd. 108, 1929.

should not be a decisive object of psychological investigation. Considering such "will power" unable to produce acts, they thought that behind this subjective process there must flow some definite stimulations impelling the person to that or another reaction, having only the appearance of spontaneity. Really at the basis of the "willed action" lies some necessity, instinct, or tendency. The internal character of the stimulus gives realisation to this necessity and makes it appear spontaneous, but back of this there is a simple administrative function acting from within this necessity. The first group of psychologists made the problem one of will-power; the second, a problem of stimuli; the first group worked with a freely acting subject, the second, with a problem of automata directed by the physiological tension. The first school of psychologists sought to find in the will something specific for the human; the second group, counting this premise false, looked for the will where they observed the primitive forms of activity automatically discharging the internal tension; by the investigation of necessity and tendency they hoped to decide the problem of the extreme complexity of the will regulators. . . .

It is not difficult to see how two important schools of thought were erected on the basis of these two systems of belief—the idealists, holding freedom of will, and the mechanists choosing the scientific path as the only correct one.

A careful study of the problem convinces us that the cause of the disagreement is not only to be sought in the difference in the views and settings of the authors, but in their extreme simplification of the problem; they strive to envisage a unified and single process where there exist many interesting mechanisms of the apparatus. Precisely this situation—leading the authors of the first group to postulate a pure spontaneity of the willed act, and the second to consider the will as an automatic tendency—brings about a divorce from reality and is the root of all those errors which are responsible for the lack of understanding of the mechanisms of voluntary activity.

The investigations of many psychologists have shown that the structure of the willed process cannot be considered as a simple one, leading to spontaneous acts as was formerly thought.[1] It had already been established that its essential part, the existence of the "willed act," could not be reckoned as spontaneous, but on the contrary, it manifested all the characteristics of an involuntary, automatic mechanism. Then, that which had always been

[1] See A. Michotte et N. Prum: *Etude Experimental sûr le Choix Volontaire et Ses Antecedents Immediates,* Archives de Psychologie, vol. 10, 1910.

counted as will *par excellence* was shown to have nothing to do with will, and the realisation of the intention or purpose, of the preliminary choice or postulated problem, approximated so closely in its structure the reflex act that in a detailed analysis they practically merged.

We make our choice perhaps with "freedom," guided by certain intellectual rules, emotional motives and accepted decisions, but once having chosen, we become slaves of our choice and execute purely automatically that act which we have prepared. "The willed act is involuntary; the problem of the will consists in the problem of connections."

In the first of these theories there was a discrepancy, and the willed act, including, as an executive apparatus, the reflex mech-anism, ceased to be so simple as it had formerly appeared. Precisely this fact leads us to believe that the question itself concerning the will process must be cast in another form, and that the problem of the will consists not in conjectures of the spontaneous behaviour but in the problem of the spontaneous, "willed" control of the prepared automatic mechanisms. This brings concreteness to the investigation, although by no means solving it.

If the specificity of the "willed process" actually leads to a control of the automatic apparatus, then in what way is this control produced? Can we not suppose that the voluntary be-haviour of the human is analogous to the performance of a machinist starting an engine, and that some free activity—a series of modernised spirits—directs the automatism of the body? Evi-dently we are not saved from the metaphysical and idealistic points of view, and the problem still remains difficult.

The authors trying to solve this question belong to the second group. Considering the voluntary act as automatic, they claim that these automatisms direct the free "I," and they posit that the executive of the automatisms is necessity, inclination, emo-tion. In the more primitive of these systems the problem of will leads to the problem of emotion and the theory of will takes on a primitive, hedonistic character. The most representative of this group is K. Lewin, who has shown the possibility of the elaboration of quasi-necessities (*Quasi-Bedürfnisse*) creating an artificial tension, which is then discharged, diverting our activity to the side.[1]

The primitive hedonistic theory of will does not convince us; we cannot believe that the will is such a "slave of passion" as

[1] K. Lewin: *Wille, Vorsatz und Bedürfniss,* 1925.

is represented by this system. The behaviour of the social human is sharply distinguished from the behaviour of an animal in this: it is often directed toward the overcoming necessity, inhibiting it, controlling it; and the complex forms of human labour presupposing the "will expressed in attention" (Marx) cannot be understood as a simple discharge of the tension created by necessity. The researches concerning the mechanisms of the "artificial necessity" (*Quasi-Bedürfnisse*) help us better to comprehend the mechanics of the voluntary processes, but they fall far short of telling us by what means the human establishes the new requirements, and they do not explain the process of human voluntary action in all its specificity.

Nevertheless, the study of the *Quasi-Bedürfnisse* put us on the right path to the decision of these complicated questions. In view of the fact that the "voluntary mechanism" is a mechanism of subordination especially by the artificially created stimuli, which may replace the natural necessity, this theory makes an actual step forward in the scientific understanding of this problem.

Even though the existing mechanisms enter into the composition of the "voluntary act," this theory still does not disclose the specificity of the resulting behaviour; the mechanism of the *Quasi-Bedürfnisse* and subordination to them are component parts of the voluntary act, but they are always something more because they are not specific for the resulting behaviour. When the child is interrupted and prevented from completing whatever he is about, he returns to it again, thanks to that tension which is created in the broken structure of the action,[1] then this is completed by virtue of the *Quasi-Bedürfnisse*, the act is characterised by its not having an origin, and the problem of will remains undecided.

Now we feel that we are nearer to the problem of the origin of behaviour when we consider it a question not of action, but of the origin of such artificial stimuli, and with the hope of explaining the nature of those of them which are specific for the willed act, we attempt to follow the investigation along the path of the genetic development.

The question which arises is this: What is the origin of the establishment of such artificial necessities and of the subsidiary internal stimuli which distinguish the human from the animal, and to some extent the child from the adult? Not only how do we spontaneously establish the problems impelling us to definite

---

[1] Ousjankin: *Uber die Wiederaufnahme Unterbrochener Handlungen*, Psychologische Forschungen, Bd. X.

action, but how do we elaborate those methods which help us to realise the action?

There is undoubtedly a great difference between the simple subordination of the necessity—whether natural or arising in the process of some activity—and those complex forms of behaviour characterised by the ability to create and to make use of the *Quasi-Bedürfnisse*. This difference is what primarily distinguishes the human from the animal, and the fact that the human is able to control not only the external world but his own behaviour indirectly by the creation of artificial necessities and stimuli produced artificially especially for the purpose is a cardinal factor in the development of behaviour.

We have good reason to believe that such behaviour is a compound product of psychological growth, in the process of which the primitive, natural forms of behaviour are complicated by new cultural ones, and as a result of this there is elaborated a new relation of the personality to its own behaviour.

This cultural development is the means whereby the human may include the dynamical mechanism which allows him to master his behaviour and automatically to bring about the corresponding actions. Whilst in the first stages of his development the human was able to act only on the surroundings, making instruments which helped him to gain the mastery over the external situation—in his further growth he began to elaborate those artificial stimuli that enabled him to think of himself as an object of action and that aided him in controlling his own behaviour.

Many observations support our view that the consideration of the voluntary act as accomplished by "will-power" is a myth, and that the human cannot by direct force control his behaviour any more than "a shadow can carry stones." The development of the voluntary processes comes about as a result of the elaboration of the various forms of behaviour, the mobilisation of the *Quasi-Bedürfnisse* to achieve his ends. *Voluntary behaviour is the ability to create stimuli and to subordinate them;* or in other words, to bring into being stimuli of a special order, directed to the organisation of behaviour.

Our researches [1] convince us that such a control comes from without, and that in the first stages of the control the human creates certain external stimuli, which produce within him definite forms of motor behaviour. The primordial voluntary mechanism

[1] See L. C. Vuigotsky: *History of the Cultural Development of the Child.* L. C. Vuigotsky and A. R. Luria: *Studies on the History of Behaviour,* Moscow, 1930.

evidently consists in the external setting, the production of cultural stimuli mobilising and directing the natural forces of behaviour. This external auto-stimulation is substituted by an internal one; and the "spontaneous" establishment of the complicated *Quasi-Bedürfnisse* seen in the adult are a result of the profound cultural reconstruction of the activity depending on the cortical apparatus, without which we could not understand the complex psychological functions.

Of such nature is the structure of the "voluntary act" in its most complicated as well as in its elementary manifestations. Although the human cannot make a path by virtue of his will power, he is able to follow a circuitous route by acting upon himself just as he formerly acted upon nature, making use of the laws of nature and consciously subordinating them. The problem of will is much clearer to us when we examine it in the light of historical evolution, creating in the human new qualitative elaborations.

We cannot attempt to decide these questions completely; in a series of experiments we shall try only to demonstrate how the indirect forms of behaviour can attain the same end as was reached through the "will power." Our experiments are but an insignificant part of the material necessary for the decision of the problems concerning the control of behaviour, but, nevertheless, they point out the path along which they will be some day decided.

We have good reasons for thinking that voluntary acts should not be investigated in the material of the forms of behaviour natural for the subject, though differing by great intensity and stability; necessity and inclination, although stable, do not interest us. On the contrary, we are concerned with the forms of behaviour having to do with control, with those factors appearing when the human overcomes his customary reactive processes and replaces them by other less habitual ones. From this point of view, the voluntary action begins at the end of that action provoked by direct necessity and inclination; James was entirely right when he gave as a typical example of a voluntary act the instance of a person forcing himself to jump out of bed on a cold morning.

We shall do better by beginning with a difficult case and studying the voluntary processes in situations where the subject succeeds in mastering some idiosyncrasy of his behaviour; and then we can approach the mechanism of the psychological processes of interest to us.

Can such control of those forms of behaviour customary for the subject be effected by the aid of will power? We feel inclined to answer this in the negative. Our experiments must, however, give experimental verification for our answer; we may expect negative results, and in the setting of the experiment we shall find that question which was present in the theory: How is the subject able to control his behaviour? Upon an ingenious experiment depends the creation of a situation which will lead the subject to control his behaviour and at the same time reveal the means whereby he accomplished this.

The chief problem of all our experiments is the proof of the fundamental law: *direct attempts to control his behaviour always lead to negative results; its mastery is achieved only by indirect means.* The mechanism of the will is the least of all included in the direct will power, and it always consists in the use of certain external or internal means, in the reconstruction of the psychological process.

In these experiments we occupy ourselves with material especially adapted to this purpose; it is difficult and without avail to use normal human adults whose psychological processes attain a considerable degree of complexity and whose activity is so rooted in their usual behaviour that it colors each of their actions. It is more profitable to try to bring about control of behaviour where it is more obstructed. We are in possession of such cases; they are as a rule associated with those disturbances in structure of the usual reactive process which we have described in two previous chapters. To restrain the diffuse character of the processes in the *child,* to create a functional barrier in the *hysteric,* making him normally control his behaviour, to overcome the motor rigidity associated with the organised destruction in *paralysis agitans,* having produced conditions more favourable for him— here is the material which we have chosen to investigate.

The peculiarity of such comparative material leads us to resort to the clinical methods of exposition, sometimes using observations on single cases to illustrate our results.

2. EXPERIMENTS WITH DIRECT CONTROL: PROBLEMS OF STIMULUS AND MEANS

WE began by attempting to have the subject control his behaviour and overcome the defects of the reactive processes by the application of direct force. We have previously pointed out that such a direct control is well-nigh impossible. If we show that in the child the reactive processes are diffuse, and that in the hysteric his behaviour lacks the functional barrier and that he reacts impulsively, then we have confirmation of our view that all these subjects are unable to overcome the reactive processes characteristic of them.

We can easily verify this by asking him to mobilise his maximal strength to overcome certain defects, and all our efforts produce only inconsiderable results. That which we are accustomed to call "voluntary behaviour" is actually so involuntary that these primitive forms of behaviour should not be given this name: the young child is absolutely unable to restrain his impulsive pressures; the hysteric, even with the exercise of maximal will power, cannot decrease the speed of his motor reactions; the patient with paralysis agitans, try as he may, is just as tremulous and just as rigid. We might multiply these examples indefinitely, showing that the efforts to control directly the "voluntary" phenomena are vain; we have already adduced a sufficient number of examples to indicate this in the presence of seriously disturbed reactive processes.[1]

In the experiments with young children in whom we attempt to control behaviour we see through the naïve efforts complete inability to effect control. Young children, who in our experiments apply all of their strength to master the problem, express this failure in many external movements. Here is an example:

Experiment of the 27th April, 1930. The subject Jenny C., 5½ years old, is told to inhibit the inadequate pressures and to respond only to the signal. Jenny mobilises all of her strength to follow the instructions; the face expresses tension, and she concentrates upon the hand applied to the apparatus. However, she gives impulsive pressures without the signals. Then she grasps the apparatus and tries with her thumb to restrain the extra pressures; but she does not succeed in this and continues to give impulsive pressures, reacting with the whole hand and even with the thumb which she has used as a regulator.

This experiment is of interest in showing the naïve psychology in the behaviour of the child, who is unable to restrain the primitive impulses. The child's applications here are evidence of the direct character of the attempts to control its behaviour, and it is evident that the "will" is powerless as long as it is not transferred to an adequate system.

What process have we here? Is the child unable to accomplish its wishes, or has it not a strong enough desire to do this? We may say that the child does not know how to want things and is therefore unable to control his behaviour. The child cannot concentrate his attention on instructions given him; such symptoms are present in the hysteric also, and thus the defect in activity is attributable to a defect in the stimuli, making it impossible for the child to mobilise its attention—and will.

[1] See Chapters X and XI.

Does the question of "will" consist in the problem of the stimuli? This may be decided only experimentally. We shall reinforce the stimuli acting on the child to control its behaviour in order to determine this. The problem of voluntary behaviour, according to many authors, consists in the problem of interest, needs and motives.

In order to introduce in the child maximum motives it is only necessary to offer rewards or threaten punishment. These are methods of the old school of pedagogy. They have both been used in our experiments, without perceptible results.

The child was brought into our usual laboratory and the motor reactions registered, according to the experiment. After obtaining the level of the diffused, reactive processes the child was given an apple or confection only when he followed the instructions exactly—not making extra pressures. After this, the experiment was repeated.

As a punishment we threatened to take the sweet away from him if the instructions were not obeyed, or we gave our instructions more sternly, or finally we threatened to accompany each error with an electric shock.

Such stimuli increased the motives of the child, but there was no improvement in his actions. The comparatively slight improvement seen in a few of the subjects could be attained without rewards or punishment, but by using other motives, such as competition, or by having the child give his maximum attention to the experiment.

However, these motives were never specific, they did not bring about any marked improvement, and they never changed the diffuse process into a differentiated, organised one. Not infrequently, the reverse happened; the excitation increased, the reactive processes became more diffuse than they were before.

Figure 120 is a typical case of the influence of a threat. The effort to follow our instructions is increased and also the excitability, but the diffuse and impulsive pressures are augmented. Threats, although having little effect in normal children, often produce shock and complete disorganisation of the processes in psychopaths. As an example of this we cite the case of a boy 11 years old, with a traumatic psychoneurosis, in whom a single threat caused disorganised behaviour and wide-spread tremor with many extra pressures.

The question of the mechanisms of the control of behaviour remains an open one; reinforcing the stimuli is insufficient to increase the effectiveness of the voluntary act.

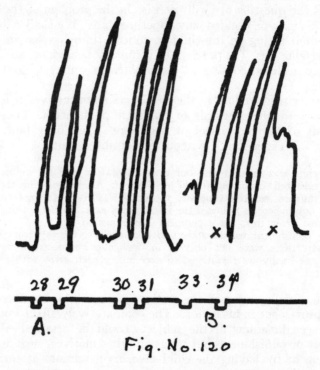

Fig. No. 120

INFLUENCE OF PUNISHMENT ON THE REACTIVE PROCESSES
OF A CHILD 7 YEARS OLD

A. SIMPLE REACTION TO A SIGNAL
B. SAME REACTIONS UNDER THREAT OF PUNISHMENT

3. EXPERIMENTS WITH THE CIRCUMVENTION OF BEHAVIOUR: THE ROLE OF THE EXTERNAL METHODS

As the direct application of force has proven to be ineffectual in aiding the human to realise his wishes, we shall investigate other methods. The human readily controls things surrounding him, and in addition, reacts to external stimuli, but he is at the same time unable to control his own behaviour. He has the motives but not the means to realise these motives and before us is the experimental question of finding the means enabling him to master his behaviour. Thus we approach more closely the mechanism of the voluntary act.

Several considerations lead us to postulate the control of behaviour from without. By choosing an external problem, he has

before him the artificial establishment of certain situations. We
have shown above that the human has before him two possibilities: he may produce changes in things, and modify the stimuli
proceeding from them; it is necessary to unite these actions and
to create those stimuli which correct the behaviour.

Our experiments will be very elementary, and they attempt to
register the results in situations analogous to those in which we
have obtained negative results by the employment of will power.

We shall first study this method in hysterical patients. We have
already shown that delayed movements are for them very difficult. A stimulus ordinarily provokes in them a transfer of excitation to the motor system and impulsive pressures, as is shown by
the vertical curve. Slow pressures are almost impossible for them
or they become delayed so that they fall in the passive part of the
curve. This diffusion of the reactive process makes the realisation
of a problem difficult, and the instructions to produce slow
movements provoke impulsive actions. It is necessary to substitute the usual interrupted stimulus (tapping or a flashing light)
by one lasting for some time (for example, a whistle) in order
to change the picture. The protracted signal produces in our subject an organised action, and the subject delays his movements
so long as the signal continues.

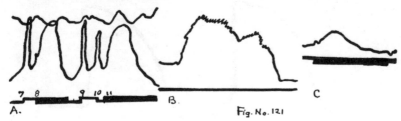

A.   B.   C

Fig. No. 121

A AND B = SIMPLE REACTIONS TO DIFFERENT CONTINUOUS SIGNALS
(HYSTERIA)
B AND C = DELAYED REACTIONS DURING CONTINUOUS SIGNALS (HYSTERIA)

Figure 121 shows two such examples. Part A records the motor
reaction in a hysterical patient to a continuous signal (buzzing)
which has replaced the interrupted one. Analogous results are
obtained with spontaneously retarded movements. While the
spontaneous retardation of the motor pressure in the subject
shown in Curve B is characterised by marked excitability (expressed in the acute tremor), the introduction of a prolonged
signal removes this excitation and makes the process of spontaneously delayed movements much less difficult.

This result was associated with a change in the very structure of the reactive process. In the first case, after the stimulus the subject gave independent spontaneous movements; in the second instance, the movement lost its spontaneous action during the prolonged stimulus and became regular. This phenomenon is related to echopraxia and suggestibility, which is often seen in marked form in hysterics. The movements which cannot be re-

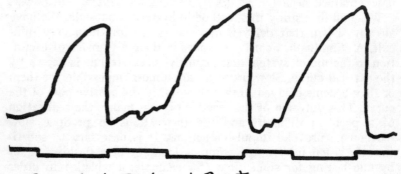

Sub. Mozh. Delayed Reaction

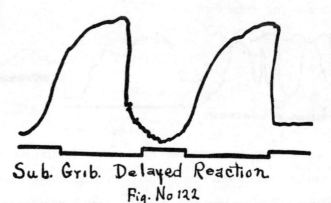

Sub. Grib. Delayed Reaction
Fig. No 122

tarded by spontaneous force or effort, may be easily regulated by substitution of certain external stimuli.

In the left hand of the subject we placed the electric button which when pressed produced the buzzing sound and told the patient to give himself auto-signals, pressing the button with the left hand and making the corresponding delayed movements with the right. The impulsive, quick movements became quite regular. The subject thus brought about control of his behaviour by measures which he applied himself; the direct control is replaced by the indirect, and will power is substituted by regulation from without.

Figure 122 proves that these movements of the hysteric are comparable to those of the normal person.

If the transfer to the indirect method produces delayed movements which were impossible to produce by effort, we may expect that during the obstructed voluntary active processes this may produce the opposite effect. To verify this we shall describe experiments with Parkinson's disease. Such patients are especially suitable for this. The pathologic condition of the subcortical ganglia and the considerable disturbance in the tonus make their movements very difficult or almost impossible. On the other hand, the healthy cortex enables him to use external stimuli and to construct a compensatory activity for the subcortical automatisms. We are able to trace here the mechanism of the voluntary processes in those instances where the will, deprived of its subcortical mechanisms, is powerless. The problem of making this person who cannot move his finger, control his behaviour and execute a fairly complex action is extremely interesting.

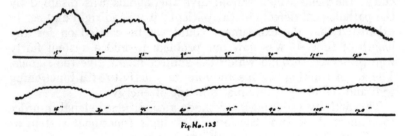

Fig No. 123

RHYTHMICAL PRESSURES IN PARKINSON'S DISEASE (SUBJECT ROZ.)

In order to define the problem confronting us we must elucidate those defects which distinguish the motor system of the *paralysis agitans* patient under the experimental conditions. A simple experiment shows that the spontaneous activity of this patient is very difficult, and in serious cases almost impossible; the great rigidity and quickly ensuing exhaustion prevent the patient from making more than four or five pressures.

In Figure 123 is the record of a patient with this disease in severe form. The instructions to make rhythmical pressures with the pneumatic bulb produce fairly intensive results. But the rigidity causes extreme tremor; the second pressure is weaker and there is more rigidity, and after six pressures complete exhaustion ensues, with inability to give any motor reactions. Appeals to the will of the subject are unavailing, and he is not able to move his hand.

Such paralysis agitans patients which we have observed could not turn over when on the level floor, but could climb a ladder; they could not ordinarily walk, but they could do so freely if we put on the floor some pieces of paper to stimulate each separate step. Their automatisms were lacking but they were successful in connecting the single reactions to separate stimuli (climbing the ladder or stepping according to the pieces of paper); the insufficient automatisms were replaced here by cortical activities, much more complex in their structure but accessible to the patient.

The problem before us, then, is to give auto-stimulations, and to replace the direct methods of "will power" by signals by which the subject might react to definite movements. First we thought of repeating the experiment with the hysterical patient, giving him an electric button to press by which he might produce stimulating signals and change from the system of automatic actions to a chain of isolated reactions. However, we met with this difficulty: the hand which should give the signals was disabled by the pathological defects of the patient; it was so rigid and easily exhausted that the experiment could not be carried on for any length of time. It was now our problem to find a system fairly well preserved through which the subject might give the signals. The act of winking was a semi-voluntary activity still functioning well and requiring a minimal amount of energy.

This activity (winking) was made a conditioned signal in order to connect these two reactions in a single functional system as we did in the experiment with the hysteric.

The subject was given a signal to which he should close his eyes and press the rubber bulb with his hand. Then he was told to give himself the signals by closing his eyes and simultaneously pressing with his hand. As a result we obtained a series of pressures analogous to the spontaneous rhythmical pressures but representing a chain of reactions to a series of auto-stimulations. (Figure 124.)

A comparison of the reactions to the auto-stimulations (A) with those of the spontaneous ones (Curve B) shows that the former is much more regular and intense while the latter quickly falls off, after the seventh pressure.

In both of the cases we proceeded apparently along the line of greatest resistance, in making the subjects give up their usual

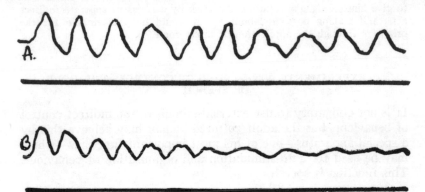

Fig. No. 124

REACTIONS IN A PARALYSIS AGITANS PATIENT (SUBJECT ROZ.)

A = PRESSURES WITH AUTO-STIMULATIONS
B = SPONTANEOUS RHYTHMICAL PRESSURES

form of activity, and in both we proved that the direct "will power" is futile, and that the control of behaviour was achieved by the indirect voluntary act, with the inclusion of accessory stimuli.

The path we have taken is analogous to that of the history of culture. Students of the psychology of primitive peoples agree that the weakest point of the behaviour of the savage is his inability to do systematic work; as we have shown above he energetically accomplishes his direct needs, but is unable to do independent work when the needs are absent. Therefore it is of special interest to note that in the control of behaviour of the worker, culture has made use of indirect external stimuli. In certain Egyptian drawings representing work together with the overseer there is painted another regulating the work. In the primitive person the indirect job of keeping time with sand-glasses and other signals represents the factor described in our experiments.

A number of applications of rhythm in the process of work is of paramount psychological significance.[1] In Borneo, as described by Bucher, there was found a primitive instrument for digging, consisting of a stick with a smaller one at the other end. Every time that the instrument was forced into the ground the smaller stick struck the larger one, producing a sound. We cannot evaluate this except as a primitive attempt of the human to control his behaviour (labour) by the aid of auto-stimulation. To the instrument acting upon the external world there is added another one influencing the worker. This latter, automatically giving a signal at every stroke of the worker, can be construed as a means

[1] K. Bucher: *Work and Rhythm*, Moscow, 1923.

to give himself signals, counting the work by a series of separate indirect acts, and making possible labour which would be unattainable for the primitive through the application of direct force.

4. EXPERIMENTS WITH INDIRECT CONTROL: THE ROLE OF SPEECH

It is not obligatory to use external stimuli in the indirect control of behaviour, but the adult cultured human may achieve this by a special apparatus—one of his most important functions—which may be used for auto-stimulation and organisation of behaviour. This function is speech.

For a long time psychologists have thought of speech as a means of communication and of expressing thoughts and feelings. Together with these communicating and emotional functions of speech, an intellectual one has been added: speech is a powerful means of formulating thoughts, and some psychologists have supposed that all the intellectual processes occur by virtue of internal, inaudible speech.

However, a number of recent works, a part of which were done in Moscow [1] prove that besides these functions, speech plays a rôle in human behaviour of no less importance. It is the means of regulating and organising the external world, including the separate elements and stabilising the picture, and on the other hand, it is the agent of organising the behaviour, of planning further actions, saving the human from sub-ordination by direct optical situations and activating his behaviour.

In genetic investigations this function of speech comes out clearly. While some authors, such as Piaget, consider the speech of the young child as egocentric, merely accompanying the activity of the child, we have proven that the "egocentric" speech has the function of planning the activity of the child and thus stimulating it. This new planning rôle of speech, its rôle in stimulating and organising behaviour, begins with cases of speech auto-commands and ends with the complex forms of judgment.

After this the disturbances in behaviour associated with the failure of speech become clear; and those facts showing that in aphasia the primary defect is one of "volition"—the inability to elaborate intentions, the dependence upon external situations, marked distractability of the subject—are comprehensible when we study that central rôle of speech which it plays in the organisation of human behaviour.

In experiments having to do with very elementary actions, we have been able to investigate the organising rôle of speech in its primitive stages. Even simple auto-commands replacing external stimulations may help the human to control his behaviour, and

[1] L. C. Vuitogsky: *Pedagogy of the School Age,* 1929.
Idem and A. R. Luria: *Function and Fate of Egocentric Speech,* Proceedings of the Ninth International Psychological Congress, 1929.

where the direct control is not attainable, by the inclusion of the speech system in the reactive process, we often obtained fairly good results.

These experiments were analogous to those in which we applied external stimuli for the control of behaviour. For this purpose we chose the hysteric patient whose behaviour we regulated by the application of continuous signals. For the external signal we may substitute speech reinforced by sound (auto-dictation). The same results were obtained as formerly, and after a few trials the patient could produce delayed regular pressures, which he was not able to do by direct effort.

If the application of speech can help to inhibit the impulsive movements, then in the cases where the control of movement means acceleration, in the overcoming of the organic rigidity, language may serve as a psychological compensation for the motor defects. In our experiments with paralysis agitans we attempt to show whether a word can act as a stimulating agent just as the external motor stimulus did. If so, the problem of auto-stimulation and control of behaviour in Parkinson's disease could be solved by the use of speech in functionally reconstructing the activity of the neuropsychical apparatus. However, we met here at first with the same elementary difficulties: our subject was unable to pronounce a word or to execute a movement, and we at first met with failure in our attempts to employ speech as an auto-stimulating factor in the behaviour of the Parkinsonian patient.

However, there naturally arises the question here, whether it is sufficient to pass over from the external speech to the internal and to be limited by the problem of giving oneself the auto-command, not pronouncing the words aloud, in order to attain the result which we seek. But along this path we meet with considerable difficulty: the internal command connected with speech is a spontaneous act which is extremely trying for the patient with paralysis agitans, and the interruption of this command in the automatic experiment is thus impossible. The experiment shows that it supports the spontaneous chain movements, and we do not see the changes which are carried into the motor activity.

The problem of the experimenter is thus altered. Instead of striving to stimulate directly the movements, he now inquires: How is it possible to stimulate speech, to overcome its rapid exhaustion, and to bring about stimulation of the motor activity? We again come to the problem of the control of the behaviour by the aid of a number of roundabout paths.

Many theoretical considerations suggested by the Berlin school of psychologists (Lewin) helps us to decide this question. Studying the energy relations in the processes of activity, Lewin proved that a monotonous repetition of the separate acts is characterised by a dynamical tension different from the activity included in the definite structure. The first can be interrupted in any part of the chain without manifesting any modification in the tension, but every moment of the structural work is characterised by a certain tension striving to discharge itself (*Entladung*); this activity draws toward its end, and the tension increases as the activity nears its completion.

If we wish to increase the activity of any function, to augment the tension, we should include it in a definite structure and bring it fairly close to the purpose of the subject.

In our experiments with paralysis agitans the unsuccessful results in working with internal speech were due to such a difficulty; the activity which we attempted to produce was monotonous; it did not tend to a definite goal; and it was deprived of

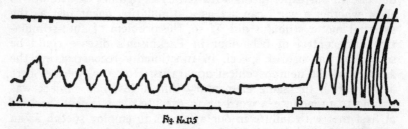

Fig. No. 125

REACTIONS WITH COUNTING IN PARALYSIS AGITANS (PARKINSON'S DISEASE)

A. MONOTONOUS COUNTING   B. COUNTING UP TO "8"

that degree of cortical tension necessary for the compensation of the sub-cortical tension in Parkinson's disease. The problem before us is to increase tension connected with internal speech, to include it in a definite system, having given it a structural rather than a chain character. We could easily do this by having the subject count to a definite number, noting the pressures associated with each figure. The experiment showed that we were on the right track, and that this transfer to the structural character of the speech activity leads to the production of the behaviour which we seek. The picture here is different from that seen in the attempts to connect the movements with the monotonous counting.

In Figure 125 we see a curve which is very significant. We tell the subject to make spontaneous rhythmical pressures, simultaneously counting each one; we do not limit the number of pressures, and we see in Curve A that it differs little from the motor reactions customary in this subject; they are tremulous and disappear after the eighth reaction. The inclusion of the speech does not give the expected result and the rigidity and rapid exhaustion are still present. Without interrupting the experiment we give him another problem: to press eight times, simultaneously counting—we limit the number of pressures to create a chain. This includes the voluntary activity in a definite structure, and we obtain a revolution in the motor activity of the subject; instead of the exhaustion and the rigidity we have well-marked movements proceeding to their terminus.

We replace the usual spontaneous type of movements by movements included in a certain cortical structure, and the result is an overcoming of the movements present in a given pathological process.

Such a transfer of the movements, including them in a well-defined, cortical structure modifies the whole dynamics of the behaviour, so that one application is sufficient to overcome the complete exhaustion and to establish along these new paths a restored activity. Figure 125 demonstrates this: the patient is told to make spontaneous, rhythmical pressures, and the experiment is continued until complete exhaustion, inability to press any more, and refusal to continue the experiment. Suddenly without any pause in the experiment, we tell him to "count to eight," and entirely unexpectedly he is able to produce eight regular pressures without signs of fatigue.

Then that which was impossible to accomplish by direct will force becomes attainable when the action is included in another complex system.

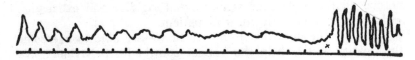

Fig. No. 126

SPONTANEOUS PRESSURES BEFORE AND AFTER BEING INSTRUCTED TO
"COUNT TO EIGHT"

Experimentation shows that the observed phenomenon is a very constant one. After a year we saw this patient again, although he was in a much worse condition. Figure 127 convinces us that the simple rhythmical pressures, rapidly leading to fatigue, are not reinforced by any direct will force.

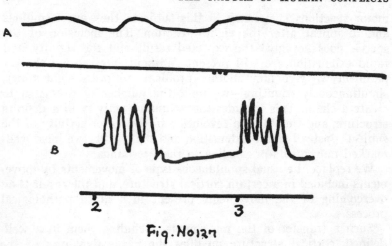

Fig. No 127

A. SPONTANEOUS RHYTHMICAL PRESSURES, NOTED DURING THE INSTRUCTION: PRESS MORE QUICKLY.

B. RESPONSE TO THE QUESTIONS: (2) HOW MANY WHEELS ON A WAGGON? (3) HOW MANY POINTS TO A STAR?

All attempts to appeal to the subject to make spontaneous pressures come to naught, and the curve remains flat. However, when we give him some intellectual problem, including the hand in the system of its execution, this defect immediately disappears. It is not necessary to make the subject count aloud, accompanying the counting by pressing; we may have him answer by tapping. Curve B illustrates such an experiment. We ask him: How many wheels on a waggon? How many points to a star? and we obtain the corresponding answers by tapping, and these have a normal character without signs of that rigidity and exhaustion which are characteristic for this patient.

What are the mechanisms by which we are able to overcome the rigidity and to help the patient control his behaviour? We believe that the complex system of cortical compensation is associated with the exchange of the very structure of the reactive processes. It is likely that the problem to "count to eight" or "how many wheels to a waggon" not only creates in the patient a strong cortical structure, but decides the problem of means.

The movements of response are here not direct, but produced through a fairly complex system of the intricate participating speech mechanisms.

The picture here is the reverse of that seen in the aphasiac. In the latter case everything that is connected with the speech mechanisms falls out, and the movements become automatic, and primitive. The paralysis agitans patient is capable of giving movements only if the speech component is included, even though it may be concealed.

It is not difficult to prove this, by using with the Parkinsonian patient motor tests which the aphasiac is unable to handle, owing to the presence of concealed speech mechanisms. The test of Head was employed: once the patient was asked to imitate the raising of the hand by the mirror image, the other time by the speech instructions. The aphasiac could accomplish the first problem (the operator facing him and requesting him to repeat the movements as he makes them), but not the second; but the patient with paralysis agitans could hardly raise the hand in imitation of the experimenter, although he could more easily, rapidly and with less rigidity execute the movements according to the language instructions. This experiment explains the nature of the compensation here and indicates its close relation to the stimulations similar in type to those which suffer most in the aphasiac.

The concealed speech mechanisms, serving as internal stimuli, help the patient to control his motor system, which he is absolutely powerless to do by the direct application of "force of will."

If the organising and stimulating rôle of speech is a powerful means of controlling the behaviour, then it is one of the early factors overcoming the primitive diffuseness of the reactive processes and aiding the child in his first attempts to organise his reactions. Our first trials to produce in the child the maximal ability to organise his behaviour (see Section 2 of this chapter) were unavailing because we presented to the child the stimulus for the organisation of his behaviour but not the means by which he might accomplish this. The acquisition of speech at once gives him this means, and leads to the regulation of the behaviour and the overcoming of the diffused reactive processes.

Above we have cited simple reactions of the child to external auditory signals. They are characterised by acute diffusion, inadequate mobilisation of the excitation and inability to restrain the extra impulses. However, it is sufficient for us to include in this reactive process the simple counting of the given pressures in order that this one factor might organise the diffuse reactive process. The speech can be included so that it represents a fairly well organised process even in children 3½ or 4 years old.

Figure 128 illustrates how the single inclusion of speech leads to the coordination of the motor processes.

Our opinion, although contradicting what has been held concerning the coordinating processes in the child, is as follows: the first coordination arises by no means as a simple habit, but it pre-

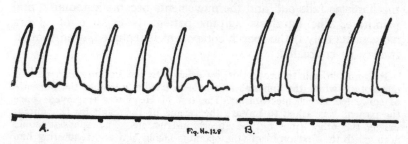

REACTION OF A CHILD 4½ YEARS OLD

A = SIMPLE REACTIONS TO A SIGNAL, WITHOUT SPEECH
B = REACTIONS WITH THE INCLUSION OF SPEECH

supposes an organised inclusion of the higher psychological mechanisms; the secret of the functional barrier is decided genetically in the first stages by the path of inclusion of these psychological systems; every movement, however simple, is constructed not only from below, but from "above" by the inclusion of the higher psychological mechanisms.

The earliest aspect of the organised reaction is not a simple responsive movement to an external signal, but a movement including the complex speech mechanisms, and—strange as it may seem—the earliest forms of organised movements are seen in the cases of the associated reactions of the motor system.

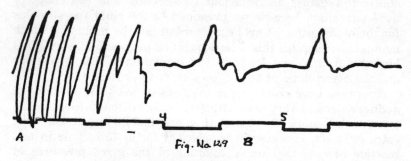

REACTIONS OF A CHILD 2 YEARS 3 MONTHS

A = REACTIONS TO A SIGNAL WITHOUT SPEECH
B = MOTOR REACTIONS ACCOMPANIED BY THE SPEECH RESPONSES:
4. DOLL—4.8"—PLAY; 5. BALL—4.0"—RED

In Figure 129 we show the simple reactions to a signal in a child 2 years and 3 months old in Curve A, and in Curve B the reactions connected with the associated answers; in the first case there are diffused and uncoordinated movements; and in the second instance organised reactions with restrained preliminary impulses and perfect coordination with the speech responses.

According to the clinical method of presentation, we shall submit only this one case, but we have numerous others manifesting the same tendencies. The inclusion of speech at first provokes an organisation of the voluntary reactive processes, and if in the child of 2 years and 3 months we can obtain such a result, we are not surprised when in the child of 3 or 4 years the inclusion of speech leads to a reactive process externally approaching the reaction of an adult and containing only several remaining signs of the dominating excitation.

5. COMPLEX FORMS OF CIRCUITOUS REACTIONS

THE experiments which we have just described indicate that the control of behaviour presupposes profound changes in the structure of the reactive processes. We have seen that direct force is ineffectual in this control and that it is possible only by a transfer to some other complex cultural mechanism. The human is unable to govern his behaviour directly; he creates some auxiliary stimulus which acts upon him and makes him automatically accomplish his goal. The problem of the control of behaviour consists in the change of the direct impulsive reactions by those of a complex system; and only in this cultural operation of the employment of auxiliary means, the establishment of stimuli having an opposite effect on the subject, does he find the possibility to control his behaviour.

This modification of the structure of the reactive processes is not limited by the simple cases of introducing auto-signals, or the application of stimuli accelerating or retarding the movements. The most striking forms of the indirect control of behaviour are seen in those cases when there is provoked not only a simple realisation of the movements, but a preparation of the complex activity having to do with the higher psychological functions of the subject. Our experiments prove that the control of human behaviour is impossible without this process of transfer, and that to this mechanism are applicable only the most involved auxiliary means.

The experiments with the reactions of choice often brought us close to our problem, and using this as an example we attempted to show that the overcoming of the primitive, diffuse, neurodynamical processes occurred in the complex strata of behaviour.

Characteristic of the child [1] is the diffused, impulsive and primitive reaction of trial and error, in contrast to the reactions of the adult which are divided into two functionally different phases and in the movement there is only the execution of the act prepared in the preliminary process.

Now we may inquire by what mechanisms is this evolution effected? What is hidden behind this overcoming of the primary diffusion, and how should we explain the divided and organised reactions of the adult?

We shall attempt to give an answer to these questions. The degree of organisation of the reactive processes of the adult, in comparison with the child, is not to be explained on the ground of the maturity and easy-flowing character of the former. They are two structurally different reactions, having to do with different natures. The diffused character of the reaction of choice is seen whenever there is absent the auxiliary means, when the process of application of the child to the complex situation is direct; it becomes substituted by the organised, subdivided reaction at that moment when the subject turns his attention to some other process, and, discarding his efforts to control the problem by direct force, applies auxiliary stimuli, means and signals.

The process of elaboration of the functional barrier consists in the transfer from the direct action to the cultured, indirect operation. The delay of the immediate impulses, the isolation of the excitation from a direct discharge into the motor sphere, and the turning to the preliminary, central preparation of the process means the refusal of the direct attempts to decide the question and the creation of those preliminary connections which might by an automatic path produce the corresponding movement.

The mechanism of the functional barrier consists in the circuition of the reactive process by the higher psychological functions, and this gave us the occasion to encounter the idea of the morphological understanding of the phenomenon and led us to seek for its roots in the stable anatomical elaborations. The functional barrier characterising the whole development of the reactions is a product of the cultural activity, a result of the ability to use the indirect operations not only in the control of the external mechanisms, but in the control of himself.

The conclusion to be drawn from this is: we no longer have the right to consider the reactive process of the human as a habit, but we must recognise in him higher psychological mechanisms, and our interest centres about these.

[1] See Chapter X, Section 5.

If we are correct in our assumption, and if actually the suppression of the diffused nature of the reactive processes is associated with the transfer to an indirect operation, then it is sufficient to include in the reactive process such an indirect factor that will provoke in the subject a transfer from the diffused structure of the reaction to its organisation on a new, higher basis.

The position which seems to us theoretically incontrovertible encounters many practical difficulties, which are so interesting that we shall discuss them before going on to the experiments. Not every child is capable of applying one or another means for the organisation of its indirect processes. The use of instruments for the external world appears very early in the life of the child, and is already present at 1½ or 2 years of age. Much later, however, comes the application of measures to himself, and a long time is required before they effect the indirect operations having to do with the control of his own behaviour, memory, attention, thinking.[1] Notwithstanding what psychological functions we were studying, the scheme of development remained the same: at first the child is able to solve the given problem only by the direct application, and only much later does he begin to employ external measures, the activity of his own psychological processes, and only at a late age does he resort to the internal, indirect processes.

The suppression of the diffusion in the simple reactive processes occurs only when the complex psychological mechanisms appear in the behaviour of the child; the time of manifestation of the organised structure in the reaction of choice stands in relation to the development of the use of the external signals, the ability to establish external stimuli, concerned with the organisation of his behaviour and its use in the psychological operations. The usual conception of the development as a gradual progression from the lower forms to the higher, gives way here to another, based on the reciprocal relations of the forms, and in accordance with this, the processes which we consider simple, depend upon much more complicated ones, including them as hidden mechanisms.

From this point of view the subordination of the primitive, diffused, reactive processes becomes comprehensible; we begin to understand it not as a process of gradual maturing, but as a result of the inclusion within it of the higher systems developing at that time.

In the experiments with the control of the reactions of choice we proceed thus: we attempt to include in the reactive process the auxiliary stimulus, which at this time is not a simple stimulus, neither provoking nor inhibiting the movement, but it shunts the whole reactive process, replacing the direct trials of the arising reaction of choice by complicated, organised acts.

[1] On the initiative of L. S. Vuigotsky and together with him we have studied the development of the indirect processes in children. See L. S. Vuigotsky: *Pedagogy of the School Age*, Moscow, 1929; *The Problem of the Cultural Development of the Child*, Jour. of Genetic Psychology, 1929. A. R. Luria: *The Problem of the Cultural Behaviour of the Child, idem*, 1928; Luria and Vuigotsky: *Studies in the History of Behaviour*, Moscow, 1930.

Proceeding on the principle that the stimulus presented causes an impulsive movement, complicating the organised reaction of choice, we proposed to the subject to make use of the auxiliary signal, in order to organise his choice and make the act a mnemonic one. The subject was instructed to close a key in front of him on the presentation of a certain drawing, and by every key we placed an auxiliary stimulus, an object which would become associated with the fundamental stimulus and would help to orient the subject in regard to the reaction of choice. Thus if to the picture of a hammer he must press the first key, we place near the first key an auxiliary, orienting [1] stimulus, a nail; if the second key must be pressed on the presentation of the picture of a lock, we put a key near it, etc. While in the very young children only an object closely connected with the stimulus may be used as the orienting signal, in older children almost anything can be employed. [2] This comes about because the subject includes the object in the speech structure. Thus in the child 9 years old we made a rubber tube an auxiliary sign for closing the key to the picture of a "forest," "because in the forest it is dark and in the tube it is also dark"; "nail" is the signal for the sketch "mother," "because the mother is ill in bed and the nail also lies down," etc.

We shall not give a detailed discussion of how these operations develop along with the child, but rather we shall show that the whole structure of the reactive processes becomes reconstructed. In the reaction of choice we have shown that the stimulus in the child produces a direct tendency to react to the movements, and the excitation is transferred to the motor system before the answer is prepared, but in the introduction of the auxiliary signals the process is changed; the stimulus provokes in the subject a structure of the speech which connects the stimulus with the auxiliary signs, leading not to movement but to the search for the auxiliary sign, and later the excitation is connected with the motor area, and the prepared act is quickly effected.

A young child is able to control its behaviour, not by direct force, but by inclusion in a complicated auxiliary system.

6. EXPERIMENTS WITH SYMBOLIC CIRCUITION

IN the control of behaviour the chief rôle is played by the mechanism of circuition, the mechanism of coupling-up the impulse

---

[1] See works of Morozov and of Faivunovich, from our laboratory.

[2] Orienting in this discussion is used in its general setting and meaning and not in the sense in which it is applied by Pavlov.—*Translator*.

and the motor appearance of some intervening link regulating the process of excitation. Experiments with children and hysterics showed that this process overcomes the primitive diffusion of the reaction, transforming it into organised, complex forms. Speech is a preeminent factor as an auto-regulator of behaviour, and helps to bring about the above transformation. The regulating and organising rôle of speech may be applied to any system. Conditioned optical symbols should play the same organising rôle as the activity of speech does.

The symbolic application included in the system of behaviour, diverts the reaction, in the same way as does speech, separates the excitation from the direct transfer to the motor system, and leads to a complex organised structure of the reactive process. Every symbolic system may be a powerful means of organising affect. This can be proved by the part that symbolic systems as images have played in the history of culture; they are connected with emotions and are widely employed in art, in the theatre, etc., to organise affect. We shall try to show how the control of affect is brought about by symbolic measures. For this we shall use experiments with hypnosis, indicating that the affective behaviour takes on a new structure after the introduction of symbolic forms.

To the subject under hypnosis we suggest the necessity of explaining the definite affective states seen directly, or by the help of the symbols.[1]

Subject K., a hysterical woman 30 years old, had been under the observation of psychiatrists some weeks. Her complex was connected with the fact that her husband was an alcoholic, and wasted all of his money on drink, and furthermore grossly mistreated her. Every recollection about this situation produced an acute affect.

In three successive séances it was suggested to the woman that she would want to describe the feelings which had been troubling her. In the first experiment, however, the conditions are created for a more direct manifestation of these experiences, and for this reason speech is included; in the second séance the subject is told to express her feelings with paper and pencil; and finally in the third, to express them with direct symbols.

Below is a description of the results.

The first experiment. To the patient in deep hypnosis it was suggested: "When you awake you will have an intense desire to relate what you

[1] Experiment done by Dr. Kannabich.

have been through recently. But you will not be able to talk about this, but you will show what has been worrying you." On awakening the subject slowly opens her eyes, looks first to one side, then the other, and begins to look in her pocket-book, at first quietly and then more rapidly, grabs the money in it and throws it down, then starts to cry, tears her dress, wrings her hands. The experiment ends with an attack of severe sobbing and the subject is put to sleep again.

The second experiment. The subject was again told to express her experiences but with paper and pencil. On awakening, she slowly goes to the table, takes up a pencil indecisively, begins to draw figures, increases the speed of her movements, draws irregular circles. Figure 132 shows

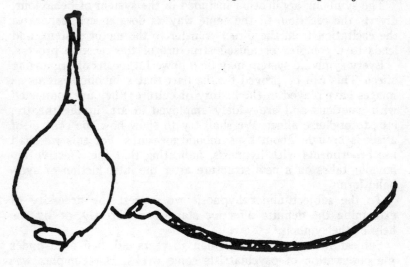

Fig. No. 131

a drunkard with a bottle and a glass. Around this is written: "spend-thrift, with one hand," the rest is illegible. The drawing shows impulsive-ness, the handwriting is deformed, individual words are helter skelter.

The third experiment. The subject was put to sleep, and the suggestion made that she express her experiences in symbolic forms which would completely describe her state, but not be intelligible at once to everyone. The patient on awakening goes to the table and makes a drawing shown in Figure 131—a bottle and near it a snake. Her behaviour is tense but without manifestation of affect. Finally she puts down the pencil and does not attempt to make any further drawings.

The three experiments manifest the affective state, but they are characterised by different structures of the affect. In the first instance, the subject began with the direct reproduction of the affective situation; the affective images are connected with the motor system and are excitatory in character. The first experiment shows a motor storm, the artificially produced affect and the diffused excitation, and finally, a severe emotional attack. The

Fig. No. 132

second experiment is similar; the motor storm here occurs on paper, also showing diffused excitation.

The third experiment is entirely different: the affective state is not expressed directly, but through symbols; the reproduction of all the experiences connected with the drunkard husband who wastes his money is substituted by the bottle and snake—the symbols of drunkenness.[1] What is of interest for us is that the

[1] A green snake is a common symbol in Russia for drunkenness.

whole structure of the behaviour is changed by these symbols; there is no sobbing, etc. The suggestion, "to express everything that troubled her," is limited by the drawing, without any motor disturbances. The symbol here overcame the affect and the subject had control of her behaviour, diverting it through conditioned symbols, and passing from the direct biological forms to the cultured forms of behaviour.

This experiment brings us to an understanding of the mechanics underlying the action of symbols as emotional signals, and, on the other hand, it helps us to see how the mechanism of the substitution of the primitive process by cultural signals is the most important factor in the control of behaviour.

The genesis of behaviour control is as follows: the regulation of behaviour comes about not through the origin and growth of voluntary processes, but by the development of the use of external signals in the problems. . . . The late appearance of the organisation of the child's behaviour is due not to the want of development in the nervous system, but to the late inclusion of the substituting systems in the reactive processes.

Experiments were done with children analogous to the preceding. The child is told to draw images illustrating something, and if these are fairly active we obtain three stages of the child's development. The child who is not yet able to distinguish signs imitates and draws indifferent figures, and then finishes with a dramatisation of the image. Thus "Slava B.," in Figure 133 A when asked to draw "war" produces unintelligible figures, but afterwards dramatises it, jumping, going through the motions of shooting, crying "boom, boom." The poverty of the sketch is compensated for by the actions.

The next child, 11 years old, Figure 133 B, puts on paper what the younger one has acted, but does not go through the bodily movements of dramatising the sketch. In the third drawing, Figure 133 C, by a child 13 years old, the motor discharge of the image disappears, as soon as the child is able graphically to give definite, specific components for the image. The imitating components are replaced by the external graphic signs. . . .

The former empirical psychology failed in the examination of the individual psychological processes and the behaviour of the living, concrete personality. Will and intellect were considered as separate entities, and the latter was not seen as the key to the development of will. Simple motor phenomena, associations, emotions and strivings, thinking and speech were subjects of special divisions of psychology, usually relegated to the final chapters of the text-book to illustrate the laws previously described.

We may consider that the preliminary period in the development of psychology has been passed. Psychology finds itself in a

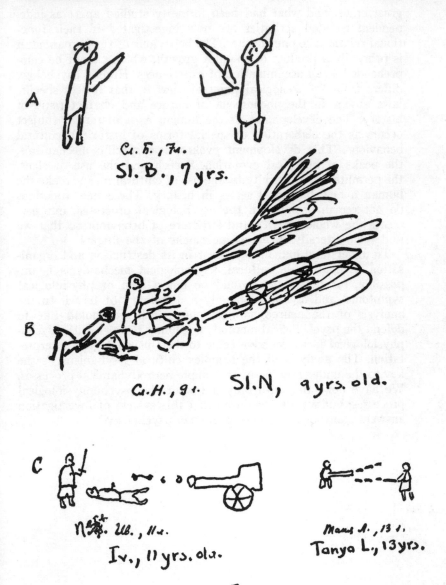

A

Сл. Б., 7л.
Sl. B., 7 yrs.

B

Сл. Н., 9л.   Sl.N, 9 yrs. old.

C

Ив., 11л.
Iv., 11 yrs. old.

Маня Л., 13 л.
Tanya L., 13yrs.

Fig. No. 133

great crisis, and what had been formerly studied apart as independent isolated activities are now investigated in their functional relations to one another. The behaviour of the human adult is primarily a product of complex growth, which cannot be comprehended as an accumulation of experiences. Human psychology differs from the zoological point of view in that it sees specific laws absent in the phenomena of nature and characteristic of history. The development of the human as a historical subject occurs as the elaboration of special forms of historical, cultural behaviour. This development evokes new specific mechanisms, the peaks of historical evolution. Speech and the use of signs, the permutation of activity by the use of cultural means make the human a new biological series in history. These new functions do not remain isolated in the psychological processes, but permeate the whole activity and structure of behaviour so that we find them literally in every movement of the fingers.

To understand human behaviour in its destruction and organisation without these cultural, psychological mechanisms is impossible, for destruction would be but a sum of physiological symptoms, and organisation only a dictionary of terms. In the analysis of the neurodynamical phenomena we should like to defend the psychological method; beginning to work with psychophysiological facts, we have come to their psychological interpretation. The analysis of the complex cultural mechanisms is the key to the understanding of the simple neurodynamical processes. We have done this with only a few of the psychophysiological processes, but we are convinced that this system of investigation answers many of the riddles of human psychology.

INDEX